Lecture Notes in Computer

Commenced Publication in 1973
Founding and Former Series Editors:
Gerhard Goos, Juris Hartmanis, and Jan van i

T0230535

Welf Löwe   Mario Südholt (Eds.)

Software Composition

5th International Symposium, SC 2006
Vienna, Austria, March 25-26, 2006
Revised Papers

 Springer

Volume Editors

Welf Löwe
Växjö University
School of Mathematics and Systems Engineering
Software Technology Group
351-95 Växjö, Sweden
E-mail: welf.lowe@msi.vxu.se

Mario Südholt
École des Mines de Nantes
Département Informatique
4, rue Alfred Kastler, 44307 Nantes Cedex 3, France
E-mail: Mario.Sudholt@emn.fr

Library of Congress Control Number: 2006930915

CR Subject Classification (1998): D.2, D.1.5, D.3, F.3

LNCS Sublibrary: SL 2 – Programming and Software Engineering

ISSN   0302-9743
ISBN-10   3-540-37657-7 Springer Berlin Heidelberg New York
ISBN-13   978-3-540-37657-6 Springer Berlin Heidelberg New York

Springer is a part of Springer Science+Business Media

springer.com

© Springer-Verlag Berlin Heidelberg 2006
Printed in Germany

Typesetting: Camera-ready by author, data conversion by Scientific Publishing Services, Chennai, India
Printed on acid-free paper   SPIN: 11821946   06/3142   5 4 3 2 1 0

Preface

Research in software composition investigates models and techniques to build systems from predefined, pretested, reusable components instead of building them from scratch. In recent years, this idea has largely been adopted by industry. In the shape of service-oriented architecture, software composition has become an influential design paradigm, especially for the (re-)organization of the IT infrastructure of organizations. On the technical level, the standardization of Web services and other composition technologies has further matured.

Current research in software composition aims at (further) developing composition models and techniques. The aspect-oriented programming and design paradigm, for instance, has gained interest in the research community as a composition (support) model. Other current research questions concern the specification of component contracts, in particular making explicit its observable behavior, and methods of correct components composition. The International Symposium on Software Composition provides a premier forum for discussing these kinds of research questions and presenting original research results.

This LNCS volume contains the proceedings of the 5th International Symposium on Software Composition, which was held as a satellite event of the European Joint Conferences on Theory and Practice of Software (ETAPS) in Vienna, Austria, March, 25-26 2006. The symposium started with a keynote on "Semantically Enabled Service-Oriented Architectures" given by Dieter Fensel, Director of the Digital Research Institute. The main program consisted of presentations of research papers on software compositions. These proceedings contain the revised versions of the papers presented at SC 2006.

We selected 21 technical papers out of 60 submissions. Each paper went through a thorough revision processes and was reviewed by three to five reviewers followed by an electronic Program Committee discussion. We would like to thank the Program Committee members and the external reviewers for selecting a set of diverse and excellent papers and making SC 2006 a success.

We would like to express our gratitude to the European Network of Excellence on Aspect-Oriented Software Development (AOSD-Europe) and to the International Federation for Information Processing, Technical Committee on Software: Theory and Practice (IFIP, TC 2) for sponsoring this event. Finally, we would like to thank the organizers of ETAPS 2006 for hosting and providing an excellent organizational framework for SC 2006.

June 2006

Welf Löwe, Växjö University, Sweden
Mario Südholt, INRIA - École des Mines de Nantes, France
Program Co-chairs
SC 2006

Organization

Program Committee

Brian Barry	(Bedarra Research Labs, Canada)
Alexandre Bergel	(Trinity College Dublin, Ireland)
Judith Bishop	(University of Pretoria, South Africa)
Pierre Cointe	(Ecole des Mines de Nantes, France)
Vittorio Cortellessa	(University of L'Aquila, Italy)
Thierry Coupaye	(France Telecom, France)
Birgit Demuth	(Technische Universität Dresden, Germany)
Flavio De Paoli	(University of Milano Bicocca, Italy)
Dieter Fensel	(DERI Galway/Innsbruck, Ireland/Austria)
Volker Gruhn	(University of Leipzig, Germany)
Thomas Gschwind	(IBM Research, Switzerland)
Arno Jacobsen	(University of Toronto, Canada)
Mehdi Jazayeri	(University of Vienna, Austria)
Tom Henzinger	(EPF Lausanne, Switzerland)
Kung-Kiu Lau	(The University of Manchester, UK)
Karl Lieberherr	(Northeastern University, USA)
Welf Löwe (Co-chair)	(Växjö University, Sweden)
Mira Mezini	(Darmstadt University of Technology, Germany)
Claus Pahl	(Dublin City University, Ireland)
Arnd Poetzsch-Heffter	(University of Kaiserslautern, Germany)
Elke Pulvermüller	(Karlsruhe University of Technology, Germany)
Lionel Seinturier	(INRIA & LIP6, France)
Mario Südholt (Co-chair)	(INRIA & EMN, France)
Wim Vanderperren	(VU Brussels, Belgium)

Referees

U. Aßmann	E. Della Valle	S. Hu
O. Barais	M. D'Hondt	A. Jackson
D. Beyer	J. Feng	E. Kilgarriff
M. Book	D. Gao	L. Ling
F. Cabitza	V. Gasiunas	S. Loecher
O. Caron	M. Gawkowski	M. Loregian
A. Chakrabarti	F. Hartmann	A. Maurino
P.-C. David	T. Haselwanter	I. Ntalamagkas
B. De Fraine	M. Haupt	J. Oberleitner

Sponsoring Institutions

IFIP, Laxenburg, Austria
AOSD-Europe, European Network of Excellence in AOSD, Lancaster, UK

Table of Contents

Automatic Checking of Component Protocols in Component-Based Systems

Wolf Zimmermann[1] and Michael Schaarschmidt[2]

[1] Martin-Luther Universität Halle-Wittenberg, Institut für Informatik,
06099 Halle/Saale, Germany
`zimmer@informatik.uni-halle.de`
[2] Martin-Luther Universität Halle-Wittenberg, Rechenzentrum,
06099 Halle/Saale, Germany
`michael.schaarschmidt@urz.uni-halle.de`

Abstract. We statically check whether each component in a component-based system is used according to its protocol and provide counterexamples if such a check fails. The protocol is given by a finite state machine specifying legal sequences of procedure calls of the interface of a component. The main contribution is that we can deal with call-backs without any restrictions. We achieved this by using context-free grammars instead of finite state machines to describe the use of components.

1 Introduction

The construction of component-based systems became increasingly important in software construction. However, software architects have to deal with new problems stemming from component-based system architectures. An important issue is whether a component is correctly used. Usually components implement one or more interfaces specifying the services they offer. For the purpose of this paper, a *service* is simply a procedure or function signature. However just the knowledge of services does not provide sufficient information for the construction of systems. Often the source code of a component is not available after its deployment or even not physically available as e.g. Web Services. However, for a component industry the unavailability of source code is essential – Web Services may even be offered on a pay-per-use basis.

A major problem for construction of component-based systems is to check whether the components can be composed and possibly provide own components to adapt them. A failure to use a component correctly might cause a system abortion while executing the system – this might happen even after the system is delivered to the customer. In this context abortion means that a system stops with an uncaught exception internal to a component (e.g. dereferencing of null reference, illegal array accesses, division by zero etc.). Since the source code of components is often unavailable, other approaches are necessary to check whether components are used in such a way that the system does not abort. Our goal is to provide a mechanizable approach for checking statically component-based systems for abortion freeness on an almost black-box basis.

W. Löwe and M. Südholt (Eds.): SC 2006, LNCS 4089, pp. 1–17, 2006.

Our approach currently restricts the architecture of component-based systems to sequential systems and to one client using services of other components. However any component may use services of other components or even of the client. In particular we do not exclude call-backs. We assume that each component implements one or more interfaces and each interface I specifies services as a set of procedure signatures Σ_I. The *services* Σ_C of a component C is the union of the interfaces implemented by the component. Informally, a *protocol* of a component is a set of sequences $L_C \subseteq \Sigma_C^*$. The aim of protocols is to guarantee certain properties, e.g. that the component doesn't abort if its services are called according to a sequence in L_C. A component C might call other services specified as interfaces used by a component. The *profile* of a component C specifies for each interface I required by C the set of sequences $P_C(I) \subseteq \Sigma_I^*$ of services possibly being called by C. A component-based system S is a multi-set of components (i.e. there might be multiple copies of a component called *instances*) where each interface used by a component is instantiated with an instance of a component. The *use of an instance* c of a component C in a component-based system S is the set of possible sequences of services $U_c \subseteq \Sigma_C^*$ that are called to c during execution of S. The use of an instance c of a component C *conforms* to its protocol iff $U_c \subseteq L_C$, i.e. any sequence of services called to c agrees with the protocol of C. Therefore, if the conformity check succeeds for each instance in a component-based system S and each component of S is correctly implemented then the abortion-freeness of S is guaranteed. We assume that each component contains in its deployment description its protocol and its profile.

Many approaches (e.g. [13,17,18,22]) use finite state machines (short: FSM) A_P and A_R to specify protocols $L(A_P)$ and profiles $L(A_R)$ for each interface of a component where $L(A_P)$ and $L(A_R)$ are the languages accepted by A_P and A_R, respectively. Since connectors connect profiles for an interface of one component with an interface of another component it is checked whether $L(A_R) \subseteq L(A_P)$ and counter-examples are provided in the case such a check fails. The idea behind these local checks is that protocol conformance checks can be executed incrementally. It implicitly assumes that any checked connection cannot be invalidated as long as the protocols of the component providing the profile are satisfied. In this paper, we show that these approaches have several drawbacks: First, local checks cannot be applied if the interfaces of a component cannot be used independently. Second, it cannot be applied if the component system contains recursive call-backs.

Other works use model-checking approaches [8,9,7,11,3,5] to prove that programs satisfy certain properties. They use context-free model checking because finite state machine models are not an adequate abstraction if the program may contain recursive procedures. However, these works assume that the whole program is completely available.

Our method combines and generalizes these approaches in order to allow dependencies between different interfaces of a component and arbitrary recursive call-backs. FSMs are used for describing protocols. In contrast to the above

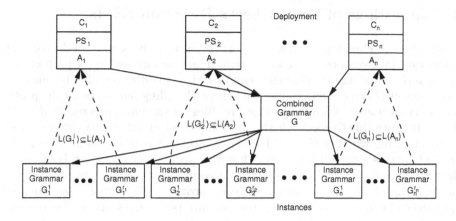

Fig. 1. An Approach to Conformance Checking

works, a single FSM A_C is used for the whole component C. Hence, interaction of procedure calls to different interfaces of C are taken into account. Instead of FSMs for describing uses of components our approach uses context-free grammar (short: CFG) G_C for this purpose. Thus, for each instance c of a component C it is checked whether $L(G_c) \subseteq L(A_C)$. It is a well-known result from the theory of formal languages that this test is algorithmically decidable. We show how counterexamples can be provided if such a check fails. From the global system and the profiles of each component the use of components is derived. However, a profile of a component C cannot be described itself as a context-free grammar since only the use of interfaces is known but not how these are instantiated. Therefore, we generalize context-free grammars by parameterizing non-terminal and terminal symbols with the interfaces. The obtained structure is called a *parameterized context-free scheme* (pCFS). These pCFSs can be mechanically computed from the source code of the components. The pCFSs are used in a component-based system S to compute a context free grammar specifying all sequences of calls to all instances of the components by instantiating the interfaces of the pCFS analogous to the corresponding instances in S. Context-free grammars for uses of instances of components in a component-based system can now be derived by projection. Hence, it is now possible to check for each instance c of component C of S whether $L(G_c) \subseteq L(A_C)$, i.e. whether to use of c conforms to the protocol. Fig. 1 illustrates the summary of our approach. The paper is organized as follows: Section 2 demonstrates the limitations of local checks and the use of FSMs for profiles. Section 3 summarizes how to check $L(G) \subseteq L(A)$ for CFGs G and FSMs A and shows how counterexamples are provided. Section 4 introduces parameterized context-free schemes. Section 5 shows their use in specifying profiles of components and how they can be generated from source text. Finally, Section 6 shows how CFGs specifying the use of a component are generated from the profiles. A short appendix introduces some of the notations from formal languages used in this paper.

2   Limitations of Local Checks Based on FSMs

Local protocol checking approaches (e.g. [18,20,13]) check independently each connection in a component-based system. They usually assume a protocol for each interface and assume that they can be independently used. I.e. instances of a component C can accept all interleavings of all calling sequences by the protocols of its interfaces. Then they deduce profiles for the interfaces required by C. Hence, it is possible to check whether a profile U for an interface conforms to its protocol P, i.e. whether $U \subseteq P$. For these checks, it is often assumed that the profile U also is a regular language. Thus, protocol conformance can be decided. However, in practice it often happens that components cannot accept arbitrary interleavings of the calling sequences to its protocol. Thus, more sophisticated approaches introduce coordination components (sometimes also called connectors) that accept arbitrary interleavings and the other components only have one interface. Therefore a component has a single protocol. In this section, we show that even if each component has one interface and if each connection is succesfully checked, the absence of global protocol errors is not guaranteed. The main reason for these violations are recursive call-backs. Thus, for the same reasons as in the works of software model checking [8,9,7,11,3,5], CFGs are more adequate than FSMs to describe the use of components.

Our examples are denoted similar to Java. The main difference is that classes are components and we do not inherit from components. Procedures and functions can only have parameters whose types are interfaces or basic types (for simplicity, we only use here the type *int*). Any procedure or function that is not defined by an interface of a component is *internal* to that component. There is exactly one component, the *client*, containing a parameterless procedure *main* which is executed upon on system start. The client has parameters that represent interfaces to be instantiated with components upon composition time. Thus, all instances of components in a component based system are known upon composition time. Note that all instances of a component can be referenced by a name. Procedures allow to pass by reference instances of components. Values of basic types are passed by value. This model is similar to commercial component systems such as COM, EJB, CORBA except that all components are known upon composition time. Dynamic instances of components are possible. The operation $new(x)$ computes a new instance of the component refered to by variable x. In this paper, we assume for simplicity that all services of components are procedures. The parameters of the client can only be used in *main*. The identifier *this* denotes the instance of the component currently being executed.

Example 1. Consider the component system in Fig. 2. c is an instance of C_2. The component system starts its execution by executing *main*. Suppose we read 2, i.e. $i = 2$. Then, the body of the loop will be executed and it calls $c.a(2, this)$. Thus, when executing this call on c it is $n = 2$ and x refers to the client. Since the condition becomes true, the call $x.b(1, this)$ is being executed. Since x refers to the client, this is a call-back and the execution of b on the client starts with $k = 1$ and z referring to c. After the first assignment it holds $n = 1$ which also

client $C_1[J\ c]$ **implements** I {
    int $n = 0$;
    void $b(int\ k, J\ z)$ {
      $n = (n + 1)\%2$; $n = 1/n$;
      $z.a(k, this)$;
    }
    void $d()$ { $n = 1/n - 1$; }
    void $main()$ {
      int i;
      $read(i)$;
      $while(i > 0)$ { $c.a(i, this)$; $i--$; }
    }
}

interface I {
    void $b(int, J)$;
    void $d(J)$;
}

component C_2 **implements** J {
    void $a(int\ n, I\ x)$ {
      if$(n > 0)$ { $x.b(n - 1, this)$; $x.d()$; }
    }
}

interface J {
    void $a(int, I)$;
}

Composition: $C_1[C_2]$

Fig. 2. A Component-Based System

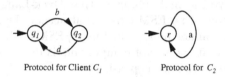

Protocol for Client C_1 Protocol for C_2

Fig. 3. Protocols for the Client and Component in Fig. 2

holds after the second assignment. Thus, the call $z.a(1, this)$ is executed. Note that this is a *recursive* call since z refers to c and the first call of a on c is not yet completed. In this second call it is $n = 1$ and x refers to the client. Thus the condition becomes true and the call $x.b(0, this)$ is being executed. This again is a recursive call since x refers to the client and the first call of b on the client is not yet completed. After the execution of the first statement it holds $n = 0$. Hence, the second statements performs a division by 0 and therefore the system aborts.

Fig. 3 shows the protocol of the components. Note that a second execution of b and a second execution of d on the client lead to a division by zero. The client requires that b and d must be called alternating and b is called first – if at all. Otherwise divisions by zero are executed. Apparently, this protocol is violated by the system.

The following example demonstrates that recursive call-backs are the reason for protocol violations:

Example 2. According to the clients protocol, the profile for c is $L_c = \{a^n | n \in \mathbb{N}\}$ and the profile for z is also $L_z = \{a^n | n \in \mathbb{N}\}$. According to component C_2's protocol, the profile for x is $L_x = \{(bd)^n | n \in \mathbb{N}\}$.

After composition, z always refers to c and x always refers to the client. Such information could e.g. be derived from a points-to analysis. Thus there are two profiles for calling sequences to c. Even an arbitrary interleaving of L_z and L_c shows that $U_c = \{a^n | n \in \mathbb{N}\}$ is the set of all calling sequences to instance c of component C_2. Since these sequences are accepted, the use of c conforms to the protocol of C. Consider now the client. Since x is the only variable referring to the client, the use of the client is $U = \{(bd)^n | n \in \mathbb{N}\}$. Hence, the local protocol checking approach also would decide that the use of the client conforms to its protocol which is wrong according to the scenario in Example 1.

The checking approach in Example 2 considers individually each component. If there wouldn't introduced recursive procedure calls due to call-backs the above arguments would be completely legal. The individual protocol conformance checking doesn't work because these recursive calls lead to use of components that cannot be detected from one component alone. Many works of protocol checking are aware of this problem and exclude therefore recursive call-backs. In fact if a is recursively called every call b can be viewed as an open bracket that is closed by a call d. Therefore the set of sequences describing the use of the client is the Dyck-Language over the pair of brackets b and d. It is generated by the CFG $G = (\{b, d\}, \{Z\}, \{Z ::= ZZ|cZd|\varepsilon\}, Z)$. It is a well-known result from the theory of formal languages that Dyck-Languages are not regular languages and therefore no FSM exists that accepts Dyck-languages. Thus, the use of components cannot be specified using FSMs. The next section shows that even in the case that the use of components is described by CFGs, model checking of protocol conformance is possible.

3   Model Checking with CFGs

We present here the standard algorithm for checking $L(G) \subseteq L(A)$ for a CFG $G = (T, N, P, Z)$ and a FSM $A = (T, Q, R, q_0, F)$. Furthermore, we show how it can be used to provide counterexamples if $L(G) \nsubseteq L(A)$. The basic idea is instead of checking $L(G) \subseteq L(A)$ to check the equivalent condition $L(G) \cap (T^* \setminus L(A)) = \emptyset$. Any word $w \in L(G) \cap (T^* \setminus L(A))$ is a counterexample of the check. In the context of the paper, it provides a sequence of procedure calls to a component that violate its protocol. The FSM $A' = (T, Q, R, q_0, Q \setminus F)$ accepts $T^* \setminus L(A)$. Hence, we check whether $L(G) \cap L(A') = \emptyset$. It is known that the intersection of a context-free language with a regular language is context-free, and that it is decidable for context-free grammars G whether $L(G) = \emptyset$. Our model checker therefore has the following steps: First, a CFG G' such that $L(G') = L(G) \cap L(A')$ is constructed. Then, it is checked whether $L(G') = \emptyset$. If it turns out that $L(G') \neq \emptyset$, a counterexample $w \in L(G')$ is produced.

Step 1: First the CFG $G = (T, N, P, Z)$ is transformed into an equivalent grammar in *extended Chomsky Normal Form* (short: eCNF) $G_1 = (T, N_1, P_1, Z_1)$, i.e., each production has one of the forms[1] $A ::= BC$, $A ::= B$, or $A ::= t$ with $A, B, C \in N$ and $t \in T$. If $\varepsilon \in L(G)$ then $Z_1 ::= \varepsilon \in P_1$. Second, a CFG $G' = (T, N', P', Z')$ is computed such that $L(G') = L(G_1) \cap L(A')$. Define the size of a CFG $G = (T, N, P, Z)$ as $|G| \triangleq |P| + \sum_{l::=r \in P} |r|$.

---

[1] Chomsky Normal form also forbids chain productions $A ::= B$.

Lemma 1. *For any CFG G, an equivalent grammar G_1 in eCNF can be computed in time $O(|G|)$ and $|G_1| = O(|G|)$.*

Proof. (Sketch) We use the same proof as [15] except the elimination of chain productions. The elimination of chain productions would result in execution time $O(|G|^2)$ and $|G_1| = O(|G|^2)$.

Lemma 2. *Let $G = (T, N, P, Z)$ be a CFG in eCNF and $A = (T, Q, R, q_0, F)$ be a FSM. A CFG G' such that $L(G') = L(G) \cap L(A)$ can be constructed in time $O(|G| \cdot |Q|^3)$. Moreover $|G'| = O(|G| \cdot |Q|^3)$.*

Proof. (Sketch) This proof slightly extends the algorithm described in [21]. In addition to their algorithm, we have to consider chain productions. We define $G' \triangleq (N', T, P', Z')$ as follows:

$$
\begin{aligned}
N' &\triangleq \{\langle X, q, q' \rangle | X \in N \wedge q, q' \in Q\} \cup Z' \\
P' &\triangleq \{Z' ::= \langle Z, q_0, f \rangle | f \in F\} \cup \\
&\quad \{\langle X, q, q' \rangle ::= \langle B, q, r \rangle \langle C, r, q' \rangle | \\
&\qquad\qquad X ::= BC \in P \wedge q, q', r \in Q\} \cup \\
&\quad \{\langle X, q, q' \rangle ::= \langle B, q, q' \rangle | X ::= B \in P \wedge q, q' \in Q\} \cup \\
&\quad \{\langle X, q, q' \rangle ::= t | X ::= t \in P \wedge t \in T \wedge qt \rightarrow q' \in R\} \cup \\
&\quad \{\langle X, q, q \rangle ::= \varepsilon | X ::= \varepsilon \in P \wedge q \in Q\}
\end{aligned}
$$

It can be shown by induction on the length of the derivation that for any $w \in T^*$ $\langle X, q, q' \rangle \overset{*}{\Rightarrow}_{G'} w$ iff $X \overset{*}{\Rightarrow}_G w \wedge qw \overset{*}{\Rightarrow}_A q'$. The time needed for this construction is proportional to the size of G' which is $O(|G| \cdot |Q|^3)$.

Using the FSM $A' = (T, Q, R, q_0, Q \setminus F)$, Lemma 1, and Lemma 2, the following Theorem summarizes Step 1:

Theorem 1. *Let $G = (T, N, P, Z)$ be a CFG and $A = (T, Q, R, q_0, F)$ be a FSM. Then, a CFG $G' = (T, N', P', Z')$ such that $L(G') = L(G) \cap (T^* \setminus L(A))$ can be computed in time $O(|G| \cdot |Q|^3)$ and $|G'| = O(|G| \cdot |Q|^3)$.*

Step 2: The main idea is to compute all generating non-terminals from a CFG $G = (T, N, P, Z)$. A non-terminal X is *generating* if there is a $w \in T^*$ such that $X \overset{*}{\Rightarrow} w$. Obviously it holds $L(G) = \emptyset$ iff Z is not generating. Hence, only generating non-terminals need to be determined and it needs to be checked whether Z is generating. This can be done in linear time as e.g. shown in [15]. The algorithm in [15] incrementally builds a set H of generating non-terminals. Initially, $H = \{X | \exists w \in T^* \bullet X ::= w \in P\}$. A new non-terminal X is added to H if there is a production $X ::= w$ for $w \in (T \cup H)^*$. This is done until H doesn't change or $Z \in H$. If we also maintain the productions considered in this process, counterexamples $w \in T^*$ can be generated by constructing a derivation $Z \overset{*}{\Rightarrow} w$ using these productions.

Theorem 2. *It can be checked in time $O(|G|)$ whether $L(G) = \emptyset$ for a CFG G*

The following Theorem summarizes the results:

Theorem 3. *Let $G = (T, N, P, Z)$ be a CFG according to Theorem 1 and $A = (T, Q, R, q_0, F)$ be a FSM. Then, it can be checked in time $O(|G| \cdot |Q|^3)$ whether $L(G) \subseteq L(A)$. In the case of a negative answer counterexamples are provided.*

4   Parameterized Context-Free Schemes

The *profile* of a component C specifies for each interface I required by C the set of sequences $P_C(I) \subseteq \Sigma_I^*$ of services possibly being called by C. These cannot be described by context-free grammars because the isolated consideration of a component cannot assume anything on the context of its use. The main idea of parameterized schemes is similar to definite-clause grammars. Each non-terminal symbol may have typed parameters. The left-hand side of a context-free production declares them (similar to the declaration of a procedure signature). The right-hand side of a production uses them. For defining profiles, we use the parameters of interface types. In contrast to definite-clause grammars we don't dynamically evaluate parameterized context-free schemes (short: pCFS). Instead, we use them as two-level grammars and expand them to CFSs (i.e. grammars without start symbol) by substituting constants for each parameter.

In our context, we use pCFSs as follows: Their productions are derived from the procedure definitions of an interface. The head becomes the left-hand side of the production. The body is generated from the right-hand side of the production. The expansion of parameterized CFSs substitutes parameters (according to their type) by instances of components in a component system.

A *type* is a pair $(I, \{c_1, \ldots, c_n\})$ consisting of a name I and a finite set of instances $c_1, \ldots, c_n$. The set of instances of a type is denoted by $\iota(I)$. A *parameter* is pair $x : I$ consisting of a *variable* x and a *type name* I. A *parameterized non-terminal* is pair $\langle f \rangle(y_1 : J_1, \ldots, y_k : J_k)$ consisting of a non-terminal name $\langle f \rangle$ and a sequence of parameters $y_1 : J_1, \ldots, y_k : J_k$. An *partial instantiation* of $\langle f \rangle(y_1 : J_1, \ldots, y_k : J_k)$ with variables $z_1, \ldots, z_k$ is the triple denoted as $\langle f \rangle(z_1, \ldots, z_k)$. A *parameterized terminal* is a pair $\mathbf{p}(x_1 : I_1, \ldots, x_m : I_m)$ and a terminal name $\mathbf{p}$ and parameters $x_1 : I_1, \ldots, x_m : I_m$. For the purpose of the paper we only consider terminals with one parameter.

$\langle f \rangle(x_1, \ldots, x_k)$ is called an *applied occurrence of parameterized non-terminal* $\langle f \rangle(y_1 : J_1, \ldots, y_m : J_m)$ over $x_1 : I_1, \ldots, x_k : I_k$ iff $k = m$ and $I_i = J_i$ for $i = 1, \ldots, k$. The notion of an applied occurrence of a terminal is defined analogously. For a set N of parameterized non-terminals, $\Omega_N(x_1 : I_1, \ldots, x_k : I_k)$ denotes the set of all applied occurrences of parameterized non-terminals $\langle X \rangle \in N$ over a sequence of parameters $x_1 : I_1, \ldots, x_k : I_k$. The notion $\Sigma_T(x_1 : I_1, \ldots, x_k : I_k)$ is defined analogously for a set T of parameterized terminals.

A *parametrized context-free scheme* is a 4-tuple $pCFS = (TYPES, N, T, P)$ where

- *TYPES* is a finite set of type names,
- N is a set of parameterized non-terminals such that all parameters have a type in *TYPES*,
- T is a set of parameterized terminals such that all parameters have a type in *TYPES* and $N \cap T = \emptyset$,
- $P \subseteq \{\langle f \rangle(x_1 : I_1, \ldots, x_k : I_k) ::= w | \langle f \rangle(x_1 : I_1, \ldots, x_k : I_k) \in N \wedge w \in (\Omega_N(x_1 : I_1, \ldots, x_k : I_k) \cup \Sigma_T(x_1 : I_1, \ldots, x_k : I_k))^*\}$ is a set of *context-free production schemes*.

The notion of context-free production scheme means that every variable used in an applied occurrence of a terminal or non-terminal on a right-hand side of a production must be declared on the left-hand side of a production. Furthermore, the applied occurrences must be correctly typed w.r.t. to N or T. Note that overloading of parameterized non-terminals and parameterized terminals is permitted. Fig. 4 shows two pCFSs. Section 5 shows how to use pCFSs to specify profiles of components. For the purpose of the paper, we need the following property:

$pCFS_1$:
$$\begin{aligned}
TYPES_1 &= \{I, J\} \\
N_1 &= \{\langle main\rangle(this : I, c : J), \langle b\rangle(this : I, z : J), \langle d\rangle(this : I), \langle a\rangle(this : J, x : I)\} \\
T_1 &= \{\mathbf{a}(this : J)\} \\
P_1 &= \{\langle main\rangle(this : I, c : J) ::= (\mathbf{a}(c)\ \langle a\rangle(c, this))^* \\
&\quad\ \ \langle b\rangle(this : I, z : J)\quad ::= \mathbf{a}(z)\ \langle a\rangle(z, this) \\
&\quad\ \ \langle d\rangle(this : I)\qquad\quad ::= \varepsilon \qquad\qquad\qquad \}
\end{aligned}$$

$pCFS_2$:
$$\begin{aligned}
TYPES_2 &= \{I, J\} \\
N_2 &= \{\langle a\rangle(this : J, x : I), \langle main\rangle(this : I, c : J), \langle b\rangle(this : I, z : J), \langle d\rangle(this : I)\} \\
T_2 &= \{\mathbf{b}(this : I), \mathbf{d}(this : J)\} \\
P_2 &= \{\langle a\rangle(this : J, x : I) ::= \mathbf{b}(x)\ \langle b\rangle(x, this)\ \mathbf{d}(x)\ \langle d\rangle(x)|\varepsilon\}
\end{aligned}$$

Fig. 4. Parameterized Context-Free Schemes

$$\begin{aligned}
N_\iota &= \{\langle main\rangle(c_1, c_2), \langle b\rangle(c_1, c_2), \langle d\rangle(c_1), \langle a\rangle(c_2, c_1)\} \\
T_\iota &= \{\mathbf{a}(c_2), \mathbf{b}(c_1), \mathbf{d}(c_1)\} \\
P_\iota &= \langle main\rangle(c_1, c_2) ::= (\mathbf{a}(c_2)\ \langle a\rangle(c_2, c_1))^* \\
&\quad\ \langle b\rangle(c_1, c_2)\quad ::= \mathbf{a}(c_2)\ \langle a\rangle(c_2, c_1) \\
&\quad\ \langle d\rangle(c_1)\qquad\quad ::= \varepsilon \\
&\quad\ \langle a\rangle(c_2, c_1)\quad ::= \mathbf{b}(c_1)\ \langle b\rangle(c_1, c_2)\ \mathbf{d}(c_1)\ \langle d\rangle(c_1)|\varepsilon\}
\end{aligned}$$

Fig. 5. An Evaluation of $pCFS_1 \cup pCFS_2$ in Fig. 4 for $\iota(I) = \{c_1\}$ and $\iota(J) = \{c_2\}$

Property 1. Let $pCFS_1 = (TYPES_1, N_1, T_1, P_1)$ and $pCFS_2 = (TYPES_2, N_2, T_2, P_2)$ be two parameterized context-free schemes. Then $pCFS_1 \cup pCFS_2 = (TYPES_1 \cup TYPES_2, N_1 \cup N_2, T_1 \cup T_2, P_1 \cup P_2)$ is also a pCFS.

A *context-free scheme* (short: CFS) is a triple (T, N, P) that can be extended to a CFG (T, N, P, Z) for a $Z \in N$. In our approach we generate CFSs from pCFS by substituting instances of types on the left-hand side of context-free production schemes and evaluate the right-hand sides of productions in the sense that each variable x is replaced by the corresponding parameter. This is later used to generate the combined grammar specifying the set of possible sequences of all procedure calls when executing a component-based system, cf. Fig. 1.

Let $pCFS = (TYPES, N, T, P)$ be a parameterized context-free scheme. An *environment* is a list of pairs $\sigma = [c_1/x_1, \ldots, c_k/x_k]$ where $x_1 : I_1, \ldots, x_k : I_k$ is a set of parameters and $c_1 \in \iota(I_1), \ldots, c_k \in \iota(I_k)$ are instances of $I_1, \ldots, I_k \in TYPES$, respectively. The *evaluation of an applied occurrence* $\langle f\rangle(x_1, \ldots, x_k)$ of a parameterized non-terminal $\langle f\rangle(y_1 : I_1, \ldots, y_k : I_k)$ *under environment* σ is defined as $\langle f\rangle(x_1, \ldots, x_k)\sigma = \langle f\rangle(c_1, \ldots, c_k)$. The *evaluation of a word* $w = a_1 \cdots a_n \in (\Omega_N(x_1 : I_1, \ldots, x_k : I_k) \cup \Sigma_T(x_1 : I_1, \ldots, x_k : I_k))^*$ *under* σ *is defined* as $w\sigma = a_1\sigma \cdots a_n\sigma$. The *evaluation of pCFS* for the instances $\iota(I_1), \ldots, \iota(I_k)$ of its types $TYPES = (I_1, \ldots, I_k)$ is the triple $CFS_\iota = (N_\iota, T_\iota, P_\iota)$ where

- $N_\iota = \{\langle f\rangle(c_1, \ldots, c_k) \mid \langle f\rangle(x_1 : I_1, \ldots, x_k : I_k) \in N \wedge c_1 \in \iota(I_1) \wedge \cdots \wedge c_k \in \iota(I_k)\}$
- $T_\iota = \{\mathbf{p}(c_1, \ldots, c_k) \mid \mathbf{p}(x_1 : I_1, \ldots, x_k : I_k) \in T \wedge c_1 \in \iota(I_1) \wedge \cdots \wedge c_k \in \iota(I_k)\}$
- $P_\iota = \{\langle f\rangle(c_1, \ldots, c_k) ::= w[c_1/x_1, \ldots, c_k/x_k] \mid \langle f\rangle(x_1 : I_1, \ldots, x_k : I_k) ::= w \in P \wedge$
$$c_1 \in \iota(I_1) \wedge \cdots \wedge c_k \in \iota(I_k)\}$$

It is not hard to see, that CFS_ι is a context-free scheme.

If we specify a start symbol $Z \in N_\iota$ we have here all the notions of derivations, languages etc. for the grammar $G = (T_\iota, N_\iota, P_\iota, Z)$. Fig. 5 shows the evaluation of $pCFS_1 \cup pCFS_2$ of Fig. 4 for $\iota(I) = \{c_1\}$ and $\iota(J) = \{c_2\}$.

This evaluation process is used in Section 6 to determine the uses for each instance of a component such that we can apply the protocol checking approach described in Section 3.

5   Generation of Profiles

In this section we show how to derive for each component C a pCFS $pCFS_C$ for its profile. We assume that overloading is resolved, i.e. any name of any procedure is different. The main ideas for construction of $pCFS_C$ are:

- The interfaces used by C define the type names. This information can easily be extracted from the component's source code and the interface definitions.
- The procedures of the interfaces define parameterized terminals. They only have a parameter *this* : I where I is the interface containing p.
- Procedures of interfaces as well as procedures of the component C define non-terminals. They always have the first parameter *this* : I where I is the interface containing the procedure and it only contains the parameter from the procedure that pass references to instances of components (*component parameters*). If a procedure is only contained within C (i.e. internal to C), it defines analogously a non-terminal. In this case a parameter *this* : J is the first parameter where J is a (fixed) interface implementing C. If C is the client, the parameters of *main* are the parameters of C. For simplicity, we assume that these are not used outside of *main*.
- Each procedure p of component C defines a production. Its left-hand side is the parameterized non-terminal corresponding to p. Its right-hand side is an abstraction of the procedure body w.r.t. calls to other interfaces. The right-hand sides are specified as EBNF (see Appendix) and follows the following principles:
  - Internal calls are mapped to applied occurrences of non-terminals using the arguments from the call that pass references to instances of components. The implicit first argument *this* is made explicit.
  - External calls are mapped to a word consisting of a terminal (corresponding to the called procedure) followed by non-terminal as above.
  - Statement lists are mapped to concatenation words stemming from the single statements.

- Conditionals are mapped to alternatives between words stemming from the branches.
- Loops are mapped to iterations over words stemming from the words.
- Expressions are mapped according to the evaluation order used by the compiler generating binary code.

An applied occurrence of a terminal $\mathbf{p}(x)$ where $\mathbf{p}(this : I) \in T_C$ models a call to an instance of a component implementing C since the variable x refers to such an instance. If $\langle p \rangle (this : I_0, x_1 : I_1, \ldots, x_k : I_k) ::= w$ is a production then w specifies a set containing all sequences of procedure calls to interfaces when calling p (i.e. it is an abstraction of the procedure body). Furthermore the other applied of occurrences of non-terminals $y.f(y_1, \ldots, y_m)$ in w specify all sequences of procedure calls to interfaces from components stemming from the call of f to the instance of the component referred to by y. Hence any applied occurrence of a terminal must be followed by the applied occurrences of the corresponding non-terminal. *This is required for taking into account possible callbacks.* Since we allow assignments to variables containing references to instances to components, it is necessary to know all possibles instances a variable may refer to. In our earlier work [23] describing the special case that a client can only call a component, we used points-to analysis (see e.g. [14] for an overview) for this purpose. However, here we don't explicitly know the instances (except the *new*-operations). On the other hand, we know that upon composition time they stem from required interfaces, i.e., generic parameters of components or parameters of procedures. We therefore consider these parameters also as possible instances when performing points-to analysis. Thus, after a local points-to analysis of a component C, for each applied occurrence of a variable y of type I, the set $PT(y)$ contains all new-objects, all generic parameters of C, and all parameters of the procedures of C that could refered to by y. For a precise analysis, a flow-sensitive and context-sensitive analysis should be used.

We now define formally the pCFS. For this some notions are required: A component C *uses* an interface I, if it either implements I, has a parameter of type I (in case of clients), has a procedure with a parameter of type I, or uses an interface with a procedure having a parameter of type I. A *component parameter* is a parameter $x : I$ where I is an interface. $\pi_C(pars)$ denotes the projection of a parameter list to component parameters. The notion is analogously defined for a list of arguments. $proc(I)$ denotes the set of procedures defined by interface I, $proc(C)$ for the set of procedure declarations $p(pars)$ *Body* of C, and $internal(C)$ denotes the set of procedure heads of C that are internal to C , i.e. not declared by an interface implemented by C. Note that all these informations can be derived from the source text of the component and the interfaces used by the component. Fig. 6 shows the formal definition of profiles. We have chosen a left-to-right evaluation order according to semantics of Java or C#. If this evaluation order is implementation-dependent one has to choose here the order used by a compiler. Note that such a transformation can easily be generalized to real-life programming languages if variables containing references to components are distinguished from other variables.

A *profile* of a component C is a pCFS $\mathsf{pCFS}_C = (TYPES_C, T_C, N_C, P_C)$

$$TYPES_C = \{I | C \text{ uses } I\}$$
$$T_C = \{\mathbf{p}(this : I)| I \in TYPES_C \wedge p(pars) \in proc(I)\}$$
$$N_C = \{\langle p\rangle(this : I, \pi_C(pars))| I \in TYPES_C \wedge p(pars) \in proc(I)\} \cup$$
$$\{\langle p\rangle(this : J, \pi_C(pars))| p(pars) \in internal(C)\}$$
$$P_C = \{\langle p\rangle(this : I, \pi_C(pars)) ::= [\![Body]\!]|$$
$$p(pars)\ \{Body\} \in proc(C) \wedge \langle p\rangle(this : I, \pi_C(pars)) \in N_C\}$$

where J is an interface implemented by C and $[\![\cdot]\!]$ is the following transformation:

$[\![p(args)]\!]$	$= \langle p\rangle(this, \pi_C(args))$	internal procedure calls
$[\![y.p(args)]\!]$	$= \mathbf{p}(y_1)\ \langle p\rangle(y_1, \pi_C(args))|\cdots|\mathbf{p}(y_n)\ \langle p\rangle(y_n, \pi_C(args))$	
	for external calls with $PT(y) = \{y_1, \ldots, y_n\}$	

$$
\begin{aligned}
[\![S_1; S_2]\!] &= [\![S_1]\!]\ [\![S_2]\!] \\
[\![\mathbf{if}(e)\ S_1;]\!] &= [\![e]\!]([\![S_1]\!]|\varepsilon) \\
[\![\mathbf{if}(e)\ S_1\ \mathbf{else}\ S_2]\!] &= [\![e]\!]([\![S_1]\!]|[\![S_2]\!]) \\
[\![\{D; S;\}]\!] &= [\![S]\!] \\
[\![\mathbf{while}(e)\ S]\!] &= [\![e]\!]([\![S]\!]\ [\![e]\!])^* \\
[\![v = e]\!] &= [\![e]\!] \\
[\![e_1 + e_2]\!] &= [\![e_1]\!]\ [\![e_2]\!] \\
[\![e_1 \&\& e_2)]\!] &= [\![e_1]\!]([\![e_2]\!]|\varepsilon] \\
[\![v]\!] &= \varepsilon \qquad\qquad \text{if } v \text{ is an integer variable or a constant} \\
[\![new(v)]\!] &= \varepsilon
\end{aligned}
$$

Fig. 6. Profile of a Component C

$$
\begin{aligned}
N &= \{\langle main\rangle(c_1, c_2), \langle b\rangle(c_1, c_2), \langle d\rangle(c_1), \langle a\rangle(c_2, c_1)\} \\
T_{c_1} &= \{\mathbf{b}, \mathbf{d}\} \\
P_{c_1} &= \{\ \langle main\rangle(c_1, c_2) ::= (\langle a\rangle(c_2, c_1))^* \\
&\qquad \langle b\rangle(c_1, c_2) \quad ::= \langle a\rangle(c_2, c_1) \\
&\qquad \langle d\rangle(c_1) \qquad\quad ::= \varepsilon \\
&\qquad \langle a\rangle(c_2, c_1) \quad ::= \mathbf{b}\ \langle b\rangle(c_1, c_2)\ \mathbf{d}\ \langle d\rangle(c_1)|\varepsilon\} \\
T_{c_2} &= \{\mathbf{a}\} \\
P_{c_2} &= \{\ \langle main\rangle(c_1, c_2) ::= (\mathbf{a}\ \langle a\rangle(c_2, c_1))^* \\
&\qquad \langle b\rangle(c_1, c_2) \quad ::= \mathbf{a}\ \langle a\rangle(c_2, c_1) \\
&\qquad \langle d\rangle(c_1) \qquad\quad ::= \varepsilon \\
&\qquad \langle a\rangle(c_2, c_1) \quad ::= \langle b\rangle(c_1, c_2)\ \langle d\rangle(c_1)|\varepsilon\}
\end{aligned}
$$

Fig. 7. Computed Uses for c_1 and c_2 in the Component System of Fig. 2

Fig. 4 shows the parameterized context-free schemes $pCFS_1$ and $pCFS_2$ describing the profiles of client C_1 and component C_2 of Fig. 2, respectively. The profiles in Fig. 4 are generated from the source code of the components in Fig. 2.

6   Model Checking Component-Based Systems

This section shows how for each instance of a component c in a component-based system $C_0[C_1, \ldots, C_k]$ a CFG G_c that describes the use of c can be generated from the profiles of each component. Let $c_0, \ldots, c_k$ be the instances of $C_0, \ldots, C_k$, respectively. The steps for computing G_c for a $c = c_i$ are the following:

1. Compute the *system profile* $pCFS_S = pCFS_{C_0} \cup \cdots \cup pCFS_{C_k}$ where $pCFS_{C_i}$ is the profile of C_i, $i = 1, \ldots, k$. Note that the system profile is a pCFS according to Property 1.
2. Evaluate the system profile for ι in order to obtain a CFS $CFS\iota = (T, N, P)$, cf. Section 4, where $\iota(I) = \{c_i : C_i \text{ implements } I\}$.

3. Compute the *system interaction* $G_S = (T, N, P, \langle main \rangle (c_0, c_1, \ldots, c_k))$. Note that G_S is a CFG.
4. Define $G_{c_i} = (N, T_c, P_c, \langle main \rangle (c_0, c_1, \ldots, c_k))$ where $T_c = \{p | p(c) \in T\}$, $P_c = \{X ::= \phi^*(w) | X ::= w \in P\}$, and $\phi^* : T^* \to T_c^*$ is induced by the

mapping $\phi : T \to T_c$ defined by $\phi(x) = \begin{cases} \mathbf{x} & \text{if } \mathbf{x} \in T_c \\ \varepsilon & \text{otherwise} \end{cases}$

Figure 5 shows the CFS after Step 2. Thus, the system interaction is obtained by adding the start symbol $\langle main \rangle (c_1, c_2)$. Fig. 7 shows the CFGs describing the uses of c_1 and c_2, respectively. It can easily be seen that $L(G_{c_1})$ is the Dyck-language with open bracket b and closing bracket d.

The right-hand sides of the productions in the system interaction are an abstraction of the corresponding procedure bodies. Therefore, we have the invariant that $L(\langle p \rangle (c_1, \ldots, c_n))$ contains at least all sequences of procedure calls to all components w.r.t. to grammar G_{s_1}. A formal proof requires formal semantics of the programming languages used by the components. An induction on the height of the derivation tree could be used to show the above claim. Hence $L(G_S)$ contains all sequences of all calls made to instances of a component during the execution of a component based system. By definition of ϕ^*, in the fourth step, all sequences are projected to those calling c. Thus, we can check for each instance c of C whether $L(G_c) \subseteq L(A_C)$ where A_C is a FSM specifying the protocol of C.

7 Related Work

Many works on static protocol-checking of components consider local protocol checking on FSMs. The same approach can also be applied to check protocols of object in object-oriented systems. The idea of static type checking by using FSMs goes back to Nierstrasz [18]. Their approach uses regular languages to model the dynamic behavior of objects, which is less powerful than CFGs. Therefore the approach cannot handle recursive call-backs. [17] considers object-life cycles for dynamic exchange of implementations of classes and methods using a combination of the bridge/strategy pattern. It also based on FSMs. The approach comprises dynamic as well as static conformance checking. Tenzer and Stevens [22] investigate approaches for checking object-life cycles. They assume that object-life cycles of UML-classes are described using UML state-charts and that for each method of a client, there is a FSM that describes the calling sequence from that method. In order to deal with recursion, Tenzer and Stevens add a rather complicated recursion mechanism to FSMs. It is not clear whether this recursion mechanism is as powerful as pushdown automata and therefore could accept general context-free languages. All these works are for sequential systems. Schmidt et al. [13] propose an approach for protocol checking of concurrent component-based systems. Their approach is also FSM-based and unable to deal with recursive call-backs. Earlier work of the authors shows that CFGs are very adequate to handle internal recursion on a client-side [23]. However, the systems only allow that clients call components.

Even modeling the use of a component with context-free languages may abstract too much from the real behavior. Other approaches therefore use dynamic protocol-checking, e.g. Chambers [10] defines Predicate Classes for the language Cecil. Each object of a given class is attached to a set of predicates. Before a method call is accepted by an object, a certain set of predicates have to be true. A class is described by several property classes. These property classes correspond to the states in our finite state machine. Ramalingam et al. [19] derive dynamic checkers using abstract interpretation techniques. In particular, they abstract client programs to Boolean programs that perform runtime checking of client-component conformance. However dynamic protocol checking does not exclude protocol faults as static protocol checking does. On the other hand, they identify bugs at the right place. In particular, dynamic adapters might support avoiding protocol faults whenever possible.

An alternative approach for investigation of protocol conformance is the use of process algebras such as CSP, cf. e.g. [2,1]. These approaches are more powerful than FSMs and context-free grammars. However, mechanized checking requires some restrictions on the specification language. For example, [2] uses a subset of CSP that allows only the specification of finite processes. At the end the conformance checking reduces to checking FSMs similar to [13].

FSMs are also used for checking Liskov's substitution principle for subtyping in object-oriented systems based on class protocols. Reussner [20] generalizes on the idea of Nierstrasz and adds counters and conditions over counters to the regular types to decide, whether Liskov's substitution principle is satisfied. Freudig et al. [12] use sub-classes of CFGs for describing protocols and checking Liskov's substitution principle. They need subclasses of CFGs because the subset-problem on general context-free languages is algorithmically undecidable. They do not model calling sequences stemming from a method which is required for checking whether the use of an object of a certain class conforms to its protocol.

The work on model checking context-free processes and pushdown systems started with [8,9]. The model checking of LTL-formulas can be done within the same complexity as shown here (linear in the size of the system and cubic in the number of states) [11,3,5]. However, these approaches would require that the complete system is available as a context-free process or as a pushdown system. The framework described in [6] contains among others an algorithm for checking whether $L(G) \subseteq L(A)$ for context-free grammars G and finite state machines A with the same complexity as our approach in Section 3. In contrast to our approach, their approach is not able to generate counterexamples.

8   Conclusions

We discussed the problem of statically checking whether instances components in a component-based system are used according to their protocol. As many approaches we consider sequential systems and require static knowledge of the components. Instances of components could be generated dynamically. As other approaches we used FSMs for describing component protocols. Other approaches usually check locally the conformance of each connection in a component-based system assuming that the use of interfaces is described by FSMs. We have shown that in the presence of recursive call-backs this approach fails to achieve its goals because a global view is required for describing the use of components and regular languages are not powerful enough to describe adequately recursive call-backs. The local protocol conformance checking approaches are therefore restricted to systems without recursive call-backs.

The contribution of our approach is that we are able to deal with recursive call-backs and determine the use of component instances from a global view. The reason for being able to deal with recursive call-backs is that we used CFGs to describe the use of components instead of FSMs. The problem whether a context-free language is a subset of a regular language is algorithmically decidable (even in time linear to the size of the grammar). The reason for being able to handle a global view is the use of two-level CFSs for specifying how a procedure of a component uses other interfaces. The parameters of the CFSs are the same as provided by the component and the interfaces it uses. Upon component composition, these parameterized context-free schemes are composed in the same way as the components are composed in order to obtain for each instance of a component the CFG specifying its use.

Our approach is a model-checking approach in the sense that if a conformance check fails, it is able to provide counterexamples. Since the CFGs are an abstraction of the use of instances of components, a failure might be caused because abstractions may contain words that do not represent a sequence of procedure calls to that instance, i.e., false negatives may occur. Further work should consider how certain counterexamples can be avoided. This would require more knowledge of the code that might be encoded in the parameterized CFSs for the components.

Certainly, for practical reasons, our approach for sequential systems needs be extended to concurrency as well as to composition with statically unknown components. If we would be able to deal with concurrency and composition with statically unknown components it would be possible to deal with most classical component systems such as Web Services, CORBA, COM, .NET, EJBs. A further challenge is certainly to deal with more recent composition principles such aspect-oriented programming [16] or invasive software composition [4] because these approaches change at runtime the protocols of components.

Acknowledgement. We thank the anonymous referees for their helpful comments.

References

1. C. Attiogbé, P. André, G. Ardourel. Checking Component Composability In *Proc. of the 5th International Symposium on Software Composition*, this volume of *Lecture Notes in Computer Science*. Springer, 2006.
2. R. Allen and S. Garlan. A formal basis for architectural connection. *ACM Transactions on Software Engineering and Methodology*, 6(3):213–249, 1997.
3. R. Alur, K. Etessami, and M. Yannakakis. Analysis of recursive state machines. In *Proceedings of the 13th Conference on Computer Aided Verification*, volume 2102 of *Lecture Notes in Computer Science*, pages 207–220. Springer, 2001.

4. U. Assmann. *Invasive Software Composition*. Springer, 2003.
5. M. Benedikt, P. Godefroid, and T. Reps. Model checking of unrestricted hierarchical state machines. In *Proceedings of the 28th International Colloquium on Automata, Languages, and Programming ICALP'2001*, volume 2076 of *Lecture Notes in Computer Science*, pages 652–666. Springer, 2001.
6. A. Bouajjani, J. Esparza, A. Finkel, O. Maler, P. Rossmanith, B. Willems, and P. Wolper. An efficient automata approach to some problems on context-free grammars. *Information Processing Letters*, 74(5-6):221–227, 2000.
7. A. Bouajjani, J. Esparza, and O. Maler. Reachability analysis of pushdown automata: Application to model checking. In *CONCUR'97: Proceedings of the 8th International Conference on Concurrency Theory*, volume 1243 of *Lecture Notes in Computer Science*, pages 135–150. Springer, 1997.
8. O. Burkart and B. Steffen. Model checking for context-free processes. In *CONCUR'92: Proceedings of the 3rd International Conference on Concurrency Theory*, volume 630 of *Lecture Notes in Computer Science*, pages 123–137. Springer, 1992.
9. O. Burkart and B. Steffen. Pushdown processes: Parallel composition and model checking. In *CONCUR'94: Proceedings of the 5th International Conference on Concurrency Theory*, volume 836 of *Lecture Notes in Computer Science*, pages 98–113. Springer, 1994.
10. C. Chambers. Predicate classes. In *Proceedings of the 7th European Conference on Object-Oriented Programming*, volume 707 of *Lecture Notes in Computer Science*, pages 268–296. Springer, 1993.
11. J. Esparza, D. Hansel, P. Rossmanith, and S. Schwoon. Efficient algorithms for model checking pushdown systems. In *Proceedings of the 12th Conference on Computer Aided Verification*, volume 1855 of *Lecture Notes in Computer Science*, pages 232–247. Springer, 2000.
12. J. Freudig, W. Löwe, R. Neumann, and M. Trapp. Subtyping of context-free classes. In *Proceedings 3rd White Object Oriented Nights*, 1998.
13. H. W. Schmidt, B. J. Krämer, I. Poernemo, and R. Reussner. Predictable component architectures using dependent finite state machines. In *Proc. of the NATO Workshop Radical Innovations of Software and Systems Engineering in the Future*, volume 2941 of *Lecture Notes in Computer Science*, pages 310–324. Springer, 2002.
14. M. Hind, M. Burke, P. Carini, and J.-D. Choi. Interprocedural pointer alias analysis. *ACM Transactions on Programming Languages and Systems*, 21(4):848–894, 1999.
15. J. E. Hopcroft, R. Motwani, and J. D. Ullman. *Introduction to Automata Theory, Languages and Computation*. Addison Wesley, 2nd edition, 2001.
16. G. Kiczales, J. Lamping, A. Mendhekar, C. Maeda, C. Lopes, J.-M. Loingtier, and J. Irwin. Aspect-oriented programming. In *ECOOP'97 – Object-Oriented Programming*, volume 1241 of *Lecture Notes in Computer Science*, pages 220–242. Springer, 1997.
17. W. Löwe, R. Neumann, M. Trapp, and W. Zimmermann. Robust dynamic exchange of implementation aspects. In *TOOLS 29 – Technology of Object-Oriented Languages and Systems*, pages 351–360. IEEE, 1999.
18. O. Nierstrasz. Regular types for active objects. In *OOPSALA '93*, volume 28 of *ACM SIGPLAN Notices*, 1993.
19. G. Ramalingam, A. Warshavsky, J. Field, D. Goyal, and M. Sagiv. Deriving specialized program analyses for certifying component-client conformance. In *Proceedings of the ACM SIGPLAN 2002 Conference on Programming Language Design and Implementation*, pages 83–94. ACM, 2002.

20. R. H. Reussner. Counter-constraint finite state machines: A new model for resource-bounded component protocols. In *Proceedings of the 29th Annual Conference in Current Trends in Theory and Practice of Informatics*, volume 2540 of *Lecture Notes in Computer Science*, pages 20–40. Springer, 2002.
21. A. K. Salomaa. *Formal Languages*. Springer, 1978.
22. J. Tenzer and P. Stevens. Modelling recursive calls with uml state diagrams. In *6th International Conference on Fundamental Approaches to Software Engineering (FASE'03)*, volume 2621 of *Lecture Notes in Computer Science*, pages 135–149. Springer, 2003.
23. W. Zimmermann and M. Schaarschmidt. Model checking of client-component conformance. In *2nd Nordic Conference on Web-Services*, number 008 in Mathematical Modelling in Physics, Engineering and Cognitive Sciences, pages 63–74, 2003.

A   Grammars and Automata

An *alphabet* Σ is a finite set of symbols. A word w over Σ is a concatenation of n symbols of Σ, i.e. $w = a_1 \cdots a_n$ where $a_1, \ldots, a_n \in \Sigma$. A word w is *empty* iff $n = 0$. The empty word is unique and is denoted by ε. Concatenation can be easily extended to words, i.e. uv denotes the concatenation of words u and v. Σ^* denotes the set of all words over the alphabet Σ. A *formal language* (or short language) is a subset $L \subseteq \Sigma^*$. A *context-free grammar* (short: CFG) is a quadruple $G = (T, N, P, Z)$ where T and N is an alphabet (the *terminal symbols* and *non-terminal symbols*, resp.), $T \cap N = \emptyset$, $P \subseteq N \times (T \cup N)^*$ (the set of *productions*, and $Z \in N$ (the *start symbol*). We denote non-terminals by capital letters and terminals by lower case letters. A production is denoted by $X ::= w \in P$. A *direct derivation* w.r.t. G is a pair of words $x, y \in (T \cup N)^*$, denoted by $x \Rightarrow_G y$, such $x = uXv$ $y = uwv$ for some $u, v \in (T \cup N)^*$, $X ::= w \in P$. The *derivation relation* $\stackrel{*}{\Rightarrow}_G$ is the reflexive, transitive closure of $\Rightarrow_G$. We omit the index G if it is clear from the context. The *language generated by CFG G* is defined as $L(G) \triangleq \{w \in T^* | Z \stackrel{*}{\Rightarrow}_G w\}$. We use often *Extended Backus-Naur Form* (short: EBNF) to describe CFGs. For this, we assume that $[,], *, | \notin \Sigma$ and use the following abbreviations:

$X ::= u|v$ abbreviates $X ::= u$ $X ::= v$ where A is a new non-terminal.
$X ::= u^*$ abbreviates $X ::= A. A ::= \varepsilon|uA$

A *finite state machine* (FSM) is a quintuple $A = (T, Q, R, q_0, F)$ where T is an alphabet, Q is a finite set of *states* such that $Q \cap T = \emptyset$, $R \subseteq Q \times T \times T$ is a set of *rules* (rules are denoted as $qa \to q'$, $q_0 \in Q$ is the *initial state*, and $F \subseteq Q$ is the set of *final states*. A accepts in state q a letter a iff there is a rule $qa \to q' \in R$. q' is called the successor state of q on input a. A *direct derivation* w.r.t A is relation $\Rightarrow_A$ defined by $qau \Rightarrow_A q'u$ where $qa \to q' \in R$ and $u \in T^*$. The *derivation relation* $\stackrel{*}{\Rightarrow}_A$ is the reflexive, transitive closure of $\Rightarrow_A$. We omit the index A if it is clear from the context. The FSM A *accepts* a word $w \in T^*$ iff there is a final state $f \in F$ such that $qw \stackrel{*}{\Rightarrow}_A f$. The *language accepted by* A is defined as $L(A) \triangleq \{w \in T^* | A \text{ accepts } w\}$. In this work we visualize finite automata as labeled directed graphs. The states are the vertices, and there is a directed edge $q \stackrel{a}{\to} q'$ iff $qa \to q' \in R$. Fig. 3 shows an example.

Checking Component Composability

Christian Attiogbé, Pascal André, and Gilles Ardourel

LINA CNRS FRE 2729 - University of Nantes
F-44322 Nantes Cedex, France
{Christian.Attiogbe, Pascal.Andre, Gilles.Ardourel}@univ-nantes.fr

Abstract. Component-Based Software Engineering (CBSE) is one of the approaches to master the development of large scale software. In this setting, the verification concern is still a challenge. The current work addresses the composability of components and their services. A component model (Kmelia) is introduced; an associated formalism, simple but expressive is introduced; it describes the services as extended LTSs and their structuring as components. The composability of components is defined on the basis of the composability of services. To ensure the correctness of component composition, we check that an assembly is possible via the checking of the composability of the linked services, and their behavioural compatibility. In order to mechanize our approach, the services and the components are translated into the LOTOS formalism. Finally the LOTOS CADP toolbox is used to perform experiments.

Keywords: Components, Services, Behavioural Interface Description, Composability, Behavioural Verification.

1 Introduction

The rigorous development of large systems with methods that scale up and that are reusable in various projects is still a challenging research topic. Component-Based Software Engineering (CBSE) motivates a number of works on this topic [19,15,6,12]. The component approach promotes the (re)use of components coming from third party developers to build new large systems. The success of the large scale development of component-based systems depends on the availability of: reliable components libraries, tools to search for components (in libraries), expressive languages of composition of the components and especially tools for checking the correct use of components.

The *motivation* for this work lies on the need of a sound basis for developing correct components, for studying composition and for implementing related tools. While many component approaches focus on the structural aspects of component composition, we insist on the functional (services) and dynamic (behaviour) aspects of the components because they are important criteria for component reuse. In this perspective, related works deal with the behavioural compatibility for simplified abstract component models [6,8,5]. On the other hand there are mechanized approaches such as Tracta [10] or SOFA [17] but their component models are restricted. These works associate behaviour(s) to

W. Löwe and M. Südholt (Eds.): SC 2006, LNCS 4089, pp. 18–33, 2006.

components and not to services. But this is a limitation since the services provide a finer description of the component usage.

The *goal* of the work is to provide the designer of component-based systems with a high level component model and also with the methods to assist his/her use of the components. We are interested in building an experimental toolbox for component study and development.

The main *contribution* of this article is a simple formal model (named Kmelia) for modelling and composing components; it supports the verification of composability. We define composability of components by considering the links between their services and the behavioural compatibility of these services. Therefore, we get a hierarchical definition of composition and assemblies. In our work, a component is viewed and used through the *services* which constitute its interface. The use of services is central for the verification of composability when assembling components. It is important to detect the defects which could lead to a faulty behaviour of the developed system early in the development. A bad interaction between a called service and the calling one may lead to a blocking of the whole system. To ensure a good level of correctness of the components and their assemblies, the formal verification of the service descriptions with respect to the desired properties of the component is necessary. Consequently, the specifications of components and their service behaviours should be abstract and formal. The use of an abstract formal model makes it possible to hide the implementation details of the components in order to have general reasoning techniques which are adaptable to various implementation environments.

The article is structured as follows. Section 2 presents the Kmelia model through the description of services and components. It is illustrated with an example of a bank Automatic Teller Machine system. Further details on Kmelia are given in [3]. The Section 3 introduces the service links and sublinks used to describe component assemblies and compositions. Section 4 is devoted to the composability of services and components. Behavioural compatibility between component services is also treated there. In the Section 5 we present the mechanization approach undertaken to support the Kmelia model. Experiments are done with LOTOS. Section 6 concludes with a discussion and the perspectives.

2   A Component Model Based on Services: Kmelia

In the Kmelia model, a component is characterised by: a name (the component identifier), a state (variables and an invariant predicate on them), an interface made of *services* and the description of the services. The *interface* specifies the component interactions with its environment [1,15]. A Kmelia component interface is made of *provided services* and *required services*. A provided service offers a functionality, while a required service is the expression of the need of a functionality. This need is fulfilled when the component is combined with other components (in an *assembly*), one of them supplying the corresponding required service. Therefore, in Kmelia, component services interact with synchronous communication supported by message exchanges or service calls/responses via *communication channels.* Related works [17,18,16] associate dynamic behaviours (or protocols) to components and services are atomic operations (*messages*). Unlike these approaches, we consider *services* as units of interaction and they are equipped with dynamic behaviours (service behaviours). This provides finer component descriptions where services are the main entities [2].

2.1   Service Specification

A *service* s of a component C is defined with an *interface* I_s and a (dynamic) *behaviour* $\mathcal{B}_s$: $\langle I_s, \mathcal{B}_s \rangle$. Usually a required service does not have the same level of detail as a provided service since a part of these details is already in the (provided) service that calls it.

The interface I_s of a service s is defined by a 5-tuple $\langle \sigma, P, Q, V_s, S_s \rangle$ where σ is the service signature (name, arguments, result), P is a precondition, Q is a postcondition, V_s is a set of local declarations and the *service dependency* S_s is a 4-tuple $S_s = \langle sub_s, cal_s, req_s, int_s \rangle$ of disjoint sets where sub_s (resp. cal_s, req_s, int_s) contains the provided services names (resp. the services required from the caller, the services required from any component, the internal services) in the scope of s. Using a required service r in cal_p of a service p (as opposed to a component interface) implies r to be provided by the component which calls p. Using a provided service p in the sub_r of a service r but not in the component interface, means that p is accessible only during an interaction with r.

The behaviour $\mathcal{B}_s$ of a service s is an *extended labelled transition system* (eLTS) defined by a 6-tuple $\langle S, L, \delta, \Phi, S_0, S_F \rangle$ with S the set of the states of s, L the set of transition labels and δ the transition relation ($\delta \in S \times L \to S$). S_0 is the initial state ($S_0 \in S$), S_F is the finite set of final states ($S_F \subseteq S$), Φ is a state annotation partial function ($\Phi \in S \to sub_s$). An eLTS is obtained when we allow nested states and transitions. This provides a flexible description with optional behaviours named *branching states* and also reduces the LTS size. A branching state is the one annotated with sub-service names (using the Φ function), which are (sub-)services of the component C that may be called when the evolution reaches this state (but the control returns to this state when the launched sub-service is terminated). Formally, the unfolding of (the branching states of) an eLTS results in an LTS.

Transitions: The elements $((ss, label), ts)$ of δ have the concrete Kmelia syntax `ss--label-->ts` where the labels are (possibly guarded) combinations of actions: `[guard] action*`. The actions may be *elementary actions* or *communication actions*. An elementary action (an assignment for example) does not involve other services; it does not use a communication channel. A communication action is either a *service call/response* or a message *communication*. Therefore communications are matching pairs: *send message(!)-receive message(?), call service(!!)-wait service start(??), emit service result(!!)-wait service result(??)*. The Kmelia syntax of a communication action (inspired by the Hoare's CSP) is: `channel(!|?|!!|??) message(param*)`.

Channels: A communication channel is established between the interacting services when assembling components. A channel defines a context for the communication actions. At the moment one writes a behaviour, one does not know which components will communicate, but one has to know which channels will be used. A channel is usually named after the required service that represents the context. The placeholder keyword CALLER is a specific channel that stands for the channel open for a service call. From the point of view of a provided service p, CALLER is the channel that is open when p is called. From the point of view of the service that calls p, this channel is named after one of its required service, which is probably named p. The placeholder keyword SELF is a specific channel that stands for the channel opened for an internal service call. In this case, the required service is also the provided service.

2.2   Component Specification

A component (C) is a 8-tuple $\langle \mathcal{W}, Init, \mathcal{A}, \mathcal{N}, I, \mathcal{D}_S, \nu, \mathcal{C}_S \rangle$ with:

- $\mathcal{W} = \langle T, V, V_T, Inv \rangle$ the state space where T is a set of types, V a set of variables, $V_T \subseteq V \times T$ a set of typed variables, and Inv is the state invariant;
- $Init$ the initialisation of the V_T variables;
- $\mathcal{A}$ a finite set of elementary actions;
- $\mathcal{N}$ a finite set of service names;
- I the component interface which is the union of two disjoints finite sets: I_p the set of names of the provided services that are visible in the component environment and I_r the names of required services.
- $\mathcal{D}_S$ is the set of service descriptions; it is partitioned into the provided services $(\mathcal{D}_{S_p})$ and the required services $(\mathcal{D}_{S_r})$.
- $\nu : \mathcal{N} \to \mathcal{D}_S$ is the function that maps service names to service descriptions. Moreover there is a projection of the I partition on its image by ν:
  $n \in I_p \Rightarrow \nu(n) \in \mathcal{D}_{S_p} \wedge n \in I_r \Rightarrow \nu(n) \in \mathcal{D}_{S_r}$
- $\mathcal{C}_S$ is a constraint related to the services of the interface of C in order to control the usage of the services.

The behaviour of the component relies on the behaviours of its services. The constraint $\mathcal{C}_S$ describes general conditions on the service usage: it may be an ordering of services or a predicate (temporal condition, mutual exclusion...). A specific service offered (like a *main*) as a single provided service may *implement* a *Component Behaviour Protocol* in the sense of [10,17].

2.3   Component Assembly

Assembling Kmelia components consists in linking their pairwise services: required services may be linked to provided services. Formal details are given in the Sect. 3.3. Let consider two main semantics for the link operator: the *monadic* and the *polyadic semantics*. With the *monadic semantics*, only one provided service may be associated to a required service; a component is both a component type and the unique instance of it; a required service may be linked to at most one provided service (no overloading); only one instantiation of a service exists at any time. The service evolutions are concurrent processes with shared component state. With the *polyadic semantics* a provided service may be linked with various required services (allowing broadcast communications); in the same way a required service may be linked to various providers. As an example, a chat application provides services for multiple clients. Only the monadic semantic is considered in this article.

2.4 Illustration

We illustrate the model with a simplified real-world problem: a bank Automatic Teller Machine (ATM). Since the case is very common, the details are omitted here. Fig. 1 shows a simplified component assembly for the ATM, that includes four components: the central ATM_CORE which handles the ATM bank services, the USER_INTERFACE component which controls the user access, the AAC stands for the bank management and the LOCAL_BANK holds the local management access. The component usage is quite flexible: an assembly may be correct for the services whose dependency chains are fulfilled. The *USER_INTERFACE*

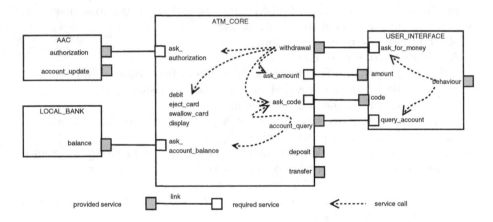

Fig. 1. Assembly for an ATM System

component offers the (provided) code service only in the interface of the behaviour service; it means that the *USER_INTERFACE* only gives its code during a withdrawal operation that it has initiated. In such a situation, code is a sub-service. The component services are detailed in the Fig. 2. Note that the *USER_INTERFACE* may also call a withdrawal service that does not require its code. In the following we focus on the withdrawal provided service which is linked to the required ask_for_money service, called by the behaviour service. This triple constitutes a context for a service verification (see Sect. 4.4). The links associated to withdrawal are:

```
(p-r ATM_CORE.withdrawal, USER_INTERFACE.ask_for_money
 //p-r stands for provided-required
 //sublinks
 (r-p ATM_CORE.ask_code, USER_INTERFACE.code)
 (r-p ATM_CORE.ask_amount, USER_INTERFACE.amount) )
```

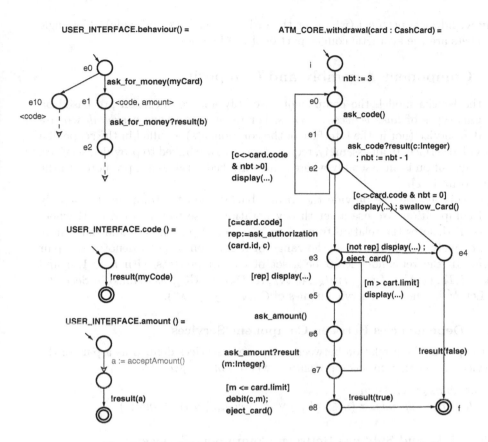

Fig. 2. LTS of the two main services (with the sub-services)

The withdrawal starts with an identification step: card insertion, password control, authentication by ACD/ATM controller (AAC). If the AAC accepts the transaction, the ATM asks for the amount of cash, otherwise the card is ejected and the withdrawal transaction ends. The user enters an amount which is compared with the current card policy limit. When the allowed amount is lower than the requested one or if the current ATM cash is not sufficient, the ATM asks again for the amount of cash. Otherwise the ATM asks the AAC to process the transaction, updates the card limit, gives the cash and prints a receipt when it is possible. In any case the withdrawal transaction ends after a card ejection. There are four elementary actions (*debit, eject_card, swallow_card, display*). The channels may be omitted and deduced either from the context or from default rules. This syntactic sugar is not currently implemented in our prototype.

The interaction description is made *flexible* by enabling the call of sub-services when the evolution reaches branching states. For example, the notation e1 <code, amount> expresses that the services code and amount may be called in the e1 (branching) state. Thus the ask_for_money service may operate with any withdrawal protocol (whatever the order for amount and code). The angle brackets are the syntactic counterpart of the Φ function.

3   Component Assembly and Composition

In the Kmelia model, the component assembly and composition are based on various types of *links between services*. For instance we have a *sublink* when a hidden service (not in the interface of the components) is called in the scope of a provided service. In an assembly, required services are linked to provided services. A composition is an assembly where some unlinked services are promoted to the composite level.

In this section, we provide the formal background for component assembly and composition. We use a set theory notation close to that of Z or B where $X \leftrightarrow Y$ denotes the relation from X to Y (a set of pairs); dom and ran denote respectively the domain and the range of a relation; $a \mapsto b$ denotes the pair (a, b). In the remainder let $\mathcal{C}$ be a set of C_k components with $k \in 1..n$ and $C_k = \langle \langle T_k, V_k, V_{Tk}, Inv_k \rangle, Init_k, \mathcal{A}_k, \mathcal{N}_k, I_k, \mathcal{D}_{Sk}, \nu_k, \mathcal{C}_{Sk} \rangle$ as defined in Sect. 2.

Let $\mathcal{N}$ be the set of service names of $\mathcal{C}$ ($\mathcal{N} = \bigcup_{k \in 1..n} \mathcal{N}_k$).

3.1   Dependencies Between Component Services

Let $depends_k$ be a relation between component services defined as a part of the service dependency in a component C_k where $sm = \nu_k(m)$:

$depends_k : \mathcal{N}_k \leftrightarrow \mathcal{N}_k$
$\forall(n, m) : depends_k \bullet (n \in cal_{sm}) \vee (n \in req_{sm}) \vee (n \in sub_{sm})$

3.2   Links and Sublinks Between Component Services

Basically, the links are 4-tuple of component and service names with the following properties: (1) the service names are those of their owner components, (2) any component service is not linked to itself (not recursive).

$BaseLink : \mathbb{P} (\mathcal{C} \times \mathcal{N} \times \mathcal{C} \times \mathcal{N})$
(1) $\forall(C_i, n_1, C_j, n_2) : BaseLink \bullet n_1 \in \mathcal{N}_i \wedge n_2 \in \mathcal{N}_j$
(2) $\forall C_i : \mathcal{C}, \ n_1 : \mathcal{N}_i \bullet (C_i, n_1, C_i, n_1) \notin BaseLink$

A link connects two services of the interfaces of their owner components.

$Link \subseteq BaseLink \wedge \forall(C_i, n_1, C_j, n_2) : Link \bullet n_1 \in I_i \wedge n_2 \in I_j$

A sublink is a base link between two services such that one of them at least is hidden. For instance we have a sublink when a hidden service is called in the scope of a provided service.

$SubLink \subseteq BaseLink \wedge \forall(C_i, n_1, C_j, n_2) : SubLink \bullet n_1 \notin I_i \vee n_2 \notin I_j$

The *sublink* makes explicit the relation between the service dependencies declared in the interfaces of the services involved in a *Link*. In the following these relationships are constrained in order to define component assembly and component composition.

3.3 Component Assembly

A component assembly is a triple $A = (\mathcal{C},\ links,\ subs)$ where $\mathcal{C}$ is a set of components, $links$ is a set of links between the services of $\mathcal{C}$ and $subs$ is a relation from links to sublinks.

> $links \subseteq Link\ \wedge$
> (1) $(\forall(C_i, n_1, C_j, n_2) : links \bullet C_i \in \mathcal{C} \wedge C_j \in \mathcal{C} \wedge$
> $((n_1 \in I_{p_i} \wedge n_2 \in I_{r_j}) \vee (n_1 \in I_{r_i} \wedge n_2 \in I_{p_j})))$
> $subs : Link \leftrightarrow SubLink\ \wedge$
> (2) $\mathrm{dom}\ subs = links\ \wedge$
> (3) $(\forall((C_i, n_1, C_j, n_2) \mapsto (C_k, n_3, C_l, n_4)) \in subs \bullet C_i = C_k \wedge C_j = C_l)\ \wedge$
> (4) $(\forall(C_i, n_1, C_j, n_2) : \mathrm{ran}\ subs \bullet ((\nu_i(n_1) \in \mathcal{D}_{S_{p_i}})\ \mathrm{xor}\ (\nu_j(n_2) \in \mathcal{D}_{S_{p_j}})))$

The components of the links are the components of the assembly (1). The sublinks are related to links (2) that concern the same components (3). Provided services are linked to required services (1 and 4).

The triple A is a *well-formed component assembly* if the following property holds: the services in the sublinks are not in the involved component interfaces, but they are in the dependencies of the involved services (w.r.t *sublinks*).

> (5) $\forall(l, sl) \in subs \mid l = (C_i, n_1, C_j, n_2) \wedge sl = (C_k, n_3, C_l, n_4) \bullet$
> $((n_3, n_1) \in depends_i{}^* \vee (n_4, n_2) \in depends_j{}^*)$

where $depends_i{}^*$ is the transitive closure of $depends_i$.

Practically a *link* establishes an implicit communication channel between the involved services. This channel is shared with the sub-services.

3.4 Component Composition

A *composition* is a well-formed component assembly which is encapsulated within a component. We define an operator named compose that builds a new component by combining one or several components.

The parameters of the compose operator are:

- an outer component oC (the composite) together with its interface, new services and services of its constituents;
- a well-formed assembly $A = (\mathcal{C},\ links,\ subs)$ (see section 3.3);
- the desired *promotions*, that are set of links between the services of oC and those of $C_k \in \mathcal{C}$.

The promotion is a relation between a service of the composite oC and an unlinked service of the components in A, that preserves existing sublinks; such promoted service becomes usable at the composite level.

> $promotions \subseteq BaseLink\ \wedge$
> $(\forall(C_i, n_1, C_j, n_2) : promotions \bullet$
> (1) $(C_i = oC) \wedge (C_j \in \mathcal{C}) \wedge$
> (2) $((\nu_{oC}(n_1) \in \mathcal{D}_{S_{p_{oC}}} \wedge n_2 \in I_{p_j}) \vee (\nu_{oC}(n_1) \in \mathcal{D}_{S_{r_{oC}}} \wedge n_2 \in I_{r_j})))$

The resulting component is an enhancement of oC: it contains every provided and required services of oC and provides/requires the promoted services from other components in C (using *promotions*). Here the sub-services of the promoted services are also promoted.

From a methodological point of view, the composition operator may be used to refine an abstract component with a component assembly; it may also be used to structure simple components or to provide a more restrictive interface of existing components.

4   Formal Verification of Components and Assemblies

Formal verification of components is performed according to various aspects. In the Section 4.1, we overview the main issues of component formal verification so as to situate the composability of components. Thereafter we focus on one specific aspect: the verification of the correct interaction between components. Indeed, a part of the service composability lies on the behavioural compatibility of the services: a correct service interaction is a guarantee for the composition of components. In the following, both static aspect and dynamic aspect of the verification are considered to check composability.

4.1   Formal Analysis of Components

The *safety* and *liveness* verifications apply to software components; but they should be adapted to component features. The *behavioural compatibility* between components is related to both safety and liveness. It is a widely studied topic [21,8,4,7]. Behavioural introspection (discovering the component behaviour) is one way to deal with behavioural compatibility; but one has to prove compatibility. Checking behavioural compatibility often relies on checking the behaviour of a (component based) system through the construction of a finite state automaton. However the state explosion is a limitation of this approach [8,4]. More generally, the following properties should be considered for verification.

- *Correctness of functional properties*: do the components do what they should do? These properties may be independently checked on the components which are used and also on the composition of the components;
- *Flexibility of maintenance (modifiability, evolution)*: that means the components should be simply updated when needed, without drastically affecting the third party components which use them. The update of a component includes the modification of the implementation of its service(s), the removing/adding of a service; etc.
- *Heterogeneity*: within the CBSE approach, the components coming from various providers may be composable to develop large systems. This is a challenging concern because the components may have different models;
- *Compositionality*: the properties of a global system should be deduced from the properties of the composed components;

- *(Static) Interoperability properties*: the compatibility of signatures and interfaces (naming and typing); does a component give enough information about its interface(s) in order to be (re)usable by other components?
- *Architectural properties*: they involve the availability of the required components, the availability of the needed services, the correctness of the links between interfaces of components (providers and callers);
- *Behavioural compatibility*: it is about the correct interaction between two or more components which are combined. Several points need to be considered: various kinds of interaction, synchronous or not, atomic actions or non atomic ones.

The last three categories of properties are related to composability.

4.2 Composability

We define composability at different related levels: service level and component level.

Definition 1 (Service Composability)
A provided service $sp_{C_i} = \langle\langle\sigma_p, P_p, Q_p, V_{sp}, S_{sp}\rangle, \mathcal{B}_{sp}\rangle$ of a component C_i and a required service $sr_{C_j} = \langle\langle\sigma_r, P_r, Q_r, V_{sr}, S_{sr}\rangle, \mathcal{B}_{sr}\rangle$ of a component C_j are s-composable (noted s-composable(sp_{C_i}, sr_{C_j})) when sr_{C_j} is required in the behaviour $\mathcal{B}_s$ of a service s of C_j if:

1. *the interfaces of sp_{C_i} and sr_{C_j} are compatible; that is,*
   (a) *their signatures are matching (no type conflict: σ_p and σ_r are identical),*
   (b) *the assertions (pre/post) are consistent ($post(sp_{C_i}) \sim post(sr_{C_j})$) and*
   (c) *their mutually dependent services S_{sp}, S_{sr} (see service dependencies in Sect. 2.1) are not conflicting: the inner required-provided relationship is preserved: that means they involve a well-formed assembly(see Sect. 3.4).*
2. *the behaviour $\mathcal{B}_{sp}$ of sp_{C_i} and $\mathcal{B}_s$ of s are compatible: compatible($\mathcal{B}_{sp}, \mathcal{B}_s$); that is, their eLTSs are matching; either they evolve independently or they perform complementary communication actions until a termination without a deadlock.*

The conditions 1.c. and 2. are checked in the context of each service s that calls sr_{C_j}. $\mathcal{B}_{sr}$ is nul since the required sr_{C_j} does not have a behaviour. The compatibility of behaviours is dealt with in more details in the following.

Definition 2 (Component Composability)
Two components C_i and C_j are c-composable according to a set of service pairs ss, if all the pairs (s_i, s_j) of ss are composable:
c-composable(C_i, C_j, ss) $\Leftrightarrow$ $\forall(s_i, s_j) \in ss \bullet$ s-composable(s_i, s_j)

Proposition 1 (Assembly 'Checkability'). *When two components C_i and C_j are c-composable w.r.t to a list of services ss, then C_i and C_j can be linked in a well-formed assembly via ss. This generalises to several components.*

Accordingly Kmelia component assemblies and compositions may be formally checked for correctness.

4.3 Checking Composability: Static Analysis

The interface of a component contains the sets of provided and required services (with the naming and typing informations); additionally, informations on required or called sub-services are attached to the interface. In a similar way, these informations are available for the service descriptions. Accordingly, the static analysis of the interface of a component is achieved using:

  i) simple correspondence checking algorithms and possibly standard typing algorithms;
  ii) a deep investigation on the availability of required or called sub-services.

The definitions given above are used to perform this static level analysis. At this stage, some incompatibilities may be detected. We cover by the way the main part of (static) interoperability properties and architectural properties.

4.4 Checking Composability: Behavioural Compatibility Analysis

At this stage, we assume that a verification of the *static and architectural properties* is already performed for a given assembly. This implies that each service of the components is completely and correctly described. Now, the main concern is to check that a given component interacts correctly with others (which may be provided by a third party developer) over the links. Remind that each service is described with an eLTS where the transitions are labelled with guarded elementary actions and communication actions (see Sect. 2.1).

The component interacts correctly with its environment if its services are composable with the other services. We consider only one caller service and one called service at time. We check that Bp a given eLTS matches with Br a second eLTS: *compatible(Bp, Br)*. A complete interaction between the services of several components results in a pairwise local analysis between the LTS of a caller and that of the called service. The eLTSs are unfolded to obtain LTSs. Therefore, two services interact until a terminal state if the labels of their associated LTSs are in correspondence according to a set of rules that define *compatible*. They are based on the labels of the transitions going from a current state to the following states (output transitions). The rules indicate the correct evolutions according to the current states of two involved services: from a current state considered in each LTS, we explore the labels on the output transitions. In the case of elementary actions on the labels, each LTS evolves independently, their current states are updated. In the case of communication actions on the labels, the transitions match if for the considered services (hence the appropriate channels), we have the matching pairs: *send(!)-receive(?), call service(!!)-wait service start(??), emit service result(!!)-wait service result(??)*. In this case each LTS evolves in its next state. If the labels do not match, an incompatibility or a deadlock is detected.

After a final state of a called service, the caller may continue with independent transitions or with transitions that imply other (sub-)services. When the final states are reached without deadlock, the services are compatible.

In the following we focus on a practical verification of the *behavioural compatibility* aspect, that (re)uses an existing verification toolbox.

5   Formal Verification with LOTOS/CADP

We use LOTOS [14] and its associated CADP [9] toolbox to experiment on the composability checking. We encode the Kmelia components into LOTOS processes which are the input of the CADP tools. In order to exploit the CADP tools, the behavioural compatibility is based on communication between processes.

5.1   LOTOS

LOTOS [14] is an ISO standard formal specification language. It is initially designed for the specification of network interconnection (OSI) but is also suitable for concurrent and distributed systems. LOTOS extends the process algebra CCS and CSP and integrates (algebraic) abstract data types. A LOTOS specification is structured with process behaviours. It has the main behaviour description operators of the basic process algebra CCS and CSP. LOTOS uses the "!" and "?" operators of CSP which denote respectively emission and reception. The salient features of LOTOS are: the powerful multi-way synchronisation; the use of communication channels called *gates*; the synchronous interaction of processes; the use of algebraic data types to model data part of systems; the availability of the CADP toolbox [9].

A process is the description in the time of the observational behaviour of a given system. The description is given as the non-deterministic combination of the sequence of events feasible by the system. The set of events of a behaviour is called the *alphabet* of the process. In a process specification, a sequence of events is denoted with ";". The choice between alternative behaviours B and C is described with B [] C. The notation [Bterm] -> B describes a process behaviour B guarded with a boolean term Bterm. The inaction is denoted with stop. A successful termination is denoted with exit. The sequential composition of behaviours B and C is described with B >> C.

Three parallel composition operators are used to compose processes: ||| is used for the interleaving behaviour of the composed processes; || is used for the strict (on all the events) synchronisation of the involved processes; |[L]| where L is a synchronisation list (of events) is used to synchronise the processes on the events within the list L; when L is empty this results on a interleaving. The use of L forces the related processes to perform matching communication actions. Both synchronous and asynchronous communications may be described in LOTOS.

The ISO LOTOS has an operational semantics in terms of labelled transitions systems. The semantic rules define the behaviour of the LOTOS processes and their communication. As far as the data part is concerned, algebraic term rewriting is considered to evaluate data terms and each variable may be instantiated by the values corresponding to its type.

5.2   Translating the Services into LOTOS Processes

Our working hypotheses are the followings. To deal with the communication, each service has a *default channel* made by prefixing the service name with the keyword "Chan_". Thus, Chan_serv denotes the default channel of a service named *serv*. This channel is used as an alphabet element of the process corresponding to the service. In the same way, the channels associated to the services with which a service *serv* communicates (service calls appearing in the behaviour) are listed in the alphabet. We treat the activation of a service with a communication (to enter the initial state of the called service). A process corresponding to a service waits for a call. The caller service sends a call. Initially each service (the associated process) waits for a communication using its default channel. A caller service calls a service by sending a message (with the called name as parameter) on the default channel of the called service. The parameters are also sent using the default channel of the called process.

Translation Principle and Result

Remind that the behaviour of a component service is a transition system where each label is a combination of actions which may be elementary actions, or communication actions. From each state of a service there are one or several (outgoing) transitions going to other states.

LOTOS processes are basically state machines. Therefore the transition system which describes a service is described with one or several LOTOS processes; one main process is associated to the service and one or several subprocesses are used to describe the former one. Basically, each state is translated into a process. The behaviour of the latter describes the transitions which are attached to the corresponding state.

The translation procedure is performed as follows: each service state is examined; each outgoing transition of the state corresponds to a LOTOS action followed by the translation of the reached state. The used channels, the communication actions and the elementary actions are collected to form the current process alphabet. According to these working hypotheses, we define a semantic encoding (namely *LotosEncoding*) of the service specifications. The encoding into LOTOS of service specifications is inductively performed by considering: service interface without formal parameters; service interface with formal parameters; service states (initial, final, intermediary and branching) and the transitions related to each service state.

During the translation process, the data type spaces are reduced[1] to avoid the state explosion problem: we use enumerated or byte types. For each service *ServName*, we define a LOTOS data type. It has a constructor which is named according to the service; this permits the call of the service. Besides, all the messages which are sent to the default channel associated to a service are used as constructors of the data type associated to this service. Enumerated data are translated with constructors of abstract data types. The expressions used within actions are not evaluated; they are translated by simple actions in the LOTOS process. The guards are not evaluated; each guard is encoded by an action.

---

[1] Model checking tools consider all the possible values of a type.

5.3   Using CADP to Check the Behavioural Compatibility

The behavioural compatibility checking is based on LOTOS processes communication. We use the | [L] | composition operator. A compatibility checking involves a pair of services: the caller service and the called one; for example behaviour and withdrawal in our case (see Fig. 2). The withdrawal service is required by behaviour via the name ask_for_money. A renaming of withdrawal with ask_for_money is performed. These two services (the caller and the called) are translated into LOTOS processes (say Lbehaviour and Lask_for_money); each process has its alphabet (alphabet in the following); the processes are then composed using the | [L] | operator to get a resulting process called Res in the following. L is instantiated with the list of channels and actions used for the communication between both services as illustrated above.

```
Res =  Lbehaviour[alphabet]
     |[chan_behaviour, chan_ask_code, chan_ask_amount, ...]|
       Lask_for_money [alphabet]
```

Consequently, the services are compatible if the obtained Res process has no conflict according to the composition operator.

As far as the running example is concerned, we check that USER_INTERFACE and ATM_CORE are composable according to the services (ask_for_money, withdrawal): the interface checking is easy. The behaviours of ask_for_money and withdrawal are compatible.

To make it easy the experimentation of our component model, we implement an analyser (using Antlr[2] and Java) of component specifications. A prototype (named kml2lotos) to translate the component services into LOTOS is also developed using Java.

Given an input component specification (in Kmelia), the analyser parses the specification and generates the corresponding internal structure. The latter is read by the kml2lotos prototype; it generates communicating LOTOS processes which are used as input to the CADP toolbox. In the ATM case study (see Section 2), the experiment deals with an assembly of components. Specific services (a caller with a called one, branching node with the sub-services) are checked. The CADP functionalities raise failures when there are lack of channels, wrong channels, incompatible types, blocking or incompatible behaviours.

The experiment using CADP helps us to discover specification errors; for example when a wrong communication channel is used. When the errors are recovered and the communications are fine, the CADP caesar utility generates the (execution) graph corresponding to the system. The graph is very large in the case of brute translation; but when we erase independent alphabet actions and minimise the generated graph, we get a graph with less than hundred states. Stepwise simulation (using CADP executor utility) is performed to analyse the evolution of the system.

---

[2] www.antlr.org

6   Discussion and Perspectives

We have presented a model where a component provides several behaviours via services. This flexibility offered to the user results in a non trivial formalisation of the model and its composability. A formal model is built to serve reasoning purpose and the composability is defined. Composable components may be used to build component assemblies or compositions. Some experiments are performed with the LOTOS CADP toolbox. A prototype toolbox (COSTO: COmponent Study TOolbox) is under development to support our experiments; it already integrates some modules: a Kmelia analyser, an architectural correctness checker, a translator to generate LOTOS processes from the component specifications. We also have a translator to MEC.

Compared to related works [4,13], our approach works at the abstract specification level, it offers a more flexible formalism than the ones proposed by [21,4] for the description of interacting services. We adopt a pairwise verification approach that avoids state explosion like in [4]. From the practical point of view, our proposal follows the mechanized approaches like Tracta [10] or SOFA [17]. The latter already provides many analysis tools; but we have a different component model that needs deep investigation before tool reuse and development. However we can build on the experiences gained with these works. Most of the approaches that integrate behavioural specifications to components [17,16,18] work at a protocol (or component) level while our approach is mainly based on the services, the protocol level is handled by a constraint in our model. Moreover, their communication actions refer only to messages and not to services (no service call or result). The non-regular protocols of [18] may be represented in Kmelia using guards and nested states, but using algebraic grammar provides a more efficient solution for the given applications. The work of [16] addresses assemblies and implementation issues in Java but does not deal with composition.

Many exciting investigations remain to be done. Whatever the component model, the compositionality is still a challenge [20]. The perspectives of this work are: to reinforce the correctness properties of component with supplementary study of correctness of components and services with regard to their environment; to extend the COSTO (COmponent Study TOolbox) prototype under development so as to cover more mechanized analysis concerns.

References

1. R. Allen and D. Garlan. A Formal Basis for Architectural Connection. *ACM Transactions on Software Engineering and Methodology*, 6(3):213–249, July 1997.
2. P. André, G. Ardourel, and C. Attiogbé. Behavioural Verification of Service Composition. In *ICSOC/Workshop on Engineering Service Compositions*, WESC'05.
3. P. André, G. Ardourel, C. Attiogbé, H. Habrias, and C. Stoquer. A Service-Based Component Model: Formalism, Analysis and Mechanization. Technical Report RR05.08, LINA, December 2005.
4. P. C. Attie and D. H. Lorenz. Correctness of Model-based Component Composition without State Explosion. In *ECOOP 2003 Workshop on Correctness of Model-based Software Composition*, 2003.

5. P. C. Attie and D. H. Lorenz. Establishing Behavioral Compatibility of Software Components without State Explosion. Technical Report NU-CCIS-03-02, College of Computer and Information Science, Northeastern University, 2003.
6. K. Bergner, A. Rausch, M. Sihling, A. Vilbig, and M. Broy. A Formal Model for Componentware. In G. T. Leavens and M. Sitaraman, editors, *Foundations of Component-Based Systems*, pages 189–210. Cambridge University Press, New York, NY, 2000.
7. A. Bracciali, A. Brogi, and C. Canal. A Formal Approach to Component Adaptation. *Journal of Systems and Software*, 74(1):45–54, 2005.
8. L. de Alfaro and T. A. Henzinger. Interface Automata. In *Proceedings of the Ninth Annual Symposium on Foundations of Software Engineering (FSE)*, pages 109–120. ACM Press, 2001.
9. J-C. Fernandez, H. Garavel, A. Kerbrat, R. Mateescu, L. Mounier, and M. Sighireanu. CADP: A Protocol Validation and Verification Toolbox. In R. Alur and T. A. Henzinger, editors, *Proc. of the 8th Conference on Computer-Aided Verification (CAV'96)*, volume 1102 of *LNCS*, pages 437–440. Springer Verlag, 1996.
10. D. Giannakopoulou, J. Kramer, and S.C. Cheung. Behaviour Analysis of Distributed Systems Using the Tracta Approach. *ASE*, 6(1):7–35, 1999.
11. T. Gschwind, U. Aßmann, and O. Nierstrasz, editors. *Software Composition, 4th Int. Workshop, SC 2005, Edinburgh, UK*, volume 3628 of *Lecture Notes in Computer Science*. Springer, 2005.
12. G. T. Heineman, I. Crnkovic, H. W. Schmidt, J. A. Stafford, C. A. Szyperski, and K. C. Wallnau, editors. *Component-Based Software Engineering, 8th International Symposium, CBSE 2005, USA, May, 2005*, volume 3489 of *LNCS*. Springer, 2005.
13. P. Inverardi, A. L. Wolf, and D. Yankelevich. Static Checking of System Behaviors using Derived Component Assumptions. *ACM Transactions on Software Engineering and Methodology*, 9(3):239–272, 2000.
14. ISO LOTOS. *A Formal Description Technique Based on The Temporal Ordering of Observational Behaviour*. International Organisation for Standardization - Information Processing Systems - Open Systems Interconnection, Geneva, 1988.
15. N. Medvidovic and R. N. Taylor. A Classification and Comparison Framework for Software Architecture Description Languages. *IEEE Transactions on Software Engineering*, 26(1):70–93, january 2000.
16. S. Pavel, J. Noyé, P. Poizat, and J.C. Royer. A Java Implementation of a Component Model with Explicit Symbolic Protocols. In Gschwind et al. [11], pages 115–124.
17. F. Plasil and S. Visnovsky. Behavior Protocols for Software Components. *IEEE Transactions on SW Engineering*, 28(9), 2002.
18. M. Südholt. A Model of Components with Non-regular Protocols. In Gschwind et al. [11], pages 99–113.
19. C. Szyperski. *Component Software: Beyond Object-Oriented Programming*. Addison Wesley Publishing Company, 1997.
20. F. Xie and J. C. Browne. Verified Systems by Composition from Verified Components. In *ESEC/FSE-11: Proc. of the 9th European software engineering conference*, pages 277–286, New York, NY, USA, 2003. ACM Press.
21. D.M. Yellin and R.E. Strom. Protocol Specifications and Component Adaptors. *ACM Transactions on Programming Languages and Systems*, 19(2):292–333, 1997.

Static Verification of Indirect Data Sharing in Loosely-coupled Component Systems

Lieven Desmet, Frank Piessens, Wouter Joosen, and Pierre Verbaeten

DistriNet Research Group, Department of Computer Science
Katholieke Universiteit Leuven, Celestijnenlaan 200A, B-3001 Leuven, Belgium
Lieven.Desmet@cs.kuleuven.be
http://www.cs.kuleuven.be/~lieven/research/

Abstract. To maintain loose coupling and facilitate dynamic composition, components in a pipe-and-filter architecture have a very limited syntactic interface and often communicate indirectly by means of a shared data repository. This severely limits the possibilities for compile time compatibility checking. Even static type checking is made largely irrelevant due to the very general types given in the interfaces. The combination of pipe-and-filter and a shared data repository is widely used, and in this paper we study this problem in the context of the Struts framework. We propose simple, but formally specified, behavioural contracts for components in such frameworks and show that automated formal verification of certain semantical compatibility properties is feasible. In particular, our verification guarantees that indirect data sharing through the shared data repository is performed consistently.

1 Introduction

Current component systems often promote loosely-coupled components to enhance component reuse. The pipe-and-filter style [1] for example is a very popular architectural style for constructing flow-oriented component frameworks. It is often combined with the repository style [1] to support anonymous communication between components. Current state-of-the-art web component frameworks such as Java Servlets [2] or the popular Struts framework [3] are examples of such frameworks.

The main advantage of this kind of architecture is that it makes "wiring" of components at the syntactical level very simple: components are independent entities and interact with the shared data repository through a generic untyped interface. The corresponding drawback is that semantical compatibility checks are absolutely minimal: even compile-time or composition-time type checking is circumvented. For instance, retrievals from the repository are done under the Object type, and the retrieved object is then downcasted to the expected type at run time, potentially leading to exceptions at run time. This in turn significantly hinders independent extensibility of applications built in such frameworks, and reuse of components in new compositions. It is for instance up to the composer to make sure that all data that a given component expects to find on the repository

W. Löwe and M. Südholt (Eds.): SC 2006, LNCS 4089, pp. 34–49, 2006.

is guaranteed to be present in the constructed composition. Oversights of the composer can lead to run-time errors.

To enhance component reuse and third-party composability, a precise documentation of the semantical behaviour of the components is essential. By making parts of the component contract formal, automated tool support for verifying some level of semantical compatibility at composition time becomes feasible. As a consequence, certain types of bugs can be detected at compile time or at composition time instead of at run time.

In this paper we propose formal component contracts written in JML, the Java Modeling Language [4], that specify part of the behaviour of components in the Struts framework and we show that static verification with state-of-the-art verifiers for JML is feasible. Our contracts specify for instance what data a component expects on the repository, and what data the component puts onto the repository. Verification checks whether (1) implementations of components honour their contract, and whether (2) compositions always respect the contracts of their constituents. Our approach has been validated on GatorMail [5], an open-source, Struts-based webmail application.

While we have worked out our contracts for the case of Struts, the same idea is applicable to any framework based on the pipe-and-filter and repository architectural styles.

The rest of this paper is structured as follows. Section 2 provides some background information on the web technologies used, component contracts and static verification. Next, the problem statement is elaborated in Sect. 3 and solutions for verifying two composition properties are proposed in Sect. 4. Section 5 validates the proposed solutions in the open-source webmail application GatorMail. In Sect. 6, the presented work is related to existing research and, finally, Sect. 7 summarises the contributions of this paper.

2   Background

2.1   Java Servlets, JavaServer Pages and the Struts Framework

Java Servlets. The Java Servlet technology is part of the J2EE specification [6]. It is a server-side component model for extending the functionality of a web server [2]. A J2EE web application is typically a collection of Java Servlets, deployed in a servlet-based web container such as Tomcat, JBoss or WebSphere. A container casts incoming HTTP requests into an object-oriented form (i.e. a *HTTPServletRequest* object) and checks to see if there is a servlet registered for processing that request. During request processing, a servlet can decide to either dispatch the request to another servlet (and by doing so, form a pipe of servlets) or to return a response to the user.

Within a web application, servlets are loosely-coupled with each other (through a very generic interface) and support for dispatching between servlets is provided by the web container. The servlets can communicate anonymously by means of a shared data repository.

JavaServer Pages. The JavaServer Pages (JSP) technology is also part of the J2EE specification and is built upon Java Servlets. JSP enables separation of content from presentation in developing dynamic websites.

JavaServer Pages are used to develop the user interface (or view) of a web application. They are also loosely-coupled, and can communicate anonymously with other JavaServer Pages or Servlets by using the same shared data repository.

The Struts Framework. Apache Struts [3] is a widespread, open-source application framework on top of Java Servlets and JavaServer Pages. Struts encourages developers to use the JavaServer Pages Model 2 architecture [7], a variation on the Model-View-Controller design pattern for web applications.

In a Struts application (illustrated in Fig. 1), incoming HTTP requests are encapsulated in *HTTPServletRequest* objects and dispatched to the *ActionServlet*. This *ActionServlet* is the Controller of the Struts application. According to the requested URL, an appropriate action is selected and the *HTTPServletRequest* (*Req* in Fig. 1) is processed. An action interacts with the Model and fetches the necessary data for the View. After processing the request, an *ActionForward* object(*AF* in Fig. 1) is returned to the *ActionServlet*, indicating which action or view has to be processed next. This process continues until a JSP view is reached and output is sent back to the web browser. In this architecture only the implementations of the different actions and JSP views are application-specific, the other parts are provided by the Struts framework.

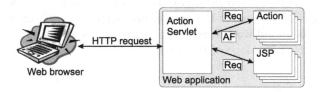

Fig. 1. Request processing in Struts

Actions resemble Java Servlets in that they both process a *HTTPServletRequest* and that both are able to use the associated shared data repository that is propagated through the flow together with the request.

In order to achieve reusable actions, an extra forward indirection is used in Struts. Actions use logical names to identify forwards, and the Struts configuration file (which is specific for each configuration) specifies the declarative mapping between logical forwards and actual forwards. In this way, the logical names are mapped to actual forwards at run time using the *ActionMapping* class. The mapping can either be action-specific (local forward) or composition-wide (global forward).

What is important in the context of this paper is the fact that the declarative forwarding and indirect data sharing ensure that actions, servlets and JSP views are very loosely-coupled from a syntactical point of view.

2.2   Component Contracts and Static Verification

Component contracts have already often been proposed before for various purposes [8]. For components written in Java, The Java Modeling Language (JML) [4] is a popular formal contract specification language. In this paper, JML notation is used to specify pre- and post-conditions as well as frame conditions for methods that process HTTP requests. Frame conditions specify what part of the state a method is allowed to modify.

One of the main advantages of JML is the large amount of tool support that is available [9]. Tools are available for run-time contract checking, test generation, static verification and inference of specifications. Of particular interest to us are tools for static verification of JML contracts. A variety of verification tools is available that make different trade-offs in verification power and need for user interaction. In the experiments reported on in this paper, we used the ESC/Java2 verifier [10]. The main advantage of this verifier is that it requires no user interaction. On the downside, the verifier is far from complete, and has some known sources of unsoundness [11,12]. In Sect. 4.3, we explain how this impacts verification of our proposed contracts.

3   Problem Statement

Although the declarative forwarding mechanism and indirect data sharing in Struts highly facilitate the composition of a web application from a syntactical point of view, they also introduce hidden complexities for the software composer. In order to achieve correctly functioning compositions, the software composer needs to bear in mind all the hidden data interactions through the shared data repository, and anticipate all possible forwards of the actions.

This hidden complexity should not be underestimated. We investigated Gator-Mail [5], an open-source webmail application of the University of Florida, built upon the Struts framework. In this web application (consisting of about 20.000 lines of code), we identified 36 Struts actions and 29 JSP views, reused in 52 request processing flows [13]. The *FolderAction* for instance was reused in more than 20 processing flows. All the flows contributed to 147 declarative control flow transitions in the webmail application, and to 1369 data repository interactions. The control flow transitions were specified in the composition configuration by means of global and local forwards, but none of the data interactions with the shared repository were documented.

It should be clear that under these circumstances it is not obvious how to reuse existing components or to contribute to an open-source project such as GatorMail, without breaking any of the existing, hidden data dependencies between actions, or without leaving some dangling control flow transitions[1], unless of course, a full source code study is undertaken to identify the declarative forwards and the data repository interactions.

---

[1] With a dangling control flow transition, we mean that at run time the action returns a logical forward, but that no mapping can be found to an actual forward in the list of local or global forwards of the running configuration.

To focus on the essence of the problem, we now define a simplified version of the Struts application model. This simplified version mainly takes the declarative forwarding mechanism and the indirect data sharing into account. The presented application model is then used to define some desired composition properties at the end of the section. The problem we address in this paper is how we can verify these properties statically.

The simplified application model is sufficiently generic to reflect the common characteristics of many pipe-and-filter applications with a shared data repository. Hence, the proposed solution of Sect. 4 is generally applicable to this kind of applications. In Sect. 5, the simplified model is further specialised towards the Struts application framework in order to apply our solution to real, existing Struts applications.

3.1   Simplified Application Model

In the simplified application model (shown in Fig. 2), an application is still a composition of actions. All actions implement an *execute* method taking two parameters: a *Request* and a *Form*. A *Request* is a first class entity representing the request that is being processed and the request provides access to the shared data repository (*setDataItem*, *getDataItem* and *removeDataItem*) associated with the request. The *Form* encapsulates the request parameters provided by the client for processing the request.

The *execute* method of an *Action* returns a string, logically indicating which control flow transition should be taken. A *Configuration* object encapsulates the local and global forwards of a composition and maps the strings to corresponding actions. The *RequestProcessor* then repeatedly executes an action for a given request and based on the return value it selects an appropriate succeeding action from the *Configuration*. JSP views are reduced to normal actions in the simplified application model, but they do not produce a forward.

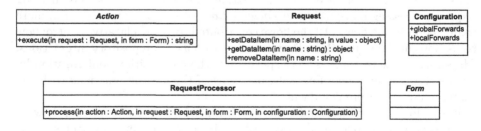

Fig. 2. The simplified application model

3.2   Composition Example

To illustrate the simplified application model, a basic composition example is now introduced. The composition is part of an online calendar system and allows a user to schedule a meeting with several participants at a given time slot and location. The composition consists of four actions and is shown in Fig. 3. The rounded boxes represent actions and the solid arrows indicate control flow transitions.

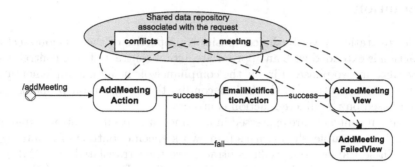

Fig. 3. Composition example: scheduling a meeting

The first action to be executed in scheduling a meeting is the *AddMeetingAction*. This action tries to schedule the requested meeting. On success, the request is processed by an *EmailNotificationAction* which sends a notification to the participants of the meeting. Afterwards, the scheduled meeting is shown to the web user (*AddedMeetingView*). On failure, the *AddMeetingFailedView* lists the different conflicts which make the scheduling impossible.

The labels on the control flow transitions represent the return values of the different actions. The *AddMeetingAction* can either return "success" or "fail", indicating whether or not the scheduling was successful. The *EmailNotification-Action* only returns "success", whereas views do not produce a forward.

The interactions with the shared data repository are indicated by dashed lines. The *AddMeetingAction* stores the meeting information (containing the participants, time slot and location) on the shared repository. In case the meeting cannot be scheduled, a list of conflicts is saved as well. All other actions retrieve the meeting information from the shared repository. In addition, the *AddMeetingFailedView* also reads the list of conflicts.

3.3 Desired Composition Properties

Based on the simplified application model, a number of desired composition properties can be defined in loosely-coupled compositions with a declarative control flow and indirect data sharing. Some examples are:

No dangling forwards: Every logical forward in the composition is mapped to an actual forward in the configuration.
No broken data dependencies: A shared data item is only read after being written. For each shared data read interaction, the shared data item that is already written on the repository is of the type expected by the read operation.

In the next section, solutions are proposed to statically verify these composition properties in the simplified application model.

4   Solution

In order to statically verify the composition properties of the previous section, each action is extended with an appropriate action contract. These contracts are then verified in two phases. Firstly, the compliance of the action implementation with the action contract is checked. Secondly, the composition properties are checked based on the different action contracts.

The action contracts are expressed in a framework-specific contract language. Listing 1.1 for example, shows such a framework-specific contract of *AddMeeting-Action*. These framework-specific contracts are then translated into JML contracts in order to verify them with existing verifiers. For the rest of the paper we have chosen to show the translated JML contracts since JML is a fairly well-known contract language.

Listing 1.1. Framework-specific contract of AddMeetingAction

```
//spec: forwards {"success","fail"};
//spec: writes {Meeting meeting};
//spec: on forward == "fail" also writes {Vector conflicts};
```

This section only highlights key points of the solution. Some additional specification decisions and the full action contracts of the composition example (in the framework-specific contract language and in JML) can be found on the paper's accompanying website [14].

4.1   No Dangling Forwards Property

Action Contracts for the No Dangling Forwards Property. In order to verify the no dangling forwards property, the action contract needs to include sufficient information about the possible declarative forwards (i.e. the different return values). This can simply be done in a JML specification by restricting the return values of an action as part of the action's post-condition. In Listing 1.2 for example, two possible return values are declared in the action's contract: the strings "success" and "fail".

Listing 1.2. Contract for declarative forwarding (AddMeetingAction.spec)

```
public class AddMeetingAction extends Action {
    //@ also
    //@ ensures \result == "success" || \result == "fail";
    public String execute(Request request, Form form);
}
```

Static Checking of the No Dangling Forwards Property. To check the compliance of the action's contract with its implementation, a very pragmatic approach such as applying a simple search pattern on the Java source could be used. If however the source code is not that straightforward anymore (e.g. if programming constants are used, or if the return value is constructed in several statements), a static checker tool such as ESC/Java2 can be used to verify the compliance with the ensures clause.

Verifying the no dangling forwards property itself is trivial and can be done by using a simple algorithm that verifies that for each possible return value of the action either a corresponding local forward or global forward exists in the composition-specific configuration. In practice, the declarative forwarding property is not individually verified, but is verified in combination with the no broken data dependencies property as will be explained in Sect. 4.2.

4.2 No Broken Data Dependencies Property

Action Contracts for the No Broken Data Dependencies Property. The action contracts have to specify the interactions between actions and the shared data repository. These interactions can be expressed in terms of the pre- and post-state of the repository by using the *getDataItem* method of the *Request*.

Because methods used in specifications may not have side-effects, the *get-DataItem* method is declared *pure*, i.e. the method will not modify the program state. A more precise definition of purity can be found in [15].

For read interactions, the action's contract indicates that the action requires that a non-null data item of the specified type can be read from the shared repository, as is shown in Listing 1.3.

Listing 1.3. Contract for indirect data sharing (EmailNotificationAction.spec)

```
public class EmailNotificationAction extends Action {
    //@ also
    //@ requires request != null;
    //@ requires request.getDataItem("meeting") instanceof Meeting;
    //@ ensures \result == "success";
    public String execute(Request request, Form form);
}
```

For write interactions, the ensures pragma states which data items on the shared repository will be non-null and of the specified type after method execution. In Listing 1.4 for example, the JML contract of the *execute* method of *AddMeetingAction* states that the shared data item *meeting* will be a non-null *Meeting* object. Since write interaction may also depend on certain conditions (e.g. if a write interaction occurs in an if-then-else structure), this must also be reflected in the action's contract. In Listing 1.4 an implication expression (==>) is used to express that the data item *conflicts* is only written in case the return value equals "fail".

Listing 1.4. JML contract for indirect data sharing (AddMeetingAction.spec)

```
public class AddMeetingAction extends Action {
    //@ also
    //@ requires request != null;
    //@ ensures request.getDataItem("meeting") instanceof Meeting;
    //@ ensures \result == "fail" ==> request.getDataItem("conflicts") instanceof Vector;
    //@ ensures \result == "success" || \result == "fail";
    public String execute(Request request, Form form);
}
```

Static Checking of the No Broken Data Dependencies Property. To verify the no broken data dependencies property, ESC/Java2 is used to verify both the compliance of the implementation of the *execute* method with the contract, and the composition property itself.

To check the compliance of the action, a specification of the shared repository is introduced, as listed in 1.5. Hereby, *explicit JML pragmas* and a *ghost variable* are introduced for each shared data item, since the current version of the ESC/Java2 tool does not support reasoning about hashtable indirections.

Listing 1.5. JML contract of the shared data repository (Request.spec)

```
public class Request {
    //@ public ghost Object meeting;
    //@ public ghost Object conflicts;

    //@ requires isKey(name);
    //@ ensures name == "meeting" ==> this.meeting == value;
    //@ ensures name == "conflicts" ==> this.conflicts == value;
    public void setDataItem(String name, Object value);

    //@ requires isKey(name);
    //@ ensures name == "meeting" ==> \result == this.meeting;
    //@ ensures name == "conflicts" ==> \result == this.conflicts;
    public /*@ pure @*/ Object getDataItem(String name);

    //@ ensures \result <==> key == "meeting" || key == "conflicts";
    public /*@ pure @*/ boolean isKey(String key);
}
```

To verify the first and second composition property, *a composition-specific check method* is automatically generated and then verified by ESC/Java2. The check method (shown in Listing 1.6) firstly initializes the different actions used in the composition. Secondly, based on the local and global forwards of the composition configuration, a complete control flow graph is statically constructed, similar to what would happen at run time by repeatedly using the *RequestProcessor*.

The *unreachable* pragmas are able to detect violations to the no dangling forwards property, since they are only reachable if an action returns a value that does not match any of its local or global forwards.

The no broken data dependencies property is implicitly verified. Since, for every method call in the method body, ESC/Java2 checks that the preconditions are fulfilled, each data item read must be preceded by a data item write in the execution path and comply with the type requirements in order to satisfy the JML contract of the read interaction.

Listing 1.6. Composition-specific check method to be verified by ESC/Java2

```
//@ requires request != null;
public void check_addMeeting(Request request, Form form){
    AddMeetingAction addMeetingAction = new AddMeetingAction();
    EmailNotificationAction emailNotificationAction = new EmailNotificationAction();
    AddedMeetingView addedMeetingView = new AddedMeetingView();
    FailedAddedMeetingView failedAddedMeetingView = new FailedAddedMeetingView();

    String forward1 = addMeetingAction.execute(request,form);
    if(forward1.equals("success")){
        String forward2 = emailNotificationAction.execute(request,form);
        if(forward2.equals("success")){
            addedMeetingView.execute(request,form);
        } else { //@ unreachable; }
    } else if(forward1.equals("fail")){
        failedAddedMeetingView.execute(request,form);
    } else { //@ unreachable; }
}
```

4.3   Unsoundness with ESC/Java2

ESC/Java2 has a number of known sources of unsoundness [11,12]. One of these sources also impacts the soundness of our approach, namely ESC/Java2's default handling of framing. As defined in JML, ESC/Java2 has a default for missing modifies clauses (i.e. *modifies \ everything*) to unhide unexpected changes to variables caused by calling a routine, but logic to reason about routine bodies that contain these modifies clauses has not yet been implemented in ESC/Java2 [12]. As a result, methods without explicit modifies clauses can be verified since the default frame condition includes everything. However in calling such methods, the current implementation of ESC/Java2 does not take this default frame condition into account resulting in an unsound verification. In our case this means that an intermediate action can break the dependencies between one action writing shared data and another action retrieving that data, without ESCJava/2 being able to detect that violation.

To counter this unsoundness, each action annotation is extended with a frame condition, explicitly stating which data items on the shared repository are changed. Also the methods in the *Request* to store and retrieve data from the repository need to have explicit frame conditions. By doing so, ESCJava/2 is able to detect unspecified write interaction with the repository. In addition, other methods interacting with the repository (such as library methods) also require an explicit modifies clause and their contracts need to be verified as well.

Since the current JML notations do not support modifies pragmas in terms of pure methods or hashtable values, the inserted pragmas in the actions are quite verbose (Listing 1.7). In the examples of this paper the modifies pragmas are omitted, but the full annotation with frame conditions can be found at [14].

Listing 1.7. Frame condition of EmailNotificationAction

```
//@ ensures (\forall String s; request.isKey(s) ==>
                    \old(request.getDataItem(s)) == request.getDataItem(s));
```

5 Validation

In this section, we validate the solutions of Sect. 4 in the open-source web-mail application GatorMail. Firstly, we introduce some slight refinements to the presented solution in order to be applicable to real Struts web applications. Secondly, we investigate the JML annotation overhead of the presented approach and the performance of the ESC/Java2 verification tool while verifying the GatorMail web application. Finally, we discuss our validation results.

5.1 Verifying Struts Applications: An Example

To illustrate the verification of Struts applications, a small composition example extracted from the GatorMail application is used. In GatorMail, the web URL */createFolder.do* is mapped to the composition of Fig. 4 and allows a web user to create a new IMAP mailfolder. The composition consists of three Struts actions and two JSP views. Four control flow transitions occur in the composition: all three action can return a "success" forward, and in addition the *CreateFolder-Action* can return a "fail" forward. The interactions of the composition with the shared data repository are listed in table 1.

Verifying the Declarative Forwarding. In the Struts framework, the *execute* method of an action returns an *ActionForward* object instead of a string. This *ActionForward* does not only encapsulate the declarative forward, but also contains the composition-specific forward path associated with the declarative

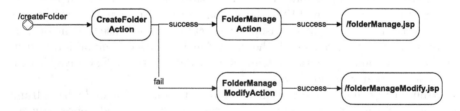

Fig. 4. /createFolder.do composition in GatorMail

Table 1. Indirect data dependencies in /createFolder.do

Folder folder:
FolderManageAction (write)
folderManage.jsp (read)
FolderManageModifyAction (write)
folderManageModify.jsp (read)

ResultBean result:
CreateFolderAction (write)

List quotaList:
FolderManageAction (write)
folderManage.jsp (read)
FolderManageModifyAction (write)
folderManageModify.jsp (read)

String requestStartTime:
CreateFolderAction (read/write)
FolderManageAction (write)
folderManage.jsp (read)
FolderManageModifyAction (write)
FolderManageModifyAction (write)

String isSubscribed:
FolderManageModifyAction (write)
folderManageModify.jsp (read)

List folderBeanList:
FolderManageAction (write)
folderManage.jsp (read)

forward. To do so, the Struts application framework loads the local and global forwards of the composition into the *ActionMapping* object at run time, and the returned *ActionForward* is then constructed by calling the *findforward* method on the *ActionMapping* parameter (Listing 1.8).

Listing 1.8. Declarative forwarding in Struts

```
public class FolderManageAction extends Action {
    public ActionForward execute(ActionMapping mapping, ActionForm form,
            HttpServletRequest request, HttpServletResponse response) throws Exception {
        // ...
        return mapping.findForward("success");
    }
}
```

To be able to express the local forward string in the JML contracts of the actions, extra specification is introduced for *ActionMapping* (Listing 1.9). The specification states that the declarative forward used as parameter of the *find-Forward* method is equal to the name property of the returned *ActionForward*. By doing so, the declarative forwards can be expressed in term of the name property of the returned result (Listing 1.10).

Listing 1.9. JML specification of ActionMapping

```
public class ActionMapping extends ActionConfig {
    //@ requires name != null;
    //@ ensures \result != null;
    //@ ensures \result.getName() == name;
    public ActionForward findForward(String name);
}
```

Listing 1.10. Declarative forward specification of FolderManageAction

```
//@ ensures \result.getName() == "success";
```

Verifying Indirect Data Sharing. Since indirect data sharing via a shared repository in Struts is identical to the simplified application model, the solution of Sect. 4 can be applied to Struts applications without any modification.

5.2   Results of the GatorMail Experiment

To validate the applicability of our approach, we annotated 12 actions and 8 views of the GatorMail webmail application. With these annotations we were able to verify the declarative forwarding and indirect data sharing properties in 17 composition flows (i.e. one third of all flows in GatorMail). We used this subset of the application to investigate the annotation overhead and the performance of the verification. Only the results are reported in this subsection. The full annotations and a short description of how to verify both the implementation conformance and the composition properties can be found at [14].

JML Annotation Overhead. As a quantification of the annotation overhead, a JML line count is performed on the annotated actions. As shown in table 2, at most 15 lines of JML annotation are used in an action contract to express the control flow transitions and the shared repository interactions. The JML contract of *FolderAction* for example, consists of 9 annotation lines, illustrated in Listing 1.11. But this quite verbose JML contract is actually generated from a more concise, Struts-specific contract specified in Listing 1.12.

The Struts-specific contracts are at most 4 lines of annotations, and they are much easier to write by a Struts developer or to read by a software composer. The Struts-specific contracts of the GatorMail case and a tool for converting them into the verifiable JML annotation can be found at [14].

Table 2. JML notation overhead in GatorMail

Action	# JML lines	Action	# JML lines
ChangeSubscribedAction[2]	14	FolderManageAction	10
CheckSessionAction	7	FolderManageModifyAction	11
CreateFolderAction	10	ModifyFolderAction[2]	15
DeleteFolderAction	10	MoveCopyAction	11
DeleteMessagesAction	10	PerformDeleteFolderAction[2]	15
FolderAction	12	RenameFolderAction	9

Listing 1.11. JML contract of FolderAction

```
//@ also
//@ requires request != null;
//@ requires mapping != null;
//@ ensures \result != null;
//@ ensures \result.getName() == "success" || \result.getName() == "inbox";
//@ ensures request.requestStartTime instanceof Long;
//@ ensures \result.getName() == "success" ==> request.folderBeanList instanceof List;
//@ ensures \result.getName() == "success" ==> request.folder instanceof Folder;
//@ ensures \result.getName() == "success" ==> request.messages instanceof List;
//@ ensures \result.getName() == "success" ==> request.quotaList instanceof List;
//@ requires form instanceof FolderForm;
```

Listing 1.12. Struts-specific contract of FolderAction

```
//struts: forwards {"success","inbox"};
//struts: writes {Long requestStartTime};
//struts: on forward == "success" also writes {List folderBeanList, Folder folder,
                                                List messages, List quotaList};
```

Verification Performance with ESC/Java2. To evaluate the performance of the verification process, the verification time and memory usage is measured for

---

[2] These actions extend the *LookupDispatchAction*, and have alternative substitutes of the *execute* method. Thus, it's obvious that these actions have a higher JML line count, since several methods are annotated.

verifying the implementation compliance and the composition properties. The performance tests were run on a Pentium M 1.4 with 512MB RAM, running Debian Linux, while using Java 1.4.2_09, ESC/Java2 2.0a9 and Simplify 1.5.4.

Table 3 shows the performance results of verifying a subset of GatorMail. Both verification steps can be done in a reasonable amount of time (less than 15 seconds per verification) and limited memory resources (not exceeding 25MB). If also the frame conditions are checked, the verification takes up to 700 seconds, but since most bugs are already found without checking the frame conditions, this type of verification has to be run less regularly. In addition, since the verification is done modularly (i.e. action per action), the verification complexity is linear and the the the verification process is scalable to larger software projects as well.

Table 3. Verification performance

Action	Verification time (with frame cond.)	Mem. usage	Composition flow	Verif. time	Mem. usage
ChangeSubscribedAction	1.960 s (13.151 s)	16 MB	/folder.do	0.853 s	14 MB
CheckSessionAction	0.252 s (2.241 s)	13 MB	/folderManage.do	0.506 s	15 MB
CreateFolderAction	0.951 s (5.106 s)	15 MB	/folderManageModify.do	0.555 s	15 MB
DeleteFolderAction	0.978 s (61.193 s)	17 MB	/createFolder.do	1.639 s	17 MB
DeleteMessagesAction	4.607 s (24.542 s)	20 MB	/renameFolder.do	1.741 s	17 MB
FolderAction	14.18 s (711.654 s)	24 MB	/changeSubscribed.do	1.733 s	18 MB
FolderManageAction	1.407 s (10.475 s)	16 MB	/deleteFolder.do	1.145 s	18 MB
FolderManageModifyAction	2.126 s (205.791 s)	16 MB	/performDeleteFolder.do	2.497 s	19 MB
ModifyFolderAction	0.831 s (1.699 s)	14 MB	/modifyFolder.do	7.638 s	22 MB
MoveCopyAction	4.334 s (20.957 s)	19 MB	/deleteMessages.do	1.819 s	23 MB
PerformDeleteFolderAction	1.390 s (5.833 s)	16 MB	/moveMessage.do	2.468 s	24 MB
RenameFolderAction	0.844 s (4.993 s)	15 MB	/copyMessage.do	1.960 s	25 MB
			/moveMessages.do	2.338 s	17 MB
			/copyMessages.do	1.936 s	19 MB
			/errorCopy.do	0.435 s	20 MB
			/errorCopyToSent.do	0.725 s	20 MB
			/errorCopyTrash.do	0.446 s	18 MB

5.3 Discussion

One of the problems that we were confronted with was ESC/Java2's poor support to reason about hashtable indirections. Since the dynamics of loosely-coupled component systems such as Struts strongly rely on hashtable indirections in the implementation, we were forced to circumvent this lack of support by introducing very verbose specifications or statically constructing the complete control flow graph. Additionally, ESC/Java2 is far from complete, for instance reasoning about loops is fairly weak. Also, known sources of unsoundness, related to framing and reentrancy need to be avoided. Again, this made specifications more verbose than they could be. This is however a temporary problem and future versions of the tool are expected to improve in the different domains.

Another issue that we encountered in verifying GatorMail was the violation of the Liskov substitution principle. The *DeleteMessagesAction* for example extends the *FolderAction*, while having a stronger precondition regarding the expected data items on the shared repository for the *execute* method. Since verification tools rely on the Liskov substitution principle, we had to slightly refactor GatorMail in order to comply with the Design by Contract concept.

While the GatorMail case study shows that annotation overhead and verification performance are fine, it can not give us data about the usefulness of our approach for detecting bugs early. Since GatorMail is a mature application, bugs due to broken dependencies have been ironed out already. Therefore, it would be interesting to apply our approach to less mature software systems or to study a development process that incorporates our approach in future research.

6 Related Work

To the best of our knowledge, this is the first proposal for automatic verification of indirect data sharing in Java-based component frameworks. However, our approach is strongly inspired by ongoing research in several research domains.

In software architecture research, several Architecture Description Languages (such as Wright, Darwin and Rapide) are proposed to support architecture-based reasoning, ranging from semi-formal diagrams with boxes and lines to formal notations [16]. Architecture analysis techniques have already been developed to detect problems such as deadlock and component mismatch [17,18].

Comparable approaches (such as CL [19] and Piccola [20]) are proposed in the domain of coordination and software composition. CL, for example, is a composition language for predictable assembly from certifiable components. In CL, the run-time behaviour of an assembly of components can be predicted from known properties of components and their patterns of interaction [19].

The use of JML or related languages such as Spec# [21] for verifying component properties is a very active research domain. For example, Smans et al. [22] specify and verify code access security properties, Jacobs et al. [23] verify data-race-freeness in concurrent programs, and Pavlova et al. [24] focus on security properties of applets. Other applications of JML are surveyed in [9].

7 Conclusion

This paper has focussed on two desirable composition properties in pipe-and-filter and repository based component systems. We proposed framework-specific component contracts to specify a component's possible forwards and its interactions with the shared repository and translated them into JML annotations. The contracts are sufficiently simple to have an acceptable annotation overhead and a very reasonable automatic verification time.

Although, as discussed in Sect. 5.3, there are still some drawbacks with the current state of the verification tool, the conducted experiments show that using existing contract annotation languages and verification tools in order to achieve more robust compositions looks promising.

Acknowledgements

The authors would like to thank Bart Jacobs, Adriaan Moors and Jans Smans for their useful comments and insights while proofreading this paper.

References

1. Shaw, M., Garlan, D.: Software Architecture - Perspectives on an emerging discipline. Prentice-Hall (1996)
2. Java Servlet Technology. (http://java.sun.com/products/servlet/)
3. The Struts Framework. (http://jakarta.apache.org/struts/)
4. The Java Modeling Language (JML). (http://www.jmlspecs.org/)
5. GatorMail WebMail. (http://sourceforge.net/projects/gatormail/)
6. J2EE platform specification. (http://java.sun.com/j2ee/)
7. Seshadri, G.: Understanding JavaServer Pages Model 2 architecture. (http://www.javaworld.com/javaworld/jw-12-1999/jw-12-ssj-jspmvc.html)
8. Szyperski, C.: Component Software: Beyond Object-Oriented Programming. Addison-Wesley Longman Publishing Co., Inc., Boston, MA, USA (2002)
9. Burdy, L., Cheon, Y., Cok, D., Ernst, M., Kiniry, J., Leavens, G.T., Leino, K.R.M., Poll, E.: An overview of JML tools and applications. International Journal on Software Tools for Technology Transfer (STTT) 7(3) (2005) 212–232
10. KindSoftware: The Extended Static Checker for Java version 2 (ESC/Java2). (http://secure.ucd.ie/products/opensource/ESCJava2/)
11. Leino, K.R.M., Nelson, G., Saxe, J.B.: (ESC/Java User's Manual)
12. Cok, D.R.: (ESC/Java2 Implementation Notes)
13. Desmet, L., Piessens, F., Joosen, W., Verbaeten, P.: Dependency analysis of the Gatormail webmail application. Report CW 427, Department of Computer Science, K.U.Leuven, Leuven, Belgium (2005)
14. Desmet, L., Piessens, F., Joosen, W., Verbaeten, P.: Static verification of composition properties. (http://www.cs.kuleuven.be/~lieven/research/SC2006/)
15. Leavens, G.T., Baker, A.L., Ruby, C.: Preliminary design of JML: A behavioral interface specification language for Java. Technical Report 98-06-rev28, Iowa State University, Department of Computer Science (2005)
16. Medvidovic, N., Taylor, R.N.: A classification and comparison framework for software architecture description languages. IEEE Trans. Softw. Eng. 26(1) (2000) 70–93
17. Inverardi, P., Tivoli, M.: Automatic synthesis of deadlock free connectors for com/dcom applications. In: Proceedings of the 8th ESEC held jointly with 9th ACM SIGSOFT FSE, ACM Press (2001) 121–131
18. Allen, R., Garlan, D.: A formal basis for architectural connection. ACM Trans. Softw. Eng. Methodol. 6(3) (1997) 213–249
19. Ivers, J., Sinha, N., Wallnau, K.: A Basis for Composition Language CL. Technical Report CMU/SEI-2002-TN-026, SEI, Carnegie Mellon University (2002)
20. Achermann, F., Nierstrasz, O.: Applications = Components + Scripts — A Tour of Piccola. In Aksit, M., ed.: Software Architectures and Component Technology. Kluwer (2001) 261–292
21. Barnett, M., Leino, K.R.M., Schulte, W.: The Spec# Programming System: An Overview. Lecture Notes in Computer Science 3362 (2004)
22. Smans, J., Jacobs, B., Piessens, F.: Static verification of code access security policy compliance of .NET applications. Journal of Object Technology 5(3) (2006)
23. Jacobs, B., Leino, K.R.M., Piessens, F., Schulte, W.: Safe concurrency for aggregate objects with invariants. In: Proceedings of the Third IEEE International Conference on Software Engineering and Formal Methods, IEEE Computer Society (2005) 137–146
24. Pavlova, M., Barthe, G., Burdy, L., Huisman, M., Lanet, J.L.: Enforcing high-level security properties for applets. In: CARDIS. (2004) 1–16

Enforcing Different Contracts in Hierarchical Component-Based Systems

Philippe Collet[1], Alain Ozanne[2], and Nicolas Rivierre[2]

[1] University of Nice - Sophia Antipolis, I3S Laboratory, France
philippe.collet@unice.fr
[2] France Telecom R&D, MAPS/AMS Laboratory, Issy les Moulineaux, France
{alain.ozanne, nicolas.rivierre}@francetelecom.com

Abstract. Using different specification formalisms together is necessary to leverage better reliability on component-based systems. The *ConFract* system provides a contracting system for hierarchical software components, but currently, only executable assertions are supported.

In this paper, we describe how TLA, taken as an instance of behavioral sequence-based formalism, was integrated in *ConFract*. A domain specific language is proposed in order to enable designers to describe the observations needed to appropriately verify their specifications. These observations are automatically generated for assertions and in the case of TLA, we show what kind of observations must be provided to link the specifications to the concrete application.

1 Introduction

Software engineering is now concerned with more complex, dynamic, evolving and long-living systems. Recently, the concept of component has been revisited to provide a more adapted framework to master software complexity. The notion of contract is then part of the definition of software components [26], in order to organize the guarantee of properties all along the software life cycle. Besides combining different specification formalisms is desirable to leverage reliability on component-based systems, but this task is rather complex, given the diversity of formalisms that express behavior, their numerous common points and differences, and the separation between static and dynamic approaches. The very term *behavioral* is even differently interpreted according to approaches. For example, works on executable assertions provide behavioral contracts as state-oriented expressions before and after method calls [19,14]. Other approaches describe component behaviors as protocols or interaction sequences [1,17,23].

In this context, the *ConFract* system [7] provides a contracting model for the *Fractal* hierarchical components platform [4] and aims at combining different specification techniques. But currently, *ConFract* only supports an executable assertion language, and properties are checked at configuration and run times. We thus propose to integrate TLA [12] as an instance of sequence-based specification formalism. In this paper, we describe its integration in *ConFract*, by enhancing the underlying metamodel and providing a domain specific language

W. Löwe and M. Südholt (Eds.): SC 2006, LNCS 4089, pp. 50–65, 2006.
© Springer-Verlag Berlin Heidelberg 2006

(DSL) that acts as a pivot model. This DSL enables designers to describe, on a *Fractal* system, the observations that are needed to appropriately verify their specifications. The definition of observations is based on a scope (where the observation takes place in the hierarchy of components), moments or times during the system life cycle (including design, configuration and run times) and the values observed. Observations are finally linked to appropriate verification methods that have been integrated in *ConFract*. In the case of executable assertions, we show that these observations can be automatically generated. As for TLA, we describe what kind of observations must be provided to link the specifications to the concrete application. As our contributions only rely on the very general assumptions made on components by the *Fractal* model [4], they are applicable to other component models.

The rest of the paper is organized as follows. The next section gives an overview of the *ConFract* system through a running example. In section 3, a TLA specification of the example is described. Section 4 presents the integration of this new formalism in the *ConFract* system. Relationships to other works are covered in section 5. Section 6 concludes this paper and gives some indications on future work. An appendix gives an overview of both TLA and the used checking technique.

2   The ConFract System

The purpose of the *ConFract* system [7] is to specify and verify, on *Fractal* software components, properties that go beyond interface signatures. Integrated in *Fractal* as a non functional feature, it reifies contracts between components. *ConFract* aims at taking into account the specificities of the life cycle of component-based applications (design, (re-)configuration, deployment, runtime) as well as their hierarchical and dynamic nature in the case of *Fractal*.

Fractal [4] is a general component model with the following main features: composite components (to have a uniform view of applications at various levels of abstraction), shared components (to model resources and resource sharing while maintaining component encapsulation), reflective capabilities (introspection capabilities to monitor a running system and re-configuration capabilities to deploy and dynamically configure a system) and openness (in the model, almost everything is optional and can be extended). Components can be connected through server (provided) and client (required) interfaces. The content of a composite component is composed of other components, called subcomponents, which are under the control of the enclosing component. A Java-based reference implementation is also available[1].

2.1   A Running Example

Throughout this paper, we illustrate our approach with a cruise control system inspired from [16]. This system is controlled by three buttons: *resume, on* and *off*.

---

[1] The reader can find more detail in [5] and at http://fractal.objectweb.org.

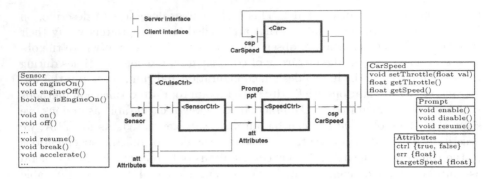

Fig. 1. The Cruise Control System in *Fractal*

When the engine is running and *on* is pressed, the cruise control system records the current speed and maintains the car at its speed. When the accelerator, brake or *off* is pressed, the cruise control system disengages but retains the speed setting. If *resume* is pressed, the cruise control system accelerates or de-accelerates the car back to the previously-recorded speed (see figure 1 for the *Fractal* architecture and the Java interfaces).

From an external point of view, the component <Car> provides the interface *csp*, of Java type *CarSpeed*, whose methods permit to set the throttle and to get the current speed at which the car is travelling. The cruise component <CruiseCtrl> represents the main control system, providing a *Sensor* interface, some attributes representing the cruise operation, its target speed and a possible error code. This component also requires a *CarSpeed* interface in order to interact with the car. Internally, the <CruiseCtrl> is made of two subcomponents. The <SpeedCtrl> is controlled through its provided *Prompt* interface, and when it is enabled, it adjusts the throttle to maintain the target speed. The <SensorCtrl> pilots the <SpeedCtrl> according to the method calls on its *Sensor* interface.

2.2   Main Principles of ConFract

The *ConFract* system dynamically builds contracts from specifications at assembly time and updates them according to the dynamic reconfigurations of components. A contract is thus a first class entity, always up-to-date regarding the architecture and which also refers to components needed for its evaluation. Among them, the *ConFract* system determines the responsibilities associated to each specification, distinguishing a *guarantor*, which must be notified in case of violation and can react to it, from *beneficiaries*, that are components which can rely on the property. It is then possible to use these concepts to negotiate on contracts at assembly or run times [6].

Currently in *ConFract*, specifications are written in the *CCL-J* language (*Component Constraint Language for Java*) which is inspired by *OCL* [20] and enhanced to be adapted to the *Fractal* model. *CCL-J* is an executable assertion language supporting classic constructs such as preconditions, postconditions and invariants. The scope of specifications can be on a type interface, on a specific *Fractal* interface or on a component instance, type or template.

2.3 Types of Contract

The *ConFract* system distinguishes several types of contracts according to the specifications given by the designers.

Interface contracts are established on the binding between a client and a server interface, only retaining specifications on the interface scope. They are similar to object contracts [19,14]. For example, the following specifications of the *setThrottle* and *getSpeed* methods are used to build the interface contract between the two interfaces based on the *CarSpeed* Java type.

```
context void CarSpeed.setThrottle(float val)
  pre: 0.0 <= val <= 10.0
  post: getThrottle() == val

context float CarSpeed.getSpeed()
  post: 0.0 <= result <= speedParam.MAX
```

External composition contracts are located on the external side of each component. They consist of specifications which refer only to external interfaces of the component. They thus express the usage and external behavior rules of the component. For example, the following specification scope is on the <SpeedCtrl> component and states the postconditions of the method *enable* from the interface *prt*. The postconditions refer to other interfaces on the component, namely *atb* and *csp*, to define its behavior, that is the *ctrl* attribute is true and the target speed is the current speed of the car.

```
on <SpeedCtrl>
  context void prt.enable()
    post: atb.ctrl == true
    post: atb.targetSpeed == csp.getSpeed()@pre
```

Internal composition contracts are located on the internal side of a composite component. In the same way, they consist of specifications which refer only to internal interfaces of the component and to external interfaces of its subcomponents. They express the assembly and internal behavior rules of the implementation of the composite component. The following specification concerns the <CruiseCtrl> component, but also refers the interfaces of one of its subcomponents <SpeedCtrl>. It asserts that the method *on* must only be called to engage the cruise when the engine itself is on, and affects the <SpeedCtrl> attributes, setting *ctrl* to true and *err* to zero.

```
on <CruiseCtrl>
  context void sns.on()
    pre: sns.engineIsOn()
    post: <SpeedCtrl>.atb.ctrl == true
    post: <SpeedCtrl>.atb.err == 0
```

Runtime checking of assertions. When building the contract, the *ConFract* system includes, in each provision of a contract, the specification predicate (currently a *CCL-J* assertion), an interception context (the times and locations where the provision is supposed to be satisfied) and the necessary references to the context (component, interfaces, etc.). The contracts are then evaluated when the appropriate event occurs : preconditions are checked at method entry, postconditions at exit, etc.

2.4 Motivations

In order to validate the general nature of the *ConFract* system, it must integrate formalisms that allow designers to specify and verify different aspects of component assemblies. Formalisms such as temporal logic or process algebra make possible the specification of the correct behaviors of a system at the desired abstraction level. The specifications can be formally verified, using theorem provers or model checker tools, but can also serve to check the adherence of a component implementation to its specification - typically by producing oracles from the system specifications, in order to (runtime) check execution traces against a verified model. Integrating such formalisms and verifications is thus very interesting, to validate and evolve the *ConFract* metamodel and to show the combination of different behavioral descriptions under the control of contracts.

3 TLA Specification

In this section we formulate in the Temporal Logic of Action (TLA) some properties of the cruise system and the associated oracles (see the appendix for a TLA overview). For the sake of brevity we focus on the component <CruiseCtrl> and its refinement by the sub-component <SpeedCtrl> of figure 1.

3.1 Specifications

<CruiseCtrl> We first specify in TLA the cruise component, taking into account a simplified requirement: the distance between the current speed of the car and the target speed cannot increase when the cruise is engaged.

──────────── MODULE *CruiseCtrl* ────────────

EXTENDS *Integers*
CONSTANT *MAX*
VARIABLE *cruise*
$TypeInv \triangleq cruise \in [ctrl : \text{BOOLEAN} , err : 0 .. MAX]$

$Init \triangleq cruise = [ctrl \mapsto \text{FALSE}, err \mapsto 0]$
$Next \triangleq \land cruise' \in [ctrl : \text{BOOLEAN} , err : 0 .. MAX]$
$\qquad \land cruise.ctrl \Rightarrow cruise.err' \leq cruise.err$
$\qquad \land \neg cruise.ctrl' \Rightarrow cruise.err' = 0$
$Spec \triangleq Init \land \Box[Next]_{\langle cruise \rangle}$

THEOREM $Spec \Rightarrow \Box TypeInv$

Fig. 2. The CruiseCtrl module

The specification is as follow (cf. figure 2). *MAX* represents the maximum speed at which the car can travel. *TypeInv* defines what values the state variable *cruise* can assume in a behavior that satisfies the specification - a record whose *ctrl* and *err* fields[2] represent cruise attributes (cf. figure 1). *Spec* is formula 1 of the annex, ignoring liveness requirements. *Init* starts any correct behavior in a state where the cruise is disengaged. *Next* defines the possible moves (using the prime notation of TLA to distinguish values in the successor states). The first conjunct ensures that the next state is conform to *TypeInv*, the second that the error cannot increase when the cruise is engaged. The last conjunct sets the error to 0 when the cruise disengages. The theorem asserts that the specification implies the invariance properties *TypeInv*.

<**SpeedCtrl**> The correct behaviors of the speed controller component are specified in figure 3. The role of this sub-component of the cruise (cf. figure 1) is to set the throttle when the car is cruising in order to decrease the error. Its specification refines the cruise specification of figure 2. The state has an additional field *trg* representing the previously-recorded speed (the attribute *targetSpeed* of figure 1). The possible moves of the speed controller are defined as a disjunction of four statements, representing the incoming calls - *enable, resume, disable* - on its interface (Prompt) and the outgoing calls - *setThrottle* - on its interface (CarSpeed). The speed controller can always record the current speed with no error when it engages (*Enable*). It can also engage with the previously-recorded speed and the current error when it is disengaged (*Resume*). The error cannot increase when it is engaged since it accelerates or de-accelerates the car back to the recorded speed (*Throttle*). Finally, it can always disengage retaining the speed setting with no error (*Disable*).

──────────────────────── MODULE *SpeedCtrl* ────────────────────────

EXTENDS *Integers*
CONSTANT *MAX*
VARIABLE *speed*
$TypeInv \triangleq speed \in [ctrl : \text{BOOLEAN} , trg : 0 .. MAX, err : 0 .. MAX]$

$Init \triangleq speed = [ctrl \mapsto \text{FALSE}, trg \mapsto 0, err \mapsto 0]$

$Enable \triangleq \exists r \in 0 .. MAX : speed' = [ctrl \mapsto \text{TRUE}, trg \mapsto r, err \mapsto 0]$
$Resume \triangleq \neg speed.ctrl \land \exists e \in 0 .. MAX : speed' = [speed \text{ EXCEPT } !.ctrl = \text{TRUE}, !.err = e]$
$Throttle \triangleq speed.ctrl \land \exists e \in 0 .. speed.err : speed' = [speed \text{ EXCEPT } !.err = e]$
$Disable \triangleq speed' = [ctrl \mapsto \text{FALSE}, trg \mapsto speed.trg, err \mapsto 0]$
$Next \triangleq Enable \lor Resume \lor Throttle \lor Disable$

$Spec \triangleq Init \land \Box[Next]_{\langle speed \rangle}$

THEOREM *Spec* $\Rightarrow \Box TypeInv$
$Cruise \triangleq \text{INSTANCE } CruiseCtrl \text{ WITH } cruise \leftarrow [ctrl \mapsto speed.ctrl, err \mapsto speed.err]$
THEOREM *Spec* $\Rightarrow$ *Cruise!Spec*

Fig. 3. The SpeedCtrl module

---

[2] *ctrl* abstracts the activity of the cruise as a boolean, *err* represents the distance between the current speed of the car and the target speed when the cruise is engaged.

Refinement. The last theorem of figure 3 asserts that the speed controller implements the cruise (i.e. every behaviors satisfying *Spec* also satisfies the specification *Cruise!Spec* of the cruise), according to the state substitution obtained by removing the field *trg* when instantiating the cruise.

Correctness. We applied the TLC model checker [13] to these specifications, describing finite-state models by giving explicit value to the constant *MAX*. These specifications and the refinement being simples no error was reported.

3.2 Oracles

As mentioned above, the intent of an oracle is to check execution traces of a system under test against a verified model. Oracles address only safety properties (whose violation can be illustrated on finite behaviors) but are a practical way to check if the system behaviors are correctly implemented, or to provide counter-examples when they are not. An approach to produce oracles from TLA specifications of a system is discussed in the appendix. We apply now this approach in the context of the speed controller - the principle is similar for the cruise.

<**SpeedCtrlOracle**> An oracle for the speed controller component is specified in figure 4. The specification first extends the modules *SpeedCtrl* and *IO*. The module *SpeedCtrl* (cf. figure 3) contains the state variable *speed* and the formula *Spec* specifying the correct behaviors of the speed controller. The module *IO* defines the *io*-operators representing observations of primitive values (cf. annex). The operator *ObsVal* represents observations of the speed controller state. Its definition relies on *io*-operators (e.g. *ioNat* to valuate the *err* integer field) and is used to set the state in the initial state predicate *InitObs* and the next-state relation *NextObs* of the observer specification *Obs*. *Obs* and *Oracle* are respectively formula 2 and formula 3 of the annex.

┌──────────────── MODULE *SpeedCtrlOracle* ────────────────┐

EXTENDS *SpeedCtrl, IO*

──

$ObsVal \triangleq [ctrl \mapsto ioBool,\ trg \mapsto ioNat,\ err \mapsto ioNat]$

──

$InitObs \triangleq speed = ObsVal$
$NextObs \triangleq speed' = ObsVal$
$Obs \triangleq InitObs \wedge \Box[NextObs]_{speed}$
$Oracle \triangleq (Init \wedge InitObs) \wedge \Box[(Next \wedge NextObs)]_{speed}$

└──┘

Fig. 4. The SpeedCtrlOracle module

Discussion. A behavior of an actual speed controller might result in the following execution trace:

```
ctrl    trg   err
─────────────────
FALSE,  50,   0     // the cruise is disengaged
TRUE,   50,   10    // the button resume is pressed (err = 10)
```

```
TRUE,   50,  6    // the cruise sets the throttle (err = 6)
TRUE,   45,  0    // the button on is pressed
TRUE,   45,  0    // the cruise maintains the current speed
FALSE,  45,  0    // the cruise is disengaged
. . .
```

This behavior is valid but verifying manually its correctness would be labor intensive. As discussed in annex, a runtime checker applied to formula *Oracle* automatically computes behaviors from this kind of trace and checks their correctness against a verified model, reporting faulty behaviors when an error is detected.

4   Integration

4.1   Requirements

As discussed above, the *ConFract* system currently makes verification by checking assertions in the context of the execution flow, using directly the computation data. Formal behavioral languages, on the other hand, make possible the specification of the correct behaviors of a system, the composition of sub-systems and refinement reasoning about a system specified at multiple levels of abstraction. These specifications, as illustrated above with TLA, can be verified on a model or serve to check execution traces acquired from an implementation of the system.

As the means of verification may differ from a formalism to another the contract system should embed different kinds of verification. People integrating a formalism should then be able to define several verifications. In the case of TLA, runtime checking of a specification requires specific oracle specifications to capture execution traces. More generally, the integration of a formalism is concerned by the definition of appropriate observations on a system. Integrating such code in *ConFract* is not an easy task. To facilitate it, a domain-specific language[3] can enable formalism integrators to focus on the semantics of observations and verifications rather than on technical particularities.

4.2   A Language for Observations and Verifications

The proposed DSL is dedicated to the definition of observations with associated verification methods, thus acting as a pivot model in the *ConFract* system. This language enables designers to define a set of rules. A rule describes where and when observations occur, what values they capture, and the verifications to be made.

Rule definition. A rule is defined according to the following syntax pattern:

---

[3] A domain-specific language (DSL) is a programming language or executable specification language that offers, through appropriate notations and abstractions, expressive power focused on, and usually restricted to, a particular problem domain [28].

```
On <a component>
   Observe {
        ( val: <some value> at: <some times>; )+
   }
   Verify <some properties>
```

Its semantics is rather close to the assertion clauses introduced in section 2, as executable assertion languages are rather operational in their expression. The *On* block defines what spatial domain of the system is visible to the rule, that is a component scope. The *Observe* block describes the observations operated in the scope. The *Verify* block describes the checking part, which can of course use the observed values.

The *Observe* part contains a list of observations that are defined by the statements *val:... at:...*. The *at* block gives the times at which the value described in the *val* block can be observed. Whereas the *On* blocks always refer to a component, the *val* part contains a sequence of functional expressions that can be evaluated in the *On* scope at defined times. Results may be bound to names if needed. Finally, the *Verify* property is a predicate that takes the *val* values as parameters.

For example, the third assertion from the internal composition contract of section 2 can be automatically translated to the following rule:

```
On <CruiseCtrl>
   Observe {
        val:  error = <SpeedCtrl>.atb.err
        at:   exit void sns.on();
   }
   Verify error == 0
```

It means that the attribute err of <SpeedCtrl> should be 0 for any of its observations made on the *on()* method exit from the *sns* interface of the <CruiseCtrl> component. The *val* block specifies that *<SpeedCtrl>.atb.err* should be observed and bound to name *error*, when events described in *at* occurs.

Event definition. In order to define when observations should occur, some atomic observable events are provided. Inside a rule, events are considered as sets. For example, in the following definition:

```
at: entry boolean sns.isEngineOn()
```

the considered set of events contains only one event, the entry in the *sns.isEngine-On()* method. Basic regular expressions enable designers to denote more easily sets of events that encompass several method calls or several interfaces:

```
at: entry * sns.*(*) , exit * sns.*(*)
```

This set of events contains all events that are determined by an entry or exit of any method on the *sns* interface. This kind of events are common in aspect-oriented systems [11].

Classic set operations are also provided (union, intersection, etc.) and an interval is defined as the set of all occurring events between two events. Open intervals can also be defined by referring to all events before or after another one. Moreover, events that are specific to components life cycle are also manipulable so that design or configuration events can be taken into account. For example, adding or removing a component to/from a composite one, binding and unbinding between two interfaces, starting or stopping a component. As the *Fractal* platform provides these control features through extensible interfaces [4], it is quite straightforward to be notified of these events.

It should be noted that a rule can refer to design time verifications that are done, for example, on an ADL. Indeed, main architectural descriptions of an ADL (containment, binding) can be translated into successive configuration events, thus enabling the checking system to do appropriate verifications.

4.3   TLA Application

We now consider the use of the DSL to integrate TLA specifications and the associated verifications in *ConFract*. Runtime and design time verifications are considered.

Implementation adherence. To check at runtime the adherence of a component's implementation to its TLA specification, the context is the set of all events at which the execution can be observed to complete the trace. We assume that they may enter the trace in any order and number of times. A trace can be checked against a verified model using an oracle specification, as proposed in section 3.2. For example, the rule shown below considers the runtime checking of an implementation of the component <SpeedCtrl>.

```
On <SpeedCtrl>
   Observe {
      val:  att.ctrl, att.err, arr.targetSpeed
      at:   exit void csp.setThrottle(float),
            exit * ppt.*(*);
   }
   Verify TlaTrace("SpeedCtrlOracle")
```

Taken the component <SpeedCtrl> as the scope reference, observation events described in the *at* construct are defined by all exits of the method *setThrottle* from the *csp* interface and of all methods from the *ppt* interface. The *val* block specifies that the attributes *atb.ctrl*, *atb.err* and *atb.targetSpeed* of <SpeedCtrl> should be observed when events described in *at* occurs.

The *Verify* clause finally states that checking is done through the *TlaTrace* technique, taking the *SpeedCtrlOracle* specification (cf. figure 4) as additional parameter. *TlaTrace* refers to a TLA runtime checker, which is called by the *ConFract* system. As mentioned in 3.2, the trace of the specified values from the *val* block are used by the runtime checker, when evaluating *SpeedCtrlOracle*, to compute a behavior and check its correctness against a verified model. Doing so, we runtime check an external composition contract of the *SpeedCtrl*, i.e. the correctness of the behaviors observed on its external interfaces against a verified model.

Design time verifications. Given the TLA specifications ofthe components <SpeedCtrl> and <CruiseCtrl> (cf. section 3.1), one can consider checking their correctness and the refinement that link them. For example, one can define the following rule on the <CruiseCtrl> before its sub-component <SpeedCtrl> starts. This rule considers the correctness of the *SpeedCtrl* specification (cf. figure 3). It must be noted that this specification explicitly asserts that the speed controller implements the cruise controller. So verifying the correctness of *SpeedCtrl*, using a model checker tool, automatically checks the refinement property.

```
On <CruiseCtrl>
   Observe {
      val:   at: before <SpeedCtrl>.start;
   }
   Verify TlaModel("SpeedCtrl")
```

The definitions of before and after constructs in the *ConFract* metamodel enable developers to implement a more specific observation. In this example, it would enable developers to check this property on an ADL or just before the application starts, and not to check it again if dynamic reconfigurations occur. The *Verify* clause states that checking is done through the *TlaModel* technique, taking the *SpeedCtrl* specification (cf. figure 3) as additional parameter. *TlaModel* refers to a TLA model checker, called by the *ConFract* system. We thus model check an internal composition contract of the *CruiseCtrl*, i.e. if the speed controller specification implements the cruise controller specification.

4.4   Enhancing the ConFract System

Using the proposed DSL, the observations and associated verifications are now made explicit. Depending on the formalism, they must be provided by the designer or can be directly generated by the *ConFract* system (see figure 5). In the case of assertions, as illustrated in section 2, *ConFract* now generates the observation rules from the specifications. Verification is then simply the evaluation of the assertion.

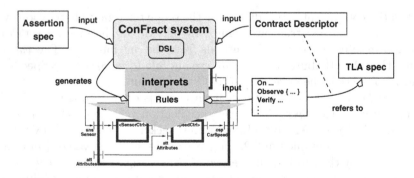

Fig. 5. The enhanced *ConFract* system

As for TLA, designers have to provide the observation rules associated to the specifications and oracles. This is illustrated in figure 5 by the three input files on the right. The *ConFract* system then interprets the rules to operate the observations and their associated verifications. But as the system does not impose any naming convention on the TLA specifications, one must provide for each contract a descriptor denoting the specifications and their oracle. In this contract descriptor, the type of contract and the concerned components are also described so that responsibilities can be deduced in the *ConFract* system [7]. On the contrary, the verification methods (TlaTrace and TlaModel in previous section) are provided once and for all when TLA is integrated into *ConFract*.

More generally, using our DSL, it is possible to define observations at design, configuration or run times. Observations can also be about components' interactions or configuration actions, so that one can capture the behavior of both components and architectures. Moreover, the DSL allows the specifier to choose the verification method for each observation rule, so that it is possible to run the verification at different times of the application life cycle. For example, the TLA oracle checking can be done at runtime or with post mortem traces (see appendix), and this can be simply configured in the system. Finally, the descriptor enables the specifier to explicitly bind its specification to a specific kind of contract. As contracts contain responsibilities between components, this makes possible to map specifications in very abstract models (such as TLA) to a concrete interpretation in the final running application.

5   Related Work

Assertions and DbC. Since the *Eiffel* language [19], numerous works focused on executable assertions in object-oriented languages, notably for *Java*. *JML* [14] combines executable assertions with some features of abstract programs. It allows the developer to build executable models which use abstraction functions on the specified classes. Works on contracting components focus on using adapted formalisms to specify component interfaces. Contracts on *.NET* assemblies have been proposed [2], associating abstract programs that are written in *AsmL* to interfaces, and interpreting them in parallel with the code. Several works have also proposed contracts for *UML* components. In [21], contracts between service providers and service users are formulated based on abstractions of action and operation behavior using the pre and postcondition technique. A refinement relation is provided among contracts but they only concerns peer to peer composition in this approach. In the same way, a graphical notation has been defined [29] to express functional and extra-functional contracts on UML components ports. All these works focus on interface specifications, whereas *ConFract* supports in addition two forms of composition contracts.

ADLs. A number of Architecture Description Languages (ADLs) have been proposed for capturing software architectures in terms of components and their overall interconnection structure [18]. Many of these languages support formal notations to specify components and connectors behaviors. For example, Wright [1] and Darwin [17,16] use CSP-based notations, Rapide [15] uses partially ordered sets of events and supports simulation of reactive architectures. These formalisms allow to verify correctness of component assemblies, checking properties such as deadlock freedom. Some ADLs support implementation issues, typically by generating glue code to connect component implementation. However most of the work on applying formal verifications to component interactions has focused on design time. A notable exception is the SOFA component model and its behavior protocol formalism based on regular-like expressions [23,22]. This formalism (recently adapted to *Fractal*) is designed to specify communication among components and permits the designer to verify the adherence of a component's implementation to its specification at runtime, while the correctness of refining the specification can be verified at design time.

Runtime verifications. The idea of testing a running system to check its conformity with a behavioral specification is not new, e.g. [8,24]. Recent works aim at developing practical testing environments for software developers as well as formal frameworks for defining finite trace monitoring logics. For example, the objective of the PathExplorer project [10] is to construct a flexible framework for efficient monitoring of program executions. It provides support to check whether an execution trace violates some Linear Temporal Logic (LTL) formula. A review of several other attempts to develop runtime verifications systems is provided in [3]. In this paper, the authors propose a rule-based framework dedicated to the definition and implementation of a large class of finite trace monitoring logics. In [9] they present JSpy, a system for instrumenting Java bytecode which aims at providing runtime analysis of Java programs. JSpy's input consists of a collection of rules, where a rule is a pair of predicate (syntactic constraints on a Java statement) and action (logging information to be inserted in the bytecode). Our work is quite similar, but it provides observation means on an architecture of components rather than on bytecode.

6   Conclusion

The work presented here targets both design and runtime verifications. However, rather to introduce a new specification language, we focus on a framework intended to integrate different formalisms for contracting component behaviors. The integration relies on a DSL dedicated to the association of observations with verification methods, and specialized to hierarchical component-based systems. It particularly takes into account the components structure (interfaces, bindings, nested components...) and life cycle (design, re-configurations, runtime).

The integration of an assertion-based language and a temporal logic have been described for illustration. These two formalisms clearly show different needs in the handling of specifications, oracles, observations and verifications. With the proposed DSL and the appropriate descriptors, the integration of a formalism is characterized. People involved in formalisms integration can now describe the formalism in *ConFract* and determine which part can be generated or must be provided by final designers. Besides, events are always confined in a component scope, facilitating monitoring. Moreover, as the contract writer can choose observation points, it is easy to accommodate the quantity of observations to specific deployment constraints.

This work can be seen as a first step to put together different specification languages, formal and semi-formal, under the control of a contracting system, so that they can be used at best all along the life cycle of component-based systems. For example, assertions are close to the developer. Temporal logics are more expressive but require a less trivial capture of the state.

Future works include the extension of the proposed DSL to add actions in observation rules. We also plan to integrate other formalisms well-suited to specify communication among components, such as behavior protocols [22], as well as languages dedicated to extra-functional properties.

Acknowledgements. This work was partially supported by France Telecom under the collaboration contracts number 422721832-I3S and 46132097-I3S.

References

1. ALLEN, R. J., AND GARLAN, D. A formal basis for architectural connection. *ACM, Transactions on Software Engineering and Methodology 6* (July 1997).
2. BARNETT, M., AND SCHULTE, W. Runtime Verification of .NET Contracts. *Journal of Systems and Software 65*, 3 (2003), 199–208.
3. BARRINGER, H., GOLDBERG, A., HAVELUND, K., AND SEN, K. Rule-based runtime verification. In *VMCAI* (2004), B. Steffen and G. Levi, Eds., vol. 2937 of *Lecture Notes in Computer Science*, Springer, pp. 44–57.
4. BRUNETON, E., COUPAYE, T., LECLERCQ, M., QUÉMA, V., AND STEFANI, J.-B. An Open Component Model and Its Support in Java. In *ICSE 2004 - CBSE7* (May 2004), vol. 3054 of *LNCS*, Springer Verlag.
5. BRUNETON, E., COUPAYE, T., AND STEFANI, J.-B. The Fractal component model. Specification, Technical Report v1, v2, The ObjectWeb Consortium, 2002/2003. http://fractal.objectweb.org.
6. CHANG, H., AND COLLET, P. Fine-grained Contract Negotiation for Hierarchical Software Components. In *31th EUROMICRO Conference 2005, 30 August - 3 September 2005, Porto, Portugal* (2005), IEEE Computer Society.
7. COLLET, P., ROUSSEAU, R., COUPAYE, T., AND RIVIERRE, N. A Contracting System for Hierarchical Components. In *CBSE'2005, St. Louis, MO, USA, May 14-15, 2005, Proceedings* (2005), vol. 3489 of *LNCS*, Springer Verlag, pp. 187–202.
8. DIAZ, M., JUANOLE, G., AND COURTIAT, J. P. Observer – a concept for formal on-line validation of distributed systems. *IEEE Trans. on Software Engineering 20*, 12 (Dec. 1994), 900–913.
9. GOLDBERG, A., AND HAVELUND, K. Instrumentation of java bytecode for runtime analysis. *Fifth ECOOP Workshop on Formal Techniques for Java-like Programs (FTfJP'03))* (July 2004).
10. HAVELUND, K., AND ROŞU, G. Efficient monitoring of safety properties. *International Journal on Software Tools for Technology Transfer (STTT) 6*, 2 (Aug. 2004), 158–173.
11. KICZALES, G., LAMPING, J., MENHDHEKAR, A., MAEDA, C., LOPES, C., LOINGTIER, J.-M., AND IRWIN, J. Aspect-oriented programming. In *Proceedings European Conference on Object-Oriented Programming*, M. Akşit and S. Matsuoka, Eds., vol. 1241. Springer-Verlag, Berlin, Heidelberg, and New York, 1997, pp. 220–242.
12. LAMPORT, L. The Temporal Logic of Actions. *ACM Trans. on Programming Languages and Systems 16*, 3 (May 1994), 872–923.

13. LAMPORT, L. *Specifying Systems: The TLA⁺ Language and Tools for Hardware and Software Engineers.* Addison Wesley, July 2002.
14. LEAVENS, G. T., BAKER, A. L., AND RUBY, C. JML: A notation for detailed design. In *Behavioral Specifications of Businesses and Systems* (1999), H. Kilov, B. Rumpe, and I. Simmonds, Eds., Kluwer, pp. 175–188.
15. LUCKHAM, D. C., AND VERA, J. An event-based architecture definition language. *IEEE Trans. Software Eng. 21,* 9 (1995), 717–734.
16. MAGEE, J., AND KRAMER, J. *Concurrency: state models & Java programs.* John Wiley & Sons, Inc., 1999.
17. MAGEE, J., KRAMER, J., AND GIANNAKOPOULOU, D. Behaviour analysis of software architectures. In *WICSA* (1999), pp. 35–50.
18. MEDVIDOVIC, N., AND TAYLOR, R. N. A classification and comparison framework for software architecture description languages. In *IEEE Transactions on Software Engineering* (Jan. 2000), vol. 26(1), pp. 70–93.
19. MEYER, B. Applying "design by contract". *IEEE Computer 25,* 10 (Oct. 1992), 40–51.
20. OBJECT MANAGEMENT GROUP. Object Constraint Language Specification. Tech. Rep. version 1.1, ad/97-08-08, IBM **www.software.ibm.com/ad/ocl**, Sept. 1997.
21. PAHL, C. Components, contracts, and connectors for the unified modelling language UML. In *FME 2001 - Formal Methods Europe* (2001), vol. 2021 of *Lecture Notes in Computer Science*, Springer Verlag, pp. 259–277.
22. PLASIL, F. Enhancing component specification by behavior description: the sofa experience. In *WISICT '05: Proceedings of the 4th international symposium on Information and communication technologies* (2005), Trinity College Dublin, pp. 185–190.
23. PLASIL, F., AND VISNOVSKY, S. Behavior protocols for software components. *IEEE Transactions on Software Engineering 28(11)* (Nov. 2002).
24. RICHARDSON, D. J., AHA, S. L., AND O'MALLEY, T. O. Specification-based test oracles for reactive systems. In *14th International Conference on Software Engineering (ICSE'92)* (1992), pp. 105–118.
25. RIVIERRE, N., HORN, F., AND TRAN, F. D. On monitoring concurrent systems with TLA: an example. *Fifth International Conference on Application of Concurrency to System Design (ACSD'05), St Malo, FR* (June 2005), 36–47.
26. SZYPERSKI, C. *Component Software — Beyond Object-Oriented Programming*, 2nd ed. Addison-Wesley Publishing Co. (Reading, MA), 2002.
27. TLA. References to the TLA literature can be found at http://lamport.org/.
28. VAN DEURSEN, A., KLINT, P., AND VISSER, J. Domain-specific languages: An annotated bibliography. *SIGPLAN Notices 35,* 6 (2000), 26–36.
29. WEIS, T., BECKER, C., GEIHS, K., AND PLOUZEAU, N. A UML meta-model for contract aware components. In *UML 2001 - The Unified Modeling Language* (Oct. 2001), vol. 2185 of *Lecture Notes in Computer Science*, Springer Verlag, pp. 442–456.

Appendix: TLA

The Temporal Logic of Actions (TLA) has been proposed by Lamport for the specification and verification of the correct behaviors of concurrent and reactive systems[4] [12,13]. TLA allows the composition of sub-systems and refinement reasoning. A *behavior* represents an execution of the system as an infinite sequence of states where a *state* is an assignment of values to state variables. An *action*

---

[4] More precisely, the specification language is TLA⁺.

formula expresses the relation between the value of variables in two successive states. TLA specifications are usually written in the canonical form:

$$Spec \triangleq Init \wedge \Box[Next]_x \wedge L \tag{1}$$

where the state predicate *Init* characterizes the system's initial states, *Next* is an action formula typically written as a disjunction of possible moves ($\Box$ asserts that *Next* is always true), x is the tuple of state variables and L describes the liveness requirements. *Spec* represents all behaviors satisfying formula 1. Compared to other temporal logics, TLA differs in that it allows to specify both a system and its temporal properties within the same formalism. The verification of TLA specifications has been amply studied [27] and can be automated with the model checker tool TLC [13].

TLA oracles. The intent of an oracle is to check execution traces of a system under test against a verified model. An approach to produce oracles from TLA specifications of a system (applied in figure 4 of section 3.2) has been proposed in [25] as follow. Let *Spec* be the specification of the correct behaviors of a system (*Spec* is formula 1) and *Obs* be a specification of an observer of this system:

$$Obs \triangleq InitObs \wedge \Box[NextObs]_x \tag{2}$$

Obs represents arbitrary valuations of the system state at each step. Its definition relies on specific TLA operators (referred as *io*-operators) representing arbitrary values. For example, an arbitrary boolean value is defined as[5]:

$$ioBool \triangleq \text{CHOOSE } val : val \in \text{BOOLEAN} .$$

An oracle is specified as a simple form of composition of formula *Obs* and *Spec*. It represents the simultaneous advance of any observable behavior against a correct behavior.

$$Oracle \triangleq (InitObs \wedge Init) \wedge \Box[NextObs \wedge Next]_x \tag{3}$$

The intent of formula *Oracle* is to be evaluated by a (runtime) checker acting as a model-checker except for the *io*-operators. When evaluating these operators, the checker captures (online or postmortem) observations of a system under test through an input stream. That way, any execution trace captured by *Obs* but satisfying not *Spec* will not satisfy *Oracle* and be reported as a deadlock. The requirement (an executable form of few *io*-operators) can be easily achieved by the TLC model checker since this tool allows a TLA operator to be overridden by a Java method [13]. For example the operator *ioStr*, defined as an arbitrary string value, is overridden as:

```
public static BufferedReader in = ...
public static Value ioStr() { return new StringValue(in.readLine()); }
```

---

[5] The expression CHOOSE $x : F$ equals an arbitrarily chosen value x that satisfies the formula F [13]. Note that *io*-operators are required only for primitive values (boolean...), since other values are construction of primitive values.

Automated Pattern-Based Pointcut Generation

Mathieu Braem, Kris Gybels, Andy Kellens*, and Wim Vanderperren

Vrije Universiteit Brussel, Pleinlaan 2, 1050 Brussels, Belgium
{mbraem, kgybels, akellens, wvdperre}@vub.ac.be

Abstract. One of the main problems in Aspect-Oriented Software Development is the so-called fragile pointcut problem. Uncovering and specifying a good robust pointcut is not an easy task. In this paper we propose to use Inductive Logic Programming, and more specifically the FOIL algorithm, to automatically identify intensional (or "pattern-based") pointcuts. We present the tool chain we implemented to induce a pointcut given a set of identified joinpoints. Using several realistic medium-scale experiments, we show that our approach is able to automatically induce robust pointcuts for a set of joinpoints.

1 Introduction

Separation of concerns [29] is a crucial property for realizing comprehensible and maintainable software. Current software engineering paradigms do however not always succeed in cleanly modularizing all concerns. Consequently, these concerns are spread and repeated over several modules in the system. Due to this code duplication, it becomes very hard to alter such concerns within the system. These concerns are called *crosscutting* because the concern virtually crosscuts the decomposition of the system. Typical examples of crosscutting concerns are debugging concerns such as logging [19] and contract verification [33], security concerns [8] such as confidentiality and access control, and business rules [28,9] that describe business-specific logic.

Aspect-Oriented Software Development aims to provide a solution for these crosscutting concerns [19]. To this end, AOSD introduces an additional module construct, named an *aspect*. Traditional aspects consist of two main parts: a *pointcut* definition and an *advice*. Points in the program's execution where an aspect can be applied are called *joinpoints*. The declarative pointcut language allows to concisely describe a set of joinpoints where the aspect should be applied. The advice is the concrete behavior that is to be executed at certain joinpoints, typically before, after or around the original behavior of the joinpoints.

Since existing software systems can benefit from the advantages of AOSD as well, a number of techniques have been proposed to identify crosscutting concerns in existing source code (aspect mining) and transform these concerns into aspects (aspect refactoring). When refactoring a concern to an aspect, a pointcut must be written for this aspect. Pointcut languages like for instance

---

* Ph.D. scholarship funded by the "Institute for the Promotion of Innovation through Science and Technology in Flanders" (IWT Vlaanderen).

W. Löwe and M. Südholt (Eds.): SC 2006, LNCS 4089, pp. 66–81, 2006.

the CARMA pointcut language allow specifying intensional (or "pattern-based") pointcuts, so that the pointcut does not easily break when the base code is changed [11]. While existing aspect refactoring techniques also automatically generate a pointcut, they typically only provide an enumerative pointcut, which is fragile with respect to evolution of the base program. Turning this pointcut into a pattern-based pointcut is left to be done manually by the developer.

In this paper we propose to exploit Inductive Logic Programming techniques to automatically deduce an intensional pointcut from a given set of joinpoints. The next section details the problem of uncovering intensional pointcuts and introduces the running example used throughout this paper. Section 3 introduces Inductive Logic Programming and the concrete algorithms used and in section 4 we apply ILP for automatically generating intensional pointcuts. Afterwards, we present the tools created to support our approach, compare with related work and state our conclusions.

2 Background and Problem Statement

2.1 Pattern-Based Pointcuts

The main problem in maintaining aspect-oriented code is the so-called *fragile pointcut problem* [21]. Pointcuts are deemed fragile when seemingly innocent changes to the base program, such as renaming or relocating a method, break a pointcut such that it no longer captures the joinpoints it is intended to capture. When code is added to a program and introduces new joinpoints in the joinpoint model of the program, pointcuts are similarly considered fragile when some of these new joinpoints should be captured by the pointcut but it fails to do so.

```
1   public class Point {
2
3       private int x,y;
4
5       public void setX(int a) {
6           this.x=a;
7       }
8       public void setY(int a) {
9           this.y=a;
10      }
11      public int getX() {
12          return x;
13      }
14      public int getY() {
15          return y;
16      }
17  }
```

Fig. 1. A simple Point class

As described in our previous work [11] and that of others [20], pointcuts are particularly fragile when they are written in an enumerative style. As an example take the Point class of figure 1. When adding an observer aspect, we need a pointcut that captures all executions of methods on the Point class that are state changing. A purely enumerative pointcut is shown in figure 2.

The pointcut language used in the figure and the remainder of the paper is based on CARMA but is restricted to a static joinpoint model, we'll refer to it as PAGH[1] to make the distinction. CARMA [11] uses a fully dynamic joinpoint model, which for example allows conditions in pointcuts on the values associated with joinpoints. PAGH has a purely static joinpoint model, which effectively equates joinpoints with shadow joinpoints. An extension of the work presented here that takes a dynamic joinpoint model into account is left for future work. The important point however is that PAGH retains other features of CARMA which allow writing advanced intensional pointcuts: the use of logic variables, recursion and full access to the static shadow joinpoint model of the program.

```
1  stateChanges(Jpvar):
2      execution(Jpvar,setX).
3  stateChanges(Jpvar):
4      execution(Jpvar,setY).
```

Fig. 2. A pointcut for the Observer aspect, written in a purely enumerative style

The pointcut of figure 2 matches if the joinpoint at hand is either the execution of method setX or the execution of method setY. Such an enumeratively described pointcut obviously breaks easily. For example, when we evolve the point class to a three-dimensional point and add a setZ method, the stateChanges pointcut does not match the added method and thus fails to comply with the intention of capturing all methods that change the state of a Point object.

The problem with enumerative pointcuts is of course the motivation for writing pointcuts in a more pattern-based style, exploiting a pattern that is exhibited by the joinpoints that should be captured. The pointcut in figure 3 uses *quantification* over the names of methods that start with set. It remains consistent when evolving the point to a three-dimensional point. However, consider for example the addition of a reset method that resets the x and y dimension of the point to the default values. This method does not have the *begins with the keyword set* pattern in common with the other state changing methods. Conversely, consider the addition of a method setting which simply returns the value of a setting, rather than doing any assignments. This method also exhibits the *begins with keyword set* pattern but should in fact not be captured by the pointcut. We can capture the reset and setting methods as a deviation from the pattern by including an extra condition that the name of the method may also be reset and should not be setting, but this tends to add an enumerative list of exceptions to the pointcut.

---

[1] The name refers to a concept from the same realm as does Karma, see http://memory-alpha.org/en/wiki/Pagh

```
1  stateChanges(Jpvar):
2      execution(Jpvar,MethodName),
3      startsWith(MethodName,'set').
```

Fig. 3. A pointcut for the Observer aspect, written in a pattern-based style

```
1  stateChanges(Jpvar):
2      execution(Jpvar,MethodName),
3      inMethod(AssignmentJP,MethodName),
4      isAssignment(AssignmentJP,AssignmentTarget),
5      instanceVariable(AssignmentTarget,ClassName).
```

Fig. 4. A pointcut for the observer

Using an advanced pointcut language that gives access to the full static join-point model of methods, it is possible to exploit a more robust pattern [11]. Figure 4 illustrates a pointcut that exploits the pattern that all the state changing methods contain an assignment to an instance variable of an object. This pointcut does not break when adding the **setting** or **reset** methods.

2.2   Automated Support for Pattern-Based Pointcuts

The area of aspect refactoring and aspect mining is a particularly interesting research area within AOSD that is currently being explored. In performing aspect mining and refactoring, the problem crops up of finding a pointcut for the newly created aspect. Also, as with object-oriented refactoring, research is being performed on how to automate these refactorings using tool support. In such tools, it would be interesting to be able to automate the step of generating a pattern-based pointcut as well. Currently, most proposals for automating aspect refactoring simply generate an enumerative pointcut, which then too easily breaks when the program is evolved after refactoring.

In this paper we present the results of using a specific machine learning technique for deriving a pattern exhibited by examples. In particular we use *Inductive Logic Programming*, which is in fact an algorithm that works similarly to the process we've described in the previous section for coming to an evolution-robust pattern-based pointcut. We further describe this relation informally in the next section, and present in detail the ILP algorithm.

3   Inductive Logic Programming

3.1   Logic Induction of Pointcuts

The algorithm of logic induction is similar to the process we followed in section 2.1 for coming to a more evolution-robust pattern-based pointcut. Informally, the way ILP works and the relationship to this manual process is as follows:

positive examples: ILP takes as input a number of positive examples, in our setting of deriving pattern-based pointcuts these would be joinpoints that the pointcut should capture.

background information: A second input to ILP is background information on the examples. In our setting, these would be the result of predicates in the pointcut language that are true for the joinpoints, or in other words, the data associated with the joinpoints. Such as the name of the message of the joinpoint, the type of the joinpoint (message, assignment, ...), in which method or class the joinpoint occurs.

induction: ILP follows an iterative process of inducing a logic rule for combinations of the positive examples. This is similar to the manual process we followed in the previous section: we take two examples such as the methods setX and setY, and find that in the background information the fact that the names of the methods start with set holds true.

negative examples: ILP also takes as input a number of negative examples, the rules that are derived during the iterative induction should never cover negative examples. Negative examples effectively force the algorithm to use other information of the background in the induced rules. This is similar to the process followed in the previous section where we added a setting method which should not be covered by the pointcut.

3.2   FOIL

In this paper we use the FOIL ILP algorithm [30]. FOIL learns hypotheses which are sets of first-order rules, similar to Horn clauses. However, since no literals containing function symbols are allowed, the rules are more restricted than Horn clauses. On the other hand, the rules are more expressive because literals appearing in the body of the rules may be negated.

Pseudo-code for the algorithm is shown in figure 5. The algorithm takes a top-down approach to ILP. Starting with the most general rule, FOIL specializes it until no more negative examples are covered. The algorithm involves a double loop to find suitable queries. In the outer loop the algorithm generates rules, each time starting with the most general rule, covering all examples. In the inner loop, it adds clauses to the rule, until no more negative examples are covered. The algorithm halts when all positive examples have been covered.

The algorithm generates candidate literals based on the literals and variables already present in the rule, and on predicates found in the background information. Suppose the current rule is $Predicate(X_1, X_2, \ldots, X_k) \leftarrow Literal_1 \ldots Literal_n$. FOIL now considers the following literals for addition as $Literal_{n+1}$.

- $Q(V_1, \ldots, V_r)$, where Q is predicate occurring in the background information and where $V_i(\forall i, 0 < i < r)$ is either a new variable or a variable already present in the rule. At least one of the variables V_i has to be present in rule.
- $Equal(X_j, X_k)$, where X_j and X_k are variables already present in the rule.
- The negation of the literals formed in the rules above.

FOIL(*Target_predicate, Positives, Negatives, Background*)

 1: *Learned_rules* ← {}
 2: **while** *Positives* is not empty **do** {learn a new rule}
 3:     *NewRule* ← a new rule for *Target_predicate* with no preconditions
 4:     *NewRuleNeg* ← *Negatives*
 5:     **while** *NewRuleNeg* is not empty **do** {specialize *NewRule*}
 6:         *Candidate_literals* ← generate candidate new literals for *NewRule*, based on *Background*
 7:         calculate *Foil_Gain* for each literal in *Candidate_literals*
 8:         add literal with highest *Foil_Gain* to preconditions of *NewRule*
 9:         *NewRuleNeg* ← subset of *NewRuleNeg* satisfying *NewRule* preconditions
10:     **end while**
11:     *Learned_Rules* ← *Learned_Rules* ∪ {*NewRule*}
12:     *Positives* ← *Positives*\{ members of *Positives* covered by *NewRule*}
13: **end while**
14: **return** *Learned_rules*

Fig. 5. Pseudo-code for the FOIL Inductive Logic Programming algorithm

At each step of the inner loop a heuristic function is evaluated for all candidate literals. The result of this function shows how much the rule gains from adding this literal. The candidate literal which results in the highest gain is chosen as the next literal. This gain function, shown in figure 6, is a simple measure, based on the comparison of the number of covered positive (p) and negative (n) examples before (p_0, n_0) and after (p_1, n_1) the literal is added to the rule. The numbers of bindings that remain positive (t) after adding the literal to the rule is factored in.

$$Foil\_Gain(L, R) = t \left(\log_2 \frac{p_1}{p_1 + n_1} - \log_2 \frac{p_0}{p_0 + n_0} \right)$$

Fig. 6. Foil_Gain function

4 Applying ILP for Pointcut Abstraction

The FOIL algorithm is able to find rules from a set of logic facts. It requires a number of positive examples and a set of negative examples to avoid oversimplification. In addition, it expects a sufficiently large set of background information in order to be able to induce a rule. The positive examples for FOIL are the joinpoints where the aspect needs to be applied. They can either be manually selected or automatically using for example an aspect mining technique. All other joinpoints are defined as negative examples for the ILP algorithm. As background information, we construct a logic database consisting of the information that is normally available in the pointcut language on these joinpoints. These are the

Joinpoint predicates	newStatement(Joinpoint, Class)
isRead(Joinpoint, Variable)	throwStatement(Joinpoint, Variable)
isSendOf(Joinpoint, Method)	catchStatement(Joinpoint, Class)
returnStatement(Joinpoint)	finallyStatement(Joinpoint)
execution(Joinpoint, Method)	synchronizedBlock(Joinpoint, Variable)
inMethod(Joinpoint, Method)	castStatement(Joinpoint, Class, Variable)
isAssignment(Joinpoint, Variable)	instanceofStatement(Joinpoint,Class,Variable)
Structural predicates	
methodInClass(Method, Class)	methodReturns(Method, Class)
classExtends(Class, Class2)	classInPackage(Class, Package)
classImplements(Class, Class2)	isInterface(Class)
argumentOf(Variable,Method,Pos)	isClass(Class)
instanceVariable(Variable, Class)	isMethod(Method)
typeOf(Variable, Class)	isVariable(Variable)
	isConstructor(Method)
Modifier predicates	
isFinal(Arg)	isProtected(Member)
isPublic(Arg)	isPrivate(Member)
isAbstract(Arg)	isVolatile(Variable)
isStrict(Arg)	isTransient(Variable)
isStatic(Member)	isSynchronized(Method)
	isNative(Method)
	annotationOf(Member, Class)

Fig. 7. Predicates available in the PAGH crosscut language to select joinpoints, the solutions for these predicates are used as background information for the ILP algorithm

solutions of the predicates shown in figure 7, which also includes predicates about the relationships between classes etc. Because this pointcut language is based on a purely static joinpoint model, these solutions can be determined using only the program's source or compiled representation, i.e. compiled Java classes.

The algorithm will induce a pointcut that captures exactly the joinpoints currently in the program that should be captured (the positive examples), and none of the others (the negative examples). This is guaranteed by the algorithm. What we furthermore expect is that the induced pointcut also is a non-fragile or robust pointcut. In general we will not have a specific pointcut in mind that the algorithm should derive (otherwise the application of ILP would be rather pointless), though in these experiments we can use the robust pointcut we derived manually in section 2.1 as a benchmark for comparison.

4.1   Basic Point class

As an example of our approach, take the simple Point class from figure 1. In a first step we derive the static joinpoints from this code, and derive the information on all of these that is given by the predicates of the pointcut language (figure 7).

```
returnStatement(jp1).              isRead(jp12,'Point.x').
returnStatement(jp6).              isRead(jp15,'Point.y').
returnStatement(jp11).             methodInClass('Point.setX(I)I','Point').
returnStatement(jp14,).            methodInClass('Point.setY(I)I','Point').
returnStatement(jp17).             methodInClass('Point.getX()I','Point').
inMethod(jp1,'Point.setX(I)I').    methodInClass('Point.getY()I','Point').
inMethod(jp2,'Point.setX(I)I').    methodInClass('Point.Point()V','Point').
inMethod(jp3,'Point.setX(I)I').    classExtends('Point','java.lang.Object').
inMethod(jp4,'Point.setX(I)I').    methodReturns('Point.setX(I)I','int').
inMethod(jp6,'Point.setY(I)I').    methodReturns('Point.setY(I)I','int').
inMethod(jp7,'Point.setY(I)I').    methodReturns('Point.getX()I','int').
inMethod(jp8,'Point.setY(I)I').    methodReturns('Point.getY()I','int').
inMethod(jp9,'Point.setY(I)I').    isAssignment(jp2,'Point.x').
inMethod(jp11,'Point.getX()I').    isAssignment(jp7,'Point.y').
inMethod(jp12,'Point.getX()I').    instanceVariable('Point.x','Point,int').
inMethod(jp14,'Point.getY()I').    instanceVariable('Point.y','Point,int').
inMethod(jp15,'Point.getY()I').    classInPackage('java.lang.Object','java.lang').
inMethod(jp17,'Point.Point()V').   execution(jp0,'Point.setX(I)I').
isRead(jp3,'l0').                  execution(jp5,'Point.setY(I)I').
isRead(jp4,'l1').                  execution(jp10,'Point.getX()I').
isRead(jp8,'l2').                  execution(jp13,'Point.getY()I').
isRead(jp9,'l3').                  execution(jp16,'Point.Point()V').
```

Fig. 8. Part of the background information for the Point class of figure 1

This forms the background information for the logic induction algorithm, part of this generated background information is shown in figure 8.

The methods that are state changing on this simple Point class are the methods setX and setY only. We identify these two joinpoints as positive examples of our desired stateChanges pointcut, which are the joinpoints jp0 and jp5 respectively. The pointcut should not cover the other joinpoints: the joinpoints jp10 and jp13, for instance, denote the execution of the getX and getY method. Clearly, these methods are not state changing. So these and all other joinpoints besides jp0 and jp5 are marked as negative examples. We give the FOIL algorithm the positive examples stateChanges(jp0) and stateChanges(jp5). The resulting rule is shown in figure 9. The pointcut selects all executions of methods that contain an assignment.

The resulting pointcut is clearly not very robust. An evolution that easily breaks the pointcut would be to have a getX method that does an assignment to a local variable which does not mean that that method changes the state of an object, yet its execution would be captured by the pointcut. This result is however not very surprising: the Point class is small and does not include non-state changing methods that do assignments to local variables which would have served as a negative example for the FOIL algorithm. As the induced pointcut covers all positive examples and no negative ones, the induction stops and no further predicates from the background information are used to limit the rule to only the positive examples. The ILP algorithm works better on larger programs, so that more negative examples are available to avoid oversimplified pattern-based pointcuts.

```
1  stateChanges(A):
2      execution(A,B),
3      inMethod(C,B),
4      isAssignment(C,D).
```

Fig. 9. Induced stateChanges pointcut

In order to have a more realistic example, we apply our experiment to the Point class bundled with Java. We do not include a full listing of the generated background, but instead we give some statistics about the generated facts. Table 1 compares the number of facts found in the AWT Point class to the number of facts from the basic Point example.

Table 1. Generated facts statistics

	# Classes	# Facts	# Joinpoints
Toy example	1	71	10
AWT Point class	1	364	70
Complete AWT library	362	276863	65060

We identify four execution joinpoints in the AWT Point class where a state changing method is invoked and input them as positive examples to the algorithm. The remaining 66 joinpoints are defined as negative examples. The resulting pointcut is shown in figure 10. In this case, the algorithm generates a pointcut that is sufficiently robust for evolution: it is in fact the same pointcut we determined manually in section 2.1.

```
1  stateChanges(A):
2      execution(A,B),
3      inMethod(C,B),
4      isAssignment(C,D),
5      instanceVariable(D,E).
```

Fig. 10. Resulting pointcut when applying our approach to the AWT Point class

4.2   Extended Experiments

In order to provide a limited evaluation of our approach, we conduct several more involved experiments using the state-changes example on the Java AWT framework.

Large fact database: We apply our approach to the complete Java AWT library in order to evaluate whether our approach still returns a useful result when the number of facts is very large. This library contains approximately 362 classes and generates more than 250000 facts. The result is the same as for the Java AWT Point class alone: the same pointcut as was determined manually in section 2.1 is induced. For a performance evaluation, we refer to section 5.

Negation: One of the distinguishing features of the FOIL algorithm in comparison to other ILP algorithms is its ability to induce rules containing negations. As a variation of the state changing methods example, we need a pointcut for the executions of methods that change the observable representation of an object. This means the method does assignments to instance variables that are not declared transient using the modifier **transient** in Java: conceptually, these fields are not part of the object's persistent state and are not retained in the object's serialization. This is used for example when a class defines a cache in order to optimize some parts of its operations. As such, observers do not need to be notified when transient fields are altered. When applying this experiment to the Java AWT library, our algorithm induces the rule shown in figure 11, which in comparison to the pointcuts induced above adds exactly the properties in the background to distinguish these joinpoints from the negative examples that we would expect it to add, i.e. the fact that the instance variables being assigned to are not declared transient.

```
1   stateChanges(A):
2       execution(A,B),
3       inMethod(C,B),
4       isAssignment(C,D),
5       instanceVariable(D,E),
6       not(isTransient(D)).
```

Fig. 11. Resulting pointcut for non-transient field assignments in Java AWT

InEquality: The FOIL algorithm is also able to induce inequality for certain rule variables. For example, suppose we want to detect all methods that contain "illegal" assignments, namely assignments to instance variables of other classes. The rule of figure 12 is induced when we apply this experiment to the AWT library. This rule declares that a method is illegally state changing when it contains an assignment to an instance variable that does not belong to the same class as the method.

Recursion: Another advantage of the FOIL algorithm is its ability to induce recursive rules. For example, suppose we redefine state changing methods to also include execution joinpoints of methods that indirectly change the state of an object by invoking a method that is state changing. This is useful for implementations of the observer aspect that take into account the jumping aspect problem [4,11]. In order to capture this pattern robustly, two pointcut rules are

```
1  illegalStateChanges(A):
2      execution(A,B),
3      methodInClass(B,C),
4      inMethod(D,B),
5      isAssignment(D,E),
6      instanceVariable(E,F),
7      C<>F.
```

Fig. 12. Resulting pointcut for field assignments from a different class than the class defining the field

required, one of which is recursive. In this experiment our ILP implementation however did not induce such a recursive pointcut rule although theoretically the algorithm is able to induce recursive rules. The algorithm induces several rules that are unnecessarily complicated, depending on information that is irrelevant to the state changing concern. This pointcut breaks easily when the base program evolves because it is concerned with too much information. However, when we use method names as positive examples rather than joinpoints, a recursive rule is induced which does not exhibit such fragility issues, the resulting rule is shown in figure 13. All that would be necessary to turn this into a pointcut is an extra condition which gets the joinpoint associated with the method name. A possible reason that the algorithm doesn't try adding this condition may have to do with the gain function, but this needs to be investigated further in future work.

```
1  stateChanges(A):
2      inMethod(B,A),
3      isAssignment(B,C),
4      instanceVariable(C,D).
5  stateChanges(A):
6      inMethod(B,A),
7      isSendOf(B,C),
8      stateChanges(C).
```

Fig. 13. Recursive stateChanges rule

5 Tool Support

Our approach is supported by a fully automatic tool chain, which is illustrated in figure 14. The tool chain consists of the following tools:

- *FactGen:* This tool translates a range of Java class files and/or jar files to a set of facts representing these classes. The tool uses the javassist library [7] to process the binary class files. The javassist library provides a high-level reflective API that allows to inspect the full Java byte code, including method bodies. The output of the FactGen tool is the fact representation in XML format.
- *JFacts:* This tool allows to translate logic predicates from one syntax into another. Currently, the tool supports the FactGen's XML syntax, QFoil's syntax, CARMA's syntax and PAGH and Prolog syntax.

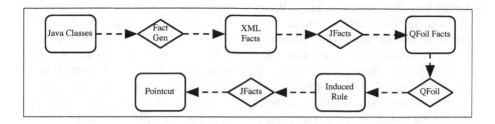

Fig. 14. The tool chain for inducing pointcuts in a logic pointcut language over static joinpoints in Java code

– *QFoil:* This tool is the implementation of the FOIL ILP algorithm by Ross Quinlan [31]. It takes a set of facts and a set of positive examples as input (negative examples are implicitly assumed) and tries to induce a logic rule that covers all of the positive examples and rejects all of the negative examples. This implementation of FOIL is particularly interesting because of its performance (see the benchmarks in the next paragraph).

In order to evaluate our approach performance-wise, we conduct several benchmark experiments with an increasingly large number of facts. The experiments were done using the state changing methods example. Table 2 shows the results[2]. In all cases, except for the toy Point class of course, the rule from Figure 10 was induced. The performance results are acceptable as the time required is not much more than compiling such a large set of classes. Considering the premature stage of the FactGen and JFacts tools, we believe that a significant improvement is still possible there.

Table 2. Benchmark results of our prototype tool chain

	# classes	# facts	# joinpoints	FactGen+JFacts (s)	QFOIL (s)
Toy Point class	1	71	10	0.461	0.01
AWT Point class	1	364	70	0.5902	0.0142
25 classes from AWT	25	11622	2855	1.8098	0.8779
50 classes from AWT	50	42870	10982	3.9702	5.4671
75 classes from AWT	75	79403	21367	6.5163	4.4448
100 classes from AWT	100	88236	23409	7.1599	5.4526
AWT (no subpackages)	118	103752	27862	7.9929	7.1708

6   Related Work

To our knowledge, there exist few approaches which try to automatically generate pattern-based pointcuts. In previous work [12] we already report on a first

---

[2] The timings were performed on an Intel Pentium 4 3Ghz. Each timing represents the average time of a single experiment, based on 100 experiments.

attempt for using Inductive Logic Programming in order to derive pattern-based pointcuts. In this work we employ Relative Least General Generalisation [27], an alternative ILP algorithm, instead of the FOIL algorithm. Using RLGG, we are able to derive correct pointcuts for some specific crosscutting concerns in a Smalltalk image. However, due to the limitations of both our implementation as well as the applied ILP algorithm (for instance, the algorithm does not support negated literals), our RLGG-based technique often results in pointcuts that suffer from some fragility: the resulting pointcuts for example frequently contain redundant literals referring to the names of specific methods or classes, which of course easily breaks the pointcut when these names are changed. Furthermore, our earlier work suffers from serious scalability issues. In the context of Adaptive Programming [24], an approach has been developed for automatically deducing traversal strategies, which are AP's counterpart of pointcuts [25], from a given class and object graph.

As mentioned earlier, the major area of application of our technique lies in the automated refactoring of crosscutting concerns in pre-AOP code into aspects. Quite a number of techniques exist [13,26,22,15] which propose refactorings in order to turn object-oriented applications into aspect-oriented ones. However, these techniques do not consider the generation of pattern-based pointcuts. Instead they propose to automatically generate an enumeration-based pointcut which, optionally, can be manually turned into a pattern-based pointcut by the developer. As is pointed out by Binkley et al. [2], our technique is complementary with these approaches as it can be used to both improve the level of automation of the refactoring, as well as the evolvability of the refactored aspects.

In the context of aspect mining, which is closely related to object-to-aspect refactorings, a wealth of approaches are available that allow for the identification of crosscutting concerns in an existing code base. The result of such a technique is typically an enumeration of joinpoints where the concern is located. Ceccato et al. [6] provide a comparison of three different aspect mining techniques: identifier analysis, fan-in analysis and analysis of execution traces. Breu and Krinke propose an approach based on analyzing event traces for concern identification [3]. Bruntink et al. [5] make use of clone detection techniques in order to isolate idiomatically implemented crosscutting concerns. Furthermore, several tools exist that support aspect mining activities by allowing developers to manually explore crosscutting concerns in source code, such as the aspect mining tool [14], FEAT [32], JQuery [17] and the Concern Manipulation Environment [16]. These approaches are complementary with our approach in that the joinpoints they identify can serve as positive examples for our ILP algorithm.

7   Conclusions and Future Work

In this paper we present our approach using Inductive Logic Programming for generating a concise and robust pointcut from a given enumeration of joinpoints. We report on several successful experiments that apply our approach to a realistic and medium-scale case study. We have applied our approach to a CARMA-based logic pointcut language restricted to a static joinpoint model, dubbed PAGH. In future work we will consider tackling full CARMA which requires taking into account in the background information that joinpoints and joinpoint shadows are not equated as in PAGH. Our approach can easily be applied to for example AspectJ [18] as well by translating PAGH pointcuts to AspectJ pointcuts. However, the FOIL algorithm must then be restricted to not generate pointcuts using features of PAGH that can not be translated to AspectJ: variables can only be used once in a pointcut (except when using the "if" restrictor in AspectJ), recursive named pointcuts are not possible, and only some uses of the structural predicates can be translated. Other points left for future work are:

- *Multiple Results:* Our current tools only generate one pointcut for a given set of joinpoints. In some cases, most notably when there is few background information (i.e. a small number of little classes), several alternative pointcuts are possible. Our current approach has a bias for short, non-negative and non-recursive rules. As we have described in the paper, this might not always lead to a (good) result. Therefore, it would be useful to allow presenting multiple pointcut results. An interesting research topic in this context would consist of uncovering poincut patterns and anti-patterns that might be used to guide the selection and generation process.

- *Other Algorithms:* There exist several algorithms for Inductive Logic Programming. In previous work, we conduct several small-scale experiments with the Relative Least General Generalization (RLGG) [27] algorithm in an aspect mining context [12]. Having several algorithms might improve the quality of the selected results to the end-user. For example, solutions that are induced by more than one algorithm might be better.

- *Run-Time Information:* Our current approach only analyzes the static program information to induce pointcuts. Pointcuts that require run-time program information, such as stateful aspects [10], cannot be induced. For this end, facts representing the run-time behavior of the program are necessary. We are currently investigating whether it is possible to induce such dynamic pointcuts using several program traces as background information.

- *Tool Integration:* Although our current tool works fully automatically, it is a stand-alone command-line tool that is not integrated in an IDE. We plan to develop an Eclipse plugin for our tool. This plugin can then be a basis for inducing pattern-based pointcuts by other plugins which provide support for the refactoring process.

References

1. Mehmet Akşit, editor. *Proc. 2nd Int' Conf. on Aspect-Oriented Software Development (AOSD-2003)*. ACM Press, March 2003.
2. D. Binkley, M. Ceccato, M. Harman, F. Ricca, and P. Tonella. Automated refactoring of object oriented code into aspects. In *21st IEEE International Conference on Software Maintenance (ICSM)*, 2005.

3. Silvia Breu and Jens Krinke. Aspect mining using event traces. In *19th International Conference on Automated Software Engineering*, pages 310–315, Los Alamitos, California, September 2004. IEEE Computer Society.
4. Johan Brichau, Wolfgang De Meuter, and Kris De Volder. Jumping aspects. In C. Lopes, L. Bergmans, M. D'Hondt, and P. Tarr, editors, *Workshop on Aspects and Dimensions of Concerns (ECOOP 2000)*, June 2000.
5. M. Bruntink, A. van Deursen, R. van Engelen, and T. Tourwé. An evaluation of clone detection techniques for identifying crosscutting concerns. In *Proceedings of the IEEE International Conference on Software Maintenance (ICSM)*. IEEE Computer Society Press, 2004.
6. M. Ceccato, M. Marin, K. Mens, L. Moonen, P. Tonello, and T. Tourwé. A qualitative comparison of three aspect mining techniques. In *Proceedings of the 13th International Workshop on Program Comprehension (IWPC 2005)*, pages 13–22. IEEE Computer Society Press, 2005.
7. Shigeru Chiba and Muga Nishizawa. An easy-to-use toolkit for efficient Java bytecode translators. In *GPCE '03: Proceedings of the second international conference on Generative programming and component engineering*, pages 364–376, New York, NY, USA, 2003. Springer-Verlag New York, Inc.
8. Bart De Win, Wouter Joosen, and Frank Piessens. Developing secure applications through aspect-oriented programming. pages 633–650. Addison-Wesley, Boston, 2005.
9. Maja D'Hondt and Viviane Jonckers. Hybrid aspects for weaving object-oriented functionality and rule-based knowledge. In Lieberherr [23], pages 132–140.
10. Rémi Douence, Pascal Fradet, and Mario Südholt. Composition, reuse and interaction analysis of stateful aspects. In Lieberherr [23], pages 141–150.
11. Kris Gybels and Johan Brichau. Arranging language features for pattern-based crosscuts. In Akşit [1], pages 60–69.
12. Kris Gybels and Andy Kellens. An experiment in using inductive logic programming to uncover pointcuts. In *First European Interactive Workshop on Aspects in Software*, September 2004.
13. Stefan Hanenberg, Christian Oberschulte, and Rainer Unland. Refactoring of aspect-oriented software. In *4th Annual International Conference on Object-Oriented and Internet-based Technologies,Concepts, and Applications for a Networked World*, 2003.
14. J. Hannemann. The Aspect Mining Tool web site. http://www.cs.ubc.ca/labs/spl/projects/amt.html.
15. Jan Hannemann, Gail Murphy, and Gregor Kiczales. Role-based refactoring of crosscutting concerns. In Peri Tarr, editor, *Proc. 4rd Int' Conf. on Aspect-Oriented Software Development (AOSD-2005)*, pages 135–146. ACM Press, March 2005.
16. William Harrison, Harold Ossher, Stanley M. Sutton Jr., and Peri Tarr. Concern modeling in the concern manipulation environment. IBM Research Report RC23344, IBM Thomas J. Watson Research Center, Yorktown Heights, NY, September 2004.
17. Doug Janzen and Kris De Volder. Navigating and querying code without getting lost. In Akşit [1], pages 178–187.
18. G. Kiczales, E. Hilsdale, J. Hugunin, M. Kersten, J. Palm, and W. G. Griswold. An overview of AspectJ. In J. L. Knudsen, editor, *Proc. ECOOP 2001, LNCS 2072*, pages 327–353, Berlin, June 2001. Springer-Verlag.

19. Gregor Kiczales, John Lamping, Anurag Mendhekar, Chris Maeda, Cristina Lopes, Jean-Marc Loingtier, and John Irwin. Aspect-oriented programming. In Mehmet Akşit and Satoshi Matsuoka, editors, *11th Europeen Conf. Object-Oriented Programming*, volume 1241 of *LNCS*, pages 220–242. Springer Verlag, 1997.
20. Gregor Kiczales and Mira Mezini. Separation of concerns with procedures, annotations, advice and pointcuts. In *European Conference on Object-Oriented Programming, ECOOP 2005*, 2005.
21. Christian Koppen and Maximilian Störzer. PCDiff: Attacking the fragile pointcut problem. In Kris Gybels, Stefan Hanenberg, Stephan Herrmann, and Jan Wloka, editors, *European Interactive Workshop on Aspects in Software (EIWAS)*, September 2004.
22. Ramnivas Laddad. Aspect-oriented refactoring, dec 2003.
23. Karl Lieberherr, editor. *Proc. 3rd Int' Conf. on Aspect-Oriented Software Development (AOSD-2004)*. ACM Press, March 2004.
24. Karl J. Lieberherr. *Adaptive Object-Oriented Software: the Demeter Method with Propagation Patterns*. PWS Publishing Company, Boston, 1996.
25. Karl J. Lieberherr, Jeffrey Palm, and Ravi Sundaram. Expressiveness and complexity of crosscut languages. In Gary T. Leavens, Curtis Clifton, and Ralf Lämmel, editors, *Foundations of Aspect-Oriented Languages*, March 2005.
26. Miguel Pessoa Monteiro. Catalogue of refactorings for aspectj. Technical Report UM-DI-GECSD-200401, Universidade Do Minho, 2004.
27. S. Muggleton and C. Feng. Efficient induction in logic programs. In S. Muggleton, editor, *Inductive Logic Programming*, pages 281–298. Academic Press, 1992.
28. H. Ossher and P. Tarr. The shape of things to come: Using multi-dimensional separation of concerns with Hyper/J to (re)shape evolving software. *Comm. ACM*, 44(10):43–50, October 2001.
29. D. L. Parnas. On the criteria to be used in decomposing systems into modules. *Comm. ACM*, 15(12):1053–1058, December 1972.
30. J. Ross Quinlan. Learning logical definitions from relations. *Machine Learning*, 5(3):239–266, August 1990.
31. Ross Quinlan. Qfoil: the reference foil implementation. Home page at http:// www.rulequest.com/Personal/, 2005.
32. Martin P. Robillard and Gail C. Murphy. Automatically inferring concern code from program investigation activities. In *Proceedings of Automated Software Engineering (ASE) 2003*, pages 225–235. IEEE Computer Society, 2003.
33. Wim Vanderperren, Davy Suvée, and Viviane Jonckers. Combining AOSD and CBSD in PacoSuite through invasive composition adapters and JAsCo. In *Net.ObjectDays 2003*, pages 36–50, September 2003.

An Aspect-Oriented Approach for Developing Self-Adaptive Fractal Components

Pierre-Charles David[1] and Thomas Ledoux[2]

[1] France Télécom, Recherche & Développement
28, chemin du vieux chêne
F-38243 Meylan
PierreCharles.David@francetelecom.com
[2] OBASCO Group, EMN / INRIA, Lina
École des Mines de Nantes
4 rue Alfred Kastler
F-44307 Nantes CEDEX 3
Thomas.Ledoux@emn.fr

Abstract. Nowadays, application developers have to deal with increasingly variable execution contexts, requiring the creation of applications able to adapt themselves autonomously to the evolutions of this context. In this paper, we show how an aspect-oriented approach enables the development of self-adaptive applications where the adaptation code is well modularized, both spatially and temporally. Concretely, we propose SAFRAN, an extension of the Fractal component model for the development of the adaptation aspect as reactive adaptation policies. These policies detect the evolutions of the execution context and adapt the base program by reconfiguring it. This way, SAFRAN allows the modular development of adaptation policies and their dynamic weaving into running applications.

1 Introduction

Nowadays, application developers have to deal with increasingly variable execution contexts. On the one hand, we find a large diversity of platforms covering a wide spectrum in terms of available resources (from embedded systems to grids), these heterogeneous machines being increasingly interconnected, and hence interdependent. On the other hand, even on a particular host the execution context of an application changes during its execution (hardware and software resources availability, mobility...). This situation makes application development more and more complex, as it is often difficult to know at development-time the conditions in which applications will be used, especially when these conditions can change unpredictably during execution. Instead of trying to hide the execution context under an abstraction layer (middleware), we believe that applications must become *context-aware* so that they can adapt to their context [1]. Such *self-adaptive applications* are able to adapt themselves autonomously [2] to the evolutions of their execution context, not only to continue functioning but also to leverage new possibilities which can appear dynamically.

W. Löwe and M. Südholt (Eds.): SC 2006, LNCS 4089, pp. 82–97, 2006.
© Springer-Verlag Berlin Heidelberg 2006

The need to build applications which adapt to their environment is not new. However, the ad hoc techniques generally used, in which adaptation decisions are hardwired in applications, are not sufficient: they mix business concerns with adaptation policies, which makes both initial development and maintenance more difficult [3]. Furthermore, it is generally impossible to predict during the development phase the actual circumstances in which applications will be used, even less the appropriate reaction. Ideally, we would like to be able to develop the adaptation code *separately* and then *integrate* it dynamically inside the business code so as to decouple these two kinds of code, both spatially and temporally.

In this paper, we use an aspect-oriented approach [4] to modularize the adaptation code in self-adaptive applications. Aspect-Oriented Programming (AOP) gives us an interesting framework to separate the adaptation concern from business code and then to dynamically weave and un-weave them. The system we propose, SAFRAN, allows to develop self-adaptive applications based on the Fractal component model [5]. SAFRAN is designed around three main principles: *(i)* the use of a dynamic component model (Fractal) to build applications which can be adapted at runtime; *(ii)* the use of AOP concepts and techniques to develop the adaptation logic separately from business code and then to dynamically weave them to yield self-adaptive applications; *(iii)* and finally the use of a Domain (or Aspect) Specific Language [6] to express this adaptation logic.

Section 2 shows how the software adaptation concern can be – conceptually – considered as an aspect. Section 3 then presents our contribution, SAFRAN, showing how this approach translates in the concrete design and architecture of SAFRAN. We finally illustrate the use of SAFRAN on a simple example (Section 4), and discuss some related work (Section 5) before concluding (Section 6).

2   Software Adaptation as an Aspect

2.1   Adaptation as a Cross-Cutting Concern

In the most general sense, an adaptation is a *modification* triggered by *changing circumstances*, by which a system becomes better suited to its new environment. In the case of software, an adaptation will be implemented by a program responsible for *(i)* observing the environment in which the target software is running to detect new conditions, *(ii)* deciding about the appropriate modifications to apply to the target software, and *(iii)* applying these modifications, adapting the target to the new conditions. With the advent of ubiquitous computing, new applications must be able to adapt themselves autonomously [2] to the various execution contexts in which they can be running. Such *self-adaptive software* applications are both the agent and the target of the adaptation.

The main issue with building such self-adaptive software is that integrating the code dealing with the adaptation concern into the application increases its complexity: the business code becomes "polluted" by non-functional concerns like observing the environment and deciding which reconfiguration is more appropriate. This also impedes the reusability of the system, which can then function properly only in the few, fixed set of situations which have been anticipated during its development. To solve these issues, we need a looser and more dynamic coupling between business code and adaptation logic.

Software adaptation thus appears as a cross-cutting concern relative to business code, which we would like to modularize so as to offer more reusability and maintainability of the business code. Aspect-Oriented Programming (AOP) [4] gives us adequate abstractions and composition mechanisms to solve these issues.

2.2   Towards an Adaptation Aspect

In "traditional" AOP systems (e.g. AspectJ [7]), an aspect is a module which regroups pairs of the form (*pointcut, advice*) where *pointcut* denotes a set of *join-points*, i.e. points of interest in the execution of a base program (in which the aspect is to be weaved) and *advice* is a code fragment to be executed whenever the pointcut matches, i.e. at each of its join-points. Together, these constructs can be used to implement in a well-defined module a concern which can modify the semantics of a base program incrementally and transparently (from the base program's point of view) [8]. The base program and the aspects are *weaved* into a consistent whole, either statically or dynamically. In the following, we propose to "aspectize" the adaptation concern.

The event-based nature of the adaptation process (when a significant change occurs, an adaptation decision is made taken and then applied) relates with the EAOP approach [9] in which point-cuts are defined in terms of sequences of runtime events in the execution of the base program (method invocation, object creation. . .). In EAOP, runtime events are only *internal*, i.e. related to the base program execution. This is not sufficient to trigger adaptations in the more general setting of context-aware applications, which must also react to *external* events regarding the evolutions of their execution context, like the appearance of a new device or the sudden decrease of the available bandwidth. Despite their different origin (the context instead of the application itself), we believe these events can also be considered as join points, as they trigger adaptation actions. Our join point model thus extends the domain of possible join points beyond internal events ("traditional" join points) to the whole execution context, which increases the expressive power of our system by allowing us to react to changes in the execution context.

Concerning the advice model, actions (triggered by events) indicate how to reconfigure the base program in order to adapt it to the new conditions. The role of the advice language is thus to adjust the target application (tuning, parameterization, architectural configuration. . .) in order to make it more adapted. Note that contrary to AspectJ [7] which is a general purpose Aspect-Oriented language, the advice language in SAFRAN is a domain-specific language whose expressive power is reduced so that it is not possible to reconfigure the application in an inconsistent state.

As for the aspect weaving model, our choice of considering adaptation in open and dynamic systems lead us to choose a dynamic approach, which is much more flexible than static weaving because the separation of concerns remains at runtime. This means that the adaptation aspect does not have to be anticipated, but can be loaded, modified and tuned at runtime, without stopping the application. This dynamic weaving process allows us to fully decouple the base program and the adaptation aspect (both spatially and temporally).

3   An Adaptation Aspect in SAFRAN

SAFRAN (Self-Adaptive FRActal compoNents) [10] is an extension to the Fractal component model [5] allowing the creation of self-adaptive applications. One of the key principles in the design of SAFRAN is the treatment of the adaptation concern as an aspect. Following the structure of a generic AOP system, SAFRAN's main elements are:

- a *base program* corresponding to a configuration of Fractal components (architecture);
- *point-cuts* corresponding to the notification of internal events (message invocations on Fractal interfaces, changes in the architecture) or external events (thanks to a framework we designed to create context-aware applications);
- *advices* voluntarily restricted to architectural reconfigurations;
- and finally the adaptation *aspect* itself, linking join points to advices, and represented by modular *adaptation policies* dynamically weaved and unweaved into target components.

The rest of this section will present in more details each of these points.

3.1   Fractal Components: The Base Program

Fractal [5] is a component model developed by France Télécom R&D and INRIA, and distributed through the ObjectWeb consortium. We chose Fractal over other component models because it is designed around a minimal but very extensible core, and is highly dynamic.

A Fractal application (see Fig. 1) is seen as an assembly of components, each made of two parts: a *controller* (in grey on the figure) and its *content*. This content can be either made of other components (*composite*) or of a single object of the underlying programming language (*primitive*). For example, the figure shows a single composite containing two primitive sub-components. The controller part of a component manages all the interactions of its content with the outside. To do this, it exposes internal and external *interfaces* (ports), which can represent services provided or required by a component. Two compatible interfaces can be connected together to create a one-way binding through which all communications must pass. On the figure, the rightmost sub-component provides a service of type "S" through an interface named "s". The other sub-component uses this service through a binding from its own required interface of a compatible type, and exposes another service "m" of a different type. This service is exported to the outside of the composite using a binding from a matching internal interface. When the composite receives an invocation on its interface "m", its controller intercepts the message, executes optional control behavior (depending on the controller configuration), and then forwards it to the sub-component through the internal binding.

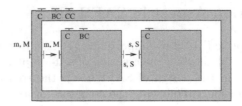

Fig. 1. Example of a simple Fractal architecture

In addition to *service interfaces*, which depends on each application ("s" and "m" on the figure), Fractal components can offer a variety of standard control interfaces. These interfaces, represented on top of the components in the figure, enable dynamic introspection and modification of various aspects of the components: discovery of the set of interfaces of a component (`component` interface, C on the figure), lookup, creation and destruction of bindings (`binding-controller`, or BC), addition and removal of sub-components from composites (`content-controller`, or CC), etc.

Fractal offers a predefined set of such control interfaces to reflectively manipulate aspects of the components. This support for architectural reflection allows us to reconfigure the architecture of an application during its execution. Compared to other component models like ArchJava [11], which supports runtime reconfigurations only if they have been programmed at compile-time, Fractal's support for reflection enables the discovery and unanticipated modification of the structure of components. This feature is essential for the creation of self-adaptive applications [12] as most of the adaptation we will want to perform are not known during the initial construction of the software.

Another advantage of Fractal is that the set of control interfaces is not fixed. Although there is a predefined set of such interfaces, all of them are optional. More importantly, Fractal and its default implementation are designed so that is is easy to add new control interfaces, thus extending the component model. We use this feature in SAFRAN to seamlessly integrate our extension into the standard model by adding a new control interface named `adaptation-controller` to manage the adaptation aspect associated to a component. Beyond the advantages inherent to the component-based approach, the specific features of Fractal make it an ideal candidate for the construction of *adaptable* applications, the first step towards fully autonomous *self-adaptive* applications.

3.2   Reconfiguration with FScript: The Advice Language

FScript is a domain-specific language [6] we designed to program the Fractal components reconfigurations. FScript is a simple procedural language with dynamic typing and lexical scoping, which gives access to all the standard operations supported by Fractal components: creation of new components, architecture introspection and reconfiguration of this architecture by manipulating composites' content and bindings between interfaces. The main features of FScript are *(i)* a special notation to navigate easily in the Fractal architecture of the base program, and *(ii)* the guarantee that reconfigurations always leave the application in a consistent state. Although it has been designed to be used in SAFRAN, FScript can also be used by itself as a scripting language to program consistent Fractal components reconfigurations.

The FPath Notation.   FScript uses a special syntax, FPath (inspired by the XPath language [13]), to easily *navigate* in Fractal architectures without modifying it and *select* elements (components, interfaces or configuration attributes) matching certain criteria. The language is based on a model of Fractal architectures as a (virtual) directed graph where nodes represent components, their interfaces and attributes, and where arcs are annotated by *labels* to denote the kind of relation between two nodes (*C1 "is a sub-component of" C2, I1 "is bound to" I2...*). In addition to basic expressions (arithmetic, boolean and comparison operators...), FPath expression can denote *relative paths* (starting from an initial node). Such a path is a series of steps, each made of three elements: `axis:` `:test[predicate]`. On each step, an initial set of nodes is converted to a new set by following all the arcs with a label corresponding to the axis, then filtering the result using the *test* (on the node names) and optional *predicates* (boolean FPath expressions applied to each candidate). More precisely, the evaluation algorithm for one step is the following:

P1. [Initialisation] $result \leftarrow \emptyset$.

P2. [Selection] Select every node connected to any of the current ones through an arc whose label matches the `axis` part: $result \leftarrow \cup\{n : c \xrightarrow{axis} n, c \in current\}$.

P3. [Test] If the test part is an identifier (as opposed to *), remove from $result$ the nodes whose name do not match: $result \leftarrow \{n \in result : name(n) = test\}$.

P4. [Filtering] Only keep the elements for which all predicates hold: $result \leftarrow \{x \in result : pred_1(x) \wedge \cdots \wedge pred_n(x)\}$.

P5. [End] The algorithm finishes and returns $result$.

For a multi-step path, this algorithm is repeated with the result of the previous step as the current node-set of the next.

FPath offers a set of axes to navigate in Fractal architectures, by selecting a component's interfaces (`interface` axis), configuration attributes (`attribute`), direct sub-components (`child`) or parents[1] (`parent`), and following the binding of an interface (`binding`). It is also possible to select in one step all the direct and indirect sub-components (resp. parents) of a component with the `descendant` (resp. `ancestor`) axis, which is the transitive closure of `child` (resp. `parent`).

For example, the FPath expression `child::server/attribute::cache-Enabled` first selects all the sub-components of the initial node(s) named `server` (test on the node name), then selects its configuration attribute named `cache-Enabled`. Using the same logic, the expression `count(interface::*[required (.) and not(bound(.))]) > 0` returns *true* if and only if the initial component has required interfaces which are not yet connected (the dot "." in predicates denote the current node to which it is applied).

FScript Actions. FScript is used to define *reconfiguration actions*, combining FPath expressions, primitive actions, simple control structures (sequence, choice, finite iteration) and variables manipulation. All the dynamic reconfiguration operations supported by Fractal components are available to FScript program as predefined, primitive actions, including the `attach()` and `detach()` actions introduced by SAFRAN to control the (runtime) weaving of adaptation policies to components. The following example shows an FScript action which could be used to adapt a component.

```
// Changes a cache's replacement strategy.
action select-strategy(cache, strat) = {
  // Gets the cache's client interface to the strategy
  itf := $cache/interface::strategy;
  if (bound($itf)) { // Is it already bound to a server interface?
    // Unbind it and stop the now unused component.
    previous := $itf/binding::*;
    unbind($itf);
    stop($previous/component::*);
  }
  // Binds the cache client interface to the
  // appropriate server interface on $strat.
  bind($itf, $strat/interface::replacement-strategy);
  // Make sure the strategy component is started.
  start($strat);
}
```

This action can be used to change the replacement strategy used by a cache component by modifying the binding between the cache and the strategy component. It uses FPath expressions to navigate in the application's structure, and primitive actions corresponding to operations supported by Fractal components (`bind()`, `stop()`...). Although this action is relatively specific to a given application, FScript can be used to program more generic reconfigurations (replacing a component by another for example) which can then be reused in multiple application (architectural patterns).

---

[1] Fractal supports component sharing, so a component can have multiple parents.

Guarantees. FScript's design and implementation guarantee the consistency of reconfigurations. Because these reconfigurations are meant to adapt running applications, we must guarantee that reconfiguration will not break the target application. To this end, we have chosen a set of consistency criterion, in particular *transactional integrity* (atomicity, consistency of the final state, isolation) and *termination* of the reconfigurations. The validation of these criteria is guaranteed in part by the language's structure itself, whose expressive power has been limited, and in part by the implementation. More precisely:

- The definition of (directly or indirectly) recursive actions is forbidden, and the only control structure available for iteration, a `for each` loop, iterates on the result of an FPath expression, which always returns a finite set of nodes. These constraints guarantee actions' *termination*, although they do not provide a time bound.
- During the execution of a reconfiguration, the language interpreter keeps a complete journal of all the primitive actions performed, together with enough information to revert them. As soon as an error occurs, the interpreters uses this journal to roll-back the current reconfiguration and return to the initial state. Given that all the primitive Fractal reconfigurations are themselves atomic and reversible, this guarantees the *atomicity* of FScript reconfigurations.
- At the end of a reconfiguration, the interpreter checks that the current configuration is consistent, i.e. that all the required client interfaces are correctly bound to a corresponding server interfaces and that all the components which have been temporarily stopped during the reconfiguration can safely be restarted. If this is not the case, the interpreters cancels the reconfiguration and rolls back to the initial state, thus ensuring the consistency of the application.
- Finally, the *isolation* of reconfigurations is currently guaranteed by globally serializing them. This works, but is highly sub-optimal and may be enhanced in future works.

3.3 Internal and External Events as Join-Points

We now describe the join-points supported by SAFRAN to trigger the adaptation actions' execution. Following the EAOP approach [9], we consider these join-points as event occurrences. Although traditional join-points only account for the execution of the base program, we extended the domain of events to consider with external events corresponding to changes in the execution context.

Whether they are internal or external, all event occurrences in SAFRAN are represented as objects with a set of properties. Some of these properties are present on every event while some are specific to certain kinds of events. Common properties are: the `type` of the event, as a string; the `source` of the event, which can be either a component or an element of the execution context (see below); and a `timestamp` indicating the time of occurrence of the event.

Event specification and detection is realized by *event descriptors*, for which the exact syntax depend on the type of event, but always follow the same general form `event-type(parameters)`. Thus, the descriptor `changed(sys://storage/memory#free)` allows to detect the variations in the quantity of memory available on the system.

Internal Events. Internal events are execution points in the base program, which in our case is a set of Fractal components. The first three types of internal events, `message-received`, `message-returned` and `message-failed`, correspond respectively to the reception of a message, the successful return of a message and the throwing of an exception. The descriptors for these three kinds of events share the same parameters, expressed using FPath, to indicate which interfaces and methods should be monitored. For example, `message-received($c/interface::logger)` can be used to detect invocations on any method of the `logger` interface of component `$c`, while `message-failed($c/interface::*)` detects errors on any interface of the same component.

The other internal event types correspond to the possible reconfigurations of Fractal components : component creation, life-cycle changes (component started or stopped), configuration (changes in configuration parameters), content manipulation (addition and removal of sub-components) and finally creation and destruction of bindings. Each of the corresponding descriptor takes arguments to specify which components, interfaces or attributes to monitor. Thus, the descriptor `component-started($c/child::*)` detects when any direct sub-component of `$c` is started.

The implementation of these events is based on the instrumentation of Fractal controllers, for example the components' `lifecycle-controller` is instrumented to generate `component-{started,stopped}` events.

External Events. In order to detect the occurrence of external events we first need to reify the application's execution context, which is normally implicit. To do this, we use WildCAT [14], a system we designed to ease the creation of *context-aware* applications [1]. WildCAT is used by SAFRAN to observe the execution context and to notify the occurrence of the external events which can trigger the execution of reconfigurations. As was the case for FScript, WildCAT can actually be used independently.

WildCAT models the execution context as a set of *context domains*, each representing a particular aspect of the context, for example hardware resources, network, geo-physical information, etc. Each of these context domains is itself modeled as a tree of *resources* described by a set of attributes (simple (*name, value*) pairs). The syntax used to denote resources and attributes is inspired by that of URIs: `domain://path/to/resource#attribute` (`#attribute` being optional). For example, `sys://storage/drives/hdc#removable` indicates whether the `hdc` drive is removable.

The context model provided by WildCAT changes dynamically to reflect changes in the actual execution context: attributes values can change, attributes and resources can appear or disappear at any moment. All these modifications generate *external events* which can be detected by an adaptation policy. The different types of external events supported by SAFRAN are:

changed(expression) : detects any modification of the value of the expression, which can reference any attribute or resource in the context[2], for example changed(geo://location/logical#room). Expressions to monitor are written in a simple language which, in addition to references to context locations, supports strings, numbers, arithmetic and boolean operations, comparisons and function calls.

realized(condition) : detects the occurrence of a boolean condition, for example realized(sys://storage/memory#free > 2*sys://storage/swap# used). This is actually a particular case of changed which only detects changes from *false* to *true*.

appears(path) and disappears(path) : detects the appearance or disappearance of a resource or attribute in the context. The path expression can be a *joker* character "*" as its last element. For example appears(sys:// devices/input/*) detects the apparition of any new input device.

3.4 Adaptation Policies: The Adaptation Aspect Language

Adaptation Aspect Syntax. Conforming to the reactive nature of the adaptation process, adaptation policies in SAFRAN are structured as sets of *reactive rules* of the form

```
when <event> if <condition> do <action>
```

where <event> is an (internal or external) event descriptor[3] (cf. Sect. 3.3) corresponding to a point-cut, <condition> is a boolean FPath expression (without side-effects), and <action> is an FScript reconfiguration (cf. Sect. 3.2) corresponding to the aspect's advice.

This type of rules is inspired by what can be found in Active Databases [15] under the name of ECA (Event, Condition, Action) rules. An adaptation rule indicates that *when* an event corresponding to the <event> expression occurs, *if* the <condition> expression holds, *then* the <action> reconfiguration is applied, thus adapting the target application to the new conditions resulting from the event.

In the SAFRAN system, the adaptation policies which are dynamically attached to Fractal components are made of (ordered) sequences of adaptation rules:

```
policy example = {
  rule { when <event1> if <cond1> do <action1> }
  rule { when <event2> if <cond2> do <action2> }
  ...
}
```

As an adaptation policy is always executed when attached to a target component, a special variable named $target can be used inside rules to access

---

[2] WildCAT automatically re-evaluates expressions when any element it depends on changes.

[3] In the future, we plan to extend this model to support more complex point-cuts, especially hybrid point-cuts which mix internal and external events and would allow finer coordination between the execution of adaptation code and the base program.

the component to which the policy is attached; it is akin to `self` of `this` in object-oriented languages.

Figure 2 summarizes the event/control flow between the different parts of SAFRAN. Internal events are generated by instrumentation code inside Fractal components, and external events are detected by WildCAT. These events are routed to the appropriate adaptation controllers, which uses its current rules to decide which adaptations to perform. These decisions are finally applied by executing FScript reconfigurations.

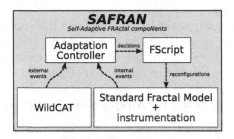

Fig. 2. Flow of events in SAFRAN

Weaving the Adaptation Aspect. SAFRAN introduces an extension to the Fractal model which enables the dynamic attachment (weaving) of adaptation policies (aspects) to components (base program). Like most Fractal extensions, it takes the form of a new control interface, in this case `adaptation-controller`. It is this controller, present on each self-adaptive component, which implements the weaving of adaptation policies into the target component, thus making it *self-adaptive*: whereas a standard Fractal component can *be adapted* by an external entity (through its standard control interfaces), a SAFRAN component embeds the adaptation code itself and becomes *autonomous*, actor of its own adaptation.

The `AdaptationController` interface (see below) enables the dynamic attachment (weaving) of one or several adaptation policies to each SAFRAN component. This interface can be seen as a special case of an aspect weaving interface, where `attachFcPolicy()` and `detachFcPolicy()` correspond to specialized versions of more general `weave(Aspect)` and `unweave(Aspect)` operations:

```
public interface AdaptationController {
  void attachFcPolicy(AdaptationPolicy policy);
  void detachFcPolicy(AdaptationPolicy policy);
  AdaptationPolicy[] getFcPolicies();
}
```

When a policy is attached to a component, the component's adaptation controller analyzes it, and depending on the join-points mentioned in the rules, instruments the target component to generate the appropriate internal events and registers itself with WildCAT to be notified of the external events. After this initialization, when the adaptation controller receives events, be they internal or external, it determines the appropriate reaction according to the current set of policies and rules on the target component (see below), and then executes this reaction in order to adapt the component to the new circumstances. This execution schema matches the reactive nature of the adaptation process, with the same three phases: observation, decision, action.

Aspect Composition Model. To handle multiple advices affecting the same join-point, SAFRAN provides an ad hoc aspect composition model. Indeed, a policy (aspect) can be made of several rules, a component can have multiple policies attached at the same time, and of course an application can contain many self-adaptive components. SAFRAN defines the following composition rules to manage the interactions between these different elements when several rules are triggered by the same event:

- Inside a given policy, the rules' reactions are composed in sequence, in the textual order of their definition, and executed in a single reconfiguration transaction. The rationale is that a given policy should implement a consistent, self-contained adaptation, and its (single) author can be expected to foresee the rules' interactions.
- On a single component, the competing reactions of multiple policies are also executed in sequence, but each in its own reconfiguration transaction. The effects of a single policy's failure is thus isolated. This is important as policies developped independently can be attached to the same component. The order in which the policies' reactions are executed depend in the order of their attachment: the oldest policies are executed first. The rationale is that once a policy P is attached to component C, the resulting component C' must be considered as a self-contained black-box by the next policies, and hence P has a greater priority over the policies attached later.
- Finally, when multiple components must react to a single event, their reactions are executed in an order defined by the components' composition relations: subcomponents are adapted before their parents. The rationale is similar to the previous one: in a component-base approach, when a composite includes a subcomponent, it should treat it as a black-box.

Although these rules are designed to be the most general possible, there are situations in which they are not appropriate. One of the main future directions of our work is the extend the execution model of our reactive rules to provide more flexibility on the semantics of composition. The challenge is to do this while without making the policies language too complex for the end users.

4   Example

The example application we chose to illustrate the use of SAFRAN is a small web server named Comanche, implemented by É. Bruneton as a tutorial on the use of Fractal. Comanche, being extremely simple, does not integrate a file cache mechanism. In order to improve its performances, we thus add a new cache component in Comanche. The cache performances depends on the amount of memory it can use. If this amount is too low, the system will not use all the cache potential. If it is too high, performances can be even lower, as the cache will force the operating system to use slow virtual memory (swap). The amount of memory we should allocate to the cache depends on the amount of free memory available on the host system, which varies dynamically and unpredictably. Our adaptation policy will thus have to dynamically adapt the maximum amount of memory allocated to the cache component in order to guarantee good performances in every circumstances. The introduction of a cache component in Comanche is very simple, as it only requires to modify the application architecture defined using Fractal's ADL (Architecture Description Language), after having coded the cache component itself, of course.

The cache component exposes two parameters accessible through its `attribute-controller` interface, `currentSize` and `maximumSize`, indicating respectively the current and maximum amount of memory the cache uses; only `maximumSize` is writable. The policy works by adjusting the value of `maximumSize` depending on the amount of free memory on the host system, which WildCAT makes available as `sys://storage/memory#free`. We now have all the information we need to write the adaptation policy:

```
policy adaptive-cache = {
  rule {
    when realized(sys://storage/memory#free < 10*1024)
    do { to-free := 10*1024 - sys://storage/memory#free;
         size := $target/cache/attribute::currentSize - $to-free;
         if ($size < 500) {
           set-value($target/cache/attribute::maximumSize, 0);
           disable-cache($target);
         } else {
           set-value($target/cache/attribute::maximumSize, $size);
         }
      } }
  rule {
    when mem:changed(sys://storage/memory#free)
    if (sys://storage/memory#free >= 10*1024)
    do { enable-cache($target);
         current := $target/cache/attribute::currentSize;
         size := 0.8 * ($mem.new-value + $current);
         max := sys://storage/memory#used - $current + $size;
         if ($max < sys://storage/memory@total - 10*1024) {
           set-value($target/cache/attribute::maximumSize, $size);
         }
      } } }
```

This file uses two user-defined FScript actions (code not shown for space reasons): the first one, `disable-cache`, disables the cache component by disconnecting it while the second action, `enable-cache`, re-introduces it in the components' pipeline. The first rule is triggered when the total amount of available memory drops below 10Mb. When this happens, the reconfiguration action tries to free memory by reducing the size of the cache, or even disabling it completely below a certain size. The second rule is triggered whenever the amount of memory changes[4] but is more than 10 Mb. In this case, the reconfiguration

---

[4] In practice, such an event is not generated each time the amount of free memory changes, but only when such a change is detected. The sampling rate and hence the system performance depends on how the corresponding sensor is configured.

adjusts the maximum cache size to use 80% of the total amount available, but only if this leaves enough free memory to the rest of the system.

This example policy illustrates *(i)* a point-cut based on two types of external events (`realized` and `changed`); *(ii)* two kinds of reconfiguration actions: parameterization and bindings manipulation. Not only the reconfiguration is dynamic, but thanks to the dynamic weaving process in SAFRAN, the policy can be updated during the execution of the base application, which is essential when developing open systems.

5 Related Work

In the last few years, numerous works have tried to make software more adaptable, in particular to take into account the needs of mobile computing and autonomous applications [2]. The most promising approach seems to be the use of dynamic and extensible component models, which enable the integration of non-functional services in a way that is adapted to the specific needs of applications, and most importantly allow dynamic reconfigurations of the application itself [16]. Some works, like ACEEL [17] or K-Components [3] are based on custom component model which impose a specific way of structuring applications. Others use existing component models but restrict themselves to particular application domains: for example PLASMA [18] which is based on Fractal like SAFRAN but limited to multimedia stream processing.

Concerning the adaptation aspect itself, Cilia *et al.* [19] have shown the links existing between AOP and reactive rules from active databases, particularly in the context of autonomous applications. Indeed, applications must be reactive in order to adapt themselves to their context, and the underlying principles of AOP allow us to introduce this reactivity in base programs in a non-invasive way. However, the authors only present abstract concepts where SAFRAN provides a concrete implementation.

We can also note the existence of FAC [20] and Fractal-AOP [21], two extensions of the Fractal model for general AOP. Although SAFRAN is heavily inspired by AOP, SAFRAN's goal is to enable the creation of self-adaptive applications, and AOP is simply a convenient framework used to structure and describe the system. The difference between the FAC/Fractal-AOP approach and SAFRAN' approach is essentially the same as between a general-purpose programming language, powerful but generic, and a DSL, more limited but better suited to its particular objective.

6 Conclusion and Future Works

In this paper, we have shown how AOP principles can be used to ease the creation of self-adaptive applications. On a conceptual level, we have shown that adaptation can be considered as a cross-cutting concern and that it is possible to use AOP's concepts (base program, point-cuts, advices and weaver) in this particular case to model the adaptation aspect. In order to support self-adaptive applications, we have *extended* the traditional notion of join-points beyond internal events related to the program's execution to include external events corresponding to changes in the execution context. Regarding the advices, we have on the contrary chosen to *restrict* the expressive power of our reconfiguration actions by designing a Domain-Specific Language (FScript) which can offer guarantees on the consistency of adaptations.

On a more concrete level, we have then described SAFRAN, an extension of the Fractal model which implements this approach and enables the modular development of reactive adaptation policies. The main features of SAFRAN are *(i)* the decoupling of adaptation policies from business components, *(ii)* a Domain-Specific Language based on reactive rules to express these policies, and *(iii)* a completely dynamic approach, where policies and reconfiguration actions – even ones which where not anticipated at compile-time – can be defined, loaded and applied during the execution of the target application without stopping it. Another interesting feature of SAFRAN is its modular design, with subsystems (WildCAT and FScript) which can be reused independently.

One of our future goals is to extend the principles of SAFRAN to allow the adaptation of distributed applications. We do not anticipate major structural changes in the system, but incremental evolutions of its different parts. A first step would be to extend FScript to support distribution-aware reconfigurations, like for example component migration and distributed bindings. New WildCAT context domains will have to be implemented to share information between remote nodes; different strategies are possible with varying degrees of invasiveness (see [14]). Finally, the execution model of adaptation policies itself will have to be extended to support coordinated adaptation of remote components.

References

1. Dey, A.K., Abowd, G.D.: Towards a better understanding of context and context-awareness. In: Workshop on The What, Who, Where, When, and How of Context-Awareness, as part of CHI 2000, The Hague, The Netherlands (2000)
2. Kephart, J.: A vision of autonomic computing. In Gabriel, R.P., ed.: Onward! proceedings from an OOPSLA 2002 track, Seattle, WA, USA, ACM (2002) 13–36
3. Dowling, J., Cahill, V.: The K-Component architecture meta-model for self-adaptive software. In: Proceedings of Reflection 2001, The Third International Conference on Metalevel Architectures and Separation of Crosscutting Concerns. Volume 2192 of LNCS., Springer-Verlag (2001) 81–88
4. Kiczales, G., Lamping, J., Mendhekar, A., Maeda, C., Lopes, C.V., Loingtier, J.M., Irwin, J.: Aspect-oriented programming. In: European Conference on Object-Oriented Programming (ECOOP). Volume 1241 of LNCS., Springer-Verlag (1997)
5. Bruneton, E., Coupaye, T., Leclercq, M., Quema, V., Stefani, J.B.: An open component model and its support in java. In: Proceedings of the 7th International Symposium on Component-Based Software Engineering (CBSE 2004). Volume 3054 of LNCS., Edinburgh, Scotland, Springer-Verlag (2004) 7–22
6. van Deursen, A., Klint, P., Visser, J.: Domain-specific languages: An annotated bibliography. ACM SIGPLAN Notices **35**(6) (2000) 26–36

7. Kiczales, G., Hilsdale, E., Hugunin, J., Kersten, M., Palm, J., Griswold, W.G.: An overview of AspectJ. In Knudsen, J.L., ed.: ECOOP 2001. Volume 2072 of LNCS., Springer-Verlag (2001) 327–353

8. Filman, R.E., Friedman, D.P.: Aspect-oriented programming is quantification and obliviousness. In: Workshop on Advanced Separation of Concerns. (2000) Minneapolis.

9. Douence, R., Fradet, P., Südholt, M.: A framework for the detection and resolution of aspect interactions. In: Generative Programming and Component Engineering GPCE 2002. Volume 2487 of LNCS., Pittsburgh, PA, USA, Springer-Verlag (2002) 173–188

10. David, P.C.: Développement de composants Fractal adaptatifs : un langage dédié à l'aspect d'adaptation. PhD thesis, Université de Nantes / École des Mines de Nantes (2005)

11. Aldrich, J., Chambers, C., Notkin, D.: Architectural reasoning in ArchJava. In: Proceedings of ECOOP'2002, Malaga, Spain, AITO (2002)

12. Redmond, B., Cahill, V.: Supporting unanticipated dynamic adaptation of application behaviour. In: Proceedings of ECOOP 2002. Volume 2374 of LNCS., Malaga, Spain, Springer-Verlag (2002) 205–230

13. World Wide Web Consortium: XML path language (XPath) version 1.0. W3C Recommendation (1999) http://www.w3.org/TR/xpath.

14. David, P.C., Ledoux, T.: WildCAT: a generic framework for context-aware applications. In: Proceeding of MPAC'05, the 3rd International Workshop on Middleware for Pervasive and Ad-Hoc Computing, Grenoble, France (2005)

15. Dittrich, K.R., Gatziu, S., Geppert, A.: The active database management system manifesto: A rulebase of a ADBMS features. In: International Workshop on Rules in Database Systems. Volume 985., Springer-Verlag (1995) 3–20

16. McKinley, P.K., Sadjadi, S.M., Kasten, E.P., Cheng, B.H.: Composing adaptive software. IEEE Computer **37**(7) (2004) 56–64

17. Chefrour, D., André, F.: Développement d'applications en environnements mobiles à l'aide du modèle de composant adaptatif ACEEL. In: LMO 2003, Vannes, Hermès (2003)

18. Layaïda, O., Hagimont, D.: Designing self-adaptive multimedia applications through hierarchical reconfiguration. In: Distributed Applications and Interoperable Systems (DAIS). Volume 3543 of LNCS., Athens, Greece, Springer-Verlag (2005) 95–

19. Cilia, M., Haupt, M., Mezini, M., Buchmann, A.: The convergence of AOP and active databases: Towards reactive middleware. In: Proceedings of GPCE'03. Volume 2830 of LNCS., Erfurt, Germany, Springer-Verlag (2003) 169–188

20. Pessemier, N., Seinturier, L.: Components, ADL & AOP: Towards a common approach. In: Reflection, AOP and Meta-Data for Software Evolution Workshop at ECOOP 2004 (RAM-SE'04), Oslo, Norway (2004)

21. Fakih, H., Bouraqadi, N.: Les aspects et les composants logiciels : Etude de cas avec le modèle de composant Fractal. Numéro spécial de la revue L'Objet sur les aspects **11**(3) (2005) 1–17 In French.

Aspects of Composition
in the Reflex AOP Kernel

Éric Tanter*

DCC – University of Chile
Avenida Blanco Encalada 2120 – Santiago, Chile
etanter@dcc.uchile.cl

Abstract. Aspect composition is a challenging and multi-faceted issue, generally under-supported by current AOP languages and frameworks. This paper presents the composition support provided in Reflex, a versatile kernel for multi-language AOP in Java. The core of Reflex is based on a model of partial reflection whose central abstractions are links: bindings between a (point)cut and an action. Reflex supports the definition of aspect languages through the mapping of aspects to links. We overview the wide range of features for link composition in Reflex—which includes extensible operators for ordering and nesting of links, and control over the visibility of changes made by structural aspects—, illustrating how they can be used to implement various scenarios of aspect composition.

1 Introduction

Aspect-Oriented Programming (AOP) provides means for proper modularization of crosscutting concerns [17]. As a matter of fact, in a typical application, *many* crosscutting concerns can be identified and modularized as aspects. This raises the issue of *aspect composition*, which includes questions such as: how to ensure that aspects are properly composed? Furthermore, since the points where an aspect applies (the *cut* of the aspect) are usually specified intensionally, how can programmers know that two aspects are affecting the same program point?

The issue of aspect composition was first analyzed in [6], where a classification of conflicts between aspects is proposed. Three classes of conflicts are identified: *(a)* inherent conflicts, related to the incompatibility of two aspects, *(b)* accidental conflicts, when two aspects happen to apply at the same program point or have semantical conflicts, and *(c)* spurious conflicts, which are conflicts that are detected whereas they are not actual conflicts. All in all, a number of approaches to aspect composition have been proposed, usually focusing on a particular dimension of aspect composition.

First of all, two aspects that apply to the same program points (text or execution) are said to interact; in other words, the intersection of their cut is not empty. When two aspects interact, there are two possibilities: either they are incompatible, and hence a *mutual exclusion* has to be specified [5, 10, 21], so as to

---

* É. Tanter is partially financed by the Milenium Nucleus Center for Web Research, Grant P04-067-F, Mideplan, Chile.

W. Löwe and M. Südholt (Eds.): SC 2006, LNCS 4089, pp. 98–113, 2006.

retract one of the aspects, or to raise an error. Otherwise, if both aspects should be applied, their *order of application* must be specified [5, 10, 31]. If aspects can act *around* an execution point of a program, then the notion of *nesting* appears, typically associated with a `proceed`-like mechanism [20, 31].

Furthermore, one may need to define that an aspect should apply whenever another applies [5, 10] (*aka. implicit cut*), or that an aspect applies onto another aspect [10, 5], for instance using a logging aspect to monitor the effectiveness of a caching aspect (*aka. aspects of aspects*). Finally, in AOP approaches where structural modifications can be done to a base program (*e.g.* adding members to a class), the visibility of these changes to other aspects should be controllable [8].

Finally, the aspect composition problem can be divided in two parts: that of the *detection* of aspect interactions, and that of their *resolution*. SOUL/Aop [5], as well as AspectJ, only address means to *specify* composition, while Klaeren *et al.* [21] focus on means to *detect* interactions. Concrete approaches to detection all deal with conflicts of aspects over a shared program point; being able to detect semantic interactions between two aspects that do not interact from a weaving point of view is to our knowledge not addressed by any proposal, as in the general case it is undecidable. If aspects are expressed using limited action languages, static analysis may be able to detect most semantic interactions (see [15] for an effort in this direction). Using static analysis in presence of Turing-complete aspect languages (at least for the part specifying the actions of aspects) is an open issue. It is also generally admitted that automatic resolution is not feasible; an exception to this is the approach of [15], where the limited expressiveness of the aspect language is used to automatically determine and resolve interactions between aspects. Nevertheless, in a general setting, unless it can be proven that the aspects commute, the resolution of their interaction has to be specified explicitly [10].

We are not aware of any proposal addressing all these dimensions. For instance, AspectJ [20] does not provide any support for mutual exclusion and visibility of aspectual changes, and is limited in terms of aspects of aspects and ordering/nesting of aspects. Furthermore aspect interactions are not detected. Other proposals are thoroughly discussed in Section 7. This paper presents the different mechanisms for aspect composition in Reflex[1], a versatile kernel for multi-language AOP [29][2]. Reflex supports:

- automatic detection of aspect interactions limiting spurious conflicts;
- aspect dependencies, such as implicit cut and mutual exclusion;
- extensible composition operators for ordering and nesting of aspects;
- control over the visibility of structural changes made by aspects;
- aspects of aspects.

---

[1] `http://reflex.dcc.uchile.cl/`

[2] In [29], we only discuss the issue of ordering/nesting of aspects, not the other dimensions. Furthermore, the part on ordering/nesting of this paper includes a number of corrections and improvements over the previously-presented work.

The major contributions of this work are a very flexible solution for ordering and nesting of aspects, and an initial solution for the under-explored issue of how structural changes made by aspects affect other aspects.

In Section 2, we briefly explain the idea of multi-language AOP, and its incarnation in the Reflex AOP kernel for Java. We then discuss the different aspects of composition in Reflex: aspects of aspects (Sect. 3), aspect dependencies (Sect. 4), ordering/nesting of aspects (Sect. 5), and visibility of structural changes (Sect. 6). We then review in Section 7 the literature in the area of aspect composition, highlighting the differences with our work. Section 8 concludes.

2   Multi-language AOP and Reflex

This section briefly introduces the necessary background concepts on multi-language AOP and the Reflex AOP kernel.

2.1   Multi-language AOP

In previous work [28, 29], we have motivated the interest of being able to define and use different aspect languages, including domain-specific ones, to modularize the different concerns of a software system. We have proposed the architecture of a so-called *versatile kernel* for multi-language AOP, and our current Java implementation, Reflex.

An AOP kernel supports the core semantics of various AO languages through proper structural and behavioral models. Designers of aspect languages can experiment comfortably and rapidly with an AOP kernel as a back-end, as it provides a higher abstraction level for transformation than low-level transformation toolkits. The abstraction level provided by our kernel is a flexible model of partial behavioral reflection [30], extended with structural abilities. Furthermore, a crucial role of an AOP kernel is that of a mediator between different coexisting AO approaches: detecting interactions between aspects, possibly written in different languages, and providing expressive means for their resolution.

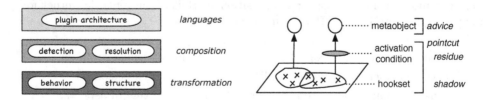

Fig. 1. Architecture of a versatile kernel for multi-language AOP

Fig. 2. The link model and correspondence to AOP concepts

The architecture of an AOP kernel consists of three layers (Fig. 1): a transformation layer in charge of basic weaving, supporting both structural and behavioral modifications of the base program; a composition layer, for detection and resolution of aspect interactions; a language layer, for modular definition of aspect languages (as plugins). It has to be noted that the transformation layer is not necessarily implemented by a (byte)code transformation system: it can very well be integrated directly in the language interpreter (VM). As a matter of fact, the role of a versatile AOP kernel is to *complement* traditional processors of object-oriented languages. Therefore, the fact that our implementation in Java, Reflex, is based on code transformation should be seen as an implementation detail, not as a defining characteristic of the kernel approach.

2.2   Reflex in a Nutshell

Reflex is a portable library that extends Java with structural and behavioral reflective facilities. Behavioral reflection follows a model of partial behavioral reflection presented in [30]: the central notion is that of explicit *links* binding a set of program points (a *hookset*) to a *metaobject*. A link is characterized by a number of attributes, among which the control at which metaobjects act (before, after, around), and a dynamically-evaluated activation condition. Fig. 2 depicts two links, one of which is not subject to activation, along with the correspondence to the AOP concepts of the pointcut/advice model. Note that our view of AOP is inherently related to metaprogramming: an aspect cut is realized by *introspection* of a program (both structure and execution), and its action consists of behavioral/structural modifications (*intercession*). Reflex does not impose a specific metaobject protocol (MOP), but rather makes it easy to specify tailored MOPs, which can coexist in a given application. This means that one can specify, on a *per-link* basis, the exact communication protocol (which method to call with which arguments) with the metaobject. A detailed case study of supporting the dynamic crosscutting of AspectJ in Reflex can be found in [25].

The aforementioned links are called *behavioral links* to distinguish them from *structural links*, which are used to perform structural reflection. A structural link binds a set of classes to a metaobject, which can both introspect and modify class definitions via a class-object structural model similar to that of Javassist [7]: an `RPool` object gives access to `RClass` objects, which in turn give access to their members as `RMember` objects (either `RField`, `RMethod`, or `RConstructor`), which in turn give access to their bodies as `RExpr` objects (with a specific type for each kind of expression). These objects are causally-connected representations of the underlying bytecode, offering a source-level abstraction over bytecode.

Reflex is implemented as Java 5 instrumentation agent operating on bytecode, typically at load time. The transformation process consists, for each class being loaded, of *(1)* determining the set of structural links that apply to it, and *applying* them, and *(2)* determining the set of behavioral links and *installing* them. The reason of this ordering is discussed in Section 6. During installation of behavioral links, *hooks* are inserted in class definitions at the appropriate places in order to provoke reification at runtime, following the metaobject protocol specified for each link.

2.3   From Aspects to Links

As said above, Reflex relies on the notion of an explicit *link* binding a *cut* to an *action*. Links are a mid-level abstraction, in between high-level aspects and low-level code transformation. How aspect languages are defined and implemented over the kernel is out of the scope of this paper (preliminary elements can be found in [29]). Composition of aspects at the kernel level is expressed in terms of link composition, which is the central matter of this paper.

A simple AspectJ aspect, comprising of a single advice associated to a simple pointcut (with no higher-order pointcut designator), is straightforwardly implemented in Reflex with a link (as in Fig. 2). However, most practical AOP languages, like AspectJ, make it possible to define aspects as modular units comprising *more than one* cut-action pair. In Reflex this corresponds to different links, with one action bound to each cut. Furthermore, AspectJ supports higher-order pointcut designators, like cflow. In Reflex, the implementation of such an aspect requires an extra link to expose the control flow information. There is therefore an abstraction gap between aspects and links: a single aspect may be implemented by several links. This abstraction gap is the matter of the language layer, as discussed in [29].

3   Aspects of Aspects

Defining aspects of aspects, *i.e.* aspects that apply to the execution of other aspects, is a feature that can be useful to handle crosscutting in aspects themselves [5, 13, 10]. For instance, a profiling aspect monitoring the efficiency of a caching aspect. Another example is an aspect resolving an accidental semantical conflict between two aspects [6]. Unsurprisingly, Reflex supports aspects of aspects, a feature supported by almost every AOP proposal (*e.g.* the adviceexecution pointcut descriptor of AspectJ). A link A can apply to the action of another link B by having the cut of A matching operations that occur in the metaobject associated to B. Since metaobjects are standard objects, a link can apply not only on the execution of the metaobject methods (similarly to adviceexecution in AspectJ), but also to all other operations occuring within the metaobject: field accesses, created objects, messages sent, etc. There is indeed no difference between controlling the execution of a base application object and that of a metaobject.

A distinguishing feature of aspects of aspects in Reflex comes if we consider aspects acting *around* an execution point, for instance a caching aspect. Typically, a caching aspect holds cached values, and when a cache fault occurs, the aspect invokes the original operation via proceed. Such a proceed is done in Reflex via calling the proceed method of an execution point closure (EPC) object, which a metaobject can request. If we want to profile the caching aspect to determine the ratio of cache hits/faults, we can define a profiling aspect that matches execution of the caching method, and separately, that of the proceed method on the EPC object. This definition is not feasible in AspectJ, because proceed is a special expression that is not visible to other aspects.

4   Aspect Dependencies

Aspect dependencies can be of two kinds: implicit cut (*"apply A whenever B applies"*) and mutual exclusion (*"never apply A if B applies"*). These dependencies between aspects are mentioned in [5, 10, 21]. In addition, we also consider the case of *forbidden interactions*, an error mechanism to forbid two aspects to interact [6].

4.1   Implicit Cut

An implicit cut is obtained by sharing the cut specification between two aspects: In AspectJ, this is done by sharing pointcuts; in Reflex, by sharing hooksets (pointcut shadows) and activations (pointcut residues). Consider an e-commerce application on which we apply a discount aspect that applies to frequent customers, implemented by link `discount`, and a tracing aspect implemented by the link `trace`. The following ensures that `trace` applies whenever `discount` does (BLink stands for *behavioral* link):

```
BLink trace = Links.get(discount.getHookset(), <mo>);
trace.addActivation(new SharedActivation(discount));
```

The first line states that `trace` has the same hookset than `discount` (`<mo>` stands for the metaobject specification, not relevant here). The second line adds an activation condition, `SharedActivation`, which ensures that the activation of `trace` is that of `discount`: even if the activation condition of `discount` evolves dynamically, the dependency of `trace` to `discount` is ensured.

```
BLink trace = Links.getSameCut(discount, <mo>);
```

The above `getSameCut` method is a convenience method equivalent to the previous version. It just hides to programmers the way the implicit cut is realized. Finally, note that an implicit cut by definition implies that both aspects apply at the same points, therefore raising the issue of their ordering/nesting. This is addressed in Section 5.

4.2   Mutual Exclusion

Mutual exclusion between two aspects is obtained in Reflex by declaring that a link should not apply if another one does. As an example, consider a bingo aspect (implemented by a `bingo` link) that is used in the same application as the discounting aspect: every 1000 buyings, a big discount is offered. If a frequent customer happens to be the winner of the bingo, then the standard discount granted to frequent customers should not apply[3]. The following statement specifies that `discount` should not apply if `bingo` does:

```
Rules.declareMutex(discount, bingo);
```

---

[3] This example is taken from an EAOP illustration [16, 14].

Following this declaration, Reflex acts differently depending on whether the dependent links are subject to dynamic activation or not. If both links are not activatable (*i.e.* no pointcut residue), the mutual exclusion dependency can be resolved at weaving time, when hooks are inserted in the code. If one of them is indeed subject to dynamic activation, then Reflex postpones the resolution of the dependency to runtime: when control flow reaches a hook shared between mutually-exclusive links, the activation condition of the dominant link (here, `bingo`) is evaluated, and consequently, only one of the two links is applied (`bingo`, or `discount` if `bingo` is not active).

In the face of multiple mutual exclusion dependencies, the current algorithm first sorts out all links which are only dominant and then eliminates dominated links if their dominant is always active, or adds a dynamic condition to the dominated links if their dominant is subject to dynamic activation. At each step, the set of rules that apply is reduced.

For instance, if links A, B and C are interacting and the mutex relations are $mutex(A, B)$ and $mutex(B, C)$, the algorithm first puts A in the remaining links set, and removes B from the links to consider (supposing A is always active). Then, only C and A remain, and since no mutex is declared between both, C is added to the remaining links. The final solution is therefore A-C. Now, if A is subject to an activation condition, B is not removed: rather, it is put in the remaining links, but subject to a dynamic condition on the activation of A. At the next step, $mutex(B, C)$ applies. Since the application of B depends on that of A, C would be kept and subject to the activation of B. Consequently, at runtime, either A-C or B result, depending on whether A is active or not.

Forbidden Interactions. A particular case of mutual exclusion is when interaction between two aspects should be considered an *error* (*aka.* an inherent conflict [6]). In this case, one does not want to specify which link to apply or not, but rather to raise an exception. This is done in Reflex using `declareError`:

```
Rules.declareError(discount, bingo);
```

Similarly to `declareMutex`, the effect of `declareError` can occur at weaving time if both links are not activatable, or at runtime otherwise. In both cases, a `ForbiddenInteraction` exception is thrown.

5   Ordering and Nesting of Aspects

As previously mentioned, the Reflex AOP kernel follows the general approach advocated by Douence *et al.*, of *automatic* detection and *explicit* resolution of aspect interactions [10]:

- The kernel ensures that interactions are detected, and reported to users upon under-specification (Sect. 5.1).
- The kernel provides expressive and extensible means to specify the resolution of aspect interactions (Sect. 5.2).
- From such specifications, it composes links appropriately (Sect. 5.3).

5.1   Interaction Detection

An aspect interaction occurs when several aspects affect the same program point (execution or structure). Two behavioral links interact *statically* if the intersection of their hooksets is not empty. Still, the cut of an aspect may include a dynamically-evaluated condition (recall Fig. 2): we say that two behavioral links interact *dynamically* if they interact statically *and* they are both active at the same time. Since link ordering is resolved statically (when introducing hooks) and activation conditions can be changed dynamically, Reflex adopts a defensive approach: any static interaction is reported, and must be considered by the developer, so that a dynamic interaction is never under-specified. Our approach limits the number of spurious conflicts because it is based on the weaving process, which occurs on a by-need basis. In the presence of open systems with dynamic class laoding, two aspects that may theoretically interact for a *given program* (as in the formal approach of [10]) but do not in a *particular run* of that program do not raise detected conflicts.

Two structural links interact if the intersection of their class sets is not empty. We do not discriminate between static and dynamic interaction, because structural links are applied directly at load time. At present our approach for structural link interactions may report spurious conflicts because two links may affect the same class orthogonally. Finer-grained detection of interactions among structural links is left as future work.

Upon interactions, Reflex notifies an *interaction listener*. The default interaction listener simply issues warnings upon under-specification (see [29] for an example), informing the user that specification should be completed. It is possible to use other listeners, *e.g.* for on-the-fly resolution.

5.2   Ordering and Nesting

At interaction points, resolution must be specified. If links are mutually exclusive, specifying their ordering is not necessary[4]. Otherwise, ordering must be specified; this section explains how this is done for behavioral links[5].

The interaction between two before-after aspects can be resolved in two ways: either one always applies prior to the other (both before and after), or one "surrounds" the other [5, 10], although AspectJ only supports wrapping. These alternatives can be expressed using composition operators dealing with sequencing and wrapping. Considering aspects that can act *around* an execution point (such as a caching aspect), the notion of *nesting* as in AspectJ appears: a nested

---

[4] We deliberately separate the issue of dependencies from ordering/nesting, although mutual exclusion and forbidden interactions could be expressed with the operators explained in this section. The reason is two-fold: first, it is easier and higher-level for the user to declare dependencies as presented in Sect. 4.2; second, it is more efficient for the weaver to "sort out" interacting links before trying to order them.

[5] The case of structural links is simpler because they are always applied sequentially at the time a class is about to be loaded; no nesting is involved.

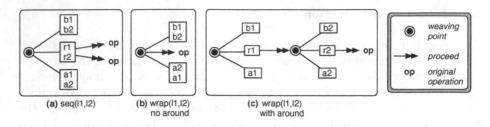

Fig. 3. Ordering and nesting scenarios

advice is only executed if its parent around advice invokes `proceed`. Around advices cannot be simply sequenced in AspectJ: they always imply nesting, and hence their execution always depends on the upper-level around advice [31].

In Reflex, link composition *rules* are specified using composition *operators*. The rule $seq(l_1, l_2)$ uses the *seq* operator to state that l_1 must be applied before l_2, both before and after the considered operation occurrence. The rule $wrap(l_1, l_2)$ means that l_2 must be applied within l_1, as clarified hereafter.

Kernel operators. User composition operators are defined in terms of lower-level kernel operators not dealing with links but with *link elements*. A link element is a pair $(link, control)$, where *control* is one of the control attributes: for instance, b_1 (resp. a_1) is the link element of l_1 for **before** (resp. **after**) control. There are two kernel operators, *ord* and *nest* which express respectively ordering and nesting of link elements. *nest* only applies to *around* link elements: the rule $nest(r, e)$ means that the application of the *around* element r nests that of the link element e. The place of the nesting is defined by the occurrences of `proceed` within r. Sequencing and wrapping can hence be defined as follows:

$$seq(l_1, l_2) = ord(b_1, b_2), ord(r_1, r_2), ord(a_1, a_2)$$
$$wrap(l_1, l_2) = ord(b_1, b_2), ord(a_2, a_1), nest(r_1, b_1), nest(r_1, r_2), nest(r_1, a_2)$$

Fig. 3 illustrates sequencing and wrapping, showing $seq(l_1, l_2)$ with all link elements (a), and the result of $wrap(l_1, l_2)$ first without around link elements (b), and then with around link elements (c). Weaving points are explained later on.

Composition operators. Reflex makes it possible to define a handful of user operators for composition on top of the kernel operators. For instance, `Seq` and `Wrap` are binary operators that implement the *seq* and *wrap* operators as defined above:

```
class Seq extends CompositionOperator {
  void expand(Link l1, Link l2){
    ord(b(l1), b(l2)); ord(r(l1), r(l2)); ord(a(l1), a(l2));
}}
```

```
class Wrap extends CompositionOperator {
  void expand(Link l1, Link l2){
    ord(b(l1), b(l2)); ord(a(l2), a(l1));
    nest(r(l1), b(l2)); nest(r(l1), r(l2)); nest(r(l1), a(l2));
} }
```

The methods b (before), r (around), a (after), ord, and nest are provided by
CompositionOperator. The expand method, evaluated whenever an interaction
between two links occurs, defines a user operator in terms of kernel operators.

Below is an example of a composition rule declared between two interacting
aspects: a timing aspect measuring method execution time, and a synchronization aspect ensuring mutual exclusion of methods. Both aspects act before and
after method executions. The declared composition implies that the timing aspect measures execution time of methods, *including* the synchronization cost:

```
BLink timer = ...; BLink synchro = ...;
Rules.declare(new Wrap(timer, synchro));
```

Another example of composition operator is Any: this operator simply states
that the order of composition of two given links does not matter (similarly to
commute in [10]); the kernel is free to compose them arbitrarily. Currently, the
Any operator is implemented as a Seq operator, but this is not something users
should rely upon:

```
class Any extends Seq {}
```

Higher-level operators. Users can define higher-level operators based on the
building blocks of Reflex. For instance, we can define a variant of Wrap that, in
addition to the Wrap semantics, specifies that the nested link does not apply if the
wrapping link is not active. We call this operator DWrap (D for "dependency"):

```
class DWrap extends Wrap {
  void expand(Link l1, Link l2){
    super.expand(l1, l2); // wrap semantics
    l2.addActivation(new SharedActivation(l1)); // active dependency
} }
```

5.3   Hook Generation

When detecting link interactions, Reflex generates a hook skeleton based on the
specified composition rules, similarly to Fig. 3. The hook skeleton is then used for
driving the hook generation process: taking into account how link elements have
to be inserted, with the appropriate calls to metaobjects. In order to support
nesting of aspects with proceed, Reflex adopts a strategy similar to that of
AspectJ described in [19], based on the generation of closures.

As mentioned earlier, in order to be able to do proceed, a metaobject is
given an execution point closure (EPC) object, which has a proceed method, as
well as methods for changing the actual arguments and receiver of the replaced

operation. Hence, for each interaction scenario with nesting, Reflex generates closures embedding the composition resolution of the following nesting level, so that calling `proceed` on the EPC object results in the execution of the links at the nesting level below. This is done down to the deepest level where `proceed` results in the execution of the replaced operation. The top-level *weaving points* on Fig. 3 represent hooks, while nested weaving points represent closures.

Since previous benchmarks [25] highlighted that executing the replaced operation reflectively implies important performance penalties, we have now adopted the generated stub solution used in AspectJ [19].

6   Visibility of Structural Changes

In the general case, aspects may change both the structure and behavior of a program as a consequence of their actions. Although several AOP proposals – such as EAOP [13, 14, 10, 11], trace-based aspects [12], AOLMP [9, 5, 18], and several others– do not consider structural aspects, languages like AspectJ do (via inter-type declarations). Reflex, as a versatile kernel for AOP, also supports structural changes, as mentioned earlier, via structural links.

As explained previously, aspects rely on *introspecting* the structure of a program to define their cut. Since structural aspects *modify* this structure, the issue of whether structural changes made by aspects are visible to others or not appears. This is a composition issue because if there is only one aspect, there is no problem: the issue arises when considering the integration of several aspects over the same application. This issue is still under-explored in the community.

Consider an aspect adding history to fields, and another aspect making fields persistent: the issue of whether the field added by the first aspect in order to record history should be made persistent appears. In Reflex, the persistence aspect is implemented by a behavioral link, monitoring field accesses; the history aspect, in addition to using a behavioral link for capturing history, makes use of a structural link to introduce a new field in appropriate classes. Therefore, the history field will only be made persistent if the cut of the persistence link actually "sees" that field. For some applications it can make sense to have history fields being persistent as well, but still, those fields may need to be hidden from other aspects.

Default visibility. Reflex applies all structural links *before* behavioral links are setup. This makes it possible for a behavioral link to affect operations related to a member added by a structural link, if so desired. But by default, all structural changes are *hidden*. This makes it possible to avoid *unwanted* conflation of extended and non-extended functionalities, as discussed in the meta-helix architecture [8].

Furthermore, changes done to the program when introducing hooks (for setting up behavioral links) are always hidden. This is motivated by the fact that behavioral changes are conceptually runtime changes: the fact that Reflex operates at load time, by introducing hooks, should be transparent; hence hooks should be hidden. Similarly, infrastructure members introduced by Reflex –such as metaobject references and initialization methods– cannot be observed. This is implemented thanks to a mirror-based structural API [3, 27], which exposes only interface types to users, rather than implementation types as in Javassist: hence Reflex can coordinate visibility of structural elements "behind the scene" (ensuring *structural correspondence* [3, 27]).

Declarative visibility. When introspecting a class for determing matching or not of its cut, a link only sees what has been declared to be its *view* of the program. By default, as we said, a link only sees the original program definition. But it is possible to declare that a link has an *augmented view* of the program, *i.e.* including changes made by other links:

```
(1) Rules.augmentViewOf(persistency, history);
(2) Rules.addToDefaultView(history);
```

Line (1) above declares that `persistency` sees all changes made by `history`. Several links can be given to `augmentViewOf`. Line (2) adopts a different focus, by promoting all changes made by `history` as part of the default view.

To support the subjectivity introduced above, Reflex automatically records the identity of the link affecting a given structural element as a metadata of the element. Metadata are stored in a general-purpose key-value property map attached to each structural element, and can be used for many purposes. In particular, it is possible for a link to *force* a new structural element to be always visible (resp. always hidden) by setting a particular property `forceVisible` (resp. `forceHidden`).

The proposed mechanism for controlling the visibility of structural changes already goes beyond existing AOP proposals, in particular AspectJ. However, our approach can still be refined and enhanced, to address more specific and fine-grained conflicts between structural changes.

7 Related Work

Our work on aspect composition in the Reflex AOP kernel is inspired by the work of Douence *et al.* in the EAOP model. It can be seen as an effort to project over a concrete and efficient implementation their formal approach to aspect composition [10, 11]. Among the notable differences is the fact that EAOP does not contemplate structural changes to programs, nor the possibilities of aspects to act around a given execution point.

Klaeren *et al.* have focused on the issue of validating combinations of aspects [21]. They use assertions to ensure the correctness of the dependencies between aspects with respect to the specification, focusing on mutually-exclusive aspects. However they do not address means to resolve interactions between aspects. Reflex also covers mutual exclusion, as explained in Section 4.2.

JAsCo [26] provides two mechanisms for aspect composition: precedence strategies and combination strategies. In JAsCo, an aspect is deployed by specifying a *connector* that determines which *hooks* should be enabled (the cut of an aspect) and which advice should be triggered when the cut is matched. Within a connector that instantiates several hooks, it is possible to specify explicitly the order in which associated advices are executed, leading to fine-grained control on precedence strategies. This is similar to what can be expressed declaratively in Reflex using the composition operators. However, this mechanism works fine only for interacting aspects that are deployed by one connector. Also, with respect to around advice however, JAsCo forces the nesting relation, while Reflex lets, at the kernel level, the possibility of having a *sequence* of around advices. For other interaction problems that are not solved by means of precedence strategies, JAsCo provides *combination strategies*: such a strategy is like a filter on the list of hooks that are applicable at a certain point in the execution. With combination strategies, one can programmatically exclude certain hooks from the current interaction. Again, this is similar to what can be achieved in Reflex; actually the low-level interface in the Reflex kernel is equivalent, except that it works on hook *trees* rather than flat lists, in order to reflect the nesting relation. However, Reflex provides a declarative layer on top of this low-level, programmatic interface, which JAsCo does not. Finally, JAsCo does not automatically report on interactions, and does not address structural aspects.

Nagy *et al.* present a declarative approach to aspect composition [23], considering two types of constraints: ordering and control. The approach for ordering constraints is similar to our kernel-level predicates: the `pre` constraint ressembles our *ord* predicate for indicating precedence. But the issue of aspect nesting (as addressed by *nest*) is not discussed. Control constraints are used to make an aspect depend on the "return value" of the action of another aspect. Although only boolean return values are considered, the approach is interesting. In Reflex, it is expressable in a more flexible manner through activation conditions. Also, Nagy*et al.* introduce two types of constraints, soft ones and hard ones, to be able to express a strong dependency between two aspects, such that one can apply only if the other one did. Mutual exclusion is however not considered. Furthermore, in our proposal, dependencies are a separate notion, although they can be embedded within user-defined composition operators (*e.g.* the `DWrap` operator, Sect. 5.2). Our approach is therefore more flexible in this sense. Finally, they do not address the issue of structural changes to base code.

Brichau *et al.* proposed the use of logic metaprogramming [32, 9] to build composable domain-specific aspect languages [5]. A logic language is used to reason about object-oriented base programs, whose description at the metalevel is done with logic facts and rules. The logic language also serves as the medium in which both aspects and aspect languages are implemented and coordinated, through logic rules in logic modules. Although no aspect-specific syntax is provided, the use of a common logic medium is extremely expressive and allows for the specification of advanced composition strategies. The proposal, called SOUL/Aop, however only considers a static joinpoint model; the more recent AOLMP system Carma [18] is based on a dynamic joinpoint model, but has not gotten to aspect composition issues yet. SOUL/Aop only deals with before/after advices, hence issues related to acting *around* an execution point are not considered; nor are structural aspects addressed. Also, advice weaving in SOUL/Aop is done by inlining advice code at appropriate places, complexifying the support for aspects of aspects. Note that Reflex, as of now, does not offer any real support for composing languages, but just aspects. Conversely, Brichau *et al.* do support composition of languages exactly in the same way as aspects are composed: by combining parameterized logic modules. We are currently exploring language composition alternatives for Reflex, in particular with the MetaBorg approach for unrestricted embedding and assimiation of domain-specific languages [4].

8   Conclusion

We have exposed different dimensions of the multi-faceted issue of aspect composition, and explained the support that the Reflex AOP kernel provides for the same. Reflex supports automatic detection of aspect interactions limiting spurious conflicts; possibilities to express aspect dependencies, such as implicit cut and mutual exclusion; extensible composition operators for ordering and nesting of aspects; the definition of aspects of aspects; and the possibility to control the visibility of structural changes made by aspects. Since Reflex is used as an experimental platform for multi-language AOP, its composition features can be used to handle composition of aspects defined in different aspect languages. The openness of the platform also makes it possible to experiment with new composition operators.

Our experience with supporting declarative aspect composition suggests that an imperative implementation in plain Java may not be the appropriate way to go, as we are facing difficulties in the implementation of some deductions, which would be straightforward using a logic engine. This remains to be explored. Furthermore, our initial solution to composition of structural aspects needs to be extended further, to deal with finer-grained conflicts and resolution schemes.

Acknowledgements. The author would like to thank Jacques Noyé for his detailed comments on a draft of this paper, as well as for his contribution on the body of work on Reflex. Guillaume Pothier, Leonardo Rodríguez and Rodolfo Toledo contributed to the implementation of the features described in this paper. The anonymous reviewers of SC'06 provided very valuable feedback that allowed us to enhance both the presentation and the work hereby presented.

References

[1] M. Akşit, editor. *Proceedings of the 2nd International Conference on Aspect-Oriented Software Development (AOSD 2003)*, Boston, MA, USA, Mar. 2003. ACM Press.

[2] D. Batory, C. Consel, and W. Taha, editors. *Proceedings of the 1st ACM SIG-PLAN/SIGSOFT Conference on Generative Programming and Component Engineering (GPCE 2002)*, volume 2487 of *Lecture Notes in Computer Science*, Pittsburgh, PA, USA, Oct. 2002. Springer-Verlag.

[3] G. Bracha and D. Ungar. Mirrors: Design principles for meta-level facilities of object-oriented programming languages. In OOPSLA 2004 [24], pages 331–344. ACM SIGPLAN Notices, 39(11).

[4] M. Bravenboer and E. Visser. Concrete syntax for objects. In OOPSLA 2004 [24]. ACM SIGPLAN Notices, 39(11).

[5] J. Brichau, K. Mens, and K. De Volder. Building composable aspect-specific languages with logic metaprogramming. In Batory et al. [2], pages 110–127.

[6] L. Bussard, L. Carver, E. Ernst, M. Jung, M. Robillard, and A. Speck. Safe aspect composition. In J. Malenfant, S. Moisan, and A. Moreira, editors, *Object-Oriented Technology: ECOOP 2000 Workshop Reader*, volume 1964 of *Lecture Notes in Computer Science*, pages 205–210. Springer-Verlag, 2000.

[7] S. Chiba. Load-time structural reflection in Java. In E. Bertino, editor, *Proceedings of the 14th European Conference on Object-Oriented Programming (ECOOP 2000)*, number 1850 in Lecture Notes in Computer Science, pages 313–336, Sophia Antipolis and Cannes, France, June 2000. Springer-Verlag.

[8] S. Chiba, G. Kiczales, and J. Lamping. Avoiding confusion in metacircularity: The meta-helix. In *Proceedings of the 2nd International Symposium on Object Technologies for Advanced Software (ISOTAS'96)*, volume 1049 of *Lecture Notes in Computer Science*, pages 157–172. Springer-Verlag, 1996.

[9] K. De Volder and T. D'Hondt. Aspect-oriented logic meta-programming. In P. Cointe, editor, *Proceedings of the 2nd International Conference on Metalevel Architectures and Reflection (Reflection 99)*, volume 1616 of *Lecture Notes in Computer Science*, pages 250–272, Saint-Malo, France, July 1999. Springer-Verlag.

[10] R. Douence, P. Fradet, and M. Südholt. A framework for the detection and resolution of aspect interactions. In Batory et al. [2], pages 173–188.

[11] R. Douence, P. Fradet, and M. Südholt. Composition, reuse and interaction analysis of stateful aspects. In Lieberherr [22], pages 141–150.

[12] R. Douence, P. Fradet, and M. Südholt. Trace-based aspects. In R. E. Filman, T. Elrad, S. Clarke, and M. Akşit, editors, *Aspect-Oriented Software Development*, pages 201–217. Addison-Wesley, Boston, 2005.

[13] R. Douence, O. Motelet, and M. Südholt. A formal definition of crosscuts. In A. Yonezawa and S. Matsuoka, editors, *Proceedings of the 3rd International Conference on Metalevel Architectures and Advanced Separation of Concerns (Reflection 2001)*, volume 2192 of *Lecture Notes in Computer Science*, pages 170–186, Kyoto, Japan, Sept. 2001. Springer-Verlag.

[14] R. Douence and M. Südholt. A model and a tool for event-based aspect-oriented programming (EAOP). Technical Report 02/11/INFO, École des mines de Nantes, Dec. 2002. 2nd edition, French version published in the Proceedings of "Langages et Modèles à Objets" (LMO'03).

[15] P. Durr, T. Staijen, L. Bergmans, and M. Aksit. Reasoning about semantic conflicts between aspects. In *2nd European Interactive Workshop on Aspects in Software (EIWAS 2005)*, Brussels, Belgium, Sept. 2005.

[16] The EAOP tool homepage, 2001. http://www.emn.fr/x-info/eaop/tool.html.

[17] T. Elrad, R. E. Filman, and A. Bader. Aspect-oriented programming. *Communications of the ACM*, 44(10), Oct. 2001.

[18] K. Gybels and J. Brichau. Arranging language features for more robust pattern-based crosscuts. In Akşit [1], pages 60–69.

[19] E. Hilsdale and J. Hugunin. Advice weaving in AspectJ. In Lieberherr [22], pages 26–35.

[20] G. Kiczales, E. Hilsdale, J. Hugunin, M. Kersten, J. Palm, and W. Griswold. An overview of AspectJ. In J. L. Knudsen, editor, *Proceedings of the 15th European Conference on Object-Oriented Programming (ECOOP 2001)*, number 2072 in Lecture Notes in Computer Science, pages 327–353, Budapest, Hungary, June 2001. Springer-Verlag.

[21] H. Klaeren, E. Pulvermüller, A. Rashid, and A. Speck. Aspect composition applying the design by contract principle. In *Proceedings of the 2nd International Symposium on Generative and Component-Based Software Engineering (GCSE 2000)*, volume 2177 of *Lecture Notes in Computer Science*, pages 57–69. Springer-Verlag, 2000.

[22] K. Lieberherr, editor. *Proceedings of the 3rd International Conference on Aspect-Oriented Software Development (AOSD 2004)*, Lancaster, UK, Mar. 2004. ACM Press.

[23] I. Nagy, L. Bergmans, and M. Aksit. Declarative aspect composition. In *2nd Software-Engineering Properties of Languages and Aspect Technologies Workshop*, Mar 2004.

[24] *Proceedings of the 19th ACM SIGPLAN Conference on Object-Oriented Programming Systems, Languages and Applications (OOPSLA 2004)*, Vancouver, British Columbia, Canada, Oct. 2004. ACM Press. ACM SIGPLAN Notices, 39(11).

[25] L. Rodríguez, É. Tanter, and J. Noyé. Supporting dynamic crosscutting with partial behavioral reflection: a case study. In *Proceedings of the XXIV International Conference of the Chilean Computer Science Society (SCCC 2004)*, Arica, Chile, Nov. 2004. IEEE Computer Society Press.

[26] D. Suvee, W. Vanderperren, and V. Jonckers. JAsCo: an aspect-oriented approach tailored for component based software development. In Akşit [1], pages 21–29.

[27] É. Tanter. Metalevel facilities for multi-language AOP. In *2nd European Interactive Workshop on Aspects in Software (EIWAS 2005)*, Brussels, Belgium, Sept. 2005.

[28] É. Tanter and J. Noyé. Motivation and requirements for a versatile AOP kernel. In *1st European Interactive Workshop on Aspects in Software (EIWAS 2004)*, Berlin, Germany, Sept. 2004.

[29] É. Tanter and J. Noyé. A versatile kernel for multi-language AOP. In R. Glück and M. Lowry, editors, *Proceedings of the 4th ACM SIGPLAN/SIGSOFT Conference on Generative Programming and Component Engineering (GPCE 2005)*, volume 3676 of *Lecture Notes in Computer Science*, pages 173–188, Tallinn, Estonia, Sept./Oct. 2005. Springer-Verlag.

[30] É. Tanter, J. Noyé, D. Caromel, and P. Cointe. Partial behavioral reflection: Spatial and temporal selection of reification. In R. Crocker and G. L. Steele, Jr., editors, *Proceedings of the 18th ACM SIGPLAN Conference on Object-Oriented Programming Systems, Languages and Applications (OOPSLA 2003)*, pages 27–46, Anaheim, CA, USA, Oct. 2003. ACM Press. ACM SIGPLAN Notices, 38(11).

[31] M. Wand, G. Kiczales, and C. Dutchyn. A semantics for advice and dynamic join points in aspect-oriented programming. *ACM Transactions on Programming Languages and Systems*, 26(5):890–910, Sept. 2004.

[32] R. Wuyts. Declarative reasoning about the structure of object-oriented systems. In *Proceedings of TOOLS-USA 98*, page 112, 1998.

A Component-Based Approach to Compose Transaction Standards

Romain Rouvoy[1], Patricia Serrano-Alvarado[2], and Philippe Merle[1]

[1] INRIA Futurs, Jacquard Project,
LIFL - University of Lille 1,
59655 Villeneuve d'Ascq Cedex, France
{romain.rouvoy, philippe.merle}@inria.fr
[2] ATLAS-GDD Team,
LINA - University of Nantes,
44322 Nantes Cedex 03, France
patricia.serrano-alvarado@univ-nantes.fr

Abstract. This paper tackles the problem of composition of transaction services, which are governed by various transaction standards. Among others, we can cite the *Object Transaction Service*, *Java Transaction Service*, or *Web Services Atomic Transaction*. However, the Web Services Atomic Transaction standard encloses legacy transaction standards to support the Web Services application platform. This encapsulation introduces an additional complexity to the system and hides the specificities of legacy transaction standards. When composing heterogeneous legacy applications, the underlying transaction services are basically not composed transparently. This paper presents an approach to build an *Adapted Transaction Service*, named ATS, which supports several transaction standards concurrently. The objective of ATS is to facilitate the transaction standards composition. To introduce ATS we detail how the Object Transaction Service, Web Services Atomic Transaction, and Java Transaction Service standards can be composed. Besides, an ATS implementation is introduced using the GoTM framework. We show that this fine-grained component-based approach does not introduce an additional overhead to legacy applications and supports well scalability. Moreover, this approach can be extended to other standards.

1 Introduction

For years, the number of transaction standards grows drastically. Among others, we can cite the *Object Transaction Service* (OTS) from the Object Management Group [1], the *Java Transaction Service* (JTS) from Sun Microsystems [2], or the *Web Services Atomic Transaction* (WS-AT) [3] published by Microsoft, IBM, IONA, BEA Systems, Hitachi and Arjuna Technologies. Current trends define new transaction standards by encapsulating existing ones. For example, the WS-AT standard encloses the JTS standard, which encapsulates the OTS standard. But this approach introduces an additional complexity for each layer, while loosing the specificities of each encapsulated transaction standard. When

W. Löwe and M. Südholt (Eds.): SC 2006, LNCS 4089, pp. 114–130, 2006.

composing heterogeneous legacy applications, the underlying transaction services are basically not composed transparently.

This drawback leads us to propose a practical approach to compose transaction standards. In this paper, we present an approach to build an *Adapted Transaction Service* (ATS) and its implementation based on fine-grained components. The ATS composes several transaction standards simultaneously and ensures the compliancy of the different functions. To design ATS, we analyze the interfaces of the transaction standards, and we identify the required *functions*. Each function is derived into various *strategies* depending on the specific semantics. Therefore, ATS is built by composition of these strategies and *adapters*. Adapters ensure the compliance with transaction standards interfaces. Finally, we use *GoTM* to build the resulting ATS. GoTM is a framework that provides various fine-grained transaction components [4]. These components are implemented with *Fractal*, a component model that provides good properties in terms of modularity and performances [5]. To illustrate our approach, we build a transaction service that composes the CORBA, Web Services and Java transaction standards.

This paper is organized as follows. The problem of transaction standard composition is presented in Section 2. Section 3 describes our approach to achieve transaction standard composition. The implementation of our solution with the GoTM framework is detailed and evaluated in Section 4. Section 5 discusses related works, and Section 6 concludes.

2 The Problem of Transaction Standard Composition

To illustrate the problem related to transaction standard composition, we use the example of *Flight Booking* and *Hotel Reservation applications*, as depicted in Figure 1.

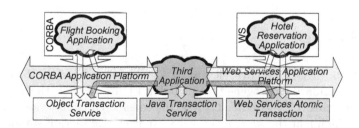

Fig. 1. Illustration of the problem of transaction standard composition

These applications are hosted by different distributed application platforms (CORBA and Web Services), which support their own transaction standard. In particular, the CORBA application platform provides the *Object Transaction Service* (OTS). The Web Services application platform provides the *Atomic Transaction Service* (WS-AT). The *Third Application* uses locally the *Java*

Transaction Service (JTS). This third application can interact with both applications remotely using the functionalities provided by each distributed application platforms.

Even if this architecture allows heterogeneous application platforms to interact, the transaction context[1] is not implicitly propagated from an application to another. That is, WS-AT, which handles Hotel Reservation transactions, does not cooperate with OTS, which controls the Flight Booking transactions. And, the third application, using JTS, can not synchronize its execution with the two other applications.

Usually, to achieve such a synchronization, the third application should control all the transaction services, and therefore use three different transaction Application Programming Interfaces (APIs). Thus, when it begins a new transaction, the third application should explicitly begin transactions in the three transaction services. But, when the transaction commits, the third application should find a way of coordinating the commit protocol of each transaction service. Existing approaches use compensation mechanisms to support the coordination of multiple transactional activities [6]. But applications can not always define compensating actions (e.g.: compensating the sending of an email). Therefore the compensating actions may be limited in some coordination situations. Moreover, the definition of a coordination algorithm at the third application level weaves the code related to non-functional properties (i.e., transaction services synchronization) with the business code.

This paper proposes an approach to deal with the heterogeneity of existing transaction standards. Instead of proposing to use a unified language or a new transaction standard, we propose to build Adapted Transaction Services (ATS) that support several transaction standards concurrently. Therefore the third application uses only the interfaces provided by JTS and transactions are automatically coordinated in the two other transaction services. With this approach, legacy systems can be transparently composed together from a transactional point of view.

3   ATS Design

This section begins with an overview of an ATS built to answer to the problem of transaction standard heterogeneity depicted in Figure 1. Thus, the approach applied to build this ATS is detailed. First, the considered transaction services are analyzed to highlight the *functions* involved in each transaction standard. Next, these functions are abstracted and dependencies are identified. Each function is extended into various *strategies* according to the semantics imposed by the considered standards. These strategies are then composed (i.e., linked together) to build the content of the *Common Transaction Service* (CTS). Finally, the ATS is built by adding to the CTS necessary *adapters* to support JTS, WS-AT, and OTS standards.

---

[1] Information related to the execution of the current transaction.

3.1 Overview of an ATS

Figure 2 introduces an ATS supporting OTS, JTS, and WS-AT standards.

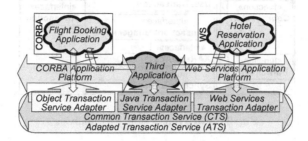

Fig. 2. An example of ATS supporting transaction standard composition

An ATS is composed of a set of *adapters* and a *CTS*. The CTS provides an implementation of a generic transaction engine. The CTS groups the behaviour of all the functions supported by the ATS. The adapters provide compliance with the considered transaction standards (OTS, JTS and WS-AT). The adapters are responsible for mapping the operation performed on a particular transaction standard to the functions provided by the CTS. The functions, required by the adapters, are provided by the CTS.

Thus, this modular architecture can be easily modified to support new transaction standards. In this case, the content of the CTS is adapted according to the chosen adapters to provide the minimal set of functions required.

3.2 Function Analysis

A **function** is a set of operations linked by their semantics. In particular, we make the hypothesis that transaction services are based on the minimal set of *Status*, *Coordination*, and *Participants* functions. Then, we identify these functions for each APIs used by the applications to ensure transactional behaviour. More specifically, we consider the CosTransactions API, Java Transaction API, and Atomic Transaction Services provided by the OTS, JTS and WS-AT standards, respectively. This analysis aims at confirming that the three identified functions are enough to compose transaction services.

JTA Analysis. The *Java Transaction API* (JTA) defines a set of Java interfaces that provide transaction support to any Java application. Figure 3 lists the interfaces involved in JTA.

Based on an analysis of this API, we establish the interface dependencies. These dependencies are illustrated with the *"uses"* UML stereotype [7] in Figure 3. For example, the `Transaction` interface depend on the `Status`, `Synchronization` and `XAResource` interfaces. The operations described in the `Transaction` interface require `Synchronization` and `XAResource` interfaces, while providing the `Status` interface.

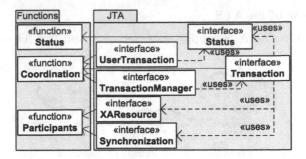

Fig. 3. Java Transaction API analysis

Next, we classify JTA interfaces according to the function indicated by their semantics. The identified functions are indicated with the *"function"* UML stereotype in Figure 3. For example, the semantics of the `UserTransaction`, `Transaction`, and `TransactionManager` interfaces refer to a *Two-Phase Commit protocol* [8]. Thus, we define the *Coordination* function to abstract the identified semantics. We apply the same approach to each operation making up the API. As a result, we extract three functions: *Coordination*, *Status* and *Participants*. The *Status* function controls the state of the transaction. The *Participants* function manages the participants involved in the transaction.

CosTransactions Analysis. The *CosTransactions* API is defined using the OMG Interface Description Language and allows CORBA applications written in different programming languages to use it. Figure 4 identifies the interfaces involved in the CosTransactions API.

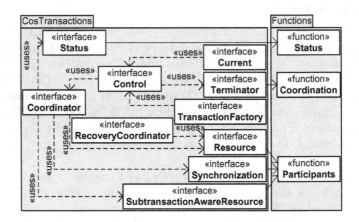

Fig. 4. CosTransactions API analysis

We apply the same process as with JTA. Interface dependencies are first inferred from the transaction API. The functions involved in the CosTransactions API are identified and we obtain the *Coordination*, *Status* and *Participants* functions.

WS Atomic Transaction Analysis. Web Services Atomic Transaction (WS-AT) is the last transaction standard specified. This standard allows transaction-aware Web Services distributed across a network to be synchronized with different policies. The WS-AT standard is structured in several services, each service providing a specific function. Figure 5 identifies the services involved in the Web Services Atomic Transaction standard.

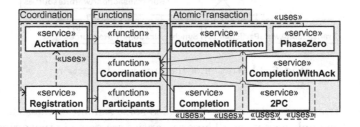

Fig. 5. WS Atomic Transactions analysis

The granularity of this standard is not the same than the two previous ones. Indeed, Web Services are based on message exchanges rather method invocations. Thus, we analyze the interaction between the services involved in the WS-AT standard. The `Registration` service depend on the `Activation` service. This is because a `Coordination Context` should be created before participants can register with the transaction. The `Completion`, `CompletionWithAck`, `PhaseZero`, `2PC` and `OutcomeNotification` services encapsulate the WS-Atomic Transaction business logic. These additional services depends on the Registration service to interact with transaction participants. As a consequence, functions involved in WS-Atomic Transaction are: *Coordination*, *Status* and *Participants*.

3.3 Strategy Definition

Function Summary. In this step, we associate each identified function with a set of generic operation signatures. This association depends on the operations declared in the CosTransactions, WS Atomic Transaction and Java Transaction APIs. Next, the dependencies between the functions are inferred from the interface dependencies established in the section 3.2.

As shown in Figure 6, the *Status* and *Participants* functions are not dependent on any other function. The *Status* function provides the operations required to handle the transaction status allowed by a given transaction model. The *Participants* function provides operations to manage the transaction participants.

The *Coordination* function updates the transaction status using the *Status* function. It also ensures the coherence between the transaction status and the resource states. For example, updating the transaction status to `commit` implies that participants validate their modifications using the *Participants* function. Thus, the `execute()` operation changes the transaction status and notifies the participants involved in the transaction.

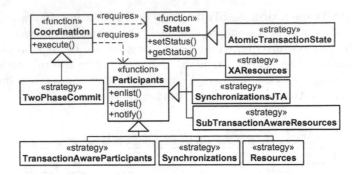

Fig. 6. Illustration of the function abstraction

However, transaction standards define also some semantics that should be respected by the implementations. These semantics are named **strategies** and are associated to identified **functions**. A strategy can be an implementation of an algorithm, a protocol (e.g., the Two-Phase Commit protocol) or a specialization of an entity (e.g., XAResource). Figure 6 shows an overview of the possible strategy derivations for JTS, WS-AT and OTS from the identified functions. These strategies are described in the following sections.

Two-Phase Commit Strategy. The *TwoPhaseCommit* strategy represents an implementation of the Two-Phase Commit (2PC) protocol for the *Coordination* function. This protocol defines, among other things, a sequence of messages that ensures atomicity. Figure 7 shows the UML Interaction diagram [7] used to describe a basic 2PC protocol.

As shown in Figure 7, the *TwoPhase-Commit* strategy extending the *Coordination* function emits a **prepare** message. The *Participants* function answers to this message with a **vote-commit** or **vote-abort** message. Depending on the collected votes, the *TwoPhaseCommit* strategy sends a **commit** or an **abort** message to *Participants* function. Once the participants have achieved the validation process, the *Participants* function sends an **ack** message to acknowledge the coordination process. Additional strategies can be defined to implement optimized versions of 2PC, such as Two-Phase Commit Presumed Commit (2PCPC) or Two-Phase Commit Presumed Abort (2PCPA) protocols (see [8] for more details).

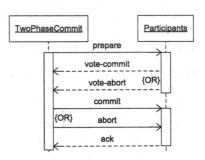

Fig. 7. 2PC Interaction Diagram

Participants Strategies. The *Participants* function is extended by six strategies, which are adapted to the different types of resources defined in the transaction standards. These strategies are the *SubTransactionAwareResources*, *Synchronizations* and *Resources* for OTS ; *TransactionAwareParticipants* for WS-AT and *SynchronizationsJTA* and *XAResources* for JTS. The differences between these strategies are the list of messages that the resources can handle. For example, the *Synchronization* strategy handles commit and abort messages. The *Resource* strategy handles these two messages plus the prepare message. Each strategy is based on a set of specific ECA rules (Event/Condition/Action). These rules define the behaviour to apply on the participants involved in the transaction depending on incoming messages.

```
1    global synchronizations
2
3    on prepare? count(synchronizations)>0:
4       foreach s in synchronizations do:
5          s.beforeCompletion()
6    on commit? count(synchronizations)>0:
7       foreach s in synchronizations do:
8          s.afterCompletion(Status.STATUS_COMMITTED)
9    on abort? count(synchronizations)>0:
10      foreach s in synchronizations do:
11         s.afterCompletion(Status.STATUS_ROLLEDBACK)
```

Fig. 8. SynchronizationsJTA Strategy ECA Rules

Figure 8 depicts the example of the *SynchronizationsJTA* strategy. The Event part corresponds to the messages received by the strategy prefixed by the on keyword. The Condition part checks that at least one participant is involved in the transaction. The Action part applies a treatment to all the participants registered in the transaction. These participants are notified before and after the completion of the transaction in which they are involved. The afterCompletion() operation parameter depends on the outcome of the transaction (i.e., committed or aborted). Additional ECA rules are defined for each strategy extending the *Participants* function.

Atomic Transaction State Strategy. The *Status* function is extended by the *AtomicTransactionState* strategy. This strategy can be configured using a state automaton describing the transaction state transitions.

The state automaton used in our example describes an atomic transaction as depicted in Figure 9. We use the UML diagram State Machine [7] to describe the states involved in the lifecycle of an atomic transaction. These states are common to each transaction standard because all of them are related to atomic transactions. As shown in Figure 9, an atomic transaction starts in an Inactive state. When it receives the start message, the atomic transaction moves to the Active state. Thus, an atomic transaction can be suspended and resumed using start and stop messages. To move to the validation phase, the atomic transaction should be in the Active state and receives a prepare, abort or aborted message.

The prepare message begins the Two-Phase Commit protocol, moving the Transaction to the Preparing state. The abort message causes the transaction to abort unilaterally. The aborted message ends the transaction without applying the Two-Phase Commit protocol. The abort and aborted messages result in the same behaviour independently of the current state of the transaction. When a transaction in the Preparing state receives the prepared message, it moves to the Prepared state to decide the out-

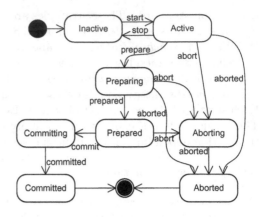

Fig. 9. Atomic Transaction State Diagram

come of the transaction. When this decision is taken by the *Coordination Protocol*, the transaction can commit if it receives the commit message. In this case, the transaction enters in the Committing state to validate the transaction and then moves to the Committed final state once the decision is acknowledged. Any abort message received by a transaction state results in moving the in the Aborting state to cancel the transaction before moving to the Aborted final state. Additional State Machine diagrams can be defined to handle new transaction states such as the Compensating state [9].

3.4   Composition of the ATS

Once the transaction standards have been described in terms of functions and strategies, the next step builds the *Common Transaction Service* (CTS) by composition of strategies following function dependencies. The CTS is a generic transaction engine that provides common facilities to the three transaction standards. This composition is implemented with the paradigm of a software bus [10]. A software bus provides facilities to compose the strategies interacting using messages. For example, the commit or abort messages are propagated from the *TwoPhaseCommit* strategy to the *Synchronizations* strategy according to the dependency that links their associated functions (*Coordination* and *Participants* respectively).

Figure 10 gives an overview of the strategy composition used to build the CTS. This composition meets the requirements of JTS, WS-AT and OTS standards. The *MessageBus* bus propagates the messages between the strategies involved in the CTS. Associations link a strategy to either a dependent strategy or the *MessageBus* in order to connect required to provided functions.

Once the CTS is built, it needs to be made compliant with the APIs of each of the considered transaction services. The result of this adaptation is the Adapted Transaction Service (ATS). In practice, the adaptation is done by constructing

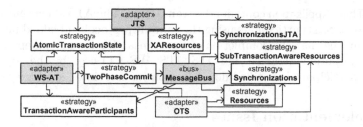

Fig. 10. CTS: composition of JTS/WS-AT/OTS-compliant strategies

adapters that provide the operations required by the associated standard APIs, and require the CTS functions identified in Section 3.2.

Figure 10 illustrates the adaptation of CTS to JTS, WS-AT and OTS transaction interfaces. In this step, an adapter for each of the transaction services is defined. Each adapter is bound to the strategies it requires. The JTS adapter requires the *TransactionState*, *TwoPhaseCommit*, *XAResources* and *SynchronizationsJTA* strategies. The OTS adapter requires the *TransactionState*, *TwoPhaseCommit*, *Synchronizations*, *Resources* and *SubTransactionAwareResources* strategies. The WS-AT adapter requires the *TransactionState*, *TwoPhaseCommit*, *TransactionAwareParticpants* strategies.

3.5 ATS Use Case

This section introduces how the ATS is used in practice. This use case describes a simple scenario applied on the example depicted in Figure 2.

1. The Third Application creates a new transaction in the ATS via the JTS adapter. An adapted transaction context is automatically initialized by the ATS. The transaction context associates the method invoked by the Third Application with the created transaction.
2. The Third Application calls the Flight Booking Application using the CORBA platform facilities. The transaction context is propagated to the target application via the CORBA Portable Interceptors mechanism [11]. In particular, the *Client Portable Interceptor* defines the OTS adapter of the ATS as the current transaction service. The *Server Portable Interceptor* replaces the existing transaction service by the OTS adapter during the execution of the application. As a consequence, the Flight Booking Application enlists `Resource` and `Synchronization` participants in the OTS adapter of the ATS.
3. The Third Application invokes the Hotel Reservation Application (see Figure 2) using the Web Services application platform. The transaction context is propagated as a *WS-Coordination Context* [12] in the header of the Web Service request. This means that the Hotel Reservation Application will enlist its `TransactionAwareParticipants` in the ATS via the Registration Service provided by the WS-AT adapter of the ATS.

4. The Third Application commits the transaction. The ATS synchronizes all the heterogeneous participants using the commit protocol embedded in the CTS. This means that the completion of the transaction is done independently of the transaction standard (i.e. OTS, JTS, WS-AT) used by the applications. Each participant is notified depending on its associated strategy.

4   Implementation Issues

In this section, we present the ATS implementation, which is based on the Fractal component model and the GoTM framework.

4.1   The Fractal Component Model

The hierarchical Fractal component model uses the usual component, interface, and binding concepts [5]. A component is a runtime entity that conforms to the Fractal model. An interface is an interaction point expressing the provided or required methods of the component. A binding is a communication channel established between component interfaces. Furthermore, Fractal supports *recursion with sharing* and *reflective control* [13]. The recursion with sharing property means that a component can be composed of several sub-components at any level, and a component can be a sub-component of several components. The reflective control property means that an architecture built with Fractal is reified at runtime and can be dynamically introspected and managed. Fractal provides an ADL, named FractalADL, to describe and deploy automatically component-based configurations [14].

Figure 11 illustrates the different entities of a typical Fractal component architecture. Thick black boxes denote the controller part of a component, while the interior of the boxes corresponds to the content part of a component. Arrows correspond to bindings, and tau-like structures protruding from black boxes are internal or external interfaces.

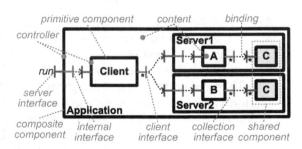

Fig. 11. The Fractal component model

Internal interfaces are only accessible from the content part of a component. A starry interface represents a collection of interfaces of the same type. The two shaded boxes **C** represent a shared component.

4.2   The GoTM Transaction Framework

Like Fractal, GoTM [4] is a project developed as part of the ObjectWeb initiative. It is a software framework that provides a set of Fractal components developed in Java and implementing generic transaction-related strategies. The static configuration of the transaction service is described using the Fractal ADL, which allows the transaction service designer to select the default strategies to use. GoTM implements efficiently various validation protocols (e.g., 2PC, 2PC-PA, and 2PC-PC) [8] and a variety of resource handlers (e.g., XAResource, Resource, and Synchronization). This list of components is not exhaustive; the GoTM framework can be extended to include new components.

The GoTM framework additionally includes different optimizations to provide good performance to the transaction services built with GoTM. These optimizations include the use of a pool of components and a caching controller to reduce the cost of component creation. GoTM uses configurable factories to describe and configure the created component instances. Finally, threading strategies (e.g., sequential, threaded, or pooled) control the propagation of messages between the components of the ATS. GoTM supports both Julia [5] and AOKell [15] implementations of the Fractal component model.

4.3   ATS Implementation with GoTM

Implementing ATS with the GoTM framework requires implementing the entities identified in Section 3 (functions, strategies, bus, etc.) with existing GoTM components when possible. GoTM provides most of the identified strategies (e.g., TwoPhaseCommit, AtomicTransactionState) as Fractal components.

The bus entity is mapped to an existing GoTM component that implements a message bus. This message bus provides various message propagation policies (e.g.: synchronous ordered, synchronous unordered or asynchronous). These policies allow implementing various 2PC protocols [8] and to provide various optimizations (e.g.: resources synchronization).

The strategy elements are mapped to similar GoTM components depending on their characteristics. As an example, the 2PC strategy is implemented by the 2PC component provided by GoTM. This composite component contains smaller components that describe the different steps of the 2PC protocol. Strategy components are composed with the message bus to form the Common Transaction Service (CTS).

The adapter components ensure the compliance with the API of each transaction standard. Therefore, the adapter components provide the standard APIs as server interfaces. The adapter component requires as client interfaces all the dependencies corresponding to the interfaces expressed in dependencies graph of Figures 3, 4 or 5. It can be easily automatically generated because all the transaction-related algorithms are implemented by strategies. To allow this generation, we use a conversion model describing how to redirect the incoming transaction standard invocations to the interfaces provided by the GoTM components (see [16] for more details).

To obtain the ATS component, the CTS component is shared between the OTS , the WS-AT and the JTS adapter components. This architecture allows the OTS, WS-AT and JTS adapters to cooperate transparently via the CTS. Figures 12 and 13 depict the resulting implementation of ATS. This implementation is composed of a *static* and a *dynamic* part. The *static* part describes the architecture of the transaction service. The *dynamic* part describes the behaviour of one transaction. Nevertheless the pattern of a common component shared between several adapter components is applied in the two parts.

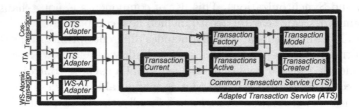

Fig. 12. An Adapted Transaction Service implementation

The *static* part of the service is depicted in Figure 12. This part corresponds to the entry point of the service. The strategies available in the static part of the CTS consist in the management of activated transactions using the `TransactionCurrent` component. The active transactions are stored in the `TransactionsActive` component. The `TransactionFactory` component provides facilities to create new instances of transactions. The transaction architecture is described in the `TransactionModel` component.

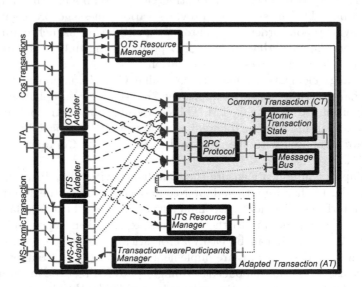

Fig. 13. An Adapted Transaction implementation

Figure 13 illustrates the model of transactions created by the transaction service. The behaviour of the transaction is grouped in the `Common Transaction` (CT). Similarly to the ATS architecture, the `Adapted Transaction` is composed of one CT and three `Adapter` components. The strategies composing the CT are GoTM components implementing the TwoPhase Commit, Atomic Transaction State, and a Message Bus. Given that JTS, WS-AT and OTS standards handle different types of resources, the associated resource managers are not placed in the CT. Finally, only the standard APIs, which are provided by the adapters, are exposed by the AT component.

4.4 Performance Analysis

This section presents a performance benchmark, which illustrates the efficiency of our approach. In particular, it shows that introducing fine-grained components to build transaction services has not a negative performance impact. ATS is compared to the JOTM 1.5.10 transaction service depending on the number of involved participants and threads. ATS uses the AOKell implementation of the Fractal component model. JOTM, a project developed as part of the ObjectWeb initiative, is a Java implementation of the JTS specification [17]. It is recognized for its reliability and efficiency. It is integrated into the JOnAS J2EE Application Server.

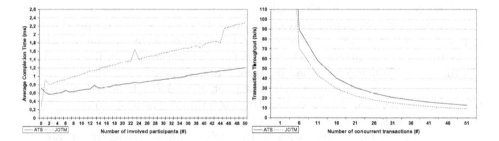

Fig. 14. Participants scalability   **Fig. 15.** Concurrent transactions

Figure 14 illustrates the result of the following scenario. A single client application creates transactions involving an increasing number of participants. The completion time of each transaction is observed depending on the number of participants. Figure 14 shows that the ATS transactions complete faster than JOTM ones. Thus, the use of a fine-grained component-based architecture does not introduce an overhead to the transaction service. This result can be explained by the optimizations available in AOKell [18].

Figure 15 applies the following scenario. An increasing number of clients create concurrent transactions involving 40 participants. The number of transactions completed per second is observed depending on the number of concurrent transactions started. Figure 15 shows that the ATS transactions complete faster than JOTM ones when the number of concurrent transactions grows. This is mainly because ATS delegates the coordination process to the transaction rather implementing this protocol at the transaction service level. This choice isolates each transaction, which completes independently. Thus, the ATS provides better scalability properties than JOTM. This speedup, estimated to 1.5 when using mock objects as transaction participants, demonstrates that the use of a fine-grained component-based transaction service introduces no additional overhead in a real application context.

5   Related Work

The Java Transaction Service (JTS) specification provides a practical solution to transaction interoperability and composition problems. Indeed JTS relies on the Object Transaction Service (OTS) to propagate transaction contexts between applications. Thus, OTS and JTS could be composed to allow heterogeneous applications to interoperate from a transactional point of view. The Arjuna Transaction Service [19] is the only transaction service that supports this architecture. Nevertheless, such a mapping is not always simple and therefore a standard may not directly depend on another one. Our approach makes abstraction of the transaction standards to avoid such dependency. Therefore, the transaction context could be propagated independently of the composed transaction standards. Moreover, our approach can be applied to consider other transaction standards (e.g., Activity Service [6,9]).

More recently, Web Services-Atomic Transactions (WS-AT) have provided an abstraction of transaction services to allow heterogeneous transaction services to be coordinated [3]. This approach extends the Web Services-Coordination (WS-Coordination) framework to handle transaction contexts [12]. Heterogeneous transaction services are reified as Participant of a global transaction service, which will act as coordinator during the execution of the validation protocol. Transaction-aware Web Services are responsible for creating a new transaction context and registering participants to the global transaction service. However, this approach requires the legacy applications to be modified to support the API introduced by the global transaction service. Our approach does not modify legacy applications because we preserve the transaction standards and we compose them rather introducing an API to support heterogeneity. Nevertheless, our approach is not orthogonal with Web Services tendency. Therefore, WS-AT can be used as an input transaction standard.

Finally, several component-based approaches have been proposed to build transaction services [20,21]. These approaches focuses on the definition of transaction services as software components to facilitate their integration in applicative systems. In this coarse-grained approach, the transaction service is encapsulated in a single component. Thus, the transaction services are hosted by a dedicated framework and made available to the application via a trading mechanism. Nevertheless, none of these works addresses the composition of the transaction standards related to the services. Our approach promotes fine-grained components, which can be reused easier than coarse-grained components to adapt the transaction service to any transaction standard.

6 Conclusion

This paper has presented an approach to build an adapted transaction service, named ATS, which supports transaction standards composition. The design of ATS has been guided by the analysis of the OTS, WS-AT and JTS transaction services. The ATS has been implemented with the GoTM framework and the Fractal component model. Our ATS implementation has been compared to the JOTM transaction service. This evaluation has shown that our approach introduces no overhead compared to existing products and supports well scalability. Our approach can be easily extended to support extended transaction standards such as Activity Services [6,9]. Consequently, the proposed solution facilitates transaction standard composition because (1) the ATS is used transparently, and (2) it increases neither complexity of existing platforms nor their performance.

Acknowledgments. This work is funded by the national institute for research in computer science and control, and the Region Nord - Pas-de-Calais.

Availability. GoTM is freely available under an LGPL licence at the following URL: http://gotm.objectweb.org.

References

1. OMG: Object Transaction Service (OTS). 1.4 edn. (2003)
2. Cheung, S.: Java Transaction Service (JTS). Sun Microsystems, Inc., San Antonio Road, Palo Alto, CA. 1.0 edn. (1999)
3. Cabrera, L.F., Copeland, G., Feingold, M. *et al.*: Web Services Atomic Transaction (WS-AtomicTransaction). 1.0 edn. (2005)
4. Rouvoy, R., Merle, P.: GoTM : Vers un canevas transactionnel à base de composants. In: Langages, Modèles et Objets Conf. (LMO). Volume 10 of L'Objet. Lille, France, Hermès Sciences (2004) 131–146
5. Bruneton, E., Coupaye, T., Leclercq, M. *et al.*: An Open Component Model and Its Support in Java. In: 7th Int. Symp. on Component-Based Software Engineering (CBSE). Volume 3054 of LNCS. Edinburgh, United Kingdom, Springer (2004) 7–22
6. Cabrera, L.F., Copeland, G., Feingold, M. *et al.*: Web Services Business Activity Framework (WS-BusinessActivity). 1.0 edn. (2005)
7. OMG: Unified Modeling Language (UML): Superstructure. 2.0 edn. (2005)
8. Serrano-Alvarado, P., Rouvoy, R., Merle, P.: Self-Adaptive Component-Based Transaction Commit Management. In: 4th Work. on Adaptive and Reflective Middleware (ARM). Volume 116 of AICPS. Grenoble, France, ACM (2005) 1–6
9. OMG: Additional Structuring Mechanisms for the OTS. 1.1 edn. (2005)
10. Eskelin, P.: Component Interaction Patterns. In: 6th Annual Conf. on the Pattern Languages of Programs (PLoP). Urbana, IL, USA (1999)
11. Wang, N., Parameswaran, K., Schmidt, D. *et al.*: The Design and Performance of Meta-Programming Mechanisms for Object Request Broker Middleware. In: 6th USENIX Conf. on Object-Oriented Technologies and Systems (COOTS). San Antonio, Texas, USA (2001)
12. Cabrera, L.F., Copeland, G., Feingold, M. *et al.*: Web Services Coordination (WS-Coordination). 1.0 edn. (2005)

13. Bruneton, E., Coupaye, T., Stefani, J.B.: Recursive and dynamic software composition with sharing. In: 7th Int. Work. on Component-Oriented Programming (WCOP). Malaga, Spain (2002)
14. Medvidovic, N., Taylor, R.: A Classification and Comparison Framework for Software Architecture Description Languages. IEEE Transactions on Software Engineering **26**(1) (2000) 70–93
15. Seinturier, L., Pessemier, N., Coupaye, T.: AOKell: An Aspect-Oriented Implementation of the Fractal Specifications. Objectweb Fractal Workshop (2005)
16. Rouvoy, R., Merle, P.: Towards a Model Driven Approach to build Component-Based Adaptable Middleware. In: 3rd Work. on Adaptive and Reflective Middleware (ARM). Volume 80 of AICPS. Toronto, Ontario, Canada, ACM (2004) 195–200
17. Mesnil, J.F.: Overview of JOTM: a Java Open Transaction Manager. In: 10th Biennal Work. on High Performance Transaction Systems (HPTS). Pacific Grove, California, USA (2003)
18. Demarey, C., Harbonnier, G., Rouvoy, R. *et al.*: Benchmarking the Round-Trip Latency of Various Java-Based Middleware Platforms. Studia Informatica Universalis Regular Issue **4**(1) (2005) 7–24
19. Little, M.: The Evolution of a Transaction Processing System. In: 11th Biennal Work. on High Performance Transaction Systems (HPTS). Pacific Grove, California, USA (2005)
20. Hérault, C., Nemchenko, S., Lecomte, S.: A Component-Based Transactional Service, Including Advanced Transactional Models. In: 5th Int. Symp. and School on Advance Distributed Systems (ISSADS). Volume 3563 of LNCS. Guadalajara, Mexico, Springer (2004) 545–556
21. Arntsen, A.B., Karlsen, R.: ReflecTS: a flexible transaction service framework. In: 4th Work. on Adaptive and Reflective Middleware (ARM). Volume 116 of AICPS. Grenoble, France, ACM (2005) 1–6

A Class-Based Object Calculus of Dynamic Binding: Reduction and Properties

Paweł T. Wojciechowski

Poznań University of Technology
60-965 Poznań, Poland
ptw@cs.put.poznan.pl

Abstract. To be able to compose and decompose software components at run time, some form of *dynamic rebinding* between components (or objects) is needed. In this paper, we identify basic properties of dynamic object (re)binding, and propose a class-based object calculus that gives precise meaning to these properties. We also define two example semantic properties that are characteristic for many concurrent programs with low-level bind/unbind operations. Our calculus has a built-in construct `atomic` that can be used to implement one of the semantic properties.

Keywords: lambda and object calculi, dynamic binding, atomicity.

1 Introduction

What do we mean by *dynamic object rebinding*? Consider a construct `bind` X a that binds a name X to an object a. The effect of binding name X to a is that we can refer to a via name X, e.g. a method m of object a can be invoked either via $a.m$ or $X.m$. The crucial point here is that the object a can be later unbound from X (using a construct `unbind` X) and another object b can be rebound to X at runtime. By the alias change, any concurrent object c that knows name X, has been therefore unbound from a and bound to b.

We must ensure that types of objects a and b that are dynamically bound to X, match the corresponding field accesses and method calls via name X. For this, X is not a pure name but it is a *signature* that declares types of fields and methods of objects that are bindable to X. Objects are defined by classes, which define fields and methods with their types. Checking the match between signatures and classes is mostly standard; for clarity, we leave therefore our calculus untyped, focusing on the operational semantics. Note that an object c invoking a method $X.m$ may not even know the object on which method m is invoked. This simple mechanism can be used to implement software components (or objects with a predefined interface) that can be *composed dynamically*.

In our previous work, we developed SAMOA [RWS06a, WRS04] – a software framework for implementing network protocols from reusable components, that provide services (a *service* corresponds to signatures presented in this paper, extended with requirement declarations). The programmers can easily encode

W. Löwe and M. Südholt (Eds.): SC 2006, LNCS 4089, pp. 131–146, 2006.

dynamic replacement of components, using high-level abstractions that are built on top of the dynamic binding feature described in this paper. A software framework, such as SAMOA, can be used for implementing dynamically composable systems. For instance, we have used our framework to design and implement an *Adaptive Group Communication (AGC)* middleware [RWS06b], in which network protocols can be replaced on-the-fly. For this, we have designed various algorithms for *Dynamic Protocol Update (DPU)*, i.e. a synchronous replacement of protocols in a distributed system [WR05].

In [RWS06a], we described the high-level architecture of a software framework for building dynamically composable systems, such as ours. In this paper, we take a more fundamental view, and investigate a small set of low-level language constructs that can be used to reason formally about dynamic object rebinding. In particular, we have used our language to give precise meaning to basic properties of dynamic object rebinding. We also define two example semantic properties that are characteristic for many concurrent programs with low-level bind/unbind operations. Our calculus has a built-in construct `atomic` that can be used to implement one of the semantic properties.

The paper is organized as follows. Section 2 introduces basic notions and defines the syntax of our calculus. Section 3 presents a set of language properties of dynamic object rebinding, and example semantic properties of programs that use the dynamic rebinding feature. To illustrate one property, Section 4 shows an example erroneous program and its fix-up. Section 5 formalizes the operational semantics of our language, thus giving precise meaning to the properties defined earlier. Section 6 presents related work. Finally, we conclude and discuss future work in Section 7.

2   The Class-Based Object Calculus

We define our language as the call-by-value λ-calculus, extended with signatures, objects, object binding/unbinding, exceptions, threads and atomic tasks. The abstract syntax of the language is in Figure 1. The main syntactic categories are signatures, classes, values and expressions. For convenience, we differentiate names: X, Y range over signature names; A, B range over class names; f ranges over object field names, and m ranges over method names. We write $\overline{x}$ as shorthand for a possibly empty sequence of variables $x_1, ..., x_n$ (and similarly for $\overline{t}$, $\overline{v}$, and $\overline{e}$). We abbreviate operations on pairs of sequences in the obvious way, writing e.g. $\overline{x} : \overline{t}$ as shorthand for $x_1 : t_1, ..., x_n : t_n$ (and similarly for $\overline{f} = \overline{v}$). Sequences of parameter names in functions and class methods are assumed to contain no duplicate names. We write $\overline{M}$ as shorthand for a (non-empty) sequence of methods $M_1, ..., M_n$ in a class. Methods of the same class must contain no duplicate names; similarly, field names are unique per class.

Types. Types include the base type `Unit` of unit expressions, which abstracts away from concrete ground types for basic constants (integers, Booleans, etc.), the type `Sig` of object signatures, the type `Obj` of objects, and the type $t \to t'$ of functions and class methods.

Variables	$x, y, a, b \in Var$	
Signature names	$X, Y \in Sig$	
Class names	$A, B \in Lab$	
Field names	f	
Method names	m	
Interface names	$n \in Sel$	$::= f \mid m$
Types	t	$::= \texttt{Unit} \mid \texttt{Sig} \mid \texttt{Obj} \mid \bar{t} \to t'$
Signatures	s	$::= \texttt{sig } X \ \{f_1 : t_1, ..., f_k : t_k,$
		$\qquad\quad m_1 : \bar{t}_1 \to t'_1, ..., m_n : \bar{t}_n \to t'_n\}$
Fun. abstractions	F	$::= \bar{x} : \bar{t} = \{e\}$
Methods	M	$::= t \ m \ F$
Classes	$C \in Class$	$::= \texttt{class } A \ \{f_1 = v_1, ..., f_k = v_k, M_1, ..., M_n\}$
Values	$v, w \in Val$	$::= () \mid X \mid \texttt{new } A \mid F$
Expressions	$e \in Exp$	$::= x \mid v \mid e.n \mid e \ e \mid \texttt{let } x = e \texttt{ in } e \mid e := e$
		$\mid \ \texttt{bind } e \ e \mid \texttt{unbind } e \mid \texttt{try } e \texttt{ catch } e \mid \texttt{escape}$
		$\mid \ \texttt{fork } e \mid \texttt{atomic } e$

We work up to alpha-conversion of expressions throughout, with $\bar{x}$ binding in e in an expression $\bar{x} : \bar{t} = \{e\}$, and x in e' in an expression $\texttt{let } x = e \texttt{ in } e'$. Names do not bind, and so are not subject to alpha-conversion.

Fig. 1. A concurrent language of dynamic object (re)binding

Signatures. A *signature* describes an *object interface*, i.e. a declaration of object fields and methods that can be accessed or called upon an object via the signature. Syntactically, a signature is a keyword $\texttt{sig}$, followed by the name of the signature, and a sequence of field and method names, accompanied with their types.

Methods. A *method* of the form $t \ m \ F$ has declarations of a type t of the values that it returns, its name m, and its body F. Access control is not modelled (all fields and methods are public). Objects can refer to their own methods with *self.m*, where *self* is a variable. A method's body is a function abstraction of the form $\bar{x} : \bar{t} = \{e\}$ (we adopted the C++ or Java notation, instead of the usual $\lambda \bar{x} : \bar{t}.e$ from the λ-calculus).

Classes. A *class* has declarations of its name (e.g. $\texttt{class } A$) and the class body $\{\bar{f} = \bar{v}, \overline{M}\}$, where $\bar{f} = \bar{v}$ is a sequence of fields (data containers) accessible via names $\bar{f}$ and instantiated to values $\bar{v}$, and $\overline{M}$ is a sequence of object methods. Classes do not explicitly declare their superclass with $\texttt{extends}$ since we do not model class inheritance. Class inheritance and object constructor methods can be easily added to the calculus definition, in the style of Featherweight Java (FJ) [IPW99]. We assume that every class implicitly extends a special class $\texttt{Object}$, like in FJ. The class $\texttt{Object}$ does not define any fields nor methods.

Values. A *value* is either an empty value () of type Unit, a signature name, e.g. X, an object instance, e.g. new A, or function abstraction $\overline{x} : \overline{t} = \{e\}$. Values are first-class, they can be passed as arguments to functions and methods, and returned as results or extruded outside objects. (Typing could be used to forbid extruding functions that contain object *self* references).

Basic expressions. Basic expressions e are mostly standard and include variables, values, field/method selectors, function/method applications, let binders, and field assignment $e := e$. The let-binder is a construct of ML-like languages, that can be used to define functions, and to bind object and immutable data to variables. For instance, let $x = $ new A in e creates a new object of class A that is bound to a variable x (where x binds in e). Then, we can write e.g. $x.f := v$ to overwrite a field f of object x with a value v, or we can write e.g. $x.m\ v$ to call a method m of object x. We use syntactic sugar $e_1; e_2$ (sequential execution) for let $x = e_1$ in e_2 (for some x, where x is fresh).

Dynamic binders and exceptions. Execution of bind $X\ a$ binds a signature X to an object a; any previous binding of signature X disappears. Execution of unbind X unbinds a signature X from any object bound to X, or raises an exception if no object is bound to X.

To catch exceptions, we have an expression try e catch e', which is similar to the one found in ML-like languages. If there was an exception thrown in e then the execution of e terminates and e' commences. Execution of try e catch e' returns either the result of e, if no exception occurred, or the result of e', if there was an exception thrown in e and no exception in e'. Exceptions can be thrown explicitly using escape, or implicitly (as in unbind). If there is no expression to catch an exception, the execution of escape blocks its thread of execution.

Threads and atomic tasks. The language allows multithreaded programs by including an expression fork e, which spawns a new thread for the evaluation of expression e. This evaluation is performed only for its effect; the result of e is never used.

Execution of atomic e creates a new concurrent thread to evaluate an expression e *atomically*; we call such expressions *tasks*. Concurrent execution of atomic tasks can be interleaved but the following property holds.

Property 1 (Isolation Property). Consider all atomic tasks in a program P, and a set N of all signatures that the tasks may refer to. A non-terminating execution of P satisfies the *isolation property*, if given any signature name X in N, the order of accessing fields or calling methods via X by the atomic tasks is the same as in an ideal execution of P in which the tasks would be executed sequentially.

An atomic task in our language can itself be multithreaded since its execution can spawn new threads using fork. The operational semantics of tasks and the atomic construct ensuring isolation will be given in Section 5.

In our previous work [Woj05], we have presented an example implementation of tasks, but for a different, more restrictive definition of isolation that considers modifications of data stores. The implementation is based on static typing and runtime *versioning*. In [WRS04], we have proposed several optimizations of the concurrency control algorithm implementing versioning.

Programs. A *program* is a pair (CT, *e*) of a class table CT and a main expression *e*, where the class table CT is a mapping from class names to class declarations. To lighten the notation, we always assume a *fixed* class table CT. To avoid uncaught exceptions we syntactically restrict the program's main expression *e* to have the form try *e′* catch *v*, where *v* is a value. We assume that a class table satisfies some sanity conditions: (1) CT(A) = class A...; (2) Object $\notin$ CT; and (3) for every class name A (except Object) appearing anywhere in CT, we have $A \in dom(\text{CT})$. Given these conditions, a class table can be easily identified with a sequence of class declarations.

3   Properties of Dynamic (Re)binding

Below we present basic properties of language constructs for binding/unbind objects in our calculus, together with some discussion of higher-level rebinding constructs that could be built on top of our calculus.

Then, we give two example semantic properties of *programs*, in which objects can be rebound dynamically. The untyped calculus presented in this paper does not have language support to declare and verify if such semantic properties hold. We leave this for future work.

3.1   Language Properties

Below are runtime properties of the language constructs. After each property, we provide a short justification of our design choice.

Property 2 (Binding Uniqueness). At run time, a signature X has two possible states: it either binds to some object or not.

This is due to the fact that we decided to have *two* language constructs: bind X v that binds a signature X to an object v, and unbind X that unbinds the signature. Our intention was to model these two operations. At the higher-level of abstraction, however, the programmers may want to have a single construct that e.g. replaces software components in one atomic step.

Property 3 (Binding Restriction). At most one object can be bound to a signature X at a time.

If more than one object could be bound to a signature X, then a method call $X.m$ would not know which object to call; similarly, a field access $X.f$ would not know which object to select. (In our language, the same field or method names can appear in different classes.) At the higher-level of abstraction, however, overwriting bindings of X could be encoded; the higher-level unbind construct could then remove the current binding and deactivate any previous binding if it exists.

Property 4 (Object Aliasing). An object can be bound to many signatures.

We allow this for expressiveness at the operational semantics. Note that $X.m$ and $Y.m$ mean something different in programs with atomic tasks, event if X and Y may bind the same object; to understand why, see the definition of the isolation property. We think that object aliasing could be useful for programmers. If any restriction is required, then it should be declared by programmers, and enforced via a type system.

Property 5 (Failures). If no object is bound to X, then unbind X fails, field access $X.f$ fails for any f, and method call $X.m$ fails for any m.

The above property with an exception mechanism built into the calculus allows for more expressiveness. We can express alternative actions on failure at the higher level of abstraction, e.g. "wait till some object is bound".

Property 6 (Concurrency). The operations of binding/unbinding a signature X, and the object field accesses or method calls via X can be concurrent.

Dynamic *re*-binding of objects in a sequential program seems to be a rarely needed feature (e.g. dynamic class loading usually occurs only on object construction). On the other hand, new emerging applications that depend on dynamic object rebinding, such as dynamic protocol updating and *adaptive systems* are often concurrent. Concurrency in these applications stems from various reasons: the old and updated protocol components may need to coexist for some time [WR05], the protocol components are themselves concurrent with the *protocol updater* [RWS06a] that dynamically rebinds the components, etc.

3.2 Semantic Properties

Below are two example properties that may be required by programs with object rebinding.

Property 7 (Reference Consistency). A set of object references $R = \{X_i.n_j : i = 1..k, j = 1..l\}$ is *consistent* in an expression e, if exists object a such that any method call or field access $X_i.n_j$ in R, as part of evaluation of e, refers to a.

In Section 4, we present an example program that requires this property. In the program, e.g. if a method call X.put has been executed upon some object, then another reference to X (a field access X.getn) in the same round of the protocol should also be executed upon the same object.

Property 8 (Signature Linearity). A signature X is *linear* in a program, if it is either unbound, or it binds the same object v during whole program execution; object v that was bound to X cannot be rebound to other signature.

If a linear signature X has been bound to some object, then it cannot be rebound to another object, and vice versa. This property could be useful in programs in which dynamic object rebinding is not a feature to mask implementations of a given signature, but to authenticate an object via a signature. If objects are communicated between machines (as part of some protocol), it may be useful to use for this an abstract signature of an object, rather than its concrete name.

4   Example of the Reference Consistency Requirement

In this section, we give a small example program to explain the need for the Reference Consistency (Property 7 in Section 3), and the use of the `atomic` construct (with the isolation property) to ensure reference consistency. The program implements a simple protocol involving the exchange of messages between a client and an anonymous server, accessible via a signature X.

The protocol uses *public key cryptography*, which can be explained as follows. The client encrypts a message m using server's public key to produce an encrypted message; only the server can decrypt this message, so this ensures secrecy. The server can sign a message m by encrypting it with its secret key (which is the inverse of the public key); any client in possession of server's public key can then decrypt this message. Public key cryptography is used, e.g. in an *authentication protocol* [Low96]).

A client obtains server's public key from a trusted key store `keyStore`, using a method `keyStore.publicKey`; the method accepts as its argument the server's name `X.getn` (see in the end of the program). The key store (omitted here) returns a public key that corresponds to this name. To send a message (a value 100) encrypted using the public key, the client invokes server's method `X.put`. Execution of `X.put` (see class A or class B) decrypts the message using server's secret key, which is stored in the object field `secretKey`.

```
sig X
{
  getn : Obj
  put : Int -> Int
}
class A
{
  getn = self      (* an object name *)
  secretKey = 1    (* a secret key of A *)
  Int put (v : Int) = { decrypt (v, self.secretKey) }
}
class B
{
  getn = self      (* an object name *)
  secretKey = 2    (* a secret key of B *)
  Int put (v : Int) = { decrypt (v, self.secretKey) }
}

class Updater
{
  Unit update (x : Sig, o : Obj) =
  {
    unbind x;   (* unbind signature x from any object *)
    bind x o;   (* bind signature x to object o *)
  }
}
```

```
let a = new A in    (* create object a *)
bind X a;           (* and binds sig X to a *)
let b = new B in    (* create object b *)
fork (new Updater).update(X, b);   (* rebind X to b *)
try
   X.put (encrypt(100, keyStore.publicKey(X.getn)))   (* The client *)
catch
   0
```

Exchange of an encrypted message between server X and the client occurs in parallel with *dynamic replacement* of the actual object implementing X. For this, we have an *updater* object Updater, with a single method update that implements a simple handover protocol: it takes as arguments a signature and an object, unbinds anything bound to the signature and binds the object. (For simplicity, we require that X is initially bound.)

In the main expression, a concurrent thread (created with fork) calls a method update that unbinds a server object a (bound to X) and binds server object b to X. The client does not know if it calls a or b; it is not aware of the hot-swapping done by the updater. The program is however problematic in twofold ways. Firstly, the client may call a server using a signature X that has been unbound by the update method and not rebound yet, thus leading to an exception error. Secondly, the following property is not true:

Property 9 (Safety). A message encrypted with a public key of object x is also received by x (for any x).

We would like this property to hold during program execution. Otherwise, the client may encrypt and send a message to the server using a public key of another server, which is like an attack on a protocol using public key cryptography.

To fix up our program, we can use the atomic construct to encode the message exchange protocol (initiated by the client) and the update protocol (in the update method) as two parallel atomic tasks. Below is an example code:

```
class Updater
{
  Unit update (x : Sig, o : Obj) =
  {
    atomic
       (unbind x;    (* unbind signature x from any object *)
        bind x o;)   (* and bind signature x to object o atomically *)
  }
}
let a = new A in    (* create object a *)
bind X a;           (* and binds sig X to a *)
let b = new B in    (* create object b *)
fork (new Updater).update(X, b);   (* rebind X to b *)
try
   atomic X.put (encrypt(100, keyStore.publicKey(X.getn)))  (* The client *)
catch
   0
```

The advantage of `atomic` with respect to coarse-grain locking is that the client-server protocol and server updating can be executed concurrently. Moreover possible deadlocks are avoided, which simplifies programming. However, isolation ensured by `atomic` is actually a stronger property than reference consistency – atomic tasks that do not do object rebinding may also be mutually isolated, even if they cannot themselves invalidate reference consistency.

The use of `atomic` in protocols depends on its implementation. Protocols have various side effects (I/O actions, network communication, etc.); these side-effects are not always revocable. The implementations of `atomic` (we give examples in Section 6) usually restrict I/O actions in atomic blocks, e.g. due to rollback support. This restriction should not be a problem if `atomic` is used to protect only short code fragments, as in our example program. Alternatively, we proposed in [Woj05] an implementation of `atomic` that does not depend on rollback-recovery of tasks. (We do not have an explicit rollback construct in our language.)

5   Operational Semantics

We specify the operational semantics of our language using the abstract machine defined in Figures 2 and 3. The machine evaluates a program by stepping through a sequence of states. A state S consists of four components: an object store Δ, a counter α of fresh atomic blocks, a bind store β, and execution threads T, organized as a sequence $T_0, ..., T_n$.

The *object store* Δ is a finite map from object field selectors to values stored in the fields, where a *field selector*, denoted $o_A.f$, is an object location o_A indexed by a field name f.

The *bind store* β is a set of pairs (X, o^A) of a signature name X and an object location o^A bound to the signature. The set difference $\beta \setminus \beta'$ is the set of elements found in β but not found in β'; the union of sets $\beta \cup \beta'$ is the set consisting of the elements of both sets, with no duplicate elements.

The expressions g in a sequence of threads T are written in the calculus presented in Section 2, extended with a new construct `task` $i\ N\ T$. The construct is not part of the language to be used by programmers; its meaning will be explained below.

We define a small-step evaluation relation $\Delta, \alpha, \beta \mid g \longrightarrow \Delta', \alpha', \beta' \mid g'$, read "expression g reduces to expression g' in one step, with Δ, α, β being transformed to Δ', α', β'". We also use $\longrightarrow^*$ for a sequence of small-step reductions. By *concurrent execution*, we mean a sequence of small-step reductions in which the reduction steps can be taken by different threads with possible interleaving.

Reductions are defined using evaluation context $\mathcal{E}$ for expressions e and g. The evaluation context ensures that the left-outermost reduction is the only applicable reduction for each individual thread in the entire program. Context application is denoted by [], as in $\mathcal{E}[e]$. Structural congruence rules allow us to simplify reduction rules by removing the context whenever possible.

Evaluation of a program (CT, e), where CT is constant, starts in an initial state with empty stores $\emptyset$, a null counter 0, and with a single thread that evaluates

State Space:

$$
\begin{array}{lll}
S \in State & = & ObjStore \times TaskId \times BindStore \times ThreadSeq \\
\Delta \in ObjStore & = & ObjLoc.Sel \rightarrow Val \\
\alpha \in TaskId & = & \mathbf{Nat} \\
\beta \in BindStore & = & Sig \times ObjLoc \\
o^A \in ObjLoc & \subset & Var \\
T \in ThreadSeq & ::= & g \mid T, T \\
g \in Exp_{ext} & ::= & x \mid v \mid e.n \mid e\, e \mid \mathbf{let}\ x = e\ \mathbf{in}\ e \mid e := e \mid \mathbf{bind}\ e\, e \mid \mathbf{unbind}\ e \\
& & \mid\ \mathbf{try}\ e\ \mathbf{catch}\ e \mid \mathbf{escape} \mid \mathbf{fork}\ e \mid \mathbf{atomic}\ e \mid \mathbf{task}\ i\ N\ T
\end{array}
$$

Evaluation Contexts:

$$
\begin{aligned}
\mathcal{E} = {}& [\,] \mid \mathcal{E}.n \mid \mathcal{E}\, e \mid v\, \mathcal{E} \mid \mathbf{let}\ x = \mathcal{E}\ \mathbf{in}\ e \mid \mathcal{E} := e \mid o^A.f := \mathcal{E} \mid \mathbf{bind}\ \mathcal{E}\, e \mid \mathbf{bind}\ X\ \mathcal{E} \\
& \mid\ \mathbf{try}\ \mathcal{E}\ \mathbf{catch}\ e \mid \mathbf{task}\ i\ N\ \mathcal{E} \mid \mathcal{E}, T \mid T, \mathcal{E}
\end{aligned}
$$

Structural Congruence

$$
T, T' \equiv T', T \qquad T, (\,) \equiv T
$$

$$
\frac{\Delta, \alpha, \beta \mid g \longrightarrow \Delta', \alpha', \beta' \mid g'}{\Delta, \alpha, \beta \mid \mathcal{E}[g] \longrightarrow \Delta', \alpha', \beta' \mid \mathcal{E}[g']} \qquad \frac{g \longrightarrow g'}{\Delta, \alpha, \beta \mid g \longrightarrow \Delta, \alpha, \beta \mid g'}
$$

Transition Relation

$$
eval \subseteq ((Lab \rightarrow Class) \times Exp) \times Val
$$
$$
eval((\mathrm{CT}, e), v_0) \Leftrightarrow \emptyset, 0, \emptyset \mid e \longrightarrow^* \Delta, \alpha, \beta \mid v_0, (\,), \cdots, (\,)
$$

Method Body Lookup:

$$
\frac{\mathrm{CT}(A) = \mathtt{class}\ A\ \{\overline{f} = \overline{v}, \overline{M}\} \qquad t\ m\ F \in \overline{M}}{mbody(m, A) = F}
$$

Fig. 2. Reduction semantics - Part I

the expression e. Evaluation then takes place according to the machine's rules in Figure 3. The evaluation terminates once all threads have been reduced to values, in which case the value v_0 of the initial, first thread T_0 is returned as the program's result. Subscripts in values reduced from threads denote the sequence number of the thread, i.e. v_i is reduced from i's thread, denoted T_i ($i = 0, 1, ..$). The execution of threads can be arbitrarily interleaved.

5.1   Reduction Rules

Below we describe reduction rules in Figure 3. The first two evaluation rules are the standard rules of a call-by-value λ-calculus [Plo75]. We write $e\{\overline{v}/\overline{x}\}$ to denote the capture-free substitution of v_i for x_i in the expression e ($i = 1, .., n$). Function application $\overline{x} : \overline{t} = \{e\}\ \overline{v}$ in (R-App) reduces to the function's body e in

$$\overline{x} : \overline{t} = \{e\}\ \overline{v} \longrightarrow e\{\overline{v}/\overline{x}\} \tag{R-App}$$

$$\texttt{let } x = v \texttt{ in } e \longrightarrow e\{v/x\} \tag{R-Let}$$

$$\frac{\begin{array}{c} o^A \notin dom(\Delta) \\ \textsc{ct}(A) = \texttt{class } A\ \{f_1 = v_1, ..., f_k = v_k, \overline{M}\} \\ \Delta' = (\Delta, o^A.f_1 \mapsto v_1, ..., o^A.f_k \mapsto v_k) \end{array}}{\Delta, \alpha, \beta\ |\ \texttt{new } A \longrightarrow \Delta', \alpha, \beta\ |\ o^A} \tag{R-New}$$

$$\Delta, \alpha, \beta\ |\ o^A.f := v \longrightarrow \Delta[o^A.f \mapsto v], \alpha, \beta\ |\ () \tag{R-Assign}$$

$$\Delta, \alpha, \beta\ |\ o^A.f \longrightarrow \Delta, \alpha, \beta\ |\ v\{o^A/self\} \quad \text{if}\ \ \Delta(o^A.f) = v \tag{R-Field}$$

$$\frac{mbody(m, A) = F}{o^A.m\ \overline{v} \longrightarrow F\{o^A/self\}\ \overline{v}} \tag{R-Invk}$$

$$\texttt{try } v \texttt{ catch } e \longrightarrow v \tag{R-Try}$$

$$\frac{\texttt{try..catch} \notin \mathcal{E}'}{\texttt{try } \mathcal{E}'[\,\texttt{escape}\,] \texttt{ catch } e \longrightarrow e} \tag{R-Esc}$$

$$\Delta, \alpha, \beta\ |\ \texttt{bind } X\ o^A \longrightarrow \Delta, \alpha, (\beta \setminus \{(X, \cdot)\}) \cup \{(X, o^A)\}\ |\ () \tag{R-Bind}$$

$$\Delta, \alpha, \beta\ |\ \texttt{unbind } X \longrightarrow \Delta, \alpha, \beta \setminus \{(X, o^A)\}\ |\ () \quad \text{if}\ (X, o^A) \in \beta \tag{R-Unbind1}$$

$$\Delta, \alpha, \beta\ |\ \texttt{unbind } X \longrightarrow \texttt{escape} \quad \text{if}\ (X, \cdot) \notin \beta \tag{R-Unbind2}$$

$$\Delta, \alpha, \beta\ |\ X.n \longrightarrow \Delta, \alpha, \beta\ |\ o^A.n \quad \text{if}\ (X, o^A) \in \beta \tag{R-Lookup1}$$

$$\Delta, \alpha, \beta\ |\ X.n \longrightarrow \Delta, \alpha, \beta\ |\ \texttt{escape} \quad \text{if}\ (X, \cdot) \notin \beta \tag{R-Lookup2}$$

$$\frac{N = \{X \in Sig\ :\ X \in e\}}{\Delta, \alpha, \beta\ |\ \mathcal{E}[\,\texttt{atomic } e\,] \longrightarrow \Delta, \alpha + 1, \beta\ |\ \mathcal{E}[()], \texttt{task } \alpha + 1\ N\ e} \tag{R-Atomic}$$

$$\mathcal{E}[\,\texttt{fork } e\,] \longrightarrow \mathcal{E}[()], e \tag{R-Fork1}$$

$$\texttt{task } i\ N\ \mathcal{E}[\,\texttt{fork } e\,] \longrightarrow \texttt{task } i\ N\ (\mathcal{E}[()], e) \tag{R-Fork2}$$

$$\frac{\begin{array}{c} \texttt{task } i\ N\ e \in \mathcal{E}\quad i < j \\ X \in N \cap M\quad X \notin e\quad (X, o^A) \in \beta \end{array}}{\Delta, \alpha, \beta\ |\ \mathcal{E}[\,\texttt{task } j\ M\ \mathcal{E}'[X.n]\,] \longrightarrow \Delta, \alpha, \beta\ |\ \mathcal{E}[\,\texttt{task } j\ M\ \mathcal{E}'[o^A.n]\,]} \tag{R-Task1}$$

$$\texttt{task } i\ N\ v \longrightarrow () \tag{R-Task2}$$

$$v_i, v_j' \longrightarrow v_i \quad \text{if}\ i < j \tag{R-Thread}$$

Fig. 3. Reduction semantics - Part II

which formal arguments $\overline{x}$ are replaced with the actual arguments $\overline{v}$. Execution of let $x = v$ in e in (R-Let) reduces the whole expression to the expression e in which variable x is replaced by value v.

Execution of new A creates a new object of class A. The object is identified by a fresh object location o_A, and represented by a new record of object fields $f_1, ..., f_k$ in the object store Δ; see the (R-New) rule. The notation $(\Delta, \overline{o^A.f \mapsto \overline{v}})$ means "the store that maps $\overline{o^A.f}$ to $\overline{v}$ and maps all other selectors to the same thing as Δ". The object fields $f_1, .., f_k$ are accessible via the object location o_A, e.g. $o_A.f_i$ ($i = 1..k$) refers to a field f_i of object o_A. The object fields in the object record are initialized with field values $v_1, .., v_k$ defined by class A.

Rules (R-Assign) and (R-Field) correspondingly, assign a new value v to the field f of an object o^A, and read the current value stored in an object field $o^A.f$. For instance, let us look at the rule (R-Assign). We use the notation $\Delta[o^A.f \mapsto v]$ to denote update of map Δ at $o^A.f$ to v. Note that the term resulting from this evaluation step is just (); the interesting result is the updated store. The (R-Assign) rule must be applied first, if not possible then we try (R-Field).

Similarly to FJ, the invocation $o^A.m \ \overline{v}$ of a method m of an object o^A applies the beta-reduction rule from the call-by-value λ-calculus; see the (R-Invk) rule. The rule first looks up in the class table CT a method body F of the form $\overline{x} : \overline{t} = \{e\}$ (using a function $mbody(m, A)$ defined in the bottom of Figure 2); then, it reduces to the method body in which $self$ is replaced by the receiver o^A. Then, the application rule (R-App) (described earlier) can be used, which applies the arguments $\overline{v}$ to the method m.

Exceptions are defined using two rules. The (R-Try) rule defines the case when no exception was thrown; it simply reduces the whole expression try ... catch with the body reduced to a value v to the value v; the catch clause is discarded. To throw an exception, the escape construct is used. If escape is in the redex position of the expression e' in the body of the innermost try e' catch e, the (R-Esc) rule reduces try e' catch e to the exception handler e.

Dynamic binder bind $X \ o^A$ in rule (R-Bind) removes from store β any previous binding $(X, \cdot)$ of a signature X, and extends β with a new element of X paired with an object location o^A. The whole expression reduces to the empty value (). Dynamic unbinder unbind X in rules (R-Unbind1) and (R-Unbind2) respectively, removes the binding $(X, \cdot)$ from store β and reduces to the empty value (), or throwns an exception with escape if no binding of X exists.

Dynamic resolver $X.n$ in rules (R-Lookup1) and (R-Lookup2) respectively, returns the field/method selector $o^A.n$, where o^A is the object location currently bound to a signature X, or throwns an exception if no binding of X exists.

5.2   Concurrent and Atomic Evaluations

Execution of an expression atomic e creates a new thread for evaluation of a *task* e with the isolation property, defined in Section 2. The task has the syntactic form task $i \ N \ e$, where i is the sequence number of the task, and N is a set of all signatures X that *may* be referred to by expression e. The (R-Atomic) rule reduces an expression $\mathcal{E}[\,\mathtt{atomic}\ e\,]$ to the context $\mathcal{E}$ with the empty value () in the redex position, and a new thread evaluating a task $\mathtt{task}\ \alpha + 1\ N\ e$; the rule also increments the task counter α.

Execution of an expression $\mathtt{fork}\ e$ in (R-Fork1) creates a new thread which evaluates e; the result of evaluating expression e will be discarded by rule (R-Thread); threads may however have side-effects, e.g. modification of object fields. Tasks can spawn their own threads using $\mathtt{fork}$; see rule (R-Fork2).

The (R-Task1) rule specifies evaluation of concurrent tasks that satisfies the isolation property. Consider evaluation of some task $\mathtt{task}\ j\ M\ e'$ in the context $\mathcal{E}$, where the redex position of expression e' is a field or method access via a signature X, i.e. $e' = \mathcal{E}'[\,X.n\,]$ for some context $\mathcal{E}'$ and an interface name n. If context $\mathcal{E}$ is such that there is some *older* concurrent task $\mathtt{task}\ i\ N\ e$ (i.e. $i < j$) that evaluates some expression e and may refer to X (since X is declared in set N), then the rule (R-Task1) applies. It reduces the expression $\mathtt{task}\ j\ M\ e'$ by replacing X by a concrete object location o^A if two conditions hold: (1) e cannot refer to X anymore (i.e. $X \notin e$), and (2) there is actually some binding of X in bind store β. If X is in e then the rule does not apply, and the other task may be evaluated. If no binding of X exists, the rule (R-Lookup2) applies.

Once evaluation of an expression e of task $\mathtt{task}\ i\ N\ e$ yields a value, the rule (R-Task2) returns the empty value as the result of the whole thread. The results of evaluating threads (except of the initial thread) are discarded by (R-Thread).

6 Related Work

Object calculi. There have been many proposals of various object calculi; we sketch some of the most known examples below.

Abadi and Cardelli [AC95] have developed an imperative calculus of objects, equipped with an operational semantics and typing (and subtyping); with addition of polymorphism, the calculus can express classes and inheritance. The object calculus of Gordon and Hankin [GH98] extends Abadi and Cardelli's imperative object calculus with operators for concurrency from the π-calculus and operators for synchronization based on mutexes. Our calculus also has a synchronization abstraction built-in (the $\mathtt{atomic}$ construct), albeit semantically richer than mutexes; we discuss the related work on atomicity below.

Igarashi, Pierce and Wadler [IPW99] have proposed a small calculus, Featherweight Java (FJ), that provides classes, methods, fields, inheritance, and dynamic typecasts, with semantics closely following Java's. The design of our calculus has been inspired by FJ, e.g. we have the same rule for method calls, which uses the call-by-value principle of the λ-calculus. However, their calculus omits interfaces and even assignment, while we have assignment and also signatures (which are similar to Java interfaces). On the other hand, we do not model typing and class inheritance in this paper since our focus is on the reduction semantics.

The above calculi have been developed mainly to reason about the implementation of objects, object encodings, typing, class inheritance, etc. We are not aware of concurrent object calculi that would have constructs for dynamic object rebinding similar to ours. We discuss some examples of (non-object) calculi with dynamic binding in the next paragraph.

Dynamic rebinding.   A lot of work on dynamic rebinding appeared in the context of functional languages (see, e.g., work of Moreau [Mor98]), focusing either on *dynamic scoping*, in which variable occurrences are resolved with respect to their dynamic environment, or *static scoping with explicit rebinding*, where variables are resolved with respect to their static environment, but additional primitives can be used to explicitly modify these environments.

Dynamic scoping exists in most modern dialects of Lisp, e.g. MIT Scheme's `fluid-let` [MIT] construct performs dynamically-scoped rebinding of local and global variables; once the construct's expression has been evaluated, the values of the variables are restored. The *quasi-static scoping* Scheme extension of Lee and Friedman [LF93] has a class of variables, which are initially unresolved. The programmer can use a rebinding primitive to specify new bindings for individual variables. The above work is different from ours; we bind whole objects to typed signatures, while the above work is on dynamic binding of variables in functional languages, with a correspondingly different semantics of rebinding.

Dynamic linking of objects in object languages such as Java, refers to resolving object components at runtime. However, once bound the code usually cannot be rebound, which is different from our approach, which aims at studying object *re*-binding. Different dynamic linking models have been described in [DLE03].

There are different applications of dynamic rebinding. For instance, Bierman *et al.* [BHS+03] proposed abstraction-safe *marshalling* and *unmarshalling* (or rebinding) values between separate programs in the λ-calculus; see also the Acute programming language [LPSW03]. An extension of Smalltalk with dynamic method redefinition in the scope of *classboxes* is described in [BDW03]; the dynamic rebinding feature is used here to support *software evolution*.

We are not aware of much discussion of concurrency issues in the context of dynamic rebinding. The existing implementations are often not satisfactory, e.g. the runtime support of type-safe dynamic Java classes in [MPG+00] aborts a thread if a class update is attempted while the thread is executing a method of that class. Our solution to this problem is to execute rebindable code fragments and code fragments that do rebinding, as concurrent (possibly multithreaded) atomic tasks, using the `atomic` construct. The semantics of the construct given in this paper eliminates the need to abort threads while doing an update.

Atomicity.   Below we sketch some work on formalizing the isolation property (also known as *atomicity* in the programming language research community), with the semantics as in transactional systems; such semantics is slightly different than the one presented in this paper. We are not aware of any formal work on using isolation (or atomicity) in the context of dynamic binding.

Vitek *et al.* [VJWH04] have recently proposed a calculi-based model of standard database transactions. They have formalized the optimistic and two-phase locking concurrency control strategies. Their approach to formalization of the isolation property is similar to ours, in the sense that both specifications refer to *order* (or scheduling) of concurrent actions.

There have recently been a lot of interest in developing language support for atomicity. For example, Flanagan and Qadeer [FQ03] presented a type system for specifying and verifying atomicity of (single threaded) methods in multithreaded Java programs. The type system is a synthesis of Lipton's theory of left and right movers (for proving properties of parallel programs) and type systems for race detection.

Harris and Fraser [HF03] have been investigating an extension of Java with (again, sequential only) atomic code blocks that implement conditional critical regions (CCRs). The programmer can guard a conditional region by an arbitrary boolean condition, with calling threads blocking until the guard is satisfied. It is also possible to terminate an execution of an atomic block and rollback, if some condition is not satisfied.

In [Woj05], we have discussed the above implementation work in more detail, including comparison with our approach to atomicity.

7 Conclusion

In this paper, we proposed a class-based object calculus with constructs for dynamic rebinding of objects to signatures; signatures describe types of object fields and methods, and can be used to call the objects. We have also discussed properties of the bind/unbind constructs.

Dynamic object binding enables developing novel applications, such as dynamic service update (as in our example). However, it also makes programming more difficult, since additional *semantic* properties may be required by programs. We have discussed an example semantic property, called reference consistency, and showed how it can be encoded using the atomic construct of our calculus that ensures isolation.

In the future work, we would like to develop tools for automatic verification of certain properties of dynamic binding/unbinding, based on the typed variant of the calculus presented in this paper.

Acknowledgments. The author would like to thank Olivier Rütti and Sophia Drossopoulou (and other members of the SLURP group) for discussions and comments. This work was supported in part by the State Committee for Scientific Research (KBN), Poland, under KBN grant 3 T11C 073 28.

References

[AC95]   Martin Abadi and Luca Cardelli. An imperative object calculus. In *Proc. TAPSOFT '95: Theory and Practice of Software Development, the 6th International Joint Conference CAAP/FASE*, LNCS 915, May 1995.

[BDW03]   Alexandre Bergel, Stéphane Ducasse, and Roel Wuyts. Classboxes: A minimal module model supporting local rebinding. In *Proc. JMLC '03: the Joint Modular Languages Conference*, LNCS 2789. Springer, August 2003.

[BHS+03]   Gavin Bierman, Michael Hicks, Peter Sewell, Gareth Stoyle, and Keith Wansbrough. Dynamic rebinding for marshalling and update, with destruct-time lambda. In *Proc. ICFP '03*, August 2003.

[DLE03]   Sophia Drossopoulou, Giovanni Lagorio, and Susan Eisenbach. Flexible models for dynamic linking. In *Proc. ESOP '03*, April 2003.

[FQ03]   Cormac Flanagan and Shaz Qadeer. A type and effect system for atomicity. In *Proc. PLDI '03*, June 2003.

[GH98]   Andrew D. Gordon and Paul D. Hankin. A concurrent object calculus: Reduction and typing. In *Proc. HLCL'98: the 3rd Int'l Workshop on High-Level Concurrent Languages*, Elsevier ENTCS 16(3), 1998.

[HF03]   Timothy Harris and Keir Fraser. Language support for lightweight transactions. In *Proc. OOPSLA '03*, 2003.

[IPW99]   Atshushi Igarashi, Benjamin Pierce, and Philip Wadler. Featherweight Java: A minimal core calculus for Java and GJ. In *Proc. OOPSLA '99*, Nov. 1999.

[LF93]   Shinn-Der Lee and Daniel P. Friedman. Quasi-static scoping: Sharing variable bindings across multiple lexical scopes. In *Proc. POPL '93*, Jan 1993.

[Low96]   Gavin Lowe. Breaking and fixing the Needham-Schroeder public-key protocol using FDR. In *Proc. TACAS '96: Workshop on Tools and Algorithms for the Construction and Analysis of Systems*, LNCS 1055, March 1996.

[LPSW03]   James Leifer, Gilles Peskine, Peter Sewell, and Keith Wansbrough. Global abstraction-safe marshalling with hash types. In *Proc. ICFP '03*, 2003.

[MIT]   MIT. *Scheme.* http://www.swiss.ai.mit.edu/projects/scheme/.

[Mor98]   Luc Moreau. A syntactic theory of dynamic binding. *Higher-Order and Symbolic Computation*, 11(3):233–279, December 1998.

[MPG+00]   Scott Malabarba, Raju Pandey, Jeff Gragg, Earl Barr, and J. Fritz Barnes. Runtime support for type-safe dynamic Java classes. In *Proc. ECOOP 2000*, LNCS 1850, June 2000.

[Plo75]   Gordon D. Plotkin. Call-by-name, call-by-value and the λ-calculus. *Theoretical Computer Science*, 1:125–159, 1975.

[RWS06a]   Olivier Rütti, Paweł T. Wojciechowski, and André Schiper. Service Interface: A new abstraction for implementing and composing protocols. In *Proc. SAC '06: the 21st ACM Symposium on Applied Computing, Track on Dependable and Adaptive Distributed Systems*, April 2006.

[RWS06b]   Olivier Rütti, Paweł T. Wojciechowski, and André Schiper. Structural and algorithmic issues of dynamic protocol update. In *Proc. IPDPS '06: the 20th IEEE Int'l Parallel and Distributed Processing Symposium*, April 2006.

[VJWH04]   Jan Vitek, Suresh Jagannathan, Adam Welc, and Antony L. Hosking. A semantic framework for designer transactions. In *Proc. ESOP '04*, LNCS 2986, March/April 2004.

[Woj05]   Paweł T. Wojciechowski. Isolation-only transactions by typing and versioning. In *Proc. PPDP '05: the 7th ACM-SIGPLAN Int'l Symposium on Principles and Practice of Declarative Programming*, July 2005.

[WR05]   Paweł T. Wojciechowski and Olivier Rütti. On correctness of dynamic protocol update. In *Proc. FMOODS '05*, LNCS 3535, June 2005.

[WRS04]   Paweł T. Wojciechowski, Olivier Rütti, and André Schiper. SAMOA: A framework for a synchronisation-augmented microprotocol approach. In *Proc. IPDPS '04: the 18th IEEE Int'l Parallel and Distributed Processing Symposium*, April 2004.

Tracechecks: Defining Semantic Interfaces with Temporal Logic

Eric Bodden and Volker Stolz

Software Modeling and Verification (MOVES)
RWTH Aachen University, 52056 Aachen, Germany
{bodden, stolz}@i2.informatik.rwth-aachen.de

Abstract. *Tracechecks* are a formalism based on linear temporal logic (LTL) with variable bindings and pointcuts of the aspect-oriented language AspectJ for the purpose of verification. We demonstrate how tracechecks can be used to model *temporal assertions*. These assertions reason about the dynamic control flow of an application. They can be used to formally define the semantic interface of classes. We explain in detail how we make use of AspectJ pointcuts to derive a formal model of an existing application and use LTL to express temporal assertions over this model.

We developed a reference implementation with the abc compiler showing that the tool can be applied in practice and is memory-efficient.

In addition we show how tracechecks can be deployed as Java5 annotations, yielding a system which is fully compliant with any Java compiler and hiding any peculiarities of aspect-oriented programming from the user. Through annotations, the tracecheck specifications become a semantic part of an interface. Consumers of such a component can then take advantage of the contained annotations by applying our tool and have their use of this component automatically checked at runtime for compliance with the intent of the component provider.

1 Introduction

Existing programs, especially large-scale applications, do not only consist of their code base and documentation. In object-oriented programs, often there exist implicit constraints e.g. in library APIs on how methods or fields may be used. Apart from simple constraints like that certain parameters must never be null, there are more complex limitations that e.g. some methods may only be invoked in special circumstances, like in a specific order. Sometimes these constraints are already checked through assertions. But the unwary developer may be tripped up by many more patterns which are only informally documented and not enforced. For example in the Java5 libraries, if a collection is added to a hash set, the set does not notice changes to the elements themselves and may hence return unsound results.

In this work we present *tracechecks*, a formalism which we consider well suited to specify such temporal relations. The proposed semantic framework is based on *linear temporal logic* (LTL) [17], which is widely known in the field of formal verification, and is often used for static Model Checking [7].

W. Löwe and M. Südholt (Eds.): SC 2006, LNCS 4089, pp. 147–162, 2006.

The first step in Model Checking is usually to derive a formal semantic model from an existing application. This model is then checked for correctness with respect to some temporal specification (e.g. in LTL). Quite often it happens that the semantic model is unsound or incomplete with respect to the actual behaviour of the implementation.

Our approach is novel in the sense that we restrict ourselves to a partial model (the one induced by a *run*) and use AspectJ to derive this partial model. The primitives of our temporal logic are AspectJ pointcuts, picking out join-points in the dynamic control flow of a Java application. That way the model is known to match the implementation because they actually coincide at well-defined points—the joinpoints. Section 2 gives two motivating examples where tracechecks enforce temporal constraints on Java interfaces. In Section 3 we explain how we derive a semantic model of an existing application using AspectJ and how LTL can be used to state *temporal assertions* over this model. We show that the model is a system where transitions are triggered by pointcuts. In Section 4 we present the syntax of tracechecks and give their semantics by example. In particular, tracechecks can access and bind objects as the application runs, hence providing a means of instance-based reasoning. Section 5 discusses details about our reference implementation as well as performance and deployment issues important to component-based software development. We also comment on possible usage scenarios and conclude with a discussion of related work.

2   Motivation

Component based software has much evolved during the last years. Where some decades ago a piece of software often existed of few large chunks of code with little recognizable structure, today we have programming languages and tool support for properly maintaining independent components—modules—on their own. This modular reasoning has lead to safer software which is easier to maintain and easier to evolve.

Yet, we find that modules as they are today lack important specification features to be fully reusable, as they are frequently only syntactically defined through their programming language interfaces. This induces a purely static view. A feature f can be accessed through a module m if and only if f is in the signature of m and if it *can* be accessed, one can usually do so at *any time*. (Sometimes exceptions are used to forbid certain access patterns but we see this as quite a cumbersome low-level solution to the problem.)

We found that this static view can lead to trouble when software is actually run. Frequently it can happen that certain functionality is only available at certain points in time when an application executes, or in other words: at certain times at runtime, certain features should *not* be allowed to be accessed for the sake of a safe and stable application.

For example, nothing should be written to an output stream, if the stream has been closed before. Such errors may be documented in APIs in the form of comments, but still the user of the output stream component has to remember

```
1   tracecheck(Collection c, Iterator i) {
2
3     sym iterator(Collection c, Iterator i) after returning (i):
4         call(Collection+.iterator()) && target(c)
5     sym modify(Collection c) after returning:
6         (call(Collection+.add(..)) || call(Collection+.remove(..))) && target(c)
7     sym next(Iterator i) before:
8         call(Iterator.next()) && target(i)
9
10    G( iterator(c,i) -> G(modify(c) -> G(!next(i))) ) {
11        throw new ConcurrentModificationException ("Collection "+c+" modified!");
12    }
13  }
```

Fig. 1. Safe iterator tracecheck

to obey this rule in order to get a safely working application. With tracechecks, such temporal assertions can be specified *right in place* and *can automatically be checked* at runtime. To further emphasize this dynamic view we would like to give a code example.

2.1 Safe Iterators

As a motivation, let us start with the *safe iterator*-pattern, which states that:

> For each Iterator i obtained from a Collection c, there must never be an invocation of i.next() after the collection has been modified.

This pattern is actually enforced in the Java5 library as follows. The *Iterator* implementation contains a mechanism to track modifications of the underlying collection by means of a modification counter. If the collection c is updated, the modification-count obtained by the iterator i on instantiation time and the current counter of the collection disagree and lead to an exception on the next access to the iterator. In this case, the specification has crept into the implementation of both the iterator and the collection.

With this work we introduce *tracechecks*, a formalism and tool to formulate such trace conditions and automatically check their violation at runtime. Java interfaces and classes (as well as AspectJ aspects) can be annotated with tracechecks to define their behaviour with respect to the execution timeline.

In our formalism the requirement from above can be specified *in a modular way* through the tracecheck in Figure 1. Line 1 declares the free variables c and i that *each* collection and iterator in question will be bound to. Lines 3–9 declare three symbols *iterator*, *modify* and *next*, which match the relevant joinpoints through pointcuts. The actual formula (expressed in LTL, see below) is stated in line 10, specifying through the outer "Globally" that this assertion should be checked on the whole execution path (and hence for *all* created iterators). For each iterator (left-hand side of the outer implication), we require of the

```
1   tracecheck(HashSet s, Collection c) {
2
3     sym add(HashSet s, Collection c) after returning:
4        call(HashSet+.add(..)) && target(s) && args(c))
5     sym modify(Collection c) after returning:
6        (call(Collection+.add(..))  ||  call(Collection+.remove(..))) && target(c)
7     sym remove(HashSet s, Collection c) after returning:
8        call(HashSet+.remove(..)) && target(s) && args(c))
9     sym contains(HashSet s, Collection c) before:
10        HashSet+.contains(..)) && target(s) && args(c))
11
12    G( add(s,c) -> G( modify(c) -> remove(s,c) R (!contains(s,c))) ) {
13      throw new ConcurrentModificationException (c+" modified while in "+s);
14    }
15  }
```

Fig. 2. Tracecheck detecting inconsistent use of collections and hash sets

remainder of the execution that after a call to *add* or *remove* no call to *i.next()* must occur. The body is executed for any instance that violates the formula. We have successfully validated this formula in practice. All examples are available on our project web-page http://www-i2.informatik.rwth-aachen.de/JLO/.

2.2   Unsafe Use of HashSets

Another practical application of our framework is based on an actual bug pattern observed by colleagues. When a collection is inserted into a *HashSet*, modifications to the contained collections influence the result of *HashSet.contains*-queries. This behaviour was not anticipated and led to unexpected results. While this is only arguably a bug but rather a mistake, the source code had to be screened for possible uses under the wrong assumptions. In this case, the JDK does not provide any builtin mechanism to detect such behaviour. We captured it in the following way:

For each HashSet s that contains a Collection c, there must be no invocation of s.contains(c) if the collection has been modified, unless the collection has been removed from the set in between.

With tracechecks, specifying this property is done by a translation into linear temporal logic (see Figure 2). Again, we define symbols matching the events of interest and then specify that globally (**G**) adding a collection to a set implies that from there on always the modification of this collection implies that the removal of the collection from the set releases (**R**) the property "not check if c is contained in s" from holding. The φ **R** ψ indicates that either ψ should hold on the whole path or at some point φ holds and in this case releases ψ from the obligation to hold any longer.

Unlike the tracechecks in those two examples, there may be application-specific tracechecks that require understanding and analysis of the application. The examples here shall demonstrate that in many cases tracechecks can be seen as a formalism to extend the interface of an aspect or class (which is currently mainly structure based) with semantic properties. Moreover those properties can automatically be checked, leading to higher confidence in the code in question.

In the next section we explain how we use AspectJ pointcuts to obtain a trace of the running application and present the underlying foundations for checking LTL formulae on a finite path. In particular we clarify the relation between the execution trace and the *model of the program*. We show how the pointcuts used as propositions in our formula influence the degree of abstraction of the model and thus the trace.

3 Introducing LTL

Linear temporal logic reasons about an *infinite path* in a *model* (usually a *Kripke structure*) [7]. It is thus an extension of *propositional logic*. A path is a sequence of states $\pi = \pi[0]\pi[1]\dots$ such that each edge $(\pi[i], \pi[i{+}1])$ is contained in the transition relation of the model. Each state $\pi[i]$ is labelled with a *set of atomic predicates* (the *propositions*). Although this section focuses on concrete examples, we briefly wish to point the reader to Figure 3, which gives the grammars for tracechecks and LTL formulae.

$\langle \text{TRACECHECK} \rangle ::= [\textbf{perthread}]$
  $\textbf{tracecheck} (\langle \text{VAR DECL} \rangle) \{$
    $\langle \text{SYMBOL DECL} \rangle +$
    $\langle \text{LTL FORMULA} \rangle$
    $\langle \text{METHOD BODY} \rangle$
  $\}$
 	
$\langle \text{SYMBOL DECL} \rangle ::=$
  $\textbf{sym} [(\langle \text{VAR DECL} \rangle)]$
    $\langle \text{NAME} \rangle \langle \text{KIND} \rangle : \langle \text{POINTCUT} \rangle;$
 	
$\langle \text{KIND} \rangle ::= \textbf{before}$
  $\| \textbf{after}$
  $\| \textbf{after returning} [(\langle \text{VARIABLE} \rangle)]$
  $\| \textbf{after throwing} [(\langle \text{VARIABLE} \rangle)]$
  $\| \langle \text{TYPE} \rangle \textbf{ around} [(\langle \text{VARIABLES} \rangle)]$
    (a) Tracecheck grammar
	$\langle \text{ARG} \rangle ::= \langle \text{SYMBOL} \rangle$
	  $\| \langle \text{LTL FORMULA} \rangle$
	  $\| (\langle \text{ARG} \rangle)$
	
	$\langle \text{LTL FORMULA} \rangle ::=$
	  $! \langle \text{ARG} \rangle \qquad\qquad \neg \varphi \quad (not \ \varphi)$
	  $\| \textbf{X} \langle \text{ARG} \rangle \qquad\quad \textbf{X} \varphi \quad (neXt \ \varphi)$
	  $\| \textbf{F} \langle \text{ARG} \rangle \qquad\quad \textbf{F} \varphi \quad (Finally \ \varphi)$
	  $\| \textbf{G} \langle \text{ARG} \rangle \qquad\quad \textbf{G} \varphi \quad (Globally \ \varphi)$
	  $\| \langle \text{ARG} \rangle \textbf{U} \langle \text{ARG} \rangle \quad \varphi \textbf{ U} \psi \ (\varphi \ Until \ \psi)$
	  $\| \langle \text{ARG} \rangle \textbf{R} \langle \text{ARG} \rangle \quad \varphi \textbf{ R} \psi \ (\varphi \ Releases \ \psi)$
	  $\| \langle \text{ARG} \rangle \textbf{\&\&} \langle \text{ARG} \rangle \quad \varphi \wedge \psi \ (\varphi \ and \ \psi)$
	  $\| \langle \text{ARG} \rangle \textbf{||} \langle \text{ARG} \rangle \quad \varphi \vee \psi \ (\varphi \ or \ \psi)$
	  $\| \langle \text{ARG} \rangle \textbf{->} \langle \text{ARG} \rangle \quad \varphi \rightarrow \psi \ (\varphi \ implies \ \psi)$
	  $\| \langle \text{ARG} \rangle \textbf{<->} \langle \text{ARG} \rangle \quad \varphi \leftrightarrow \psi \ (\varphi \ iff \ \psi)$
	    (b) Syntax of LTL formula

Fig. 3. Tracecheck and LTL grammar

They consist of the set of Boolean operators as well as the temporal operators *Next*, *Finally*, *Globally*, *Until* and *Release*, which can be used to temporally combine propositions or sub-formulae.

```
x:=1; y:=1;
while (p1) {
    f(x,y);
    if (p2) then
        { x:=1; y:=1; }
    else
        { x:=2; y:=2; }
} /* while */
```

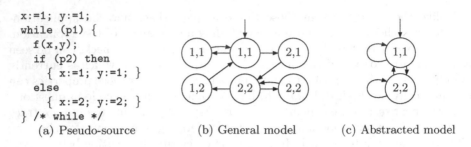

(a) Pseudo-source   (b) General model   (c) Abstracted model

Fig. 4. Simple *while*-loop with branching

For the verification of programs, these atomic propositions could be abstracted from each program state, i.e. the complete program state with heap, program counter, local variables, and call stack. Usually the program counter and a projection of parts of the state would be used to limit the model to the relevant propositions for the task at hand (cf. for example the specification language PROMELA [15]). The *model of a program* is defined by the generally undecidable set of all computation paths. We limit ourselves to reasoning about an *actual execution trace* of the program to overcome the inherent limitation of Model Checking on obtaining an appropriate model to existing source code.

Throughout the paper, the atomic propositions of our framework are point-cut expressions that select the matching joinpoints as the states of our abstract model. Each state is labelled with the set of *active propositions*, i.e. the propositions which match the current joinpoint. For example in the case of Figure 1, each state where an iterator i is created for a collection c would be labelled with a superset of $\{iterator(c, i)\}$. Although our examples only use `call` and `if`-pointcuts, any other pointcut, e.g. `cflow`, may be used.

3.1   Temporal Assertions

Reasoning about *one* such state is closely related to *assertions*. An assertion is the check of a predicate over the *current state* of a system (identified through the position in the source code). We can further abstract this to a model where we retain only those states in which assertions are actually checked by a tracecheck.

As an example, consider the program in Figure 4(a). It contains two predicates *p1, p2* that decide (possibly non-deterministically if for example I/O is involved) the number of iterations and which branch to take. Figure 4(b) shows the model we obtain if we are interested in the variables x, y. (We do not show the edges leading out of the loop.) Note that it contains two states labelled $(1, 1)$ or $(2, 2)$, but all are distinguishable from each other since they have different predecessors and successors. Figure 4(c) shows the abstracted model obtained if we are only interested in the values of the arguments of the method invocation f.

Temporal assertions use LTL path formulae as a means of reasoning about a *sequence of states*. They allow us to specify that states have to occur in a special order, e.g. that a call to a method f must eventually be followed by a method call to g, expressed by the LTL formula $\mathbf{F}(f \rightarrow \mathbf{F}g)$. The operator $\mathbf{F}$ is often pronounced "Finally" because of its meaning.

Another important LTL operator is called "Globally". It specifies that a property should hold on every state of the model. E.g. it might be desirable to confirm that in each state the values of the variables x, y are equal: $\mathbf{G}\ (x = y)$.

We observe some differences between the models above (where LTL formulae have to hold on *all* paths) and a specific path. For the aforementioned program, $\mathbf{F}(x = y)$ holds on any infinite path in both models. $\mathbf{G}(x = y)$ does not hold in the general model because of the states $(2, 1)$ and $(1, 2)$. If we are evaluating a formula at *runtime*, we might observe a path where these states are not visited and the formula might hold *on this run*. Consequently we use a finite path semantics, i.e. over a single finite *unwinding* of a model.

We conclude that the level of abstraction the model provides is essential to its validity. By the appropriate use of pointcuts as propositions in our LTL formulae unimportant intermediate states can be filtered away, hence leading to an abstracted model as in Figure 4(c), where we filtered for method calls. Specifically, the abstract model is defined through the propositions in the formula. Hence we can now formulate the query "On all invocations of f, do x and y have the same value?": $\mathbf{G}\ (f \rightarrow (x = y))$. In our implementation, we would use a *call*-pointcut to select the method invocation and an *if*-pointcut to evaluate the predicate over the variables.

In the following, we discuss the remaining temporal operators which reason about intervals and need a more thorough discussion.

Until, Release and Next. The binary operators "Until" and "Release" can be considered the low-level operators of our temporal logic. The aforementioned operators "Finally" and "Globally" can be expressed using "Until" and "Release":

$$
\begin{array}{c|c}
\mathbf{F}\ \varphi = \mathrm{tt}\ \mathbf{U}\ \varphi & \mathbf{G}\ \varphi \equiv \mathrm{ff}\ \mathbf{R}\ \varphi \\
\neg(\varphi\ \mathbf{U}\ \psi) \equiv \neg\varphi\ \mathbf{R}\ \neg\psi & \neg(\varphi\ \mathbf{R}\ \psi) \equiv \neg\varphi\ \mathbf{U}\ \neg\psi \\
\varphi\ \mathbf{U}\ \psi \equiv \psi \vee (\varphi \wedge \mathbf{X}(\varphi\ \mathbf{U}\ \psi)) & \varphi\ \mathbf{R}\ \psi \equiv \psi \wedge (\varphi \vee \mathbf{X}(\varphi\ \mathbf{R}\ \psi))
\end{array}
$$

The "Until"-operator $\mathbf{U}$ states that a formula $\varphi\ \mathbf{U}\ \psi$ holds in a state if the sub-formula φ holds from this state on until a state is reached where ψ holds. ψ is required to hold eventually, that is before the end of the program.

The dual operator "Release", $\varphi\ \mathbf{R}\ \psi$, specifies that either ψ should hold indefinitely or that ψ holds up to and including the state where φ holds. We already used this operator in the *HashSet*-example in the previous section: $\mathbf{G}(modify(c) \rightarrow remove(s, c)\ \mathbf{R}\ \neg contains(s, c))$.

A detailed discussion of the application of these specific operators is out of the scope of this paper and we point the interested reader to [18].

The last temporal operator is $\mathbf{X}$, the "Next"-operator. A formula $\mathbf{X}\ \varphi$ holds if φ holds in the next state, e.g. we might require that after pushing the start-button the engine should turn on through $start \rightarrow \mathbf{X}\ running$.

While LTL is only arguably an appropriate specification language, we consider it appropriate for a prototype. In the static verification community, several other specification languages like SUGAR [4] and FORSPEC [3] exist, which also contain additional syntactic sugar hiding the temporal logics in the semantic layer to make the input languages more user-friendly.

A comprehensive survey of existing verification patterns and how to express them in various specification formalism including LTL can be found in [11]. It can serve as a starting-point into specifying properties. The *HashSet*-requirement for example can be identified as a combination of the "Universality After"-pattern and a variant of the "Absence of P after Q until R"-pattern, where P is the *contains*, Q the *modify* and R the *remove*-action.

4   Tracechecks

The introductory examples show that tracechecks use an LTL formula with free variable bindings in order to specify conditions over the dynamic execution trace. Figure 3(a) gives the formal syntax of tracechecks. A tracecheck consists of a declaration of free variables which can be bound during evaluation, a nonempty list of symbol (proposition) declarations, an LTL formula declaration (cf. Figure 3(b)) and a body. The keyword *perthread* causes a thread-local instantiation of the formula, if a property should be checked for each thread separately.

A definition of the formal declarative semantics of tracechecks is out of the scope of this work and can be found in [5] where we also prove them equivalent to our operational semantics. In the following we want to explore the semantics *by example*, recalling the initial specification of the *iterator* requirement.

4.1   Quantification

The formula (with free variables c, i) can be written as:

$$\mathbf{G}(iterator(c,i) \rightarrow \mathbf{G}(modify(c) \rightarrow \mathbf{G}(\neg next(i))))$$

The informal requirement specification states that the condition $\mathbf{G}(modify(c) \rightarrow \mathbf{G}(\neg next(i)))$ should hold *for each pair (i,c) of iterator and collection*. With tracechecks, quantification *over objects* can be expressed by quantifying *over events*. Global quantification over a variable x can be modelled by wrapping a formula $\varphi(x)$ with a "Globally"-formula of the form $\mathbf{G}(create(x) \rightarrow \varphi(x))$. Likewise, existential quantification can be modelled by "Finally"-formulae of the form $\mathbf{F}(create(x) \wedge \varphi(x))$.

Tracechecks always specify a language of *valid traces*. That means that we are naturally interested in traces which *violate* the LTL formula of a tracecheck. A tracecheck body is executed whenever a formula is *falsified*. In cases where this falsification took place under a certain binding, this binding can be referred to by the variables declared in the tracecheck body (cf. Figure 6, line 9).

It may happen that no such binding is available. For instance the formula $\mathbf{F}(create(x))$, which states that at some point in time, some object x is created, can only be falsified at application shutdown time. If it is falsified, this means that $create(x)$ did not occur. Consequently, x cannot be bound. In such cases, x will be *null* in the tracecheck body. Future versions of our implementation will use static analysis in order to avoid accidental unchecked use of such variables.

4.2   Annotation Style Syntax

In addition to the tracecheck syntax, our implementation offers an inlined "annotation" style that can be used to deploy specifications as annotations in interfaces of ordinary classes (cf. Section 5). For the iterator example, this allows to directly attach the formula to the *iterator()* method of the *Collection* interface as shown in Figure 5. Note how the keywords *thisMethod* and *thisType* can be used to refer to the member respectively type the annotation is attached to. That way, formulae can be directly attached to the components they reason about in a reusable way. (Like in the AspectJ semantics, pointcuts over interfaces specify behaviour over *all classes implementing that interface*.)

```
1  interface Collection {
2
3  @LTL("thisType c, Iterator i:
4    G( exit(call(thisMethod) && target(c)) returning(i) ->
5      G( exit( (call(thisType+.add(..)) || call(thisType+.remove(..))) && target(c))
6        -> G(! entry(call(Iterator.next()) && target(i)) ) ) )
7  ")
8  Iterator  iterator ();
9
10 //remaining interface code
11 }
```

Fig. 5. Annotation style definitions in our prototype tool J-LO

Since tracechecks in annotation style have no body, if an error is detected, the implementation issues a message to a set of user definable observers. These may simply output an error message or apply some more sensible error handling, depending on the property. Also, such annotations are currently not automatically documented by Sun's `javadoc` API documentation tool. Future versions will likely support such a feature.

Using annotations as a means of deployment, the specification literally forms a (semantic) part of the public interface of a class. This can be useful for several purposes, comprising documentation, runtime checking (through our tool) but also static verification by third party tools. In particular, the *designer* of an interface, class or component can attach such semantic annotations to its code and have them compiled into Java bytecode. People *using* this class or component or implementing this interface respectively can then in a second, independent step simply apply our tool to have their implementation instrumented to be checked for compliance with this semantic interface. We believe that this is a unique feature which has not been provided before in practice and that it is a major contribution to the modular deployment of components.

4.3   History Access Through *if*-Pointcuts

This syntax imposes one problem: Since there is no body available, one cannot perform any further computation on the bound values. In particular, one cannot filter for unwanted valuations. As a solution, tracechecks implement an extended semantics for *if*-pointcuts, giving them access not only to valuations at the current joinpoint but also to variables which have been bound earlier on the path. Figure 6 shows a tracecheck enforcing the *Singleton* design pattern [14].

```
1   tracecheck(Singleton s1, Singleton s2) {
2
3     sym create(Singleton s) after returning (s):
4       call(static Singleton Singleton+.inst ());
5     sym createAnother(Singleton s, Singleton t) after returning (s):
6       call(static Singleton Singleton+.inst ()) && if(s!=t);
7
8     G(create(s1) -> XG !createAnother(s2,s1) ) {
9       throw new SpecViolationException ("Two singletons detected:"+s1+","+s2);
10    }
11  }
```

Fig. 6. Tracecheck enforcing *Singleton* pattern

Note that the symbol *createAnother* gets a parameter t passed in (lines 5–6), which is not provided by the symbol itself. This raises the question what happens when one must decide if a condition such as $s \neq t$ actually holds at the current joinpoint, but one of the variables has not yet been bound. Indeed such formulae are forbidden. In [5] we explain a static analysis based on abstract interpretation which assures the validity of given formulae at compile time.

5   Reference Implementation

In this section we discuss some implementation details and how well tracechecks can be used in practice. We comment on the runtime overhead and explain possible deployment outside of aspects by using annotations. Our reference implementation is based on an adaption of alternating automata [13] with free variable bindings. It allows to implement the LTL semantics quite directly. Details are given in [5], so we only briefly outline important details.

Generally, for each tracecheck with n symbols we generate $n+1$ pieces of advice where the first n construct the set of propositions holding at a joinpoint and the last advice triggers the automaton transition function. In addition, we generate a method containing the tracecheck body, which is called by the backend with the appropriate binding whenever the tracecheck fails. (The interested reader might want to have a look at the output of our tool during instrumentation as the prototype prints the generated aspects to the commandline.)

On startup of the instrumented application, the initial automaton configuration is installed in the runtime environment and then updated every time the aspect triggers a transition.

As mentioned, *if*-pointcuts in symbol declarations of a tracecheck can refer to variables which were bound earlier on in the trace. In order to evaluate an *if*-pointcut within the execution history, the compiler extracts the Boolean expression and constructs a closure which is attached to the defining proposition. The proposition is then passed in the correct variable binding at runtime through the evaluation of the transition function.

We have successfully tested our implementation with various assertions over data structures as well as on an instance of the lock order reversal pattern [18], where threads obtain locks in a way which may lead to a deadlock.

The work of Allan et al. [2] discusses an instance of the *safe iterator* pattern in *JHotDraw* (a Java drawing package, available at http://www.jhotdraw.org/) as use case. We were able to reproduce their results by executing a sequence of events violating the pattern in the graphical user interface. The error was properly picked up. If no instrumentation had been present, the error would probably have gone unnoticed. Step-by-step instructions along with all related code are available on our website.

5.1   Memory Overhead

With respect to memory leaks we made sure that our implementation uses strong references only where necessary, that is when variables are used within a tracecheck body (e.g. Figure 6, line 9). In those cases, strong references need to be kept in order to make sure that the object is still available when the tracecheck body is executed. For variables which are *not* referenced in such a way, each object bound to this variable can be garbage collected as if no tracechecks were present. All related propositions (weakly) referencing such objects are then automatically removed in the next application of the transition function. Their semantics is equal to those of *false*, because a proposition referencing an object that was garbage collected can never hold again.

As a result, when variables are not used within a tracecheck body (i.e. they are *collectable*), we observe only a constant memory overhead, since any bound object can be freed as usual. In particular this is always the case when using the annotation style syntax, because those specifications consist only of a formula and have no body which would require strong references to bound objects.

Figure 7 shows the memory consumption for our iterator example in *JHot-Draw*. The left graph shows memory consumption for the version without instrumentation, when animating an object. Consumption is constantly around 1.3 MB. (Note that this is code compiled with the *abc* compiler. Code generated

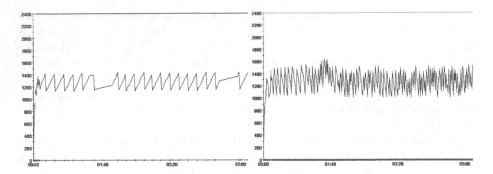

Fig. 7. Memory usage for the iterator example in JHotDraw; left: uninstrumented program (memory consumption in KB over time in minutes), right: instrumented version of the program; dots indicate garbage collection

by *javac* takes up about 2 MB.) The instrumented version shown on the right hand side shows the same constant memory consumption, however, it is triggering much more garbage collections than the original one. This is due to the fact that we have not yet optimised our application for speed. As a result, we still observe a considerable runtime overhead. Future versions will try to mitigate this problem by standard techniques such as caching. Yet the graph shall give proof of the fact that there are no memory leaks caused by our implementation.

When variables are used within a tracecheck body, Allan et al. [2] suggested a static pointer analysis which is able to identify such cases and hence may warn the user at instrumentation time. That way the user has the possibility to decide for himself whether he wants to pay for this debug information with the unavoidable memory overhead. This analysis is implemented in *abc* and can thus be reused for tracechecks.

If an application is instrumented with expensive tracechecks, they should only be active in internal debugging builds of the software, and disabled on deployment due to their performance-penalty at runtime. Test-case generation and path-coverage are essential to effectively use tracechecks. Despite the perceived overhead, with growing computer performance there is a trend to continuously monitor applications and eventually combine results of different runs to obtain asymptotic verification of analysed programs [6].

6   Related Work

Specifying aspects based on the execution history of a program has been recognized as a desirable feature for aspect oriented programming under the name of Event-based AOP (EAOP) [10]. The AOP approach which is closest to the one of tracechecks are *tracematches* introduced by Allan et al. [2].

6.1   Tracematches

They propose a matching language based on regular expressions. Those are quite different compared to LTL formulae in a way that regular expressions are well suited for *existential patterns*, i.e. patterns which anticipate certain behaviour to exist and then match this behaviour. While this is useful for the purpose of tracematches, which is using them as an *implementation language* where additional behaviour is attached to *existing* paths, the *absence of faulty behaviour* can consequently often only be expressed in a cumbersome way—by enumerating the language of all possible paths leading to an error state.

The use of LTL as a specification formalism allows here to translate *safety conditions* ("something bad never happens") in a more direct way. Such patterns are essential to checking and verifications as [11] shows.

Table 8 shows a comparison of tracematches and tracechecks: While tracechecks can be deployed in an AspectJ-like syntax, they can also be deployed as Java annotations, forming a real part of a Java interface.

Also, while tracechecks (i.e. LTL) allow the user to express negation and conjunction, this is not possible with tracematches (i.e. regular expressions). Even if the respective operations "intersection" and "complement" were added, tracematches would still not be equally expressive: For example, $a^* \cap b^*$ is only satisfied by the empty trace, while the property $\mathbf{G}(a) \wedge \mathbf{G}(b) = \mathbf{G}(a \wedge b)$ is also satisfied by the trace $[\{a, b\}\{a, b\}]$. This is due to the fact that regular expressions always have to be interpreted over *strict sequences of events*. That means that the aforementioned trace would be interpreted as a trace $[a\ b\ a\ b]$ or similar, which is not matched by $a^* \cap b^*$. Since LTL is a *propositional* logic, it can distinguish such *overlapping* events. Pure LTL in turn cannot detect patterns which require modulo counting (e.g. $(aa)^*$). We believe that such patterns are seldom useful in the context of verification.

Table 8. Comparing tracematches and tracechecks

	Tracematches	Tracechecks
Formalism	regular expressions	linear temporal logic
Deployment	AspectJ language ext.	AspectJ language ext. or Java annotations
Input symbol	$p \in \Sigma$	$\{p_1, \ldots, p_n\} \in 2^{\Sigma}$
Semantics	sequential	interleaving
Negation	implicit, through def. of Σ	explicit
Conjunction	no	yes
Concatenation	yes	no
Quantification	$\exists x$, implicit	$\exists x, \forall x$, through LTL
Shutdown	explicit	implicit

Also, the "Globally" operator, as we use it here, provides a means to universally quantify over variables (cf. Section 4). With tracematches this is not possible, since regular expressions are implicitly existentially quantified.

Last but not least, the shutdown event of an application needs to be explicitly modelled in tracematches, while our tool installs a shutdown hook, automatically notifying the verification runtime, when the application shuts down.

We conclude that tracematches and tracechecks show indeed some similarities, but in the end are both each better suited for their particular purpose.

6.2   Other Approaches

Temporal logics have already been used together with AOP: In [1], rules based on temporal logics are used to describe sequences of instructions where events should be inserted. The instrumentation happens on a static level and does not consider free variables.

Douence, Fradet and Südholt [8] developed an aspect calculus where advice can be triggered not only via a single joinpoint but via *sequences*. Although their work is targeted towards a formal model of joinpoint matching and advice execution and less on an actual implementation, there are clear similarities to our work. Their formalism describes regular sequences of joinpoints, so it can rather be compared to the sequential model of tracematches than to our's. Consequently, they cannot express overlapping events. It is implemented in the Arachne system [9], a dynamic weaver for C applications.

Other work by Südholt and Farias [12] discusses the use of explicit protocols in the interfaces of components in order to satisfy a certain notion of correctness. Hence the goal of their work is certainly similar to ours. Yet, they use another specification formalism (finite state machines) and do not employ and aspect-oriented programming. Consequently, they are unable to exploit the crosscutting nature of pointcuts, an essential stength of the formalism presented hete. Also, they provide no implementation.

Vanderperren et al. [19] propose the stateful pointcut language JAsCo also based on the above model. Pointcuts trigger transitions in a deterministic finite automaton and advice can be attached to each pointcut. JAsCo does not provide a means of quantification or bindings. These have to be implemented in the declaring aspect by hand.

In their work [20], Walkers and Viggers proposed the *tracecuts* formalism. As tracechecks and tracematches, tracecuts provide an AspectJ and pointcut based formalism for temporal reasoning. The authors describe an implementation by an AspectJ compiler extension, which gave of course some insights for our work. With respect to the formal model, the obvious difference to our approach is that tracecuts use context-free grammars for the specification of trace languages.

Additionally to context free languages, the set of languages recognisable by tracecuts is however even larger, since the implementation allows for the attachment of custom action blocks to each matching symbol. Such an action block has access to the whole execution history observed so far and can based on this decision reject the current symbol using a *fail* keyword, resuming as if the symbol had *not* just been read. A stack based implementation imposes additional overhead, although this might be optimised for regular traces.

Klose and Ostermann [16] discuss how temporal relations can be expressed in GAMMA, an aspect-oriented language on top of an object-oriented core language. Pointcuts are specified in a Prolog-like language and include timestamps that can be compared using the predicates *isbefore* or *isafter*. Their prototype requires a stored trace to analyse and is not applicable to an existing language.

In the field of annotation-based property checking, there are many tools around, such as Contract4J, JML, etc. but actually all of them support pure "Design by Contract", i.e. only pre- and postconditions and invariants. Each can be expressed through tracechecks, but tracechecks are more powerful as they allow to reason about the whole execution trace and not just a single point in the execution flow.

7 Conclusion

We have presented a specification framework for formal reasoning about object-oriented programs. The implementation is based on the *abc* compiler. Formulae in a temporal logic can be used to reason about the dynamic execution trace of a running application. The application is observed by an automaton where transitions are triggered by an aspect. Formulae can bind free variables to exposed objects on the execution path and can refer to those objects through a redefined scope of *if*-pointcuts during matching. They can be deployed using a language extension to AspectJ or by the means of Java5 annotations, yielding a fully Java compliant solution.

Through such annotations, the tasks of specification and verification is split into two parts: The designer of a component or interface adds annotations to his code representing the dynamic semantics of how the component is to be used. The annotations can then be compiled into bytecode and shipped to the user.

The user can then take advantage of the annotations for the purpose of documentation or automated runtime checking—by applying our tool. That way the user can make sure that his access to a component or implementation of an interface is compliant with the original intent of the component provider.

Our prototype, the *Java Logical Observer J-LO*, together with all presented examples is available from http://www-i2.informatik.rwth-aachen.de/JLO/.

Acknowledgements. We thank the whole *abc* group for their useful comments on this work and on extending the AspectBench compiler in general.

References

1. R. A. Åberg, J. L. Lawall, M. Südholt, G. Muller, and A.-F. L. Meur. On the automatic evolution of an OS kernel using temporal logic and AOP. In *Proc. of Automated Software Engineering (ASE'03)*. IEEE, 2003.
2. C. Allan, P. Avgustinov, A. Simon, L. Hendren, S. Kuzins, O. Lhoták, O. de Moor, D. Sereni, G. Sittamplan, and J. Tibble. Adding Trace Matching with Free Variables to AspectJ. In *OOPSLA '05, San Diego, California, USA*, October 2005.

3. R. Armoni, L. Fix, A. Flaisher, R. Gerth, B. Ginsburg, T. Kanza, A. Landver, S. Mador-Haim, E. Singerman, A. Tiemeyer, M. Y. Vardi, and Y. Zbar. The ForSpec Temporal Logic: A new Temporal Property-Specification Language. In P. S. Joost-Pieter Katoen, editor, *Tools and Algorithms for the Construction and Analysis of Systems (TACAS'02)*, volume 2280 of *LNCS*. Springer, 2002.
4. I. Beer, S. Ben-David, C. Eisner, D. Fisman, A. Gringauze, and Y. Rodeh. The temporal logic sugar. In *Computer Aided Verification (CAV'01)*, volume 2102 of *LNCS*. Springer, 2001.
5. E. Bodden. J-LO, a tool for runtime checking temporal assertions. Master's thesis, RWTH Aachen University, Germany, 2005. Available from http://www-i2.informatik.rwth-aachen.de/JLO/.
6. T. M. Chilimbi. Asymptotic Runtime Verification through Lightweight Continous Program Analysis (invited talk). In *Fifth Workshop on Runtime Verification (RV'05)*. To be published in ENTCS, Elsevier, 2005.
7. E. Clarke Jr, O. Grumberg, and D. Peled. *Model Checking*. MIT Press, Cambridge, MA, USA, 1999.
8. R. Douence, P. Fradet, and M. Südholt. Composition, reuse and interaction analysis of stateful aspects. In G. C. Murphy and K. J. Lieberherr, editors, *Proc. of the 3rd intl. conf. on Aspect-oriented software development (AOSD'04)*. ACM, 2004.
9. R. Douence, T. Fritz, N. Loriant, J.-M. Menaud, M. Ségura-Devillechaise, and M. Südholt. An expressive aspect language for system applications with arachne. In *Proc. of the 4th intl. conf. on Aspect-oriented software development (AOSD'05)*. ACM Press, 2005.
10. R. Douence, O. Motelet, and M. Südholt. A formal definition of crosscuts. In *Proc. of the 3rd. intl. conf. on Metalevel Architectures and Separation of Crosscutting Concerns*, volume 2192 of *LNCS*. Springer, 2001.
11. M. B. Dwyer, G. S. Avrunin, and J. C. Corbett. Patterns in property specifications for finite-state verification. In *ICSE '99: Proceedings of the 21st intl. conf. on Software engineering*. IEEE Computer Society Press, 1999.
12. A. Farías and M. Südholt. On components with explicit protocols satisfying a notion of correctness by construction. In *In International Symposium on Distributed Objects and Applications (DOA)*. LNCS, 2002.
13. B. Finkbeiner and H. Sipma. Checking Finite Traces using Alternating Automata. *Formal Methods in System Design*, 24(2):101–127, 2004.
14. E. Gamma, R. Helm, R. Johnson, and J. Vlissides. Design patterns: Abstraction and reuse of object-oriented design. In O. M. Nierstrasz, editor, *ECOOP'93— Object-Oriented Programming*, volume 707 of *LNCS*. Springer, 1993.
15. G. J. Holzmann. *The SPIN model checker: primer and reference manual*. Addison-Wesley, Boston, Massachusetts, USA, September 2003.
16. K. Klose and K. Ostermann. Back to the future: Pointcuts as predicates over traces. In *Foundations of Aspect-Oriented Languages workshop (FOAL'05)*, 2005.
17. A. Pnueli. The temporal logic of programs. In *Proc. of the 18th IEEE Symp. on the Foundations of Computer Science*. IEEE Computer Society Press, 1977.
18. V. Stolz and E. Bodden. Temporal Assertions using AspectJ. In *Fifth Workshop on Runtime Verification (RV'05)*. To be published in ENTCS, Elsevier, 2005.
19. W. Vanderperren, D. Suvée, M. A. Cibrán, and B. De Fraine. Stateful Aspects in JAsCo. In T. Gschwind and U. Aßmann, editors, *Workshop on Software Composition 2005*, volume 3628 of *LNCS*. Springer, 2005.
20. R. J. Walker and K. Viggers. Implementing protocols via declarative event patterns. In R. Taylor and M. Dwyer, editors, *Proc. of the 12th ACM SIGSOFT Intl. Symp. on Foundations of Software Engineering*. ACM Press, 2004.

Service Composition with Directories

Ion Constantinescu, Walter Binder, and Boi Faltings

Ecole Polytechnique Fédérale de Lausanne (EPFL)
Artificial Intelligence Laboratory
CH-1015 Lausanne, Switzerland
firstname.lastname@epfl.ch

Abstract. This paper presents planning-based service composition algorithms that dynamically interact with a potentially large-scale directory of service advertisements in order to retrieve matching service advertisements on demand. We start with a simple algorithm for untyped services, similar to a STRIPS planner. This algorithm is refined in two steps, first to exploit type information, and second to support partial type matches. An evaluation confirms that the algorithms scale well with increasing size of the directory and that the support for partial type matches is essential to achieve a low failure rate.[1]

Keywords: Service composition, planning, service discovery, semantic web services.

1 Introduction

Today the predominant way we interact with the Web is via browsers that manipulate information by rendering it in a human-readable way. However, there is an evolution towards the automatisation of many processes on the Web, which may result in computer-to-computer interactions becoming predominant over current human-to-computer interactions. For modeling computer-to-computer interactions, currently the de-facto paradigm is that of "services". But making services automatically interact with each other raises a number of difficult problems, currently under hard scrutiny by industrial and academic research.

The Semantic Web [14] is fundamental for such computer-to-computer interactions to become reality, since it provides an universally accessible platform and computer-understandable semantics for data to be shared and processed by automated tools. Experts have already developed a range of mark-up frameworks and languages, notably the revised Resource Description Framework (RDF) [29] and the Web Ontology Language (OWL) [28], which mark the emergence of the Semantic Web as a broad-based, commercial-grade platform.

Service discovery is the process of locating providers advertising services that can satisfy a service request specified by a service consumer. *Automated service composition* addresses the problem of assembling services based on their functional specifications in order to achieve a given task and to provide extra functionality. When discovery

---

[1] The work presented in this paper was partly carried out in the framework of the EPFL Center for Global Computing and supported by the Swiss National Funding Agency OFES as part of the European projects KnowledgeWeb (FP6-507482) and DIP (FP6-507483).

W. Löwe and M. Südholt (Eds.): SC 2006, LNCS 4089, pp. 163–177, 2006.

fails in locating a single service, service composition can be used instead for satisfying a service request. Thus, service composition may be regarded as a generalized form of discovery. So far, most approaches that have been suggested for automated service composition are based on planning techniques.

Due to the open and changing environment in which it is performed, service discovery needs to operate without any specific prior knowledge of existing services. Services are therefore indexed in directories, and the main goals for the implementation of these directories and the matchmaking algorithms are to maximize the success rate as well as the efficiency of processing queries.

Therefore, planning algorithms used for automated service composition have to be adapted to a situation where operators are not known a priori, but have to be retrieved through queries to these directories. Basic planning systems check all operators in the planning library against the current search state in order to determine which action to perform next. In contrast, in the case of service composition, the search state is used to extract the *specification of possible operators*. This specification together with some constraints specific to the composition algorithm is used to formulate a query to the service directory.

The original contribution of this paper is the presentation of service composition algorithms that dynamically interact with a directory to retrieve relevant service descriptions. Our approach to automated service composition is based on matching input and output parameters and world states prior and posterior to the invocation of a service in order to constrain the ways in which services may be composed. In this paper we show the stepwise refinement of a simple planning algorithm in order to take the types of input resp. output parameters into account and to support also the composition of services with *partially matching parameter types*, which significantly reduces the failure rate of the composition algorithm.

The approach presented here builds on our research on service directories [8,3,9] and refines and extends our previous work on service composition [12] by supporting a more expressive service description formalism and detailing the interaction of our service composition algorithms with a directory. Moreover, this paper includes the first detailed presentation of our composition algorithms, which we derive from a standard planning approach. New measurements of our approach complete this paper.

The rest of this paper is structured as follows: The next section discusses some related work in the area of service composition. In Section 3 we explain how we represent service advertisements and service requests. Section 4 discusses requirements and gives an overview of our service composition engine. Section 5 introduces a simple composition algorithm, which does not take type information into account. It is the basis for the subsequent refinements in Section 6 and Section 7. In Section 8 we evaluate performance and failure rate of the presented service composition algorithms. Finally, Section 9 concludes this paper.

2   Related Work

For the last years, service integration has been an active field in both the AI and database research communities, including Infosleuth [1] and work by Doan and Halevy [13].

Another approach is that of Thakkar and Knoblock [26], concretized by the Building Finder application, where a number of manually defined data-sources, such as the Microsoft Terraservice, U.S. Census Bureau information files, as well as geocoding information and different real estate property tax sites, where composed using a forward chaining technique.

Some approaches to composition require an explicit specification of the control flow between basic services in order to provide value-added services. For instance, in the eFlow system [6], a composite service is modeled as a graph that defines the order of execution of different processes. The Self-Serv framework [2] uses a subset of statecharts to describe the control flow within a composite service. The Business Process Execution Language for Web Services (BPEL4WS) [5] addresses compositions where the control flow of the process and the bindings between services are known in advance.

There is a good body of work which tries to address the service composition problem by using planning techniques based either on theorem proving (e.g., ConGolog [20,21] and SWORD [25]) or on hierarchical task planning (e.g., SHOP-2 [32]). Such approaches do not require a pre-defined process model of the composite service and return a possible control flow as result. In the scenario used by the ConGolog approach, the composition engine would have to book flight tickets and arrange ground transportation and hotel reservations. For SWORD, the example used was of a composite service giving driving directions to one's home. The composite service was formed from two services, one that mapped names to addresses and another that was giving driving directions to a given address. In the motivating example in the SHOP-2 approach, for handling a medical emergency, several data sources had to be composed and a schedule had to be computed.

Other approaches based on planning, such as planning as model checking [16], are being considered for Web service composition and would allow more complex constructs such as loops [27].

The main drawback of all previously presented approaches to service composition based on planning is that they assume that relevant service descriptions are initially loaded into the reasoning engine and that no service discovery is performed during composition. I.e., these approaches do not fit an environment where a large number of dynamically changing service advertisements are published in service directories. In contrast, the service composition algorithms presented in this paper dynamically retrieve relevant service advertisements from a potentially large-scale service directory.

3   Service Descriptions

A service description specifies aspects related to the functionality available from a service provider (service advertisement) or requested by a service consumer (service request). We represent service advertisements and service requests through variables and constraints on these variables. Variables refer to required or provided service parameters or to aspects related to the state of the world before or after the invocation of the service. Constraints specify the possible combinations of values that different variables can take.

In our formalism, each variable is defined by two elements:

- A *description* specifying the actual semantics of the data the variable is holding, including information whether the variable represents a parameter or a world state (e.g., in a travel domain the description of a variable could be $DepartureParam$ or $ArrivalParam$ and the description of a world state could be $ValidCreditState$). Usually, the description is directly associated to the name of the variable itself.
- A *type* defining the way data of the variable is represented and the set of values that the variable can take (e.g., possible values for $DepartureParam$ and $ArrivalParam$ could be represented by the sets $\{Geneva, Basel\}$ and $\{Barcelona, Nice\}$, where all four city values could be of type $Location$).

We presume that both variable *descriptions* and *types* can be defined using a class/ontological language like OWL [28]. Primitive data-types used for specifying the variable *type* can be defined using a language like XSD [30].[2]

Constraints on variables can specify either *preconditions* (set of possible parameter and world state values required to be true prior to the invocation of the service) or *effects* (how parameters and world states are affected by the execution of the service). Constraints are specified in the form of sets of possible variable assignments. Each assignment represents a set of variable/value pairs. Constraints are identified by keywords (e.g., PRE for preconditions, respectively EFF for effects).

We call parameter or world state variables appearing in PRE constraints *prior* variables, and parameter or world state variables appearing in EFF constraints *post* variables.

In a service advertisement, variables and constraints describing parameters and world states have the following semantics:

- In order for the service to be invokable, a value must be known for each of the *prior* variables and it has to be consistent with the respective semantic *description* and syntactic *type* of the variable. The value provided as *prior* parameter or world state has to be semantically at least as specific as what the service is able to accept. Regarding the variable type, in the case of primitive data types the invocation value must be in the range of allowed values, or in the case of classes the invocation value must be subsumed by the type of the variable.
- Upon successful invocation, the service returns a value for each of the *post* parameters, and the execution engine assigns a value to each of the variables representing *post* world states. Each of these values is consistent with the respective *description* and *type* of the variable.
- Regarding preconditions, in order for the service to be invokable, at least one assignment set in the constraint has to be satisfied by the current values of variables defining parameters and states of the world.
- Effect constraints represent guarantees on the possible combinations of values for variables describing *post* parameters and world states as well as how *prior* world states are maintained after the invocation of the service (e.g., the effect of an action modeling a robot picking up a block from a table will not maintain the fact that the block is on the table, which is part of the action's preconditions).

---

[2] At the implementation level both primitive data-types and classes are represented as sets of numeric intervals [8].

Service requests are represented in a similar manner but have different semantics:

- The service request's *prior* variables describe available parameters (e.g., provided by the user or by another service) or aspects of the world specifying an initial state of facts. Each of these variables has attached a semantic *description* and either a *type* or a concrete *value*.
- The service request's *post* variables represent parameters that a compatible (composite) service must provide and world states that specify aspects of the state of the world that have to be influenced by the execution of the service. The variable description defines the actual semantics of the required information and the variable type defines what ranges of values can be handled by the requester. A compatible (matching) service must be able to provide a value for each of the *post* parameters and world states of the service request, semantically at least as specific as the requested variable description, and having values in the range defined by the requested parameter type.
- Preconditions in a service request represent restrictions on the allowed combinations of values for available parameters or initial world states described by *prior* variables.
- Effects represent restrictions on the allowed combinations of values for variables describing required *post* parameters or world states that the service request is willing to accept.

We use the following functions to access the variables of service advertisements and service requests:

- $vars(prior \mid post, S)$ – Returns the set of *prior* or *post* variables for a service description S. We assume variables to be described as concepts using a language like OWL [28], conforming with the semantics for the Description Logic operators $\equiv, \sqsubseteq, \sqcap, \sqcup, \bot, \top$. As previously specified, the description of each variable specifies if it is a parameter or a world state.
- $type(V, S)$ – Returns the type of the variable named V in the frame of a service description S as the set of possible values that V can take. The $\equiv, \sqsubseteq$ and $\sqcap \neq \emptyset$ operators in conjunction with this function can be used to determine if two value sets are equivalent, subsume each other, or are overlapping.
- $constraint(PRE \mid EFF, S)$ – Returns the set of possible variable assignments (variable/value pairs) for the precondition or effect constraints in the service description S.

4   Requirements and High-Level Architecture

Classic approaches to planning assume domains with a relatively small number of operators (e.g., domains for the International Planning Competition [17] have some dozens actions). For solving planning problems in these kinds of domains, the difficulties that need to be addressed are related to the large space of possible states to be searched and to the embedded hard resource-allocation problems.

In this paper, we are concerned by the following issues, which are specific and unique to the composition of services deployed in open environments:

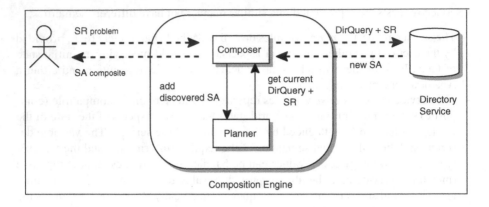

Fig. 1. Interactions of service composition engine using a directory

- **Discovery in large-scale directories** – We assume that a large number of service advertisements is stored in (possibly distributed) yellow-page directories. How can we discover exactly the services that are relevant at each step of the composition process?
- **Runtime non-determinism** – When discovered services match only partially but not completely[3], the reasoning engine has to aggregate several services as switches in order to fulfill the required functionality. The actual flow of messages will be routed based on runtime values on the appropriate paths. How can we discover and create those switches and how can we make sure that they correctly handle all possible combinations of parameter values?

The design choices that we took in our approach to service composition are driven by the above requirements and based on the following assumptions:

- **Large result sets** – For each query, the service directory may return a large number of service advertisements.
- **Costly directory accesses** – Being a shared resource, accessing the directory (possibly remotely) is expensive.

The design of our service-composition engine addresses these issues by interleaving discovery and composition and by computing the "right" query at each step. Hence, the architecture of our service composition system consists of three separate components (see Fig. 1):

- **Planner** – A component that is able to compose one or more known service advertisements (SAs) in order to satisfy an initial service request $SR_{problem}$. The composition is formulated as a service advertisement $SA_{composite}$, represented as a workflow. If using the currently known services the planner is unable to generate

---

[3] We consider as partial matches the *subsume* match type identified by Paolluci [23] and the *intersection* or *overlap* match type identified by Li [19] and Constantinescu [10].

Algorithm 1. Composer algorithm for service composition with directories

---

procedure $FindComposition(PL, DIR, SR_{problem}) : SA_{composite}$
   $PL.init(SR_{problem})$
   $SR \leftarrow SR_{problem}$
   while $(SA \leftarrow DIR.nextResult(SR, PL.getDirQuery())) \neq \emptyset$ **do**
      $PL.addService(SA)$
      if $PL.isFeasible() \wedge (SA_{composite} \leftarrow PL.solve()) \neq \emptyset$ **then**
          return $SA_{composite}$
      $SR \leftarrow PL.getServiceRequest()$

---

such a composition, the state of the current composition search can be used to extract a new service request SR. Together with a planner-specific $DirQuery$, a new directory query can be formed. See [3,9] for details concerning our directory query language that is used to specify a $DirQuery$.

- **Service directory** – Stores service advertisements and is able to process queries formulated as a pair of a service request SR and a $DirQuery$. The query result consists of one or more service advertisements SA that can be incrementally returned to the composition engine.
- **Composer** – A component that implements the interleave between planning and discovery by using the current search state of the planner to generate new service requests SRs which are used for the discovery of additional service advertisements SAs. These advertisements are then added to the planner either until the initial service request $SR_{problem}$ is satisfied or no more results can be found.

In Algorithm 1 we present our approach to service composition with directories. As outlined before, the algorithm makes use of a planner PL and directory DIR in order to solve a composition problem formulated by the service request $SR_{problem}$. If successful, the system returns a composition in the form of a service advertisement $SA_{composite}$, represented as a workflow.

The algorithm relies on the following functions:

- $PL.init(SR)$ – Initializes the planner according to a given service request $SR_{problem}$.
- $DIR.nextResult(SR, DirQuery) : SA$ – Queries the directory for advertisements consistent with the given SR according to the matching relation defined by $DirQuery$. The best ranking SA accordingly to $DirQuery$ is then returned. For details concerning the ranking of matching service advertisements, see [3,9].
- $PL.addService(SA)$ – Adds a newly discovered service advertisements SA to the planner, possibly updating search structures internal to the planner.
- $PL.getDirQuery() : DirQuery$ – Returns a planner-specific $DirQuery$ that together with a service request SR can be used for formulating a query to the service directory.
- $PL.getServiceRequest() : SR$ – Returns a service request that reflects the current state of the search for composition.

Algorithm 2. Initialization and query generation functions of a planner for untyped deterministic services

procedure $PL.init(SR)$
    $PL.states(0) \leftarrow constraint(PRE, SR)$
    $lastLevel \leftarrow 0$
    $PL.goals \leftarrow constraint(EFF, SR)$

procedure $PL.getServiceRequest() : SR$
    $SR \leftarrow newRequest()$
    $constraint(PRE, SR) \leftarrow PL.states(PL.lastLevel)$
    $constraint(EFF, SR) \leftarrow PL.goals$
    return SR

- $PL.isFeasible() : Boolean$ – This is a computationally cheap test that represents a necessary condition for the plan to be solvable using the current service advertisements. If this function returns true, the search for a plan might be successful. If it returns false, the search for a plan will certainly fail (i.e., further services have to be discovered from the directory).
- $PL.solve() : SA$ – When the plan is feasible, this function uses the currently known service advertisements to search for a composition that fulfills $SR_{problem}$.

In the next sections we present in detail several planning systems of different complexity. The first one is able to handle untyped deterministic services, the second one handles compositions of completely matching typed services (deterministic compositions), and finally the last one allows to compose typed services that partially match, where the non-determinism in the composition is addressed by the creation of *switches* in the resulting workflow.

5 Composing Untyped Deterministic Services

By untyped services we understand service descriptions (service advertisements and requests) for which all possible values in specification assignments are disjoint (e.g., for data-types their intervals must not overlap, and any two concepts must satisfy the $\cap = \perp$ relation).

Moreover, we assume that service advertisements are completely deterministic: their precondition PRE and effect EFF constraints each contain exactly one assignment set. The same applies to the precondition constraints in the service request $SR_{problem}$. We allow precondition constraints (available states) in non-problem requests (like those generated by the planner) to contain several assignments. Effect constraints (required goals) in requests can always contain several assignments.

As assignment sets with disjoint values can be seen as sets of propositions, untyped deterministic services are equivalent with actions and problems of the STRIPS planning formalism [15]. As such, the structure of our planner is similar to the structure of well-known STRIPS planners like Graphplan [4].

Internally, our planner maintains a structure of alternating action and state levels. A state level n accessible by $PL.states(n)$ represents the set of states reachable from the initial state by the application of n services. In contrast to Graphplan, we assume that only one service can be applied at each level. The planner for untyped deterministic services uses the variable $PL.lastLevel$ for holding the current number of levels and a special level (set of states) for holding the problem goals $PL.goals$.

For this planner, $PL.init(SR)$ (see Algorithm 2) uses the preconditions of the problem request SR to initialize the first level and the problem effects to initialize the goal states. $PL.getServiceRequest()$ returns a new request (created by the $PL.newRequest()$ function) for which the precondition constraint is taken from the last level and the effect constraint from the goals.

The $DirQuery$ returned by this planner's $PL.getDirQuery()$ method ensures that all inputs required by a matching service advertisement are provided by the service request SR. As all services are assumed to be untyped, the $DirQuery$ ignores the matching of types. Moreover, the assignment set of the service advertisement's precondition constraint has to be included in SR's assignment set (potentially available states). The results are sorted so that matching service advertisements providing more of the outputs or goals required by SR come first. Concrete examples of similar directory queries can be found in [3,9].

The main complexity of the planner stems in the methods for addition of services and for solving the composition problem by searching the structure of levels. The $PL.addService(SA_{new})$ procedure has three phases: First, it tries to find the level at which a newly discovered service SA_{new} should be added. Next, it propagates new states generated by the addition of the service or the application of existing services over the states stored by current levels. Finally, a fixpoint procedure is used to extend the current levels by new ones (as long as the last levels are not the same).

$PL.addService(SA)$ used two additional functions: $PL.canApply(states, SA)$ tests whether a service advertisement SA can be added to a given set of states (level), and $PL.apply(states, SA)$ computes the effect states that result from applying a service advertisement SA to the set of states. These two functions operate under the following assumptions, specific to untyped deterministic services:

– Deterministic SAs – Each service advertisement has exactly one set of assignments in its precondition and effect constraints.
– Explicit maintenance of preconditions – Variable/value tuples present in the precondition constraint of an advertisement that *do not* appear in the effect constraint are removed (delete list).

$PL.isFeasible()$ returns true if the last level contains some of the possible sets of goals.

To search for a planning solution, the $PL.solve()$ function recurses over the levels of the plan, starting from the initial level. If a sequence of services marking a solution has been found, a new composite service advertisement is created and returned. The composite service advertisement is a sequential workflow without any branches.

$PL.solve()$ maintains the state that can be achieved by currently selected services and at each step performs the following tasks: First, it checks whether a solution has been reached and if so it returns the solution. Otherwise, if the current state can be further expanded, it applies all services on the level to the current state and recursively checks for a solution. Finally, if no solution has been reached, neither by the current state nor by the recursive call, $PL.solve()$ fails. A solution is discovered if the goal states are included in the current search state.

6 Composing Completely Matching Typed Services

Typed services correspond to non-deterministic planning operators, such as e.g. those supported by the ADL language [24]. Our approach for composing this kind of services is similar to the approach of Kuter and Nau [18], in which deterministic planning algorithms are enhanced in order to support non-determinism. This relies on the fact that conceptually, deterministic planning can be seen as search in a state space, whereas non-deterministic planning can be seen as a very similar search in a belief space, where a belief is represented as a set of states. Still, a major difference between non-deterministic planning and our approach is that the process of composing typed services does not support negative effects.

Next, we present the updates that our previous procedures need to undergo in order to be able to handle sets of states (beliefs) instead of simple states.

Concerning service descriptions, we do not maintain any restriction: values of assignments can be overlapping and constraints can have several assignments. Still, we assume that initial service descriptions (service request and service advertisements retrieved from the directory) are discretized, which may result in some constraints possibly containing extra assignments. For example, the constraint $\{< A, [10 - 20] >, < B, [0 - 10] >\}$ might be discretized along the A variable by the value 15 and along the B variable by the value 5 resulting in four constraints, equivalent with the initial one: $\{< A, [10 - 15] >, < B, [0 - 5] >\}, \{< A, [15 - 20] >, < B, [0 - 5] >\},$ $\{< A, [10 - 15] >, < B, [5 - 10] >\}, \{< A, [15 - 20] >, < B, [5 - 10] >\}$. As a result, in the composer all values are disjoint and as for untyped services we can consider assignments as sets of propositions, where a proposition maps to a variable/value pair.

We call the current planner "complete matching" due to the procedure for selecting services while searching for a plan. Even though we allow for a service to produce non-deterministic effects, the current planner will create a solution where the precondition constraints of services applied at each step (the set of states for which the service can be invoked) completely match or subsume the set of possible states available until that planning step, either from the initial conditions or generated by services applied so far. This implies that applying the service at that step will always work, even in the presence of non-determinism. These kinds of plans are also described in reference [7] and are called *strong solutions*.

In the case of our non-deterministic planner, the initialization and query extraction procedures $PL.init(SR)$ and $PL.getServiceRequest()$ are the same as for the untyped planner.

The $DirQuery$ returned by $PL.getDirQuery()$ is updated such that service advertisements matching any possible state are selected. It takes types into account, which have to be at least as general in the service advertisement as in the service request SR. For precondition constraints, we require that an overlap exists between the states accepted by the service advertisement and the ones provided by SR.

As for the previous planner, the current one maintains a Graphplan-like structure of levels containing states and services. Consequently, the only difference in the procedure of adding a newly discovered service to the current structure stems in the fact that preconditions and effects might include multiple sets of states. This is reflected only in the procedures for testing the viability of applying a service $PL.canApply(states, SA)$ and actually computing the states resulting by the application $PL.apply(states, SA)$. Since a level contains the union of effects of different possible plans, the $PL.canApply(states, SA)$ function considers a service to be applicable only to level states that are supersets of states in the precondition of the service advertisement.

We use the same $PL.isFeasible()$ function as for the deterministic planner before; it returns true if some of the goal sets can be satisfied by the currently reachable states.

The main search function $PL.solve()$ is updated to deal with sets of states instead of a single state. The important difference between the current $PL.solve()$ function and the one for deterministic domains stems in the $PL.canApply(states, SA)$ function, which selects only services having the set of preconditions completely subsuming the current states of the search. In other words, we select services that will always work, no matter which of the current states will be true at runtime. The condition is similar to the one for determining the plan solution. Also the $PL.apply(states, SA)$ function is different from the one for untyped services in that no states are removed in this case (negative effects are not supported).

For determining when a given set of states represents a solution, we require that any of the possible states reachable by the current plan contains some goal states. This is equivalent with the notion of *strong solution* introduced for non-deterministic plans in reference [7].

7   Composing Partially Matching Services

Frequently, forward chaining with complete type matches is too restrictive and fails to find a solution, because the types accepted by the available service advertisements may partially overlap the type specified in a service request. For example, a service request for restaurant recommendation services across all Switzerland may specify that the integer parameter zip code could be in the range [1000,9999], whereas an existing service providing recommendations for the French speaking part of Switzerland accepts only integers in the range [1000-2999] for the zip code parameter. Nonetheless, there may be several recommendation services for different parts of Switzerland that together could cover the whole range given in the query. Hence, a service composition algorithm could create a workflow with different execution paths, depending on the concrete value provided for the zip code parameter at execution time. That is, the workflow would include a *switch* in order to select the appropriate execution path.

A novelty of our approach to composition stems in the capability of our planner to use service advertisements that partially match the current search states while the generated plans will still remain *strong solutions*. This kind of partial matching between service descriptions corresponds to the *overlap* or *intersection* match identified by Li [19] and Constantinescu [10]. In this respect, $PL.getDirQuery()$ returns a less restrictive $DirQuery$ than before, selecting service advertisements that have overlapping types with the service request [3,9].

Handling this kind of partial matches transforms our search into an AND/OR process: all states of the current belief have to lead to a solution (AND) while for each of them the process of searching for the right service advertisement(s) to be applied (OR) has to be recursively invoked.

Of course, exhaustively trying to recursively solve all states in a belief would have a tremendous impact on the performance of the search algorithm. To address this problem, the main idea of our approach relies on the fact that a belief is to be considered solved when all its states recursively lead to a solution. But for each of these states, once the fact that it leads to a solution has been established, it will remain so across different other searches and even in the case of adding new services.

Therefore, the approach that we take for enhancing our AND/OR search is to use a dynamic programming technique that globally marks the states of a belief successfully solved and re-uses this information for pruning OR branches at different invocation levels in the current search or in other further searches. It has to be noted that due to the nature of the search, we cannot anymore represent the planner solution as a sequential workflow, but have to create a tree structure in order to represent the switches.

8   Experimental Evaluation

We evaluated the service composition algorithms explained in Section 6 and Section 7 with our testbed presented in [11]. The testbed covers several application domains and

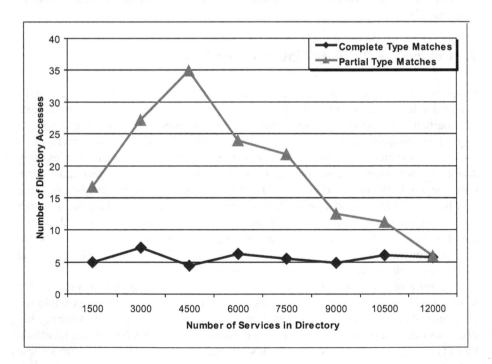

Fig. 2. Algorithm performance for successful compositions, measured in the number of directory accesses

allows to generate randomized service advertisements and service requests for these domains. We populated our directory [3,9] with an increasing number of generated service advertisements (1500–12000) and executed our service composition algorithms using the generated service requests as input. Each measurement represents the average of 50 runs with different service requests.

We used the number of directory accesses as performance metric. As it can be seen in Fig. 2, service composition with complete type matches scales well, because even in the presence of large numbers of service advertisements in the directory the number of required directory accesses does not increase significantly. Service composition with partial type matches is more costly concerning the number of directory accesses, in particular when composition problems are very hard (in our experiments when the directory contains about 4500 services). This is due to the fact that when the directory contains some services but not enough, failure of the composition cannot be determined easily since a good number of services are relevant but not enough of them can be composed to fully satisfy the given service request.

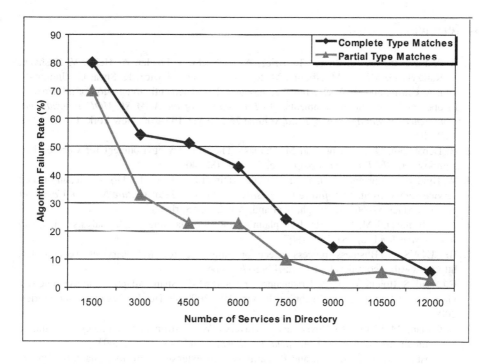

Fig. 3. Algorithm failure rate

As shown in Fig. 3, a major drawback of the service composition algorithm with complete type matches is the high failure rate of the composition, in particular when the directory does not contain too many services (up to 80% failure rate). Service composition with partial type matches significantly reduces the failure rate.

9   Conclusion

With the move towards Web services, tools for service composition are becoming increasingly important. Prevailing approaches to automated service composition, which are often straightforward adaptations of standard planning algorithms, require all service advertisements to be pre-loaded into the reasoning engine. Such techniques are not applicable in an open environment populated by a large number of dynamically changing services.

In this paper we presented planning-based service composition algorithms that dynamically access a separate, potentially large-scale directory in order to retrieve relevant service advertisements. We started with a simple planning algorithm for untyped services and refined it to first exploit type information, and second to support partial type matches. Experiments show that our algorithms scale well with the number of service advertisements stored in the directory. Moreover, the support for partial type matches brings significant gains in the number of problems that can be solved by automated service composition with a given set of service advertisements.

References

1. R. J. Bayardo, Jr., W. Bohrer, R. Brice, A. Cichocki, J. Fowler, A. Helal, V. Kashyap, T. Ksiezyk, G. Martin, M. Nodine, M. Rashid, M. Rusinkiewicz, R. Shea, C. Unnikrishnan, A. Unruh, and D. Woelk. InfoSleuth: Agent-based semantic integration of information in open and dynamic environments. In *Proceedings of the ACM SIGMOD International Conference on Management of Data*, volume 26,2, pages 195–206, New York, 13–15 1997. ACM Press.
2. B. Benatallah, Q. Z. Sheng, and M. Dumas. The self-serv environment for web services composition. *IEEE Internet Computing*, 7(1):40–48, 2003.
3. W. Binder, I. Constantinescu, and B. Faltings. Directory support for large-scale, automated service composition. In *Software Composition*, volume 3628 of *Lecture Notes in Computer Science*, pages 57–66, Edinburgh, Scotland, Apr. 2005. Springer.
4. A. L. Blum and M. L. Furst. Fast planning through planning graph analysis. *Artificial Intelligence*, 90(1–2):281–300, 1997.
5. BPEL4WS.   Business process execution language for web services version 1.1, http://www.ibm.com/developerworks/library/ws-bpel/.
6. F. Casati, S. Ilnicki, L. Jin, V. Krishnamoorthy, and M.-C. Shan. Adaptive and dynamic service composition in eFlow. Technical Report HPL-2000-39, Hewlett Packard Laboratories, 2000.
7. A. Cimatti, M. Pistore, M. Roveri, and P. Traverso. Weak, strong, and strong cyclic planning via symbolic model checking. *Artificial Intelligence*, 147(1-2):35–84, 2003.
8. I. Constantinescu, W. Binder, and B. Faltings. An extensible directory enabling efficient semantic web service integration. In *3rd International Semantic Web Conference (ISWC 2004)*, pages 605–619, Hiroshima, Japan, Nov. 2004.
9. I. Constantinescu, W. Binder, and B. Faltings. Flexible and efficient matchmaking and ranking in service directories. In *2005 IEEE International Conference on Web Services (ICWS-2005)*, pages 5–12, Florida, July 2005.
10. I. Constantinescu and B. Faltings. Efficient matchmaking and directory services. In *The 2003 IEEE/WIC International Conference on Web Intelligence*, pages 75–81, 2003.

11. I. Constantinescu, B. Faltings, and W. Binder. Large scale testbed for type compatible service composition. In *ICAPS 04 workshop on planning and scheduling for web and grid services*, 2004.

12. I. Constantinescu, B. Faltings, and W. Binder. Large scale, type-compatible service composition. In *IEEE International Conference on Web Services (ICWS-2004)*, pages 506–513, San Diego, CA, USA, July 2004.

13. A. Doan and A. Y. Halevy. Efficiently ordering query plans for data integration. In *ICDE*, 2002.

14. D. Fensel, W. Wahlster, and H. Lieberman, editors. *Spinning the Semantic Web: Bringing the World Wide Web to Its Full Potential*. MIT Press, Cambridge, MA, USA, 2002.

15. R. Fikes and N. J. Nilsson. Strips: A new approach to the application of theorem proving to problem solving. In *IJCAI*, pages 608–620, 1971.

16. F. Giunchiglia and P. Traverso. Planning as model checking. In *European Conference on Planning*, pages 1–20, 1999.

17. International Conference on Planning and Scheduling. International Planning Competition, http://ipc.icaps-conference.org/.

18. U. Kuter and D. S. Nau. Forward-chaining planning in nondeterministic domains. In *AAAI*, pages 513–518, 2004.

19. L. Li and I. Horrocks. A software framework for matchmaking based on semantic web technology. In *Proceedings of the 12th International Conference on the World Wide Web*, 2003.

20. S. McIlraith, T. Son, and H. Zeng. Mobilizing the semantic web with DAML-enabled web services. In *Proc. Second International Workshop on the Semantic Web (SemWeb-2001)*, Hongkong, 2001.

21. S. A. McIlraith and T. C. Son. Adapting Golog for composition of semantic web services. In D. Fensel, F. Giunchiglia, D. McGuinness, and M.-A. Williams, editors, *Proceedings of the 8th International Conference on Principles and Knowledge Representation and Reasoning (KR-02)*, pages 482–496, San Francisco, CA, Apr. 2002. Morgan Kaufmann Publishers.

22. OWL-S. DAML Services, http://www.daml.org/services/owl-s/.

23. M. Paolucci, T. Kawamura, T. R. Payne, and K. Sycara. Semantic matching of web services capabilities. In *Proceedings of the 1st International Semantic Web Conference (ISWC)*, 2002.

24. E. P. D. Pednault. ADL: Exploring the middle ground between strips and the situation calculus. In *Proceedings of the First International Conference on Principles of Knowledge Representation and Reasoning (KR'89)*, pages 324–332, Morgan Kaufmann Publishers, 1989.

25. S. R. Ponnekanti and A. Fox. Sword: A developer toolkit for web service composition. In *11th World Wide Web Conference (Web Engineering Track)*, 2002.

26. S. Thakkar, C. A. Knoblock, J. L. Ambite, and C. Shahabi. Dynamically composing web services from on-line sources. In *Proceeding of the AAAI-2002 Workshop on Intelligent Service Integration*, pages 1–7, Edmonton, Alberta, Canada, July 2002.

27. P. Traverso and M. Pistore. Automated composition of semantic web services into executable processes. In *International Semantic Web Conference*, volume 3298 of *Lecture Notes in Computer Science*, pages 380–394. Springer, 2004.

28. W3C. OWL Web Ontology Language 1.0 Reference, http://www.w3.org/tr/owl-ref/.

29. W3C. RDF Primer, http://www.w3.org/tr/rdf-primer/.

30. W3C. XML Schema Part 2: Datatypes, http://www.w3.org/tr/xmlschema-2/.

31. WSMO. Web Service Modeling Ontology, http://www.wsmo.org/.

32. D. Wu, B. Parsia, E. Sirin, J. Hendler, and D. Nau. Automating DAML-S web services composition using SHOP2. In *Proceedings of 2nd International Semantic Web Conference (ISWC2003)*, 2003.

Modeling Composition in Dynamic Programming Environments with Model Transformations

Uwe Zdun and Mark Strembeck

Institute of Information Systems, New Media Lab
Vienna University of Economics and BA, Austria
{uwe.zdun, mark.strembeck}@wu-wien.ac.at

Abstract. Although dynamic programming environments are in widespread use, only basic runtime composition mechanisms are covered by today's modeling languages. Thus, it is common in real-world development projects that dynamic compositions are not modeled formally and are consequently hard to use, for example together with the model-driven paradigm where formal models are essential to generate source code. In this paper, we propose an approach based on model transformations between the valid structural and behavioral runtime states that a system can have. We use UML 2.0 class and activity diagrams for specifying the structural and behavioral model states and provide a UML 2.0 meta-model extension for describing the valid model transformations between corresponding model states.

1 Introduction

Each software composition mechanism defines the possible binding time(s) for the software elements it composes. The binding time is the point in time where the decision for a composition of particular software elements is made. Examples of binding times include development time, source instantiation time, source reuse time, build time, packaging time, installation time, start-up time, and execution time (runtime) [11].

Many different approaches exist to model software compositions that affect binding times before runtime. Examples for such approaches are UML class or component diagrams [21,23] and most architecture description languages (see, e.g., [12,2]). Some modeling languages also allow to specify runtime reconfigurations of components to a certain degree (see, e.g., [1,22]), but not beyond the level of changing the relationships of component or class instances. The specification of effects resulting from more sophisticated runtime composition mechanisms is only sparsely addressed in contemporary modeling languages.

At present, static programming languages such as Java, C++, or C# are still more prevalent than dynamic languages, such as CLOS, Perl, Python, Ruby, Smalltalk, or Tcl. However, together, the dynamic programming languages[1] have a substantial user base and are applied in a widespread application spectrum. Furthermore, some of the

---

[1] Not all dynamic composition mechanisms are directly realized as language features of programming languages – some are based on frameworks and tools. We thus use the more generic term *dynamic programming environments* below.

W. Löwe and M. Südholt (Eds.): SC 2006, LNCS 4089, pp. 178–193, 2006.

more static languages, like Java and C#, increasingly introduce dynamic language features such as limited forms of class reloading or reflection. In addition, aspect-oriented software composition frameworks [10] add language constructs that allow to produce similar effects to those of dynamic composition mechanisms. Furthermore, recent approaches also propose dynamic AOP features (see, e.g., [4,20]).

Given the broad use and increasing importance of dynamic composition mechanisms, it is obvious that modeling support for them is essential for the engineering, understanding, and maintenance of corresponding software systems. In case a software development project follows the model-driven paradigm [19] or the software factory approach [7], we even require a formal specification of the respective composition mechanisms. Such a formal definition is mandatory since it is impossible to generate source code from modeling level artifacts without a formal representation of model elements. Current modeling approaches, however, support dynamic software composition only to a minor degree. The UML 2.0, for example, does not support the specification of runtime changes of most UML modeling elements. For instance, in a class diagram it is not possible to model changing inheritance relations or the introduction of a new method to a class definition at runtime.

In this paper, we present an approach to model structural and behavioral system changes that result from the use of dynamic composition mechanisms. In particular, our approach is based on model transformations [3]. Because UML is the de-facto standard modeling language for software systems, we exemplify our approach by providing a UML meta-model extension (see [23]).

The remainder of this paper is structured as follows. In Section 2 we give a high-level introduction to our approach before we provide a detailed specification of Model Transformation Diagrams in Section 3. Subsequently, Section 4 presents an example for the use of Model Transformation Diagrams. In Section 5 we discuss related work before we conclude the paper and give an outlook on future work in Section 6.

2   Motivation and Approach Synopsis

In essence, this paper aims to provide a well-defined and widely applicable modeling approach to enable the systematic specification of dynamic changes in the structure of software systems as well as resulting changes in system behavior. From our experiences, it is equally important to model structural and behavioral changes, as they most often appear together and they represent two essential views to specify, comprehend, and maintain software systems.

Since the UML is by far the most important modeling language in the area of software engineering, we chose to define an extension to the UML 2.0 standard to realize our approach. However, the general approach does not depend on the UML and may also be realized with any other modeling language.

We especially aim to model a specific subset of the dynamic composition features that can be found in dynamic object-oriented programming environments: changes to structural object-oriented features of classes or components, and the behavior changes that result from them. Here the term "structural feature" relates to:

- the methods of a class,
- the fields of a class,
- the relationships of classes, such as superclass (generalization) relationships, dependencies (e.g. to an interface), associations, compositions, and aggregations,
- the relationships (e.g. the instance-of relationship) and slots of an instance, and
- the classes and objects defined in a system.

In addition, there are many other features that may be subject to dynamic composition, such as non-object-oriented structural features (e.g. procedures in procedural dynamic languages), data that is evaluated as code in homoiconic languages [9], or cross-cutting in aspect-oriented environments [10]. Even though these composition features might possibly be modeled with our approach, in this article we focus on the object-oriented features.

To further motivate our approach, let us consider a typical dynamic composition task that we also use as an example in Section 4. A storage interface abstracts a number of persistent storages, such as different databases. Objects can be made persistent using different persistence strategies that, in turn, must be configured with a storage to which they write the data. Any object can be made persistent or transient at any time. In a static programming environment we would need to instrument all classes that can potentially be made persistent. After that, we could turn persistence on and off at runtime. In a dynamic programming environment, however, we can perform the necessary changes at runtime. For instance, we can configure the storage dynamically with the persistence strategy, and then add the persistence class as a type to all objects (or classes) that should be made persistent. Unfortunately, these dynamic class changes cannot be modeled in most modeling languages.

Moreover, changing the class of an object usually has consequences for other structural elements. For example, fields that belong to the "old" class might get removed from instances, while other fields might be added. The behavior of the methods of the affected class changes as well. For instance, in the example above two different persistence strategies, e.g. eager persistence and lazy persistence, introduce new activities, and these activities are different for the two strategies. Again, switching between these behaviors cannot be modeled in most modeling languages. Furthermore, class changes might also have constraints. For instance, a persistence strategy must be associated with a storage (e.g. a flat file storage or a database), otherwise it must not be used for an object.

Similar concerns appear for all dynamic composition features listed above. Such features are, however, not well supported in contemporary modeling languages. Though, a static "snapshot" of the dynamic programming environment at a particular point in time can well be modeled using modeling languages like the UML. Our concept is thus to extend modeling languages so that legal snapshots of a system can be modeled to describe the valid states of a dynamic software system. To specify snapshot states of static system structures, we use UML class diagrams and variants of class diagrams, such as component diagrams[2]. UML activity diagrams are used to model system behavior and dynamic system facets.

---

[2] Please note that we allow the structure diagrams to contain instance specifications.

To describe changes in a system's structure or behavior we use model transformations. Our approach introduces a new type of UML diagram called *Model Transformation Diagram* (MTD). In essence, an MTD is a special type of state machine. Each MTD state includes a diagram that defines a valid structure or behavior specification of the system under consideration. The MTD also defines the possible changes of the system's structure or behavior as transformations of the model, and excludes changes that are not allowed. The details of MTD diagrams are defined in the following section.

3   Model Transformation Diagrams

In this section, we describe our meta-model extension to the UML 2.0 standard. We introduce a new type of model called *Model Transformation Diagram* (MTD). To define MTDs formally, we specify the new package *ModelTransformations*. Figure 1 shows the meta-model for MTDs that constitutes the base model of the ModelTransformations package. Names of abstract classes are printed in italic letters, as customary in

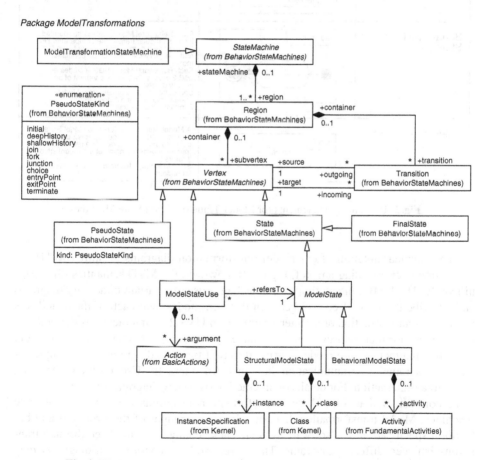

Fig. 1. UML Meta-Model Extension for Model Transformation Diagrams

UML. Relevant UML2 classes from other packages are included in the figure (the "from" clause indicates the corresponding source package in the UML2 superstructure specification [23]).

NODE TYPE	NOTATION	Explanation & Reference
Model Transformation State Machine Frame	mtd name	Each Model Transformation State Machine is surrounded by a rectangular frame around the diagram. The compartment in the upper left corner contains the three letter token "mtd" and optionally the name of the state machine. See ModelTransformationStateMachine from ModelTransformations.
Structural Model State	cd name — ClassName — variable a / variable b — method x / method y	Each Structural Model State is surrounded by a rectangular frame. The compartment in the upper left corner contains the token "cd" and optionally the name of the contained model. Each Structural Model State includes an UML2 class diagram or a variant of a class diagram, such as a component diagram. See StructuralModelState from Model-Transformations and Class from Kernel.
Behavioral Model State	ad name — ●→ ActivityName →◉	Each Behavioral Model State is surrounded by a rectangular frame. The compartment in the upper left corner contains the token "ad" and optionally the name of the contained model. Each Behavioral Model State includes an UML2 avtivity diagram or a variant of an activity diagram. See BehavioralModelState from Model-Transformations and Activity from FundamentalActivities.
Model State Use	mref — name	A Model State Use refers to a Model State. The compartment in the upper left corner contains the token "mref". The rectangular frame contains the name of the model state it refers to. See ModelStateUse from ModelTrans-formations.

Fig. 2. Basic notation elements for Model Transformation State Machines

The graphical notation of our model transformation diagrams is similar to UML2 interaction overview diagrams (cf. Figure 2), however, the MTD semantics differ significantly. The UML2 interaction overview diagrams are a variant of activity diagrams and describe the flow of control between different nodes, and each of these nodes is itself either an Interaction or an InteractionUse. In UML2 an Interaction is defined as a unit of behavior that focuses on the exchange of information between different model elements. Interactions are modeled using different types of diagrams, for example sequence diagrams or communication diagrams. An InteractionUse, on the other hand, refers to an Interaction. For details on interaction overview diagrams see [23].

In contrast to that, our Model Transformation Diagrams are a variant of state machines. Model transformation diagrams describe changes of the structural and behavioral specification of a software system. These changes are modeled through transitions between different diagrams. Therefore, model transformation diagrams may include two different types of states: each *structural model state* refers to an UML2 class diagram, and each MTD *behavior model state* refers to an UML2 activity diagram (see Figure 2).

As shown in Figure 1 the corresponding meta-model classes, StructuralModelState and BehavioralModelState, inherit from an abstract ModelState class, which is itself a State. A StructuralModelState aggregates elements of the types Class and InstanceSpecification, whereas a BehavioralModelState aggregates elements of the type Activity. Variants of the respective diagram types, such as component diagrams which specialize class diagrams, can thus also be contained in ModelStates.

In UML2, all elements of state machines that can have transitions are derived from the Vertex class. In addition to ordinary states, UML2 defines pseudo states (see the classes PseudoState and PseudoStateKind), such as initial, fork, join, choice, etc., as a subtype of Vertex. The UM2 FinalState class is a subtype of the State class. All Vertexes can be connected via Transitions (for additional details on state machines see [23]).

For the definition of MTDs we derive one more class from Vertex. This additional class is called ModelStateUse. Instances of ModelStateUse have no state themselves, so the class is directly derived from Vertex. A ModelStateUse refers to a ModelState, i.e. a ModelStateUse is purely a reference. It is used as a placeholder for the referred ModelState, which contains either a structural model state (modeled as a class diagram) or a behavioral model state (modeled as an activity diagram).

The ModelTransformationStateMachine is a state machine that contains MTDs. Like any other state machine it contains Vertexes and Transitions, which may be organized in Regions (see Figure 1). For the purposes of our ModelTransformations package, we need to constrain the ModelTransformationStateMachine so that it can only have vertexes of the types ModelState, ModelStateUse, FinalState, or PseudoState. That is, ordinary states must not be used in MTDs. The corresponding OCL constraint is given below:

```
context ModelTransformationStateMachine
inv: self.region->forAll(r | r.subvertex->forAll(v |
    v.oclIsKindOf(ModelState) or v.oclIsKindOf(ModelStateUse)
    or v.oclIsKindOf(FinalState) or v.oclIsKindOf(Pseudostate)))
```

The main transition type used in MTDs are *transform transitions*. Transform transitions express that the source model state of the transition is transformed to the target model state of the transition. Thus, transform transitions typically connect ModelStates and ModelStateUses. A transition from one model state to another means that the structure or behavior of a certain system aspect is transformed so that after the transition the system structure or behavior conforms to the state specified by the transition's target. A transform transition from an empty source model state to another target model state means that the model elements contained in the target are added to the system during the transformation.

To define transform transitions we extend the Transition class with the stereotype «*transform*» (see Figure 3). In principle, all transitions in MTDs are transform transitions. There are, however, some exceptions: most PseudoStates and FinalStates have no transform semantics, and are thus connected through ordinary transitions. For instance, the "initial" PseudoState defines the starting point of a certain State Machine. Therefore, the transition from the "initial" PseudoState to a connected model state involves

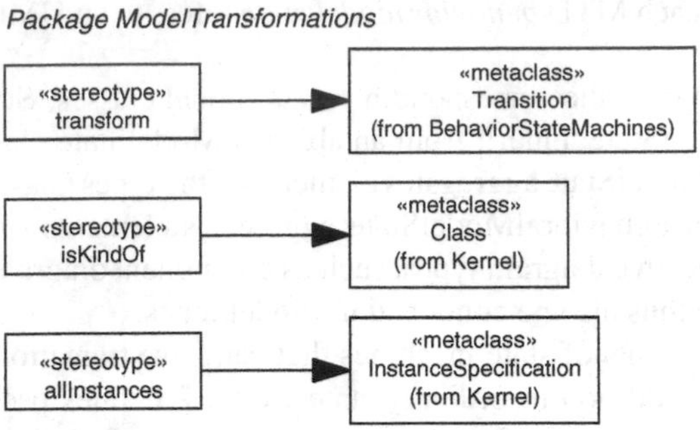

Package ModelTransformations

Fig. 3. Stereotype Definitions for Model Transformation Diagrams

no transformations between model states. The following OCL constraint thus defines that all Transitions in a Model Transformation State Machine which are not connected to PseudoState or FinalState vertexes, must be typed with the «*transform*» stereotype:

```
context ModelTransformationStateMachine
inv: self.region->forAll(r | r.subvertex->forAll(v |
  v.incoming->forAll(t1:Transition|
    if (not v.oclIsKindOf(FinalState)) and
       (not v.oclIsKindOf(PseudoState)) then
      transform.baseTransition->exists(t2:Transition| t2 = t1))
  and
  v.outgoing->forAll(t1:Transition|
    if (not v.oclIsKindOf(PseudoState)) then
      transform.baseTransition->exists(t2:Transition| t2 = t1))
))
```

As mentioned above, PseudoStates cannot have transform transitions. There are, however, a few exceptions to this generic constraint. All exception cases are shown in Figure 4. The following OCL constraint defines that PseudoStates cannot be typed by the «*transform*» stereotype, except for the outgoing connections of "join", "fork", "junction", and "choice" PseudoStates:

```
context ModelTransformationStateMachine
inv: self.region->forAll(r | r.subvertex->forAll(v |
  if v.oclIsKindOf(PseudoState) then
    v.outgoing->forAll(t1:Transition|
      if not (v.kind = #join or v.kind = #fork or
              v.kind = #junction or v.kind = #choice)
      then not transform.baseTransition->exists(t2:Transition|
          t2 = t1))
    and
    v.incoming->forAll(t1:Transition|
      not transform.baseTransition->exists(t2:Transition|
        t2 = t1)))
```

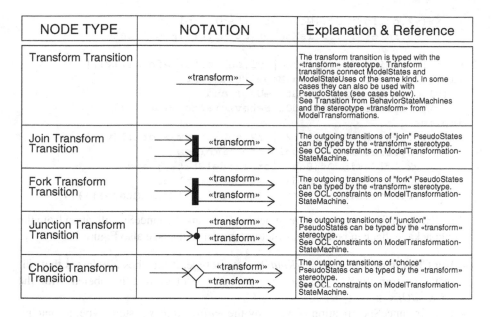

NODE TYPE	NOTATION	Explanation & Reference
Transform Transition	«transform»	The transform transition is typed with the «transform» stereotype. Transform transitions connect ModelStates and ModelStateUses of the same kind. In some cases they can also be used with PseudoStates (see cases below). See Transition from BehaviorStateMachines and the stereotype «transform» from ModelTransformations.
Join Transform Transition	«transform»	The outgoing transitions of "join" PseudoStates can be typed by the «transform» stereotype. See OCL constraints on ModelTransformation-StateMachine.
Fork Transform Transition	«transform» «transform»	The outgoing transitions of "fork" PseudoStates can be typed by the «transform» stereotype. See OCL constraints on ModelTransformation-StateMachine.
Junction Transform Transition	«transform» «transform»	The outgoing transitions of "junction" PseudoStates can be typed by the «transform» stereotype. See OCL constraints on ModelTransformation-StateMachine.
Choice Transform Transition	«transform» «transform»	The outgoing transitions of "choice" PseudoStates can be typed by the «transform» stereotype. See OCL constraints on ModelTransformation-StateMachine.

Fig. 4. Transform Transitions in Model Transformation Diagrams

Furthermore, to ensure that FinalStates never have incoming «*transform*» transitions we specify the OCL constraint shown below (remember that FinalState is *not* a PseudoState and has no outgoing transitions, see [23]):

```
context ModelTransformationStateMachine
inv: self.region->forAll(r | r.subvertex->forAll(v |
  if v.oclIsKindOf(FinalState) then
    v.incoming->forAll(t1:Transition|
      not transform.baseTransition->exists(t2:Transition|
        t2 = t1)))
```

All model states used within the same Model Transformation State Machine must be of the same kind because it is not sensible to describe a transformation from an activity diagram to a class diagram, or vice versa. Thus, each Model Transformation State Machine contains either structural model states or behavioral model states but not both. This is expressed by the following OCL constraints:

```
context ModelTransformationStateMachine
inv: self.region->forAll(r1 | r1.subvertex->forAll(v1 |
  v1.oclIsKindOf(StructuralModelState) or
    (v1.oclIsKindOf(ModelStateUse) and
    v1.refersTo.oclIsKindOf(StructuralModelState))
  implies
    self.region->forAll(r2 | r2.subvertex->forAll(v2 |
      (v2.oclIsKindOf(ModelState) implies
      v2.oclIsKindOf(StructuralModelState)) and
```

```
        (v2.oclIsKindOf(ModelStateUse) implies
         v2.refersTo.oclIsKindOf(StructuralModelState))))))

inv: self.region->forAll(r1 | r1.subvertex->forAll(v1 |
  v1.oclIsKindOf(BehavioralModelState) or
    (v1.oclIsKindOf(ModelStateUse) and
     v1.refersTo.oclIsKindOf(BehavioralModelState))
  implies
      self.region->forAll(r2 | r2.subvertex->forAll(v2 |
        (v2.oclIsKindOf(ModelState) implies
         v2.oclIsKindOf(BehavioralModelState)) and
        (v2.oclIsKindOf(ModelStateUse) implies
         v2.refersTo.oclIsKindOf(BehavioralModelState))))))
```

Finally, we define two more stereotypes for Class and InstanceSpecification from the Kernel package that can be used in structural model states (see also Figure 3):

– If a Class is typed by the «isKindOf» stereotype, it matches all classes that (directly or transitively) provide the type of the class that is labeled with the «isKindOf» stereotype.
– If an InstanceSpecification is typed by the «allInstances» stereotype, it matches all objects which are (direct or indirect) instances of the class that is labeled with the «allInstances» stereotype.

The «isKindOf» and «allInstances» stereotypes are mainly defined for convenience reasons, to allow for a compact specification of structural transitions (see also Section 4). These placeholder stereotypes especially ease situations where a StructuralModelState contains a class diagram that includes one or more class hierarchies. The use of these stereotypes, however, is optional to get smaller MTD models.

4   Example: Dynamic Composition of Persistence Strategies and Storages

In this section, we illustrate the use of MTDs via a number of dynamic composition functionalities of the scripting language XOTcl [17]. XOTcl is a dynamic language that supports dynamics in class relationships, superclass relationships, and mixin classes. Mixin classes [16] can be dynamically composed with any other class or object. A mixin class serves as a composition unit for a number of mixin methods. A mixin class is dynamically registered for an object or class as a *message interceptor*, which means that mixin classes intercept the method calls to the respective target object. Mixin classes are typically used as small building blocks to extend given classes [15]. These language functionalities are hard to model using standard UML diagrams because the corresponding dynamic changes in structure and behavior of the system cannot be captured.

As an example to demonstrate the use of MTDs, we consider the dynamic composition of persistence strategies for objects in XOTcl. The XOTcl library provides the class Storage as an abstract interface for a number of storage classes, and the class Persistence provides an abstract interface for two persistence strategies: eager and

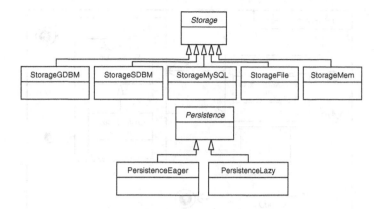

Fig. 5. Classes implementing storages and persistence strategies

lazy persistence. The respective classes are shown in Figure 5. If an XOTcl object has a type relationship to one of the `Persistence` classes, the object is persisted to one of the storages defined by the `Storage` class. This can happen eagerly, i.e. all changes are immediately written to the storage, or lazily, i.e. the effect of all changes is written to the storage when the application closes down.

In our example, we now model the dynamic structural compositions that are valid for the composition of persistence strategies. First of all, we can make all instances of a particular class persistent. In XOTcl, two dynamic language elements can be used here: we can either add a `Persistence` class as superclass for the class whose instances should be made persistent, or we can add a `Persistence` class as a per-class mixin to the corresponding class. Figure 6 models these two situations in an MTD. The simple model state in the upper left corner shows a class diagram that matches all instances (indicated by the «*allInstances*» stereotype, see Section 3) of the type `Class` (note that `Class` is the type of all classes in the XOTcl object system). That is, the transformations can potentially be applied for all classes defined in XOTcl.

The other two model states depicted in Figure 6 show state transformations that can be applied to each XOTcl class. They show the possible combinations variants of `Persistence` classes and instances of `Class`. To include all subclasses of `Persistence` we add the stereotype «*isKindOf*» (see Section 3). This means any subclass of `Persistence` can be composed with all instances of `Class`, and XOTcl classes may either have a superclass relationship or a per-class mixin relationship to a respective `Persistence` class.

Similar to the example described above, individual objects can be dynamically composed with any `Persistence` subclass. The most general class in the XOTcl object system is the class `Object`. Thus, to make an instance of the `Object` class or an instance of a subclass of `Object` persistent, a `Persistence` class is either added as a class of the respective instance, or a `Persistence` class is added as a per-object mixin to the corresponding instance. Both transformations are depicted in Figure 7.

Finally, once a class or an object is made persistent, we must configure a persistent storage, so that the persistence strategy knows to which storage it can write the data

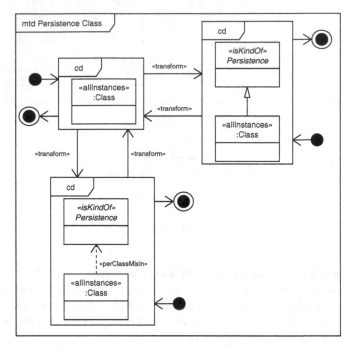

Fig. 6. All possible compositions of the Persistence class and instances of Class

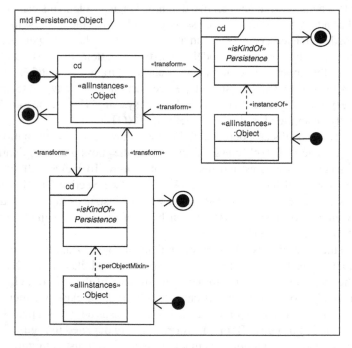

Fig. 7. All possible compositions of the Persistence class and Object instances

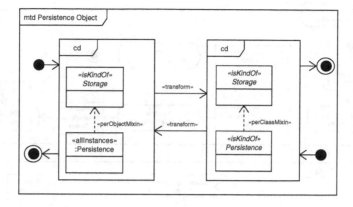

Fig. 8. Possible compositions of the Persistence and Storage classes

(see also Figure 5). There are two mutual exclusive alternatives, but it is mandatory to select one of these alternatives. Figure 8 shows the two variants modeled via an MTD:

- The `Storage` is defined as per-class mixin for the `Persistence` class, meaning that all persistence data is written to the same storage.
- The `Storage` class is defined as per-object mixin for `Persistence` instances, meaning that the storage for each persistent instance is configured individually.

After we have defined the different structural transformations, we describe the corresponding model transformations of the behavioral model states. Figure 9 shows an empty activity diagram as an initial state. This initial state can either be transformed to a behavioral model state that introduces the eager persistence strategy or to a model

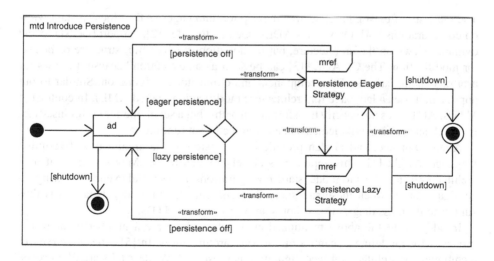

Fig. 9. Behavioral model transformations for eager and lazy persistence

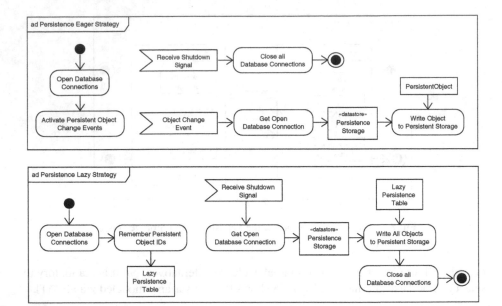

Fig. 10. Detailed behavioral model states for eager and lazy persistence

state that introduces the lazy persistence strategy. The model states in Figure 9 are given as ModelStateUse references. The detailed behavioral model states for eager and lazy persistence that these ModelStateUse states refer to are shown in Figure 10.

5   Related Work

The majority of existing architecture description languages (ADL) focus a static view on configurations [14]. Only a few ADLs, such as Rapide [12], support both static and dynamic views on the architecture, but do not support (dynamic) structure or behavior modification. The C2 ADL [13] can be seen as an exception because it allows for arbitrary modifications of the component and connector configuration. Similar to our approach, it uses a language for architecture modification (called AML). In contrast to MTDs, AML does not specify transformation paths, but a set of operations for insertion, removal, and rewiring of elements in an architecture at runtime.

Allen, Douence, and Garlan provide an extension to the architecture description language Wright [1]. This approach is closely related to our MTDs because it uses architectural snapshots to model static configurations, and special events triggering reconfiguration between these snapshots. The general idea to model dynamics is thus similar to the class diagram snapshots that we use in our MTDs.

In addition to the above mentioned approaches, there are a number of other approaches for modeling dynamics of software architectures. In [5] a recent survey of techniques for architectural reconfiguration is presented. While ADLs are often based on process algebras, other techniques used for specifying architectural reconfiguration are graph rewriting rules, graph transformation, and logic. None of the surveyed approaches, however, is based on model transformations like the approach presented in our paper.

A commonality of the approaches mentioned so far is that they focus on the addition and removal of components and connectors at runtime only. That means that, in contrast to our MTDs, those other approaches do not model other dynamic composition mechanisms. Moreover, corresponding changes in the behavioral model state which can be specified in MTDs via activity diagram snapshots, cannot be modeled using the above mentioned approaches.

Czarnecki and Antkiewicz propose an alternative way to model variants of behavioral models [6] that is comparable to our transformations of behavioral model states. The work described in [6] does, however, not cover the other elements of MTDs yet. In particular, Czarnecki and Antkiewicz use feature models to describe the possible variants of UML activity diagrams. Here a model is described via a model template, which specifies the possible composition of a system's features. Furthermore, they use a special-purpose tool to instantiate the model template from a feature configuration. Using the MTDs presented in this paper, we can use model transformations to add features in a similar fashion. In cases where many features need to be combined, the MTDs might get more complex than feature models. On the other hand, possible transformations of the models are not directly visible in feature models.

Our approach is based on the concept of model transformation. Recently, the research field of model-driven software development [19] has brought up a number of approaches for model transformations, mainly based on UML models (see, e.g., [3,18,24,7]). Our work extends these approaches with a concept for representing dynamic software compositions and with an extension of the UML standard for depicting structural and behavioral transformations suitable for these dynamic software compositions. As our general approach does not depend on a specific modeling language (as the UML for example), the transformation syntax and semantics in those other model transformation approaches could be extended, following our approach, to also support dynamic software composition. We have chosen the UML to exemplify our approach because it is the de-facto standard for software systems modeling.

Dynamic aspect-oriented approaches (see, e.g., [4,20,8]) provide an implementation of dynamic aspect-oriented transformations. However, modeling dynamic aspects is not yet in focus of the aspect-oriented community. Our approach can potentially be used to provide models for transformations implemented by dynamic aspect-oriented approaches. However, in this paper, we have only focused on modeling object-oriented language features.

6 Conclusion

In this paper, we have presented an approach to model structural and behavioral compositions in dynamic programming environments – with a special focus on object-oriented language features. Even though dynamic composition mechanisms are in widespread use, most contemporary modeling languages provide only little or even no support to specify dynamic compositions. Our paper describes an intuitive approach to resolve this problem. We use structural and behavioral snapshots of a system that are given as class and activity diagrams. These snapshots are interconnected using model transformations.

To be able to apply our approach in model-driven development, we introduced a formal meta-model extension to the UML. We chose the UML since it is a standardized modeling language that is in widespread use. Our general approach, however, is not depending on the UML. As a part of our future work, we plan to develop a model-driven tool-set for dynamic languages. So far our main focus was on structural evolution of dynamic object-oriented composition mechanisms. We plan to further extend our work in two directions: first, we want to introduce a pointcut language for model states to provide modeling support for (dynamic) AOP. Second, we will develop an approach to specify constraints on system states, e.g. via forbidden model states.

References

1. R. Allen, R. Douence, and D. Garlan. Specifying and analyzing dynamic software architectures. In *Proc. of the Conference on Fundamental Approaches to Software Engineering (FASE'98)*, Lisbon, Portugal, March 1998.
2. R. Allen and D. Garlan. A formal basis for architectural connection. *ACM Trans. Softw. Eng. Methodol.*, 6(3):213–249, 1997.
3. J. Bezivin. From object composition to model transformation with the mda. In *Proceedings of the Technology of Object-Oriented Languages and Systems (TOOLS USA)*, Santa Barbara, CA, USA, 2001. IEEE Press.
4. C. Bockisch, M. Haupt, M. Mezini, and K. Ostermann. Virtual Machine Support for Dynamic Join Points. In *AOSD 2004 Proceedings*. ACM Press, 2004.
5. J. S. Bradbury, J. R. Cordy, J. Dingel, and M. Wermelinger. A survey of self-management in dynamic software architecture specifications. In *WOSS '04: Proceedings of the 1st ACM SIGSOFT workshop on Self-managed systems*, pages 28–33. ACM Press, 2004.
6. K. Czarnecki and M. Antkiewicz. Mapping features to models: A template approach based on superimposed variants. In *Proc. of 4th International Conference on Generative Programming and Component Engineering (GPCE 2005)*, pages 422–437, Tallinn, Estonia, Sep/Oct 2005.
7. J. Greenfield and K. Short. *Software Factories: Assembling Applications with Patterns, Frameworks, Models & Tools*. J. Wiley and Sons Ltd., 2004.
8. R. Hirschfeld. AspectS – Aspect-Oriented Programming with Squeak. In *Objects, Components, Architectures, Services, and Applications for a Networked World*, LNCS 2591, pages 216–232. Springer-Verlag.
9. A. Kay. *The Reactive Engine*. PhD thesis, University of Utah, 1969.
10. G. Kiczales, J. Lamping, A. Mendhekar, C. Maeda, C. V. Lopes, J. M. Loingtier, and J. Irwin. Aspect-oriented programming. In *Proceedings European Conference on Object-Oriented Programming (ECOOP'97)*, pages 220–242, Finnland, June 1997. LCNS 1241, Springer-Verlag.
11. C. Krueger. Software product lines – binding times. http://www.softwareproductlines.com/introduction/binding.html, 2005.
12. D. C. Luckham and J. Vera. An event-based architecture definition language. *IEEE Trans. Softw. Eng.*, 21(9):717–734, 1995.
13. N. Medvidovic. Adls and dynamic architecture changes. In *Joint proceedings of the second international software architecture workshop (ISAW-2) and international workshop on multiple perspectives in software development (Viewpoints '96) on SIGSOFT '96 workshops*, pages 24–27. ACM Press, 1996.

14. N. Medvidovic and R. N. Taylor. A classification and comparison framework for software architecture description languages. *IEEE Trans. Softw. Eng.*, 26(1):70–93, 2000.
15. D. Moon. Object-oriented programming with flavors. In *Proceedings of the Conference on Object-Oriented Programming Systems, Languages, and Applications (OOPSLA '86)*, volume 21 of *SIGPLAN Notices*, pages 1–8, Portland, November 1986.
16. G. Neumann and U. Zdun. Enhancing object-based system composition through per-object mixins. In *Proceedings of Asia-Pacific Software Engineering Conference (APSEC)*, Takamatsu, Japan, December 1999.
17. G. Neumann and U. Zdun. XOTcl, an object-oriented scripting language. In *Proceedings of Tcl2k: The 7th USENIX Tcl/Tk Conference*, Austin, Texas, USA, February 2000.
18. OMG. MOF 2.0 Query / Views / Transformations RFP. Technical Report ad/2002-04-10, Object Management Group, April 2002.
19. OMG. MDA Guide Version 1.0.1. Technical report, Object Management Group, 2003.
20. A. Popovici, T. Gross, and G. Alonso. Just In Time Aspects: Efficient Dynamic Weaving for Java. In *Proc. of the 2nd International Conference on Aspect-Oriented Software Development (AOSD 2003)*, pages 100–109, Boston, USA, 2003. ACM Press.
21. J. Rumbaugh, I. Jacobson, and G. Booch. *The Unified Modeling Language Reference Manual*. Addison-Wesley, 1999.
22. G. Succi, R. Wong, E. Liu, and M. Smith. Supporting dynamic composition of components. In *ICSE '00: Proceedings of the 22nd international conference on Software engineering*, page 787, New York, NY, USA, 2000. ACM Press.
23. The Object Management Group. Unified Modeling Language: Superstructure. http:// www.omg.org/technology/documents/formal/uml.htm, August 2005. Version 2.0, formal/05-07-04, Object Management Group.
24. D. Vojtisek and J.-M. Jzquel. MTL and Umlaut NG - Engine and framework for model transformation. *ERCIM News 58*, 58, 2004.

General Composition of Software Artifacts

William Harrison[1], Harold Ossher[2], and Peri Tarr[2]

[1] Department of Computer Science
Trinity College
Dublin 2, Ireland
Bill.Harrison@cs.tcd.ie
[2] IBM Thomas J. Watson Research Center
P.O. Box 704
Yorktown Heights, NY 10598, USA
{ossher, tarr}@watson.ibm.com

Abstract. Composition is the process of creating new artifacts from a set of input artifacts by combining the content of the input artifacts according to some given specifications. Composition engines are a distinct kind of software component. Like compilers, parsers, and UI-generators, they have their own domain of discourse and base of concepts, their own structure for expressing desired results, their own internal solution structure, and their own set of research problems. Composition applies not only to artifacts representing executable code, but to any sort of artifacts, from build or configuration controls to documentation or UI. While software composition is of interest to an audience wider than that of developers applying aspect-oriented software development (AOSD) approaches, AOSD's composition of separate concerns or aspects presents more complex requirements than does object-composition. This paper describes a base of concepts suitable for expressing composition and shows how a general composition engine realizing these concepts can be used to effect the composition needs of several existing AOSD approaches.

1 Introduction

Composition is the process of creating new artifacts from a set of input artifacts by combining the content of the input artifacts according to some given specifications. Much work in component software has focused on components that are viewed as channel-connected components, whether represented as objects accessed through interfaces or other behavioral packages accessed through ports[16]. The need for bus-connected component models, in which the components contain many packages, objects, or interfaces, was also noted [6], and approaches to software development by composition of separately encapsulated concerns are the general subject of interest of several approaches to Aspect-Oriented Software Development (AOSD). While much support for AOSD is focused on executable software material[20], and on the injection of event-interceptors into executable code [2], [14], [18], composition is useful not only for programming-language artifacts, but for requirements, use case, UML design artifacts, test suites, and auxiliary resources like user-interface descriptions, menus and menu elements, and even for build-time or deployment-time directives, like Make or Ant scripts and WSDL, directories or jar files.

W. Löwe and M. Südholt (Eds.): SC 2006, LNCS 4089, pp. 194–210, 2006.
© Springer-Verlag Berlin Heidelberg 2006

In this paper, we use the term AOSD to refer to all bus-connected composition models, whether or not they employ pattern-based event interception. Implementations of higher-order composition models generally employ two common building blocks:

1. Language constructs that create additional artifacts to be woven with the developer-produced artifacts,
2. A "composition engine" or "weaver" component to actually effect the desired composition.

Composition is thus only one part of what is needed for many AOSD approaches. Composition engines are a distinct kind of software component that provide the second of these building blocks. They do not, for example, include the generation of code to track control flow as needed by AspectJ's "cflow" specifications. We are familiar with compilers, parsers and UI-generators as distinct kinds of software components, each having their own domain of discourse and base of concepts, their own structure for expressing desired results, their own internal solution structure, and their own set of research problems. A similar suite of interests applies to composition engines. This paper describes a base of concepts suitable for expressing composition and illustrates how a general composition engine realizing these concepts can be used to effect the composition needs of several existing AOSD approaches and to extend the domain of applicability beyond the application to code.

A composition component based on these concepts has been developed and is available as open source as part of the Concern Manipulation Environment (CME)[8]. It underlies the composition capabilities made available by the Concern Explorer and other tools. A description of the implementation and the research problems posed by the composition component is beyond the scope of this paper, but some additional concepts needed in realizing Java™ composition and extraction (of new artifacts from existing ones) are discussed here.

The remainder of the paper is organized as follows: Section 2 presents a *very small* example, used in following explanations. Section 3 describes a model for material to be composed, and Section 4 discusses the concepts that are used for describing composition. Section 5 describes how CCC could be employed to effect the composition needs of AspectJ, Hyper/J, Composition Filters, or Adaptive Programming.

2 A Very Small Example

Consider designing a feature for a hypothetical, pre-existing thermostatic control system as a separate concern. The existing "basic" system contains Sensor classes that record temperature, maintain an updated average, and report when asked. They have methods for "report" and "update." The system is implemented with many independent subclasses, most but not necessarily all of which are named "*Sensor," each with its own style of implementation.

The "alarm" feature to be added is to produce a fire alert if temperature exceeds some threshold. The Sensors must now know a "controller", and alert it when needed. So they need have an added field: "controller". This feature is to intercept updates, and generate an alert when necessary.

Sensors that alert the controller are to be created by composing the basic sensors and the alarm enhancements. The artifacts to be composed fit a general model that allows the meaning of the specifications to be given. The model and the specifications are discussed in Sections 3 and 4.

3   A Model for Material to Be Composed

Our implementation of the composition engine employs plug-in components called concern assemblers and informants [8] to shield it from the concrete representation of artifacts. This allows the composition task to be separated into many small artifact-representation-dependent components that are simple to build, but a single, complex artifact-independent composition engine to embody the high-level planning activities. The separation is made in terms of a common abstract representation for the artifacts themselves. The artifacts can be data objects, such as directories of files, or more complex objects, such as programs and UML diagrams stored in directories or files. Figure 1 shows that artifact and element containment are independent. Composition is similar across both, though complex objects require additional concepts, such as typing of their elements. We present a single model, based on the more complex context, with the understanding that not all capabilities of the definitions are applicable to all artifacts. This model treats artifacts as physical containers, made up of identifiable, structurally-related elements. Each of those elements can have a body of material whose structure is treated as a "black-box" but whose important characteristic is that it may contain references to other elements (or itself). Unlike a meta^n-model like the OMG's MOF, the abstract elements form a model of the relevent information in the artifacts directly; and they are realized as Java interfaces used in building the composition engine Their implementations are artifact-representation specific, but implementing them on an artifact represented using MOF is a small task. We use Java's terms for programming constructs in the discussion here, but for illustrative purposes only—the model is applicable to artifacts defined in many languages and formalisms.

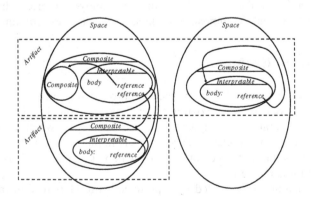

Fig. 1. Artifacts and Elements

Spaces. A *space* encapsulates a body of material with a well-defined interpretation of all names used by its elements to reference other elements. These elements must also be within the space. This makes the space "referentially complete", and independent from other spaces. Spaces only contain named container definitions. They are artificial elements, not expected to be referenced in any of the material being composed, but to provide ways of dealing with a multiplicity of separately-defined corpora of first-class elements within which the same names might be used for different purposes. In dealing with Java programs, for example, a space may be defined by a *classpath*, consisting of all classes on that path.

Container Definitions. A *container* definition specifies a collection of named elements that are its *members*. Members can be nested containers or interpretable material definitions, but not spaces. In dealing with Java programs, for example, classes and interfaces are treated as containers.

Interpretable Material Definitions. Interpretable material definitions provide the "meat" of the material subject to composition – the code, text, or image material itself. Each interpretable element definition has a *body*, generally treated as a black-box except that its correct interpretation may require proper resolution of by-name references to other elements. Each interpretable element definition may also refer to a container used, for example, to specify the type of result obtained from interpreting the body or of information retrieved by accessing it. Support for type-matching allows the model to be used to describe elements for which integrity must be preserved by type-checking.

Purely-procedural Interpretables. Interpretable definitions are purely-procedural if they have no execution-time constraint other than their interpretability; for example, they have no additional state. They can therefore be combined and may be rewritten differently for different uses when needed. For example, one can rewrite a method to delegate its call to another method. It is important that references to them be parameterized to achieve different effects on different executions, so references to purely-procedural interpretables may be qualified by a *signature*, consisting of a sequence of references to containers. The signature can be used, for example to represent parameter types. This signature is considered to be part of the interpretable's name. In dealing with Java programs, for example, methods are examples of purely-procedural interpretables.

Resource-bearing Interpretables. If not purely procedural, interpretable definitions are resource-bearing. They denote more than just their interpretable material, but also ownership of some execution-time resource like a processor, a thread, or a place in storage to which values may be assigned. The association with their resource limits flexibility of composition even though their body may still contain references that need to be interpreted, such as an initialization expression. For example, one cannot rewrite the value of a field to permit copies that share storage when on different processors. So, in dealing with Java programs, for example, fields are treated as resource-bearing interpretables, with their bodies interpreted for initialization.

References. Interpretable material may contain references, by name, to itself or other elements within the same space. In dealing with Java programs, for example, references can be found to types, fields and methods.

Methoids. It is frequently the case that a developer performing composition needs to work with constructs that lie within the element bodies that are treated as black-boxes. The injection of pattern-based event interception into element bodies is some-times seen as characteristic of AOSD because it was characteristic of Aspect-Oriented Programming [13]. But while needed to express the required recombinations, the possible constructs to be matched by the patterns are generally specific to the kind of artifact involved. For example, if an element body is the text of a paper, there might be a need to compose each page-footer with a copyright notice. Or in the coding sphere, it may be that additional behavior is needed whenever the value of some field is written or read. In this latter example, although the field access could have been written as a call to a get/set method, directly available for composition, it may not have been. Such "might-have-been" elements can be treated as explicit elements by characterizing them with some pattern to be matched in the body and asserting that occurrences of this pattern should be treated as references to synthesized elements. In general, the possible patterns that might be specified depend on the type of artifact, so we do not model each kind explicitly. Although a more explanatory term like "pat-tern-specified submodular extractions" might be preferable, we found no suitable short term, so we call these synthesized elements *methoids*, for historical reasons - in the context of OO code they are like methods (purely procedural) found by pattern-matching.

An extended treatment of the handling of open-ended methoid characterization, query, extraction and injection is beyond the scope of this paper. The key points, however, are that they are specified by artifact-kind-dependent patterns, and that once identified by query, extraction and composition mechanisms can manipulate them like other pure interpretable material. They are defined as an extension of purely interpret-able material (methods). Even though no general abstract model can be made for them because they are entirely dependent on the kind of artifact involved, combining them is described and effected in the same way as for other elements. Their final reassem-bly is again carried out by artifact-dependent concern assemblers. An example of the identification of a Java code methoid in this way appears in the next section at 4.1.e3.

Uninterpreted information: Modifiers and Attributes. Elements may have addi-tional information, not requiring interpretation of references within it. Examples of this information include *modifiers* like "public", "private", "synchronized" in Java, and *attributes*, like "association name" in UML. This information is represented and available for composition, but its composition follows a rather simple model and tends to be handled in ways that depend on the particular kind of artifact being manipulated.

4   Concepts for Describing Composition

To describe composition, it is necessary to identify *what* elements are to be com-posed, and to specify *how* those elements are to be composed. We do this by means of *correspondences* and *weaving models,* respectively. Together, these make up *weaving directives.* This section describes these concepts, discusses how multiple weaving directives interact, and then discusses the nature of implicit assumptions made by de-velopers using composition, and how those implicit assumptions are made explicit. In the implementation of our composition engine, these concepts are expressed as simple, objects passed through the engine's interfaces to carry the choices expressed by whatever tool is using the composition engine to carry out its needs.

4.1 Identifying Correspondences

The first component of a weaving directive establishes elements to be composed. The elements to be identified with one another for composition purposes may be indicated explicitly or implicitly, and a name must be given to the composite result.

The n-tuple of *input elements* that are to be composed, along with the name of the *result element* to be produced by the composition, is called a *correspondence*.

Explicit Identification. Explicit correspondences result from queries using patterns over items' names. Each query produces a set of correspondences. This model allows us to subsume the query capabilities of a variety of existing AOSD languages and tools. Correspondences supporting AspectJ advice consist, for example, of 3 parts: the "base" to which the aspect or advice is being attached, the aspect or advice itself, and the result (which is by default given the name of the "base"). The structure of AspectJ is such that the set of correspondences is formed by applying a one advice to a set of many "base" elements that are indicated by a query, called a "pointcut." Hyper/J's "by-name" matching structure, on the other hand, produces a set of correspondences for elements with matching names.

The query languages employed are not required or described here. However, it is important to note that the query processor is capable of forming tuples containing elements matched by a unification-based search. This allows embedding of both AspectJ's queries (pointcuts) and queries required to support Hyper/J's capabilities into a query structure much more powerful than that provided by either. Examples of queries that may be useful for the very small Thermostatic Control example described above are[1]:

e1: (**class basic:*Sensor, alarm:SensorAddition**)

which produces a set of correspondences, each having a pair of inputs consisting of a class in the space "basic" whose name ends with "Sensor" and the class named "SensorAddition" in the space "alarm", and defaulting the result class's name to the one in "basic." The nature of the result class is determined by the weaving model used in the weaving directive of which this query is part.

e2: (**method basic:*Sensor.update(<type>),
alarm:SensorAddition.update(<type>)**)

which produces the set of correspondences, each identifying an "update" method of a class whose name ends with "Sensor" in the space "basic" and that takes a single parameter of any type, and the method named "update" in the class "SensorAddition" in the space "alarm" that has the same type signature as the one in "basic," also defaulting the result method's name to the one in "basic." The nature of the result method is determined by the accompanying weaving model, as before.

---

[1] The syntax used here simply provides a direct reflection of the underlying concepts for expressing composition, and not meant to be suggested as an actual language in use by any approach to AOSD.

e3: **(method basic:["set" <type> av<suffix>],**
   alarm:sensorAddition.update(<type>)) as setAv<suffix>

which produces the set of correspondences, each having two parts. The first part is a "set" methoid that denotes an assignment to a field whose name starts with "av" in the space "basic". The second part identifies the method named "update" in the class "SensorAddition" in the space "alarm" that has the same type signature as the type of the field in "basic". The result method's name is based on the name of the field in "basic." The nature of the result is determined by the accompanying weaving model. An actual method can be produced, called in place of each assignment to the variable, or what would be the method body can be in-lined.

Implicit Identification. Implicit correspondences result from implicit elaboration of container definitions. Unless inhibited, a correspondence established between two container definitions also establishes implicit correspondences between members of the containers, so that the resulting containers will contain contents equivalent to the originals. Depending on the developer's expectations (see section 4.4), these correspondences can either apply to like-named members or can simply reflect "copying" of the individual definitions from the inputs in the correspondence. The names assigned in the output are generally the same as those used in the inputs, except where name-clashes arise. As described in section 4.2 on "selection", it is possible to diagnose such clashes as erroneous, if desired.

4.2 Weaving Models

The weaving model is the part of a weaving directive that provides directions on how the output named in a correspondence is to be derived from the inputs. There are two fundamental aspects to a weaving model: *selecting* from the inputs, and describing how the selected elements fit into the result's *structure*.

Selection. Each selection of inputs is governed by an ordering that applies to the elements that it selects from. We describe selection modes, then ordering.

Selecting Elements from the Inputs. Not all inputs in a correspondence are necessarily intended to be part of the result. One obvious case of this is often called *override*, where one of the inputs is intended to replace another entirely. Another obvious case arises from the desire to indicate that name clashes are not allowed. This selection is called *unique*. Other kinds of selection occur when one of the inputs is selected to be wrapped *around* one or more other members, or when a single representative member is selected as *any* of a set of allegedly equivalent inputs.

A single weaving model can contain multiple selections, such as several override selections applying to different inputs. When no special selection is to apply, the remaining inputs are all selected for combination. This default is called *merge* selection.

When applied to container definitions, an ambiguity can arise – does the selection apply to the whole container, or are the containers intended to be merged but to have the selection apply to their like-named members? As a result, many selection modes are available as pairs, like *override* and *overridemember*.

This list is clearly not exhaustive. Our implementation of CME's composition engine provides for extensibility of the selection modes made available.

An example of a simple weaving directive that might be used in the Thermostatic Control example described above is:

merge (class basic:*Sensor, alarm:SensorAddition)

using the query described in section 4.1.e1 and a weaving model with the "merge" selection. It directs that the material from the SensorAddition class in "alarm" is to be merged with the material from the selected classes in "basic" to make the result class.

Ordering the Selected Elements. The orderings provided for *override* or *around* govern which input overrides or is wrapped around which others. The ordering provided for merge is used in the case of interpretable elements, such as methods, and to the order in which they are combined within the result.

The simplest general model for ordering is that of a partial order. Supposing that names like "before" can be used to indicate previously-defined orderings, an example useful for the Thermostatic Control example is:

merge before
    (method basic:*Sensor.update(<type>),
      alarm:SensorAddition.update(<type>))

using the a query described in section 4.1.e1 and a weaving model with the "merge" selection, to put the method from the alarm feature before the corresponding method from the basic system.

Since a single weaving model can contain multiple selections, each with its own ordering, it will often be necessary to harmonize independently-specified orderings that apply to the same inputs. We address this issue in section 4.5 where we describe a extension of the concept of partial orderings that suits this need.

Specifying the Result Structure. When a composite is formed from several inputs, there are many issues that may or must be resolved about its *structure* – about how the individual inputs participate in the composite. Though exactly which issues are important to a particular composition approach vary, the ability to specify and control structure is necessary. In one analysis [7] we discuss the issues that concern the identity, the lifetime, and the delegation relationships among participants in a group, but other issues can apply as well, including specialized linkage conventions or the use of particular run-time representations. As with the other aspects of the weaving model, the exact manner in which the structure is established for a correspondence is a point at which a general composition engine component should try to provide for extensibility. Using simple names explained below, like *aspect, facet,* or *copy,* to indicate the structure allows us to phrase some of the compositions needed for the Thermostatic Control example:

e1: **merge (class basic:*Sensor as facet, feature:SensorAddition as aspect)**

This merges the classes as described in the example in section 4.1e1, but adds to that the specification that the base classes are to be treated as "facets" – object components with the same lifetime and identity as the composite object itself – while the additions are to be treated as "aspects" having a separate lifetime and identity.

e2:   **merge before (method basic:*Sensor.update(<t>) as facet, fea-
ture:SensorAddition.update(<t>) as copy)**

This merges the methods as described in the example in section 4.1.e1, but adds to that the specification that the "update" method is to be treated as a "copy" – an equal partner copied from an original, with the copy having the same lifetime and identity as the composite (but, being a copy, not as the original).

The Weaving Model as a Point of Extension. The weaving model is a part of the composition specification likely to have great natural variation. Particular needs of an approach may require weaving models that bundle choices together in particular ways. Our composition engine directly and openly provides independent choices for selections, orderings and structure.

4.3   Resolving Multiple Weaving Directives

A composite element's characteristics may be specified by multiple directives. The need to resolve separate directives requires that it be possible to provide information about how the directives themselves are related. There are two aspects to the relationship among directives for a result element: *precedence* and *exclusivity*. In addition, it can be necessary control characteristics of any output composed of particular inputs if they are present. Such specifications are called *conditional weaving* directives.

Precedence. When considering the methods indicated by examples 4.2.e1 and 4.2.e2, it is clear that the second directive is more specific than the first. In other cases, however, it is not clear which directive is more specific. Section 4.1's example e1 is a directive that adds the capabilities of the SensorAddition class to all classes with names ending in "Sensor." But the sensor subclasses provided for use in Alaska may need a different addition to accommodate the cold weather. This can be indicated with a second weaving directive:

**merge (class basic:*AlaskaSensor as facet,
alarm:ColdWeatherAddition as aspect)**

We cannot simply rely on the circumstance, obvious here, that one specification is narrower than the other, and build this in as a rule, because instances often arise where it is unclear which of two rules employing pattern-matching is more general. For generality's sake we can fall back once again on the use of partial orderings to establish precedence among weaving directives. One way to specify them is by means of "except" clauses. If several directives apply to the same result element, the precedence and exclusivity together determine the outcome.

Exclusivity. Not all the information about a composition product need be provided by a single directive. In fact, when the queries used to form correspondences are complex, each directive may direct the formation of a set of composition products, and the sets produced by different directives may overlap in non-nested ways. Attaching an indication of exclusivity (*exclusively*, *inclusively* or *initially*) to each directive allows expression of these relationships.

   If there is a unique highest-precedence directive that is marked *exclusive*, it alone is used. Otherwise, if the unique highest-precedence non-*inclusive* directive is *initially*, it is used, along with any inclusive directives with the same or higher precedence. Otherwise, all inclusive directives are used whose precedence is greater than the unique highest-precedence exclusive directive. If the partial ordering renders any of the above statements undefined, an error is reported.

Conditional Weaving Directives. It is necessary on occasion to provide directives that constrain the relationship among the inputs composed to produce a result element without actually describing the result. These are specified by means of *conditional weaving directives.* For example,

    whenever (A, B) use before

specifies that whenever inputs "A" and "B" participate in the same result, as dictated by other directives, they are to be related by the "before" ordering.

4.4 Making Implicit Assumptions Explicit

Prior experience with use of Hyper/J has indicated that, in ways described below, developers have different expectations of a composition tool, reflecting their own knowledge of the software they are manipulating. Failure to take these different expectations into account leads to results which may be expected by some but surprising to others. "Software surprise" is a situation to be shunned. This section discusses two of the most common areas of differing expectation, with ways to make the expectations explicit to avoid surprise.

Encapsulation. The implicit correspondence of like-named elements is a great convenience for developers creating new software as extensions of other software or as concurrently-developed features for later, pre-planned integration. On the other hand, these development scenarios presume some level of familiarity with the internal details of the material being composed. The use of composition to produce artifacts for further use by developers (versus for runtime execution only) makes the same presumption. When developers treat software to be composed as "black boxes," however, as they might if it is purchased or subject to change, the presumption that name correspondence has meaning may be entirely inappropriate.

The simplest way of exposing the "implicit by-name correspondence assumption" is to remove it and make all correspondences explicit by means of queries; but this is often too onerous. When the expectation is that the material is co-developed or when the correspondences involve complex uses of precedence, the implicit correspondence of like-named members may suit better. So, to control the application of implicit correspondence, each weaving directive has a property that indicates what level of *encapsulation* the developer expects – are like-named containers to correspond implicitly but not their members (type encapsulation), or like-named members (member encapsulation), or nothing at all (space encapsulation)?

Opacity. A more subtle skein of issues is illustrated by a small example. If we presume a method has implementations "a" and "A" in the classes composed using "+", the expected result of the merging the classes shown in Figure 2 is clear. If the classes are seen as "black boxes", the same result should be expected for the two classes composed in Figure 3. But this not the expectation of developers who know to use the inheritance structure shown in Figure 3 and who think the composition engine should know that they know. Knowing the structure, they might expect just "a", since it is used to override "A" where both are present.

$$a + A \Rightarrow aA$$

Fig. 2. Clear Composition Expectation

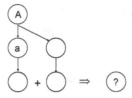

Fig. 3. Unclear Composition Expectation

We can make these implicit expectations explicit by indicating whether a space is *opaque* or *exposed*. For an opaque space, the developer disavows any claim to know how its classes were implemented – they are treated as "black-boxes" whether their members are inherited, implemented, or re-implemented locally. For an exposed space, the developer expects to know the implementation structure and also expects that the knowledge will be used by the composition engine.

4.5 Specifying Orderings for a Selection

The conceptual base described in section 4 has been used in designing and implementing the Concern Composition Component of CME, called CCC. Clients of CCC describe their weaving directives in terms of objects encoding specifications of correspondence, result, structure, selection and ordering. In most cases the encodings are simple: correspondences and results are specified in a query language, and structure and selection are specified by making choices from a provided (though extendable) set of alternatives. Orderings are specified using objects that implement an extension of the concept of partial ordering, called *combination graphs*, that provide added flexibility in their specification and combination. A combination graph has two parts: an *abstract combination graph* and a *population*. An abstract combination graph is a directed acyclic graph, each node of which 1) can be labeled with a name, called its *role* and 2) can be "pre-filled" with predefined content, such as a fixed library class to be included or around-like wrapping styles to allow the graph to execute one or more contained graphs. If there are multiple nodes with the same name (including unlabelled), they must all have the same in- and out- edges. This ensures that all nodes for a role are treated uniformly. The population maps graph nodes to selected input elements. Not all graph nodes need be mapped. *Method combination graphs* are a specialized form of combination graph with additional information attached to each edge, such as conditions for following the edge based on the value returned by (or the exception thrown by) the method that is mapped to the node from which the edge emanates. The method combination graphs in the CME Concern Assembly Toolkit [9] also realize this concept.

Figure 4 shows an abstract combination graph called PrePost, which represents the composition of a method with precondition (in the node labeled "pre:") and post-condition (labeled "post:) checks.

Fig. 4. PrePost Abstract Combination Graph

One combination graph using it might have the population (pre:A, :B). Another might have (:B, post:C). As described in the sections of 4.3 on "precedence" and "exclusivity", a result can be created according to several weaving directives. It must be possible to construct from them a merged combination graph that embeds all of them within it. In the case just mentioned, that would be a PrePost combination graph with the population: (pre:A, :B, post:C).

The ability to merge combination graphs is one of the driving reasons for adopting this form of ordering. The constraints governing the result of the merge are:

1) Each node in any input graph is assigned a node in the result graph with the same population and role (if specified).
2) Nodes of input graphs that are populated with the same input are assigned the same result node.
3) Pre-filled nodes with the same roles specified for them are expected to have the same contents, and are assigned the same result node.
4) Other nodes of input graphs are assigned different nodes.
5) If there is an edge between two nodes in an input graph, there is an edge between the nodes assigned them in the result.
6) If there an edge of a node with a specified role in any input graph to or from another node, there is an edge of each result node with that specified role to or from the node assigned the other node.
7) The resulting graph must be a valid combination graph – i.e. it must be a directed acyclic graph. Additional constraints may apply to merging specializations like method combination graphs.

These constraints produce the result described for PrePost, above, or, for example, the more complex result of combining the two graphs in Figure 5, shown in Figure 6.

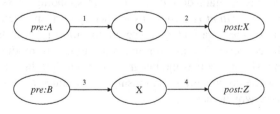

Fig. 5. Two Combination Graphs

In this combination, by rule 2, the nodes filled with X are assigned to the same result node. The unprimed result edges are directly copied from the inputs. The primed result edges are required by rule 6 – both "pre:" nodes must have edges to the node containing Q and the node containing X.

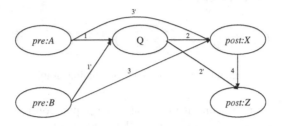

Fig. 6. Combined Combination Graph

5 Supporting Existing Approaches

Treating the composition engine as a component allows the reuse of what is a complex body of software to facilitate implementation, integration, and comparison of a wide spectrum of AOSD languages, formalisms, and paradigms. If appropriate, an approach can be applied to a new artifact representation by implementing plug-in concern assemblers and informants for the artifact. Or an approach can be supported on existing kinds of artifacts by expressing its weaving directives as objects implementing of the concepts described in section 4, passing them to guide the operation of the composition engine. To help demonstrate how this can be done, this section briefly describes the mapping of constructs contained in some existing aspect-oriented approaches to the core composition concepts described in this paper. Due to space constraints, we have not exhaustively elaborated the full mappings here, but rather, we highlight how to map some of their particularly interesting and key features to CCC. Hyper/J-like composition using CCC has been implemented or prototyped for UML class diagrams, for ANT-scripts, and for Java by implementing the appropriate plug-in concern-assemblers.

5.1 Hyper/J

Hyper/J[20] supports the representation and composition of concerns whose contents are standard Java classes and interfaces. The concerns may overlap, in the sense that multiple concerns may contain definitions for corresponding classes, interfaces, or members. It uses *composition relationships* to specify correspondences and the manner of composition of the Java material. The composition relationships are specified separately from the concerns, in a manner analogous to that of module interconnection formalisms. Composition involves the integration of multiple Java type hierarchies in a way that satisfies the composition relationships, to produce a set of composed Java types that contain the woven material.

Hyper/J's concerns map to CCC *spaces* (Section 3), containing Java classes and interfaces. Hyper/J's joinpoints are classes, interfaces, and their members (fields, operations, constructors, and types).

The composition relationships in Hyper/J specify a wide variety of weaving directives. Some control the establishment of correspondences. *NonCorresponding* and *ByName* specify whether like-named elements of related concerns should correspond. These map to CCC's space- and member-encapsulation (Section 4.4) mechanisms, respectively. Other composition relationships indicate how corresponding elements should be integrated. *Merge* and *override* map directly to CCC's *merge* and *overridemember* selection modes (Section 4.2) and the *facet* result structure (Section 4.2). The execution order of merged elements is specified with *before* and *after* order constraints, expressed using CCC's combination graphs (Section 4.5). *Bracket* specifies a "before" method and an "after" method for the same set of inputs, and would be defined as a predefined method combination graph) in CCC. Bracket's before and after methods are composed using the *copy* structure, allowing them to bracket many different methods. Hyper/J also supports *summary functions*, methods whose parameters are the return values of a set of composed methods, returning a single value computed from them as the result of the composed method. An example summary function is boolean "and," which returns true iff all the composed methods return true. Summary functions are realized in CCC with method combination graphs. Edges exiting from nodes in these graphs can contain "accumulator variables," and each node can add a value to the accumulator. At the end is a method node that calls the summary function on the accumulator.

5.2 AspectJ

AspectJ [14] is a Java extension that adds the *aspect* construct to represent concerns that cut across multiple Java classes. Aspects are class-like entities that can define their own behavior and state (standard Java fields and methods), behavior and state to be introduced into other classes (*intertype declarations*), and *advice* to be attached as specified by *pointcuts* (queries that identify the applicable join points). Advice constructs can be treated as weaving directives coupled with the code (represented as methods) to be woven with Java methods. Weaving involves the insertion of code to attach aspect objects to Java objects and to trigger advice, in a way that satisfies the advice and other weaving directives, notably, *declare* specifications.

The types (aspects, classes, and interfaces) that are to be woven are listed in AspectJ's ".lst" files. Each ".lst" file specifies a single CCC input space (Section 3), containing the set of types that are to be composed.

AspectJ's pointcuts describe execution-time events, but these events occur at a set of points in the program's static structure. As noted in Section 1, the generation of code to collect runtime information or perform runtime tests on dynamic state is an activity separate from composition. The composition activity involves composing that code, which AspectJ compiler produces, together with the applicable aspect code, at the relevant points in the program's static structure [14]. These points are specified in *correspondences* (Section 4) in CCC, queries.

If an advice is to be woven at some point in a class, the aspect containing the advice is woven with the class itself, using a specialization of CCC's *aspect attachment* [7] structure. This means the aspect is represented as a separate object with separate identity from the "base" object(s) to which it is attached. The lifetime of the aspect attachment depends on the aspect's "per" specification. By default, the lifetime is CCC's *singleton*, meaning that there is one aspect instance for all of the classes with which the aspect is woven. The other AspectJ "per" specifications—percflow, percflowbelow, perthis, and pertarget—are specified as having CCC's *dynamic* lifetime. All of these specifications depend on dynamic residue, which is, as noted earlier, treated separately from composition.

AspectJ supports three types of advice: *before*, *after*, and *around*. The before and after advice from an aspect must be run as a "bracket" around the advised join point, so the same method combination graph solution is used as for Hyper/J's *bracket* directive (Section 5.1). Two variants, *after throwing* and *after returning*, are realized using edge conditions in these method combination graphs. Around advice is not simply an ordering constraint, but rather, a different selection mode, called *around*, causing the advice to be "wrapped around" another element. Around advice can include a language construct, *proceed()*, which executes the wrapped element. A common implementation of proceed() [11] employs *AroundClosure* objects, created, passed, and used in the composed code. The run-time conventions appropriate to the continuation-related code is specific to the chosen implementation of AspectJ, and therefore, it is realized in CCC as an AspectJ-specific extension of CCC at an extension-point, called rectification, generally available for adapting specific language needs. Rectification is, in fact, the extension used to adapt general composition, for example, to Java's requirement for single-inheritance of implementations.

Most of AspectJ's *declare* and inter-type specifications are handled as compile-time checks or by treating them as though they were written as Java classes with the desired characteristics (parents, fields, etc.) and composed using "merge," as described in Section 5.1. One exception is *declare precedence*, which specifies that advice from one aspect is surrounded by the advice from another. A method combination graph is generated in each case to ensure the required precedence semantics.

5.3 Other Major AOSD Technologies

A number of other major AOSD technologies and languages exist, particularly for implementing aspect-oriented code. Space constraints preclude additional detailed mappings of these technologies to CCC, but we believe that the key features of all of them are covered by the descriptions of AspectJ and Hyper/J. For example, Aspect-Werkz [1] and JBoss [17] support an AspectJ-like composition model, but they differ in their specification languages (standard Java, with XML or tags for specifying composition), and both provide more extensive support for dynamic attachment of aspects. Support for of dynamic responses to events requires little accommodation by a composition engine, so these distinctions do not significantly affect the mapping to CCC. Mixin layers [19] are mapped to CCC like Hyper/J's concerns, with corresponding classes in different layers combined using *around* wrapping and support for *super()* in extensions that resembles the support for *proceed()* for AspectJ. Composition filters [2] are realized in a way similar to AspectJ, but with different attachment semantics and a variety of method combination graphs to realize different filter semantics. Detailed mapping of these and other important AOSD technologies and paradigms is left for future papers.

6 Summary and Related Work

This paper presented a model for composable artifacts and a base of concepts suitable for expressing composition of artifacts in a general setting independent from language or AOSD approach. The model describes artifacts in terms of a containment structure of interpretable material in which artifacts may embed by-name references to other artifacts. The conceptual base describes composition in terms of queries to form correspondences among composable elements and weaving directives providing information about selection, ordering, structure and conflict-handling. It provides examples of many useful choices that can be provided or used in particular cases. The paper shows how an existing open-source implementation based on this concept base can be used to realize the composition needs of several existing AOSD approaches.

There are existing tools for manipulation of Java classes, usually at load time, such as Javassist [4], JMangler [15], JOIE [5] and Binary Component Adaptation (BCA) [12]. These operate at a lower level than the kind of composition engine described above, generally applying to single types or methods, only combining at the level of types and not providing direct support for the combination of interpretable elements.

Section 5 also discussed other AOSD technologies that provide a high-level approach and embed a composition engine to perform their composition needs. But these existing tools and approaches, while making use of individual particularizations of the concepts presented here (like selection or ordering), do not provide a conceptual abstraction for creating a generalized composition engine. Furthermore, these systems are all specific to single kinds of artifacts like Java bytecodes or source. This paper has identified and described key concepts needed to address composition of the variety of artifacts encountered throughout the development lifecycle.

References

[1] AspectWerkz web site, http:aspectwerkz.codehaus.org
[2] M. Aksit, L. Bergmans and S. Vural. "An Object-Oriented Language-Database Integration Model: The Composition-Filters Approach." Proc. European Conference on Object-Oriented Programming, 1992.
[3] Don S. Batory, V. Singhal, J. Thomas, S. Dasari, B. Geraci and M. Sirkin. "The GenVoca Model of Software-System Generators." IEEE Software, September 1994
[4] S. Chiba, "Load-time Structural Reflection in Java." Proc. 2000 European Conference on Object Oriented Programming, LNCS 1850, Springer Verlag, 2000
[5] G. Cohen and J. Chase, "Automatic Program Transformation with JOIE", USENIX Annual Technical Conference, June, 1998
[6] W. Harrison and H. Ossher. "Subject-Oriented Programming: A Critique of Pure Objects." Proc. 8th conference on Object-oriented programming systems, languages, and applications, 411-428 (1993).

[7] W. Harrison and H. Ossher, "Member-Group Relationships Among Objects", at Work-shops on Foundations of Aspect Languages, on Aspect-Oriented Design, and on UML in Aspect-Oriented Software at International Conference on Aspect-Oriented Software De-velopment, March 2002

[8] W. Harrison, H. Ossher, S. Sutton, P. Tarr, The Concern Manipulation Environment—Supporting aspect-oriented software development. IBM Systems Journal Special Interest Issue on Open Source, Vol. 44, No. 2, 2005

[9] W.H. Harrison, H.L. Ossher, P.L. Tarr, V. Kruskal, F. Tip, "CAT: A Toolkit for Assem-bling Concerns" IBM Research Report RC22686, December, 2002

[10] Richard Helm, Ian Holland, and Dipayan Gangopadhyay, "Contracts: Specifying Behav-ioral Compositions in Object-Oriented Systems", Proceedings of the Conference on Ob-ject-Oriented Programming: Systems, Languages, and Applications, (Vancouver), ACM, October 1990.

[11] E. Hillsdale and J. Hugunin, "Advice Weaving in AspectJ", Proc. 3rd International Con-ference on Aspect-Oriented Software Development, 26-35 (2004)

[12] R. Keller, U. Hölzle, "Binary Component Adaptation," Proc. 1998 European Conference on Object Oriented Programming, LNCS 1445, Springer Verlag, 1998.

[13] Gregor Kiczales, John Lamping, Anurag Mendhekar, Chris Maeda, Cristina Videira Lopes, Jean-Marc Lo-ingtier, John Irwin. "Aspect-Oriented Programming." In proceed-ings of the European Conference on Object-Oriented Programming (ECOOP), Finland. Springer-Verlag LNCS 1241. June 1997.

[14] G. Kiczales, E. Hilsdale, J. Hugunin, M. Kersten, Jeffrey Palm and William G. Griswold. "An Overview of AspectJ." Proc. 15th European Conference on Object-Oriented Pro-gramming, 327-353 (2001).

[15] G. Kniesel, P. Constanza, M. Austermann, "JMangler – A Framework for Load-Time Transformation of Java Class Files, November 2001. IEEE Workshop on Source Code Analysis and Manipulation (SCAM),

[16] Kung-Kiu Lau and Zheng Wang, A Taxonomy of Software Component Models, Proceed-ings of 31st Euromicro Conference on Software Engineering and Advanced Applications, IEEE, August 2005

[17] JBOSS web page, http://www.jboss.org

[18] M. Mezini and K. Lieberherr, "Adaptive Plug-and-Play Components for Evolutionary Software Development." Proc. Conference on Object-oriented Programming: Systems, Languages, and Applications, 1998.

[19] Smaragdakis and Batory, Mixin Layers: An Object-Oriented Implementation Technique for Refinements and Collaboration-Based Designs, ACM Transactions on Software Engi-neering and Methodology, April 2002.

[20] P. Tarr, H. Ossher, W. Harrison and S.M. Sutton Jr. "N Degrees of Separation: Multi-Dimensional Separation of Concerns." Proc. 21st International Conference on Software Engineering, 107-119 (1999).

Dimensions of Composition Models for Supporting Software Evolution*

In-Gyu Kim[1], Tegegne Marew[2], Doo-Hwan Bae[2],
Jang-Eui Hong[3], and Sang-Yoon Min[4]

[1] Telecommunication R & D Center, Telecommunication
Network Business, Samsung Electronics, Co. Ltd., Suwon, Korea
igkim.kim@samsung.com
[2] Dept. of Electrical Engineering & Computer Science, KAIST,
373-1, Guseong-dong, Yuseong-gu, Daejon 305-701, Korea
{tegegnem, bae}@se.kaist.ac.kr
[3] School of Electrical & Computer Engineering, CBNU,
12, Gaeshin-dong, Heungduk-gu, Cheongju 361-763, Korea
jehong@chungbuk.ac.kr
[4] SOLUTIONLINK, KAIST Venture Incubator
373-1, Guseong-dong, Yuseong-gu, Daejon 305-701, Korea
sang@sol-link.com

Abstract. Software systems with constrained and dynamic environments need to adapt to local and diverse computing environments by providing highly customized services at run-time. In order to address such dynamic changes effectively, composition models addressing complicated composition issues and supporting advanced composition features are required. In order to analyze and identify the required features of composition models supporting dynamic changes, we propose the dimensions of composition models by survey and analysis of existing work. Based on the dimensions, it is possible to provide a road map to improve capability of a composition model for a specific domain such as a dynamic mobile agent domain.

1 Introduction

An important emerging requirement for software systems is the ability to address dynamic requirements changes. As the competitions among enterprises become fiercer, there is a need for each enterprise to satisfy the time-to-market requirement faster. In addition, the spread of the Internet and mobile communications with constrained devices requires software systems (e.g. mobile agent systems) to adapt to local and diverse computing environments by providing highly customized services at run-time.

Composition based techniques are practical and effective approaches for supporting software evolution because of high flexibility and increased productivity.

* This work was supported by the Ministry of Information & Communication, Korea, under the Information Technology Research Center (ITRC) Support Program.

W. Löwe and M. Südholt (Eds.): SC 2006, LNCS 4089, pp. 211–226, 2006.

In this paper, we define compositional aspects of the techniques as composition models. Composition models enable decisions to be made on how composition units are composed and which functionality the composed one provides. According to the capabilities of composition models that applications are based on, the ability of the applications to accommodate changes is decided. Thus, in order to support software evolution more effectively, composition models addressing complicated composition issues and supporting advanced composition features are required. In this paper we propose dimensions of composition models in order to analyze and identify the required features of composition models for evolvable software systems especially with dynamic requirements changes. Through surveying existing work supporting software evolution and existing criteria for comparing composition models, the dimensions are identified, collected, classified, and refined. Based on the dimensions, it is possible to find which areas are not supported or need to be more supported in existing composition models and to provide a road map to improve composition model capability. The dimensions also enable software developers to find out required features of a composition model for a new application domain where computing conditions or environments are different from other domains.

The remainder of this paper is organized as follows. Section 2 shows and analyzes briefly some existing efforts and research projects supporting software evolution. Section 3 collects and analyzes existing criteria related to comparing composition models. Based on the analysis of Section 2 and 3, Section 4 proposes dimensions of composition models and describes each dimension in detail. Section 5 compares some existing research projects by the proposed dimensions. As a case study applying the proposed dimensions to a new domain to find out the required features for effectively supporting software evolution in the domain, Section 6 shows how the dimensions can be used for choosing the required features for a composition model supporting dynamic mobile agent applications. In Section 7 we conclude our research with further work.

2   Work Supporting Software Evolution

There exist techniques or research projects for supporting software evolution. We have classified these efforts largely into 9 categories.[1] The pros and cons of each category are explained briefly in Table 1.[2] Since our paper focuses on dimensions of composition models, we are more interested in composition based techniques (row 3 in Table 1). Some of efforts in the category (i.e. composition based techniques) are explained in detail in the following.

As basic OO composition techniques, there are association, inheritance, and delegation. Association is one of the simple composition techniques which has been widely used in OO systems. It enables an object to refer to other objects, for instance, by using object variables. In association, functionality can be changed

---

[1] The classification is not mutually exclusive. Some efforts belong to more than one category.

[2] For more detailed information, [18] can be referred to.

Table 1. Comparison of Efforts Supporting Software Evolution In the Large

Efforts supporting software evolution	Pros	Cons
Code Modification	any kind of adaptation, any part can be modified, direct modification, efficient for experienced programmers.	requiring source code, error-prone, not suitable for large and complex systems.
Parameter Modification	controlled modification by parameters.	limited modification within parameter scopes.
Composition Based Techniques [1,2,5,22,23]	producing and adapting software systems fast and cost-effectively by (run-time) composition, high reuse of components.	requiring various mechanisms to support composition.
Design Pattern Based Techniques [12]	providing general solutions for addressing software evolution problems.	hard to find exact patterns for addressing given problems.
Software Architecture Based Techniques [8]	supporting high level modification by changing components, connectors, or configuration.	subjective to architectural styles, requiring further research on dynamic architecture supporting software evolution.
Transformation Based Techniques [3,4]	as powerful as code modification, supporting controlled modification by transformation templates.	requiring source code, hard to modify at run-time.
Reflection Based Techniques [11,21]	supporting run-time change by modifying meta data, used as complementing or supporting techniques for many other adaptation efforts.	requiring mechanisms to support meta-level architecture, complex to use.
Collaboration Based Techniques [16,27]	large granularity of reuse (collaboration-level), supporting separation of concerns.	requiring further research on efficient realization of the concepts and supporting mechanisms.
Industry Component Models [9,13]	providing various practical supporting tools for developing systems based on their own component models, easy to use.	not sufficiently providing component or composition models for adapting components or systems.

at run-time by changing the references. Class inheritance allows a subclass's implementation to be defined in terms of the parent class's implementation [2,26]. The advantage of class inheritance is that it is done statically at compile-time and is easy to use. The disadvantage of class inheritance is that the subclass becomes dependent on the parent class's implementation and the implementation inherited from a parent class cannot be changed at run-time. Delegation is similar to association except message handling mechanisms [2,20]. Using delegation, a method can always refer to the original recipient of the message, regardless of the number of indirections. Like association, delegation also supports dynamic composition by changing parents at run-time.

Ostermann et al. propose compound references, a new abstraction for object references, that allows to provide explicit linguistic means for expressing and combining individual composition properties on-demand [22]. They provide five composition properties to express a seamless spectrum of composition semantics in the interval between object composition and inheritance: overriding, transparent redirection, acquisition, subtyping, and polymorphism. A variety of composition mechanisms can be used by simply decorating object references with the above composition properties. A seamless transition from one composition mechanism to the other is also possible by changing composition properties, which enables applications to be adapted to have the changed functionality.

Context relation is a relation between classes which directly models dynamic evolution [23]. In Context relation, a context class defines a dynamic update for a base class. Attaching a context object to a base object alters the base object's method table based on the class updates defined by the context class. Context relation supports method-level updating.

HADAS is a decentralized framework for composition of software systems by connecting components [5]. HADAS supports dynamic adaptation, which allows for the adjustment of structure and behavior of autonomous components. Each component is split into two sections; Fixed and Extensible. Data items and methods defined in the Fixed section are not changed during the component's lifetime. In contrast, the Extensible section comprises the mutable portion of the component through which component's structure and behavior can be changed, and in which new methods can be added or removed on-the-fly. HADAS is based on 2-level method invocation mechanism which supports extensibility of the invocation mechanism itself. The mechanism partially enables "supporting multi-services" by metainvocation. Added components can access original components through "*selfObject*" construct. HADAS supports dynamic adaptation and a hybrid approach to get benefits both from class-based and instance-based changes.

DC-AOP is a platform for scalable mobile agents, which supports dynamic composition of functionality using code mobility [19]. Kim et al. categorize functionalities that mobile agents can use as follows: built-in functionality, resident functionality, carried functionality. Carried functionality enables mobile agents to add functionalities in remote nodes into their behaviors by code mobility and use the functionalities at run-time. DC-AOP supports such dynamic composition of functionality by providing four language constructs for carried functionality.

Lasagne defines a platform-independent architecture for dynamic customization of component-based systems using wrappers [28]. Lasagne introduces the concept of "Composition Policy". In Lasagne, composition logic is externalized from the code of clients, core system, and extensions by encapsulating it in a composition policy. In Lasagne, an application consists of a minimal functional core (implemented as a component-based system), and a set of potential extensions that can be selectively integrated within this core functionality. Each extension (i.e. collaboration) is implemented as a layer of mixin-like wrappers, simultaneously tailoring multiple components of the application and their interactions between each other.

GenVoca is one of program transformation approaches. GenVoca generators synthesize software systems by composing plug-compatible and interchangeable components [4]. GenVoca components are parameterized program transformations that are capable of operation refinements. The interfaces and bodies of GenVoca components are subjective (i.e. changeable). When components are composed, GenVoca checks additional constraints (e.g. precondition and postcondition) called design rules as well as type.

The CORBA Component Model (CCM) is a specification for creating server-side scalable, language-neutral, transactional, multi-user, and secure enterprise-level applications [13]. In CCM, components support a variety of interaction features, called ports. The ports includes facets, receptacles, and event sources/sinks. A component can provide multiple object references, called facets, which are capable of supporting distinct IDL interfaces. Using facets, operations can be grouped. In addition, introspection facilities associated with facets permit one to discover the set of roles provided by a component type at run-time. Other component models such as EJB ([9]) provide similar functionalities for component customization, composition, evolution, and deployment.

3   Existing Dimensions for Comparing Composition Models

This section presents and analyzes existing criteria used to compare composition models. Bosch proposes superimposition, a novel black-box adaptation technique that allows one to impose predefined, but configurable types of functionality on a reusable component [6]. He identifies the requirements that component adaptation techniques should fulfill; "transparent", "black-box", "composable", "configurable", and "reusable" requirements. Some of these requirements are useful to identify dimensions of composition models. For example, "composable" requirement implies that the adapted component should be as composable as it was without the adaptation and the adaptation should be composable with other adaptations. In addition, Bosch focuses on configurable adaptation, which is realized by a number of component adaptation types that can be configured for the specific component.

Heineman et al. present a list of requirements necessary for component adaptation techniques from surveying and analyzing some existing work and considering three additional requirements [14]. Although some requirements such as "identity" and "architectural focus" are useful as dimensions of composition models, other requirements are not suitable directly for composition models. For example, "conservative" requirement is based on the assumption that existing functionalities of components are not cancelled. However, we think that composition of two components can make a combined component with less functionalities than the sum of functionalities of two components.

Kniesel classifies component adaptation approaches according to four criteria [20]. "anticipated or unanticipated changes" and "time" are important aspects of composition models.

Buchi et al. provide requirements for a wrapping mechanism [7]. "shielding", one of the requirements, indicates that a wrapper should be able to control whether clients can directly access the wrappee or not.

Dominick et al. provide concerns which are important for extensible and configurable components [10]. "extensible and reusable extensions" concern means that components can be plugged into components recursively. They think that extensions (to components) also should have component-like properties.

Svahnberg et al. provide selection criteria of variability realization techniques for selecting an appropriate technique for implementing variability [24]. They realize variability in product line software systems through steps of identifying variant features, introducing variation points for the features, populating the variant feature with its variants (software entities), and binding variation points with specific variants. They organize variability realization techniques into 13 types by using involved software entities and binding times. They compare the 13 types of variability realization techniques in detail by five criteria: introduction times of variation points, open times for adding variants, ways of populating collection of variants, binding times, ways of binding. The criteria are focused to classify variability realization techniques especially for product line software systems.

4   Dimensions of Composition Models

Based on the analysis of Section 2 and 3, we have identified, collected, classified, and refined dimensions of composition models. The dimensions and their elements (features) are explained as follows:

Granularity: Granularity classifies composition units into attribute, method, object, component, and collaboration. Collaboration is a set of objects, together which provides a particular functionality to the application.

Composition Time: This dimension addresses when composition is performed. This dimension has the following elements:

- compile-time: Composition is performed at compile-time or before (e.g. product architecture derivation time [24]).
- deploy-time: Composition is performed at deploy-time.
- load-time: Composition is performed at load-time.
- run-time: Composition is performed at run-time.

These elements are cumulative: a later time element implies the previous time elements. For example, run-time element implies load-time, deploy-time, and compile-time elements.

Location of Delta: Where can we get "added functionality" (called as delta) at run-time? This dimension is explained in more detail from [19].

- built-in: Delta is combined into original components at compile-time.
- local: Delta in the local node (computer) is used.
- remote: Delta can be loaded and combined from remote nodes.

Elements in this dimension are cumulative.

Required Composition Information: This dimension addresses what kinds of information is necessary for composition.

- interface: It requires signature information (e.g. return type, name, parameters).
- contract: Pre&post conditions and invariants are necessary [15].
- configuration: For advanced or flexible composition such as expressing various composition semantics, more configurable composition information should be provided explicitly and could be used and manipulated by component customers. Explicit configuration information enables developers or adapters to customize components to provide different behaviors by changing the information.

Contract and configuration elements imply interface element unless explicit notes are provided.

Consistency Checking when Composition: What kind of consistency checking is performed when composing?

- signature: Signature checking is performed.
- subtype: Subtype checking is performed.
- rule: Composition rules are used for consistency checking.

Subtype element implies signature element. Usually, signature element is a minimal element to check.

Composition Capability: This dimension shows which composition semantics can be provided after composition.

- adding new services (1)
- deleting existing services (2)
- changing services (3)
- supporting multi-services (4): When a message is received, multi-services can be provided.
- overriding (5)
- wrapping (6)
- combinations (7): Combinations of composition primitives are supported. In order to provide expressive and changeable composition semantics among components, it is necessary to combine various composition operators and provide various composition semantics through the combinations.

As a note, the numbers in parentheses for the above elements are for the reference in Table 2.

Reference Primitives: When a composition unit (let's say it as a component) is composed with other components, the reference scope of the other components which the component can access is decided by reference primitives. Let's assume that two components, original and delta, are composed.

- origin (O): The delta component can access the original component.
- delta (D): The original component can access the delta component.

- identity (ID): The original and the delta are aggregated into one identity.
- based on internal structure information (ISI): This category is different from the above three categories in that the reference scope can be decided by using internal structure information of a component such as information of fixed and extensible parts. For example, an internal component of a component can access all internal components of the fixed part of the component by using "fixed" reference primitive. Reference primitives belonging to this category can be used to express more specific and various reference scopes other than original and delta components.

Identity element (ID) implies both original (O) and delta (O).

Hierarchical Composition Support: This dimension decides whether composition can be applied hierarchically or not. It is important to raise the level of abstraction in such a way that the evolution is expressed, reasoned about, and implemented. One way of raising the level of abstraction is hierarchical composition. Hierarchical composition enables component composition to be applied uniformly to both component adaptation and application assembly. It also enables components to be adapted by other components and the adapted components to be used for adapting other components as well. It increases reusability by enabling components to play both the roles: original and delta.

Composable Parts: This dimension shows which parts of a system are allowed to be composed.

- Whatever: Any part can be changed or composed.
- Designated parts: Only particular parts are allowed to be changed or composed.

Anticipation: This dimension shows whether or not unexpected functionality which original developers do not consider at design-time, can be added into the software later by using the extension mechanism which is provided by the supporting composition model.

- Expected: By using the supporting composition model, only expected functionalities which are considered at design-time are allowed to be composable.
- Unexpected: By using the supporting composition model, unexpected functionalities which are not considered at design-time can also be composed.

Who Provides Composition Codes?

- Manual (Developer): Composition logic is programmed by developers. In this manual decision of composition, anticipated composition logic is coded at compile-time and according to the fixed logic, compositions in software systems are performed.
- Automatic (AI): Reasoning engine decides what to do at run-time (e.g. which parts have to be composed and in which ways) by using inference rules together with inputs from environments. Thus, composition logic can be decided automatically at run-time by the reasoning engine.

5   Comparison of Existing Work by the Proposed Dimensions

This section compares some of work presented in Section 2 by our proposed dimensions in Section 4. The comparison results are shown in Table 2 and the detailed comparison results with respect to each dimension are explained in the following:

Table 2. Comparison of Software Composition Efforts by the Proposed Dimensions

Dimensions	Software Composition Efforts				
	HADAS	DC-AOP	Context Relation	Lasagne	GenVoca
Granularity of Composition Units	object (mainly focused on methods)	object	object	collaboration (extension)	collaboration
Composition Time	run	run	run	run	compile
Location of Delta	local	remote	local	local	local
Required Composition Information	interface	interface	interface	configuration (composition policy)	contract
Consistency Checking	signature	signature	signature	subtype	rule (design rule checking)
Composition Capability	1,2,4	1,2	1,2,3	6,7	1,6
Reference Primitive	O,D	D	O	ID	O
Hierarchical Composition	No	Yes	No	No	Yes
Composable Part	Part (Extensible part)	Part (carried-functionality)	Part (Instance-based method)	All	All
Anticipation	Expected	Expected	Expected	Expected	Unexpected
Who	Manual	Manual	Manual	Manual	Manual

Granularity of Composition Units: HADAS can add and remove items (data, methods, or objects). It mainly deals with methods. DC-AOP and Context Relation are based on objects. Lasagne wraps a set of components with extensions. GenVoca can compose collaborations of "realm".

Composition Time: In HADAS, DC-AOP, Context Relation, and Lasagne, composition is performed at run-time. GenVoca performs software composition at compile-time. Generally, compile-time composition enables better performance because it does not require intermediate invocation layers. Run-time composition enables flexible functionality change because it can change functionality at run-time.

Location of Delta: Only DC-AOP enables remote functionalities to be loaded and composed with existing functionalities.

Required Composition Information: In HADAS, DC-AOP, and Context Relation, signature information is used for composition. Lasagne and GenVoca require more information than signature. Lasagne describes components with services (interfaces), dependencies, decorators (wrappers), and intercepters. At run-time, Lasagne uses component descriptions and composition policy to combine extensions into the core system selectively. GenVoca uses contract information such as pre and post conditions.

Consistency Checking when Composition: HADAS, DC-AOP, and Context Relation perform consistency checking at the level of signature; composition is not allowed if signatures are not matched. Lasagne wraps components or uses role object patterns to compose components and deltas. Thus, it requires subtype relation between components and deltas. GenVoca performs design rule checking to detect illegal combinations of components.

Composition Capability: HADAS, DC-AOP, and GenVoca enable components to provide new services. HADAS and DC-AOP can remove existing services. Context Relation changes existing services using context objects. It also adds new services which are only invoked by the attached context objects. Those new services can be disposed by changing context objects. GenVoca can add or wraps existing services. HADAS supports multi-services by metainvocation. Lasagne supports wrapping of services and selective combination of extensions by composition policy.

Reference Primitives: In HADAS, when two components are composed, one component can access the other component through "*selfObject*" construct. Context Relation has *this* primitive to access original components. It also has *context* primitive for delta to access itself. However, it does not provide primitives for delta to access original components. DC-AOP provides "cafInvoke()" method to access deltas. However, it does not provide facilities to invoke original objects which load the deltas. Lasagne provides the notion of component identity by *variation point*. It uses *inner* primitive to access the aggregate of a component instance and its decorating wrapper instances. Lasagne enables original components and deltas to be combined into one identity. Component identity (ID) implies that deltas can access the original component (O), the original component can access deltas (D), and delta can access other deltas. In GenVoca, deltas (upper layers) can access original components (lower layers).

Hierarchical Composition Support: In HADAS and Lasagne, deltas cannot be extended by other deltas recursively. For example, in Lasagne, it is very difficult to reuse deltas because they have subtype relation with original classes. Context Relation also does not support hierarchical composition because context classes are specified only for one base class. In DC-AOP and GenVoca, deltas can be extended by other deltas recursively.

Composable Parts: In HADAS, each component has two parts; Fixed and Extensible. Functionality in only "Extensible" part can be added or deleted.

In DC-AOP, only carried-functionalities of system can be changed through the proposed language constructs. In Context Relations, instance-based methods can be updated. In Lasagne, any services of components can be wrapped. In GenVoca, any components can be composed.

Anticipation: In HADAS, DC-AOP, Context Relation, and Lasagne, developers of components have to anticipate adaptations which will be performed in the future and also provide some ways (hooks) within the components to realize the adaptations. In GenVoca, original developers do not have to anticipate future adaptations. Adapters, instead of the original developers, perform necessary adaptations. However, although GenVoca composes unanticipated functionality, it is done before run-time. In order to satisfy fast-changing requirements more fully, unanticipated adaptations should be supported at run-time as well as at compile-time.

Who Provides Composition Codes?: In all work, the change is encoded by the developers or adapters at compile-time. Specifically, in HADAS, DC-AOP, Context Relations, and Lasagne, the change is encoded by developers. In GenVoca, the change is encoded by adapters as well as developers.

6   Applying the Dimensions for Dynamic Mobile Agent Applications

As a case study applying the proposed dimensions to a new domain, this section shows how our proposed dimensions can be used to select the required features of a composition model supporting dynamic mobile agent applications.

6.1   A Testing Mobile Agent with Dynamic Requirements Changes

As an application with dynamic requirements changes, a mobile agent application is described as follows. A mobile agent, called as DTMA, navigates to various nodes (e.g. insurance company web sites) where there are insurance components differently implemented by various companies with their own business rules. At each node, DTMA tests the insurance component provided at the node. The goal of DTMA is to find the most reliable insurance component among nodes. At various nodes, DTMA performs some testing activities. At a specific node, it happens to test the insurance component in the node in more detail because the insurance component has passed all testing activities of the current DTMA. DTMA changes the existing testing functionality with a new testing functionality which has more detailed test cases, and performs new testing activities. Similarly, at another nodes, DTMA adds a new display functionality which displays texts in well formatted forms, and adds a monitoring functionality which performs some backup activities. The above scenario is shown in Figure 1.

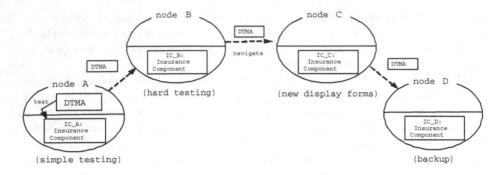

Fig. 1. A Navigating Scenario of DTMA

6.2   Required Features of a Composition Model for Dynamic Mobile Agent Applications

For the above mobile agent application, DTMA can be programmed as having all functionalities including testing, display, and monitoring functionalities at compile-time. However, it requires more memory space and increased network bandwidth when moving to other nodes. In addition, it cannot accommodate unanticipated requirements such as a new secure communication functionality. In order to address dynamic requirements changes in the mobile agent application more sufficiently, a composition model suitable for the application should be selected and used. In order to find out the required features of the composition model, we used the proposed dimensions. As a result, we decided the following features are required for the composition model:

Granularity of Composition Units: Component Based Software Development (CBSD) enables applications to be developed fast and cost-effectively by composing existing or customized components [25]. Also, CBSD is being considered as a practical and effective approach for supporting software evolution because composing components provides high flexibility and productivity. Thus, applications with dynamic requirements changes could get benefits from CBSD. As a result, the composition unit for the composition model is decided as "component".

Composition Time: DTMA changes the existing testing functionality to a newly developed testing functionality at run-time. In addition, DTMA adds a newly developed other functionality (e.g. display) at run-time. Run-time composition is very useful for satisfying dynamic changes.

Location of Delta: It is possible for mobile agents to navigate in unexpected environments. If mobile agents can add functionalities in remote nodes into their behaviors by code mobility and use the functionalities at run-time, they can use various and timely functionalities in the Internet with high robustness [19].

Required Composition Information: Components provide services through interfaces. However, in order to address dynamic requirements changes in mobile agents through component composition, (re)configurable composition information should be explicitly provided. Through changing the information, components can provide various behaviors. For example, let's assume that DTMA decides to move to an untrustworthy node. In order not to save travel information into the node, DTMA can change internal configuration to limit access to logging services.

Composition Capability: DTMA needs the following composition capabilities:

- add new services (1): DTMA adds display and monitoring functionalities.
- delete existing services (2): DTMA could delete the existing functionality.
- change services (3): DTMA changes the testing functionality.
- change configuration information (7): DTMA can change its architectural configuration information when it navigate to untrustworthy node. In addition, mobile agents move around nodes and perform some activities for each node. Each node may have different environments or requirements such as security levels and communication protocols. Thus, various composition semantics should be supported by combinations of composition primitives.

Reference Primitives: In DTMA, existing functionalities need to access new added functionalities (local or remote) and vice versa. In order to use different kinds of internal parts of DTMA effectively, DTMA needs to support "based on internal structural information" in this dimension.

Hierarchical Composition Support: If DTMA supports hierarchical composition, it will get the benefits of hierarchical composition such as increasing reusability of components and managing different composition levels uniformly.

Consistency Checking when Composition: In DTMA, signature checking is a minimum requirement. Subtyping checking is also necessary for hierarchical composition. Configuration checking is also required.

Composable Parts: Mobile agents need to manage their parts differently according to their goals. For example, one part has functionalities fundamental and very unlikely to change, and the other part has dynamically changeable functionalities. DTMA needs some basic functionalities such as a navigation functionality to be fixed for its proper operation. In the other hand, DTMA needs to use resources effectively because of limited memory space and network bandwidth. Thus, DTMA also needs composable or changeable part.

Anticipation: The ability to compose unexpected functionality is required to handle dynamic and diverse situations in mobile agent environments.

Who provides composition codes?: For the safe, reliable, and predictable operation of DTMA, the composition logic needs to be specified by developers explicitly.

The required features of a composition model for the dynamic mobile agent application are shown in Figure 2. The circles shows the chosen features for the composition model.

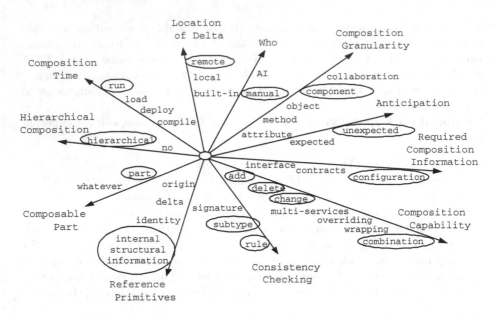

Fig. 2. Required features of a composition model for the dynamic mobile agent application

7   Conclusion and Further Work

In order to analyze and identify the required features of a composition model for software systems with dynamic requirements changes, we proposed the dimensions of composition models by survey and analysis of existing efforts supporting software evolution, especially composition based techniques, and the existing comparison criteria. The dimensions could be useful in the following areas:

- Existing work addressing dynamic requirements changes can be analyzed in various ways as shown in Section 5.
- The dimensions help to identify issues critical to improving composition capability of existing work.
- Future research directions of a specific dimension can be identified.
- When making a new composition model suitable for a specific domain such as [17], we can use, as a road map, the dimensions.

As experiments of our dimensions, first, we compared some existing software composition efforts by using the dimensions. Second, we identified the required features of a composition model supporting a dynamic mobile agent application by using our dimensions. Also, we have developed APIs for the composition model and implemented the application. For more information, please refer to "http://salmosa.kaist.ac.kr/~igkim/DCM".

While our research offers improvement in dimensions of composition models, there are some issues that are worth talking about in further research. First, it is useful to apply the proposed dimensions to various domains in order to extend the dimensions with additional features or to further refine the dimensions. We are now applying the dimensions to a hotel reservation system with continuous upgrades and changes of business requirements. Second, relations among the dimensions need to be analyzed and specified explicitly. Some of the dimensions could affect each other. They could be refined into more orthogonal dimensions, or the relations among them should be specified explicitly, for example, in documents. Finally, it is useful to identify relations between the dimensions and software quality attributes such as performance, reusability, and modifiability. For example, for modifiability, "Required Composition Information" has a higher priority than "Location of Delta". Such relations are useful to identity important dimensions that composition models should have in order to satisfy certain quality attributes or goals.

References

1. W. Aalst. "Don't go with the flow: web services composition standards exposed". *IEEE Intelligent Systems*, 18(1):72–76, 2003.
2. M. Abadi and L. Cardelli. *A Theory of Object*. Springer, 1996.
3. U. Abmann. *Invasive Software Composition*. Springer, 2003.
4. D. Batory and B. Geraci. "Composition Validation and Subjectivity in GenVoca Generators". *IEEE Transactions on Software Engineering*, 23(2):67–82, 1997.
5. I. Ben-Shaul, O. Holder, and B. Lavva. "Dynamic Adaptation and Deployment of Distributed Components in Hadas". *IEEE Transactions on Software Engineering*, 27(9):769–787, 2001.
6. J. Bosch. "Superimposition: A Component Adaptation Technique". *Information and Software Technology*, 41(5):257–273, 1999.
7. M. Buchi and W. Weck. "Generic Wrappers". In *Proceedings of ECOOP*, pages 201–225, June 2000.
8. S. Cheng, D. Garlan, B. Schmerl, J. Sousa, B. Spitznagel, P. Steenkiste, and N. Hu. "Software Architecture-base Adaptation for Pervasive Systems". In *Proceedings of the International Conference on Architecture of Computing Systems: Trends in Network and Pervasive Computing*, pages 67–82.
9. L. DeMichiel, L. Yalcinalp, and S. Krishnan. Enterprise JavaBeans^{TM} Specification, Version 2.0. Technical report, Sun Microsystems, 2001.
10. L. Dominick and K. Ostermann. "Supporting Extension of Components with new Paradigms". In *Workshop on Advanced Separation of Concerns at OOPSLA*, 2000.
11. J. Dowling and V. Cahill. "The K-Component Architecture Meta-Model for Self-Adaptive Software". In *Proceedings of the Third International Conference on Metalevel Architectures and Separation of Crosscutting Concerns, LNCS 2129*, pages 81–88.
12. E. Gamma, R. Helm, R. Johnson, and J. Vlissides. *Design Patterns: Elements of Reusable Object-Oriented Software*. Addison-Wesley, 1995.
13. O. M. Group. CORBA Components, v3.0 full specification. Technical report, OMG, 2002.
14. G. Heineman and H. Ohlenbusch. An Evaluation of Component Adaptation Techniques. Technical report, Computer Science Department, Worcester Polytechnic Institute, 1999.

15. R. Helm, I. Holland, and D. Gangopadhyay. "Contracts: Specifying Behavioral Compositions in Object-Oriented Systems". In *Proceedings of the OOPSLA/ECOOP Conference)*, pages 169–180, 1990.
16. G. Kiczales, J. Lamping, A. Menhdhekar, C. Maeda, C. Lopes, J. Loingtier, and J. Irwin. "Aspect-Oriented Programming". In *Proceedings of ECOOP*, 1997.
17. I. Kim and D. Bae. "A Dynamic Composition Model for Addressing Constrained Environments". In *OOPSLA Workshop on Reuse in Constrained Environments*, 2003.
18. I. Kim and D. Bae. Dimensions of Composition Model for Supporting Software System Evolution. Technical report, Department of Computer Science, KAIST, 2005.
19. I. Kim, J. Hong, D. Bae, I. Han, and C. Yoon. "Scalable Mobile Agents Supporting Dynamic Composition of Functionality". In *Infrastructure for Agents, Multi-Agent Systems, and Scalable Multi-Agent Systems, T. Wagner and O. Rana, eds., LNAI 1887*, pages 199–213, 2001.
20. G. Kniesel. "Type-Safe Delegation for Run-Time Component Adaptation". In *Proceedings of ECOOP*, pages 351–366, 1999.
21. P. Maes. "Concepts and Experiments in Computation Reflection". In *Proceedings of OOPSLA)*, pages 147–155, 1987.
22. K. Ostermann and M. Mezini. "Object-Oriented Composition Untangled". In *Proceedings of OOPSLA*, pages 283–299, 2001.
23. L. Seiter, J. Palsberg, and K. Lieberherr. "Evolution of Object Behavior Using Context Relations". *IEEE Transactions on Software Engineering*, 24(1):79–92, 1998.
24. M. Svahnberg, J. Gurp, and J. Bosch. "A taxonomy of variability realization techniques". *Software Practice and Experience*, 35(8):705–754, 2005.
25. C. Szyperski. *Component Software - Beyond Object-Oriented Programming*. Addison-Wesley, 1998.
26. A. Taivalsaari. "On the Notion of Inheritance". *ACM Computing Surveys*, 28(3):438–479, 1996.
27. P. Tarr, H. Ossher, W. Harrison, and S. Jr. "N Degrees of Separation: Multi-Dimensional Separation of Concerns". In *Proceedings of ICSE*, pages 107–119, 1999.
28. E. Truyen, B. Vanhaute, W. Joosen, P. Verbaeten, and B. Jorgensen. "Dynamic and Selective Combination of Extensions in Component-Based Applications". In *Proceedings of ICSE*, pages 233–242, 2001.

Context-Aware Aspects

Éric Tanter[1,*], Kris Gybels[2], Marcus Denker[3], and Alexandre Bergel[4,**]

[1] Center for Web Research/DCC
University of Chile, Santiago – Chile
[2] PROG Lab
Vrije Universiteit Brussel – Belgium
[3] Software Composition Group
University of Bern – Switzerland
[4]Distributed Systems Group
Trinity College – Ireland

Abstract. Context-aware applications behave differently depending on the context in which they are running. Since context-specific behavior tends to crosscut base programs, it can advantageously be implemented as aspects. This leads to the notion of *context-aware aspects*, *i.e.*, aspects whose behavior depends on context. This paper analyzes the issue of appropriate support from the aspect language to both restrict the scope of aspects according to the context and allow aspect definitions to access information associated to the context. We propose an open framework for context-aware aspects that allows for the definition of first-class contexts and supports the definition of context awareness constructs for aspects, including the ability to refer to past contexts, and to provide domain- and application-specific constructs.

1 Introduction

Context awareness [5,10], *i.e.*, the ability of a program to behave differently depending on the context in which it is running, has been the subject of a number of research proposals, mainly in the field of ubiquitous computing [21], self-adaptive [17] and autonomic systems [16]. In these areas, a major issue is that of *perceiving* the context surrounding an application (*e.g.*, hardware or network state, user characteristics, location, etc.). Context awareness toolkits have been proposed to address this issue of context perception (*e.g.*, WildCAT [9]). In the area of programming languages, it has been recognized that beyond perceiving context, actually *composing* context-specific behavior with the application logic results in context-related conditionals (if statements) being spread out all over the program [7]. Context awareness is therefore a crosscutting concern, which

---

[*] É. Tanter is partially financed by the Milenium Nucleus Center for Web Research, Grant P04-067-F, Mideplan, Chile.

[**] Author supported by the Science Foundation Ireland and Lero - the Irish Software Engineering Research Centre, and the Swiss National Science Foundation, Project No. 200020-105091/1 "A Unified Approach to Composition and Extensibility".

W. Löwe and M. Südholt (Eds.): SC 2006, LNCS 4089, pp. 227–242, 2006.

is a good candidate for being treated as an aspect. Doing so implies that aspects should be context aware; a *context-aware aspect* is an aspect whose behavior depends on the context. The "behavior" of an aspect includes the crosscut specification of the aspect as well as its associated action (*a.k.a.*, advice). This paper explores aspect *language constructs* to scope aspects to certain contexts, and to allow aspect advices to be parameterized by information associated to contexts.

Current approaches to AOP support several means to restrict an aspect based on some kind of *context*: *e.g.*, based on certain data associated with the join points it intercepts (*e.g.*, the value of a certain parameter), or based on their relationship to past join points (*e.g.*, current control flow or past execution history [14, 12]). However the notion of context used in context-aware applications is more general and AOP languages lack an explicit notion of context. Interestingly, context can also be related to particular application domains, such as a promotional context in an online shopping application. Also, current AOP languages are limited with respect to the kind of context dependencies that can be expressed: most do not consider *past* contexts. While there are approaches that keep track of past events and state of the program, the problem of context-dependent aspects has not been fully considered in these cases. Expressing context dependencies in aspects would imply relying on design patterns and idioms. Conversely, we believe context awareness is central enough to many systems to deserve dedicated language constructs. We therefore aim at studying appropriate aspect language constructs for context-aware aspects, including general-purpose and domain-/application-specific constructs. The contributions of this paper are: *(a)* a general analysis of the issues associated with context-aware aspects; *(b)* the description and implementation of an open framework for context-aware aspects that meets all identified requirements. This framework, implemented on the Reflex AOP kernel [19], includes a context definition framework and a framework for defining context-related aspect language constructs.

Section 2 introduces a running example on which we base our analysis of context-aware aspects, and distills a number of requirements for defining contexts and providing aspect language features for context awareness. We describe our framework for context-aware aspects in Section 3, and discuss related work in Section 4. Section 5 presents our conclusions.

2   Motivation and Requirements

2.1   Running Example

The running example is an online shop application. When a customer logs in, a shopping cart is created that can be filled with various items. When the purchase has to be ordered, the bill is calculated. Within this application, we consider a simple discounting aspect. The following is a skeleton implementation of a Discount aspect in AspectJ which is not at all dependent on current promotions but simply applies a constant discount of 10%:

```
aspect Discount {
  double rate = 0.10;
  pointcut amount() : execution(double ShoppingCart.getAmount());
  double around() : amount() { return proceed() * (1 - rate); }
}
```

There are several ways in which the discounting aspect can be related to a promotion. For instance, the discount can be based on **(D1)** the current promotion
that is active either when the customer checks out, or **(D2)** when the customer
logs in and the shopping cart is created, or **(D3)** when the item is added to the
shopping cart.

The fact that a promotion is active or not can be described as the application
being in a *promotional context* [1]. Whether the application is currently in a promotional context can be defined in several ways, e.g.: **(P1)** it can be time-based,
based on whether the current time falls in any of the given intervals during
which promotions are given; or **(P2)** the shop application can automatically
give promotions when the shop's stock area is getting overloaded and needs to
be cleared; or **(P3)** the shop's sales department may want to advertise a new
web-services-based interface to the application, the application would then be in
a promotional context if shopping is done through web-service requests.

Finally, the discount rate may **(R1)** simply be constant as in the example
above, but **(R2)** may also vary depending on the actual promotion. In other
words, instead of being in a promotional context or not, the application may
also offer promotions with different discount rates.

2.2   Example Design Analysis

Context Definition. The definition of when to apply the discount and the
definition of the promotional context should be separate. The reason for this
is simply good separation of concerns. As discussed above, there are several
variations possible both for the context definition itself and the discount aspect
that depends on it. In an evolution scenario, the shopping company may either
change when the discounts are applied without changing the definition of the
promotion, or vice-versa. Also, the definition of the promotion may apply to
other aspects besides the discount aspect, such as an advertising aspect which
adds customized banners for each customer to the shop's web pages. Hence,
separating aspects that are dependent on some contexts from the definition of
contexts themselves serves well-established engineering principles. In addition to
this logical separation between aspects and contexts, contexts should be:

- **stateful:** a context may have state associated to it. Support should be
  provided for both state internal to the context's implementation (*e.g.*, the
  time slots when a promotion is active) and publicly accessible state, such as
  for variation R2 in the example when the rate of discount depends on the

---

[1] We also use the interchangeable phrases "the application is in a given context" and
"a given context is active".

promotion. In that case, the discount aspect would define when to actually apply a discount, and would get the specific discount rate from the promotion which defines when this rate is determined. Of course, the state of a context may change dynamically.

- **composable:** a context may be defined from more primitive contexts. For instance, one can define the stock overload context independently of the promotional context; this way, other contexts can be based on stock overload, and the promotional context can combine the time-based definition with the stock overload context.
- **parameterized:** contexts can be defined generically, and parameterized by aspects that are restricted to it; for instance, the stock overload context can be parameterized by the actual threshold that leads to the context being active.

Finally, a context can be related to *control flow properties* (*e.g.*, the web-services-based promotional context), in the broad sense of the term (not only as AspectJ's cflow, but also as past event sequences [14, 12]).

Contextual Restriction. Restricting an aspect to a particular context requires the possibility to refer to a context definition in a pointcut definition. For instance:

```
pointcut amount(): execution(double Item.getPrice()) && inContext(PromotionCtx);
```

Furthermore, since the discount rate may vary on the actual promotion, the associated advice may need to access some external state of the considered context:

```
aspect Discount {
  pointcut amount(double rate): execution(double ShoppingCart.getAmount())
                        && inContext(PromotionCtx(rate));
  double around(double rate): amount(rate) { return proceed() * (1 - rate); }
}
```

The code above assumes that using rate in PromotionCtx(rate) relies on the fact that a promotional context exposes a rate property (*e.g.*, via a getRate accessor). In addition to context state exposure, it has to be possible to *parameterize* a context when expressing a dependency on it: *e.g.*, Discount could depend on both a time-based PromotionCtx, and the StockOverloadCtx, parameterized by a threshold of, say, 80%[2].

```
pointcut amount(double rate): execution(double ShoppingCart.getAmount())
        && inContext(PromotionCtx(rate)) && inContext(StockOverloadCtx[.80]);
```

The above inContext pointcut restrictor is semantically equivalent to an if restrictor in AspectJ: restricting an aspect based on whether a certain (context) condition is *currently* verified. However, it should also be possible to restrict an aspect based on whether the application *was* in a certain context previously.

---

[2] We assume the syntax: (..) for exposing context state, and [..] for context parameterization.

There is one generally-useful past context dependency: the context during which an object is created (*a.k.a.*, its *creation context*), *e.g.*, the context during which a shopping cart is created. Using an appropriate language construct createdInCtx, the following implies that Discount applies for any shopping cart that *was created* when PromotionCtx was active, without considering whether the promotion is still active when the customer checks out:

```
pointcut amount(): execution(double ShoppingCart.getAmount())
                   && createdInCtx(PromotionCtx);
```

Finally, it should also be possible to define *domain-* or *application-specific* context restrictors; *e.g.*, to refer to the context during which an item was added to the shopping cart (assuming an appropriate application-specific putInCartInCtx pointcut restrictor):

```
pointcut amount(): execution(double Item.getPrice()) && putInCartInCtx(PromotionCtx);
```

The combination of past context dependencies and stateful contexts implies the need for keeping track of past contexts and their associated state: on the one hand, contexts can be stateful and this state can vary over time; on the other hand, the actual application of the discount can depend on a past promotion context. We refer to this process of keeping track of past contexts and their states as *context snapshotting*, and to the frozen state of a context at a given point in time as a *context snapshot*. A *global* context snapshot is therefore a snapshot of all defined contexts at a given point in time.

For implementation considerations (basically, memory usage), it is obviously impossible to keep the global context snapshots at each and every point in time. It is thus important to be able to snapshot contexts only when really needed. For instance, snapshotting the creation context of an object is needed only if this object is affected by an aspect that is subject to a creation-context dependency. It is also desirable that snapshots be associated to the object they relate to in order to avoid maintaining huge global hashtables, as these would surely become bottlenecks.

Finally, the possibility of defining domain- and application-specific context restrictors implies that the corresponding snapshotting (when to snapshot, where to store the snapshots) be user-definable.

2.3 Summary

The above design analysis of the running example points out a number of requirements for appropriately modeling contexts on the one hand, and for providing aspect language features for context awareness on the other hand, which can be summarized as follows:

- Contexts and context-aware aspects must be separate entities.
- Contexts should possibly be parameterized, stateful, and composable.
- Context state should possibly be bound to pointcut variables.
- It should be possible to express dependencies on past contexts.
- New context-related constructs (possibly domain-specific) should be definable.
- Non-naive implementation of context snapshotting must be supported.

3   An Open Framework for Context-Aware Aspects

We now present an open framework for context-aware aspects that meets the above requirements. The framework is an extension of Reflex[3], a versatile kernel for multi-language AOP in Java [19]. Reflex supports AOP-like dynamic cross-cutting, and the framework supports plugins that compile languages such as AspectJ to standard Java programs using Reflex [18]. We do not discuss concrete syntax extensions for supporting context-dependent restrictions here; we focus on the extension of the framework.

3.1   Why a Framework Approach?

A major requirement we have identified is to be able to add new constructs to an aspect language, along with their corresponding semantics. Such an extensible aspect language can be achieved using one of the following alternatives:

- modifying the *interpreter* of the aspect language;
- using a *reflective* aspect language, *i.e.*, an aspect language that has an account of itself embedded within it;
- using an extensible *compiler* for that aspect language.

To the best of our knowledge, there have been no real reflective aspect language proposed to date. As regards extensible compilers, we could implement our proposal using abc, the AspectBench compiler, which is precisely an extensible AspectJ compiler [3]. Our framework-based approach has an advantage in terms of simplicity of the implementation and hence rapidity in prototyping new language features. There is no doubt though that abc would lead to a more efficient implementation as a number of static optimizations could be done: but this is not the purpose of this paper; optimized implementations of context-aware aspects is deliberately left for future research. It has to be noted that working at the framework level is conceptually equivalent to working at the level of the interpreter of the aspect language.

The following section gives a brief overview of Reflex, to give the necessary background for understanding the description of the extended framework that follows. The presentation of the extension for context-dependence is divided in four parts, following the organization depicted in Fig. 1: we first present the context definition framework, followed by the context restriction framework, and we illustrate the use of both with user-defined extensions.

3.2   Background on Reflex

Reflex is an open reflective extension of Java that supports both structural and behavioral modifications of programs. The core concept of Reflex is the *link*; we hereby only need to explain behavioral links: a behavioral *link* invokes messages on a *metaobject* at occurrences of operations specified by a *hookset* [19, 20].

---

[3] http://reflex.dcc.uchile.cl

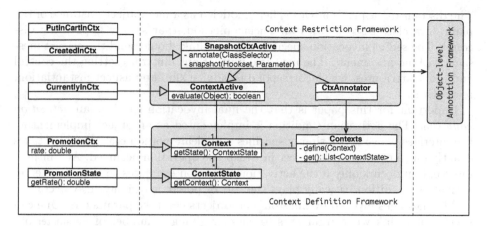

Fig. 1. The Reflex-based frameworks for context-aware aspects: the Context Definition Framework for defining when contexts are active and the Context Restriction Framework for defining context-dependent activation conditions

A hookset, like an AspectJ pointcut, is a composable entity that specifies a set of operations based on selection conditions. However, it expresses lexical crosscutting only (pointcut shadows). An example hookset and its equivalent in AspectJ is the following:

```
// execution(* WebServiceRequest+.*(..))
  Hookset hs = new Hookset(MsgReceive.class,
                  new NameCS("WebServiceRequest", true), new AnyOS()));
```

The selection conditions of a hookset are split into a selection on the type of operation, on the classes in which they occur and on the operations themselves. In the example, the hookset intercepts occurrences of MsgReceive operations, which corresponds to the execution join point type in AspectJ. The NameCS class selector specifies that the class should be WebServiceRequest – or one of its subclasses, as specified by the true parameter, which corresponds to the + in AspectJ. The operation selector AnyOS simply specifies no further conditions on operation occurrences (similar to the use of "*" wildcards).

The exact message sent to the metaobject, as well as how and even if it is really invoked, can be further controlled by setting attributes of the link. Following is an example link definition (amountHS is the hookset corresponding to the amount pointcut):

```
BLink discount = Links.createBLink(amountHS, new Discount());
discount.setCall(Discount.class, "amount");
discount.setControl(Control.BEFORE);        // before advice kind
discount.setScope(Scope.GLOBAL);            // singleton metaobject
discount.addActivation(new Condition());    // adding a dynamic condition
```

The discounting aspect's advice is here modeled as a metaobject, instance of the plain Java class Discount with an amount method, that simply applies the discount. The setCall invocation specifies that the link should send the amount message, with no arguments. The next two invocations illustrate setting the control and scope attributes, which correspond to advice kind and aspect instantiation, respectively.

Important for this paper is that the final invocation specifies an *activation condition*. The activation condition is implemented as an object implementing the interface Active which simply specifies a boolean method evaluate which takes exactly one parameter, the object in which the operation occurred. At runtime, interception occurs only if the activation condition evaluates to true. Hence, an activation condition basically plays the role of pointcut residues in AspectJ.

The messages invoked by links on metaobjects can take parameters. One can specify on a link what arguments to pass by giving a number of Parameter objects. There are several possible objects one can pass, but a number of predefined parameters are available, such as Parameter.THIS and Parameter.RESULT which represent the currently-executing object and the result of the intercepted operation, respectively.

3.3   Context Definition Framework

A simple usage of Reflex for defining context can represent contexts as objects with a boolean method active. Since Reflex supports first-class pointcuts via hooksets and activation conditions, AOP features can be used for defining when a context is active. For instance, consider the definition of the web-service-based promotion context:

```
class PromotionCtx {
    // cflow(execution(* WebServiceRequest+.*(..)))
    CFlow cf = CFlowFactory.get(new Hookset(MsgReceive.class,
                         new NameCS("WebServiceRequest", true), new AnyOS()));
    boolean active() { return cf.in(); }
}
```

The CFlow object exposes the control flow of the hookset given to the CFlowFactory The active method is defined in terms of the in message of this object, which returns true when the application is in the control flow of an operation that matches the hookset.

We also need to define how contexts are snapshot: at any point in time, we may need to snapshot a context, in order to access its state later. One way to design this is to make contexts cloneable, and clone all active contexts when doing a snapshot. But this introduces the issue of managing the depth of context cloning; also, some state of the context is related to its initial parameterization and hence does not need to be cloned.

We rather opted for a design that forces context implementors to explicitly consider the issue of context snapshots. Context definitions should extend the abstract class Context, which instead of having a boolean active method requires overriding a getState method. This method should return null if the context is not active, otherwise it should return a snapshot of the context as a ContextState object. ContextState is defined as an inner class of Context to ensure the snapshots have a relation to the originating context:

```
abstract class Context {
  Context() { Contexts.define(this); } // define context (explained later)
  abstract ContextState getState(); // null if inactive
  class ContextState {
    Context getContext() { return Context.this; }
}}
```

Suppose that PromotionCtx is characterized by a variable discount rate:

```
class PromotionCtx extends Context {
  CFlow cf = /* as above */              class PromotionState
  double rate; /* with setter */                 extends ContextState {
  ContextState getState() {                  double rate; // init in constructor
  if(!cf.in()) return null;                  double getRate() { return rate; }
  return new PromotionState(rate);        }}
  }
```

The above implementation ensures that the promotion context can be snapshot correctly: a PromotionState object holds the value of the discount rate at the time the snapshot was requested – although the *current* discount rate may be different.

The framework also includes a global context dictionary, Contexts, which keeps track of all contexts that have been defined (via define(c), as done in the constructor of the abstract Context class) and which can be asked for a global snapshot of all currently active contexts (via get). A global context snapshot is represented as a Snapshot object, which is simply a map of Context-to-ContextState objects. Recall that each context state object contains a reference to the context object that generated it.

3.4   Context Restriction Framework

The context-dependent pointcut restrictors of Section 2.2 can be defined in the Reflex framework as activation conditions on links. Two abstract classes implementing the Active interface are defined as a framework for defining context-dependent activation conditions (Fig. 1). We show here how these are specialized for defining the currentlyInCtx restrictor. The createdInCtx and putInCartInCtx restrictors are presented in the next section. First of all, the CtxActive abstract class is defined as follows:

```
abstract class CtxActive implements Active {
  Context itsContext;
  CtxActive(Context c){ itsContext = c; } // associate context to condition
  boolean evaluate(Object o){ return getCtxState(o) != null; }
  abstract ContextState getCtxState(Object o);
}
```

In the constructor, the context on which the activation condition relies is stored in an instance variable. The activation condition evaluates to true if the associated context is active, or more precisely, is *determined* to (having) be(en) active by getCtxState. This method is abstract because some context-related conditions rely on a *past* context state, and should therefore be able to retrieve the appropriate context snapshot associated to the currently-executed object. This is explained in more details in the rest of this section.

The CurrentlyInCtx condition restricts a link to be active only when the condition's context is active. So getCtxState returns the value of the context's getState method:

```
class CurrentlyInCtx extends CtxActive {
    ContextState getCtxState(Object o){ return itsContext.getState(); }
}
```

The following is an example of using this activation condition to restrict a link to activate only when the promotion context is active:

```
discount.addActivation(new CurrentlyInCtx(new PromotionCtx()));
```

Past Dependencies. The abstract class SnapshotCtxActive provides the necessary support for defining activation conditions that depend on past context snapshots.

```
abstract class SnapshotCtxActive extends CtxActive {
    ContextState getCtxState(Object o){
      Snapshot snapshot = getSnapshot(o);
      return snapshot.get(itsContext);
} }
```

When queried, such an activation condition extracts the relevant snapshot from the currently-executing object passed as parameter (getSnapshot), and queries the snapshot for the state associated to its context.

There are basically two design options for storing the snapshots of contexts associated with specific objects. One is to rely on a global map of objects to contexts, another is to associate snapshots as extra hidden state in the objects themselves. We opted for the latter option, to avoid a central bottleneck and also since it ensures that the snapshots are removed from memory when the objects they are associated with are garbage collected. We rely on a general object-level annotation framework based on Reflex and its abilities to perform structural changes to classes (not presented here due to space restrictions). To control snapshots, SnapshotCtxActive implements a number of utility methods to interact with this framework, such as:

- void annotate(ClassSelector cs) – enable annotations in classes matched by cs.
- void snapshot(Hookset hs, Parameter p) – upon operation occurrences matched by hs, store snapshot context in the parameter p of the occurrence.
- Snapshot getSnapshot(Object o) – return snapshot stored in o.

3.5   User-Defined Extensions

Having presented the whole framework for context-aware aspects, we illustrate its use by showing how new pointcut restrictors are defined. Two examples are given, one for restricting based on the creation context of a particular object, the other is an application-specific one. Since both refer to past contexts, they are extensions of SnapshotCtxActive.

Creation Context. The creationCtx pointcut restrictor is implemented as the CreatedInCtx class for activation conditions. It can be added as an activation condition to the discount link as follows:

CtxActive createdInPromo = new CreatedInCtx(new PromotionCtx(), discount);
discount.addActivation(createdInPromo);

Note that the discount link itself is passed as a parameter to the activation condition. This is done so that the link can be introspected, in order to determine which instantiations of which classes the discount aspect actually depends on; the snapshotting of the contexts can thus be limited to instantiations of just those classes. In the constructor of CreationCtx below, the class selector of the link is and used to define snapshotting on just the classes described by the selector:

```
class CreatedInCtx extends SnapshotCtxActive {
    CreatedInCtx(Context c, BLink l){
        super(c);
        ClassSelector cs = l.getClassSelector();
        annotate(cs);
        snapshot(new Hookset(Creation.class, cs, new AnyOS()), Parameter.THIS);
} }
```

The class selector cs is retrieved from the link using its getClassSelector method and is used in a call to snapshot. The hookset passed to snapshot describes all invocations of constructors in classes matching the class selector. Context snapshots are consequently stored in the newly-created object (Parameter.THIS).

In Cart Context. We now illustrate how an application-specific pointcut restrictor is defined, by considering the case of the PutInCartInCtx discussed in Section 2.2. In Reflex, the corresponding activation condition would be used as follows:

CtxActive putInCartInPromo = new PutInCartInCtx(new PromotionCtx());
discount.addActivation(putInCartInPromo);

The implementation of PutInCartInCtx states that Item objects should be annotated, and that context snapshot annotation occurs upon execution of addItem on a shopping cart; The object to be annotated, the item, is the first parameter (NthParameter(1)) of the call:

```
class PutInCartInCtx extends SnapshotCtxActive {
    PutInCartInCtx(Context c){
        annotate(new NameCS("eshop.Item"));
        snapshot(new Hookset(MsgReceive.class, new NameCS("eshop.ShoppingCart"),
                        new NameOS("addItem")), new NthParameter(1));
}}
```

3.6   State Exposure and Parameterization

Since contexts are standard objects, their parameterization is naturally done
by passing parameters at instantiation time, or by sending them configuration
messages. For instance, restricting Discount to inContext(StockOverflowCtx[.80]) is
implemented as:

```
discount.addActivation(new CurrentlyInCtx(new StockOverflowCtx(.80)));
```

Exposing context state, such as the discount rate in:

```
aspect Discount {
    pointcut amount(double rate): execution(double ShoppingCart.getAmount())
                        && createdInCtx(PromotionCtx(rate));
    double around(double rate): amount(rate) { return proceed() * (1 - rate); }
}
```

is based on the mechanism provided by Reflex to customize the invocation of a
metaobject (recall Section 3.2). The above example would be implemented as
follows:

```
Context promotionCtx = new PromotionCtx();
CtxActive inPromo = new CreatedInCtx(promotionCtx, discount);
discount.addActivation(inPromo);
discount.setCall(Discount.class, "amount", inPromo.getCtxParam("rate"));
```

The important line is the last one: the specification of the call to amount (the
advice) is changed to include one parameter, bound to the value of the rate
state property of the promotional context. getCtxParam is a method of CtxActive[4]
that returns a custom Parameter object. To evaluate the value of this parameter
at runtime, the activation condition inPromo is queried for the context state
corresponding to the currently-executing object, retrieves that context state in
the adequate snapshot (in this case, the creation context snapshot), and invokes
the getRate method on it.

3.7   More Extensions

In the current work we have only considered context dependencies related to the
currently-executing object of an operation occurrence. The two constructs we

---

[4] The implementation of getCtxParam is not shown as this would lead us too far into
details. The interested reader is welcome to ask the authors.

have presented for past context dependencies always look for context snapshots in the this: if the currently-executing object has been created in a given context, or put in the shopping cart in a given context, etc. It would be equally interesting to be able to relate to past contexts associated with other objects, such as the target or any of the arguments of an operation occurrence, or even any object that is accessible from the join point. We could define additional activation conditions that are defined to check for context-dependency related to other objects than the this. Another option fitting in the Reflex framework would be to parameterize context-related activation conditions with a Parameter object to describe on which parameter of the operation occurrence the activation condition acts. In that case, the constructors of the activation condition will also have to perform a slightly more complex introspection of the link's hookset to determine on which classes snapshotting should be performed. We expect to research such extensions in future work.

4 Related Work

We now review related work in the area of contexts, and existing proposals to restrict the scope of aspects. The term *context* can be found in different meanings and definitions in many computer science disciplines, such as human-computer interaction and ubiquitous computing. We hereby only focus on the use of context as an element of a programming language.

Context-Oriented Programming. ContextL [7] is a recent CLOS-based approach for Context-Oriented Programming (COP). While we have presented an extension of an aspect-oriented approach, COP is exploring a paradigmatically new approach. A major difference between both approaches is in the way time is dealt with. In the AOP approach an aspect can be made dependent on whether the application was previously in a certain context, while in COP this is reversed: when the application enters a state that qualifies as being in a certain context, code is redefined so that its future execution takes the "aspect" into account. As the two approaches are paradigmatically different, it is difficult to compare them, though one could state that our proposal has a more declarative nature as the conditions under which the application is in a certain context arc encapsulated in context definitions, while in ContextL context has to be more explicitly activated.

Context in other AOP Approaches. The term context has also been used in other AOP approaches: the term is meant to denote information associated with joinpoints, but is typically also limited to information directly associated with joinpoints such as arguments of messages, or the control flow "context" of the joinpoint. We have considered the term context in the more general meaning of all the information about the state of a program when a joinpoint occurs, and have also considered the use of context about past joinpoints, while limiting the amount of information that is kept about past contexts.

Technically, this can be realized in any AOP approach like it is done in the implementation of our framework, *i.e.*, by defining additional pointcuts and advices to capture contexts when needed. However, in our framework these additional pointcuts (or hooksets) are *automatically* installed, they do not have to be written by hand (Sect. 3.5). Also, in our approach context dependencies can be checked in the pointcut, not in the advice, resulting in clearer code.

In AspectJ for example, one can implement a context definition such as the promotion context as an object and the discounting as an aspect. The discounting aspect has one advice for applying the discount, and a second one for snapshotting the promotion context when, *e.g.*, a shopping cart is created. But any aspect depending on the promotion context needs an advice to snapshot the context as needed. An attempt to define a more general promotion context snapshotting aspect runs into the problem that it is not possible to analyze the pointcuts of the aspects that depend on the context. So the reusable definition of the snapshotting necessarily has to snapshot the context at all instance creations, leading to unnecessary overhead. In AspectJ, there is also the problem of defining context activation predicates as reusable named pointcuts because such pointcuts can neither be made dependent on a context using polymorphism (pointcut invocations are not late bound), nor can named pointcuts be parameterized with a context object (named pointcuts only have output arguments). In more advanced aspect languages it may be possible to achieve an implementation of context-aware aspects that is both more reusable and efficient than an implementation in AspectJ, for instance with CaesarJ [2]. Although a detailed comparison with the Reflex-based implementation presented here remains to be done, the interest of Reflex (apart that it is *sufficiently* expressive and open to cover our needs) is that it explicitly addresses the issue of extensible aspect languages on top of the framework, through the on-going integration of Reflex and MetaBorg [6]. Therefore the context-aware syntactic extensions formulated at the beginning of the paper can be provided over Reflex.

A number of proposals make it possible for aspects to depend on the past execution history, and to refer to state associated to past events [1,8,11,13]. These approaches make it possible to refer to past context, but only consider context in the sense of join point-related information, as above. Conversely, in this work we consider a more general notion of context, whose state can actually be computed arbitrarily. In other words, we can bind any context state to pointcut variables, which can then be used to parameterize advices. Although the extensions considered in this paper are not impossible to realize in, *e.g.*, EAOP, they have not been explicitly considered. Allowing aspects to refer to the full state of the program was also introduced in the user-extensible logic-based language CARMA using object reifying predicates [15]. This work could also be extended to solve context-dependency problems.

The recent introduction of a `let` construct [4] in the AspectBench Compiler [3] makes it possible to bind any context information to pointcut variables, as in our approach. This construct therefore solves the issue of being able to expose (external) context information in pointcuts. However, being an extension of

AspectJ, an *abc* solution would not do any better with respect to the other issues discussed previously with AspectJ: lack of first-class pointcuts, no late-bound pointcut invocations, no input pointcut arguments, etc.

5   Conclusion

Handling context-related behavior as aspects allows for better modularization. In this paper, we have analyzed what it means for aspects to be *context aware* and explored the associated aspect language features. We have exposed an open framework for context-aware aspects, *i.e.*, aspects whose behavior is context dependent. This includes the possibility to restrict aspects to certain contexts, both currently and in the past, as well as to parameterize aspect advices with context-related information. Furthermore, our approach makes it possible to define application- or domain-specific context-related restrictors for aspects.

Future work includes experimenting with context-aware aspects in more elaborate scenarios, and implementing a set of contexts in our framework based on a context-awareness toolkit such as WildCAT [9]. This should provide feedback on our aspect language feature approach to handling context awareness.

Acknowledgments: Many thanks to thank Johan Brichau, Pascal Costanza, Maja D'Hondt, Stéphane Ducasse, Johan Fabry, Oscar Nierstrasz and Roel Wuyts for fruitful discussions on context-oriented programming and context-aware aspects.

References

[1] Chris Allan, Pavel Avgustinov, Aske Simon Christensen, Laurie Hendren, Sascha Kuzins, Ondrej Lhoták, Oege de Moor, Damien Sereni, Ganesh Sittampalam, and Julian Tibble. Adding trace matching with free variables to AspectJ. In *Proceedings of OOPSLA 2005*. ACM Press, 2005.

[2] Ivica Aracic, Vaidas Gasiunas, Mira Mezini, and Klaus Ostermann. An overview of CaesarJ. In *Transactions on Aspect-Oriented Software Development*, volume 3880 of *Lecture Notes in Computer Science*, pages 135–173. Springer-Verlag, February 2006.

[3] Pavel Avgustinov, Aske Simon Christensen, Laurie Hendren, Sascha Kuzins, Jennifer Lhotak, Ondrej Lhotak, Oege de Moor, Damien Sereni, Ganesh Sittampalam, and Julian Tibble. abc: an extensible AspectJ compiler. In *Proceedings of AOSD 2005*, pages 87–98, New York, NY, USA, 2005. ACM Press.

[4] Pavel Avgustinov, Julian Tibble, Eric Bodden, Ondrej Lhoták, Laurie Hendren, Oege de Moor, Neil Ongkingco, and Ganesh Sittampalam. Efficient trace monitoring. Technical Report abc-2006-1, abc Group, March 2006.

[5] M. Baldauf and S. Dustdar. A survey on context-aware systems. Technical Report TUV-1841-2004-24, Technical University of Vienna, 2004.

[6] Martin Bravenboer and Eelco Visser. Concrete syntax for objects. In *Proceedings of OOPSLA 2004*, Vancouver, British Columbia, Canada, October 2004. ACM Press. ACM SIGPLAN Notices, 39(11).

[7] Pascal Costanza and Robert Hirschfeld. Language constructs for context-oriented programming. In *Proceedings of the ACM Dynamic Languages Symposium*, 2005.

[8] Thomas Cottenier and Tzilla Elrad. Contextual pointcut expressions for dynamic service customization. In *Dynamic Aspect Workshop*, 2005.

[9] Pierre-Charles David and Thomas Ledoux. WildCAT: a generic framework for context-aware applications. In *Proceeding of MPAC'05, the 3rd International Workshop on Middleware for Pervasive and Ad-Hoc Computing*, Grenoble, France, November 2005.

[10] A. K. Dey and G. D. Abowd. Towards a better understanding of context and context-awareness. In *Workshop on the What, Who, Where, When, and How of Context-Awareness, as part of the 2000 Conference on Human Factors in Computing Systems (CHI 2000)*, The Hague, The Netherlands, April 2000.

[11] Rémi Douence, Pascal Fradet, and Mario Südholt. Composition, reuse and interaction analysis of stateful aspects. In *Proceedings of AOSD 2004*, pages 141–150. ACM Press, March 2004.

[12] Rémi Douence, Pascal Fradet, and Mario Südholt. Trace-based aspects. In Robert E. Filman, Tzilla Elrad, Siobhán Clarke, and Mehmet Akşit, editors, *Aspect-Oriented Software Development*, pages 201–217. Addison-Wesley, Boston, 2005.

[13] Remi Douence, Olivier Motelet, and Mario Sudholt. A formal definition of crosscuts. In *Proceedings of Reflection 2001*, volume 2192 of *Lecture Notes in Computer Science*, pages 170–186, Kyoto, Japan, September 2001. Springer-Verlag.

[14] Rémi Douence and Luc Teboul. A pointcut language for control-flow. In Gabor Karsai and Eelco Visser, editors, *Proceedings of GPCE 2004*, volume 3286 of *Lecture Notes in Computer Science*, pages 95–114, Vancouver, Canada, October 2004. Springer-Verlag.

[15] Kris Gybels and Johan Brichau. Arranging language features for more robust pattern-based crosscuts. In *Proceedings of AOSD 2003*, 2003.

[16] J. Kephart. A vision of autonomic computing. In *Onward! Track at OOPSLA 2002*, pages 13–36, Seattle, WA, USA, 2002.

[17] P. K. McKinley, S. M. Sadjadi, and B. H Kasten, Cheng. Composing adaptive software. *IEEE Computer*, 37(7):56–64, July 2004.

[18] Leonardo Rodríguez, Éric Tanter, and Jacques Noyé. Supporting dynamic crosscutting with partial behavioral reflection: A case study. In *Proceedings of SCCC 2004*, pages 48–58, 2004.

[19] Éric Tanter and Jacques Noyé. A versatile kernel for multi-language AOP. In Robert Glück and Mike Lowry, editors, *Proceedings of the 4th ACM SIGPLAN/SIGSOFT Conference on Generative Programming and Component Engineering (GPCE 2005)*, volume 3676 of *Lecture Notes in Computer Science*, pages 173–188, Tallinn, Estonia, September/October 2005. Springer-Verlag.

[20] Éric Tanter, Jacques Noyé, Denis Caromel, and Pierre Cointe. Partial behavioral reflection: Spatial and temporal selection of reification. In *Proceedings of OOPSLA 2003*, pages 27–46, nov 2003. ACM SIGPLAN Notices, 39(11).

[21] Mark Weiser. Some computer science issues in ubiquitous computing. *Communications of the ACM*, 36(7):75–84, July 1993.

Understanding Design Patterns Density with Aspects
A Case Study in JHotDraw Using AspectJ

Simon Denier and Pierre Cointe

OBASCO
École des Mines de Nantes, INRIA, LINA,
4, rue Alfred Kastler, Nantes, France
{sdenier, cointe}@emn.fr

Abstract. Design patterns offer solutions to common engineering problems in programs [1]. In particular, they shape the evolution of program elements. However, their implementations tend to vanish in the code: thus it is hard to spot them and to understand their impact. The problem becomes even more difficult with a "high density of pattern": then the program becomes easy to evolve in the direction allowed by patterns but hard to change [2]. Aspect languages offer new means to modularize elements. Implementations of object-oriented design patterns with AspectJ have been proposed [3]. We aim at testing the scalability of such solutions in the JHotDraw framework. We first explore the impact of density on pattern implementation. We show how AspectJ helps to reduce this impact. This unveils the principles of aspects and AspectJ to control pattern density.

1 Introduction

Design patterns [1] are well-known couples of problem-solution for program engineering. They shape the structure and the interface of their targets, and redefine some behaviors. Most design patterns aim at decoupling concerns, in particular to allow separate evolution. However, the shape they impose disallows evolution in other directions. Also, the programmer must often make a tradeoff between the impact of the pattern and the properties he wants from it, which results in distortions from the standard pattern. Then implementations of design patterns suffer from lack of traceability: some elements tend to be lost and pattern identity itself is hard to trace back to the model — such that the pattern is said to "vanish" in the code [4].

The impact of design patterns on implementation, their tendency to shape evolution, and the difficulty to trace them in the code raise questions when software grows in complexity. But the implications of design patterns in complex software is not well understood. Most prominent work includes the study of relationships between design patterns, such as [1] (section "Design pattern relationships") and [5], who proposes a classification of different kind of relationships. This includes patterns making use of other patterns in their implementation as

W. Löwe and M. Südholt (Eds.): SC 2006, LNCS 4089, pp. 243–258, 2006.

well as interactions between two patterns. [2] shows in the context of JUnit that mature frameworks tend to have a high density of patterns: then they are "easy to use, but hard to change". Implementations become so entangled that it is nearly impossible to think of a pattern alone and that they can lose some of their flexibility.

Aspect-oriented languages à la AspectJ [6,7] offer new means to modularize software elements. [3] shows some general aspectizations of the GoF design patterns [1]. Aspect-oriented languages allow:

- modularization of crosscutting pattern elements;
- better separation between a generic (reusable) part and a specific part;
- language-level detection and visualization tools for interactions;
- pluggability of modules to replace a pattern implementation by another.

Our aim is to test the scalability of such aspectizations of design patterns in a real application. We experiment with the JHotDraw framework[1] as it is a well documented "design exercise" involving many design patterns.

Our guideline is to look for an incremental and reversible development of JHotDraw. We start with a basic yet functional framework (called the *base* thereafter). We then "compose" new modules into the base, incrementally enhancing the framework, but still with the option to come back to earlier versions. By doing so we underline design choices which happen through the whole program when more functions are composed together, but get lost because there is no mean to trace such choices to the module they support. Such a guideline allows for a deeper separation of concerns highlighting the development process and product versions.

Section 2 presents JHotDraw *base* (internals and design patterns), as well as the specific example of the "invalidation" concern. Section 3 examines the invasive impact of two additional concerns on the base, related to the OBSERVER, COMPOSITE and DECORATOR patterns. Section 4 shows how such impact can be modularized with AspectJ constructs. We follow with some discussions in Sect. 5, related work in Sect. 6 and conclude in Sect. 7.

2   An Overview of the JHotDraw Framework

2.1   General Architecture

Figure 1 shows main interfaces and relationships involved in the JHotDraw framework *base*. It gives a feeling of how a JHotDraw application works and what can be extended. We now explain the responsibilities and collaborations of each interface, in particular with regard to framework extension:

- **DrawingEditor** is the base interface for the application. It maintains a link to the active `DrawingView` and to the current tool. Extensions usually define the GUI, instantiate tools and drawing views.

---

[1] We use JHotDraw 5.3 – available at http://www.jhotdraw.org/

- **DrawingView** displays one drawing. It holds interactions between the user and the drawing, as well as graphics with Swing. This is apparent as it is linked to `JPanel`, maintains a link to the list of currently selected figures, and has access to the current tool *via* the editor. The default implementation class fulfills all these roles.
- **Drawing** acts as a container and a uniform layer to manage a set of figures.
- **Figure** is a central entity to the user. Depending on the application, it can spawn a large tree of derived figures, such as rectangle, circle, line, or more structured figures.
- **Tool & Handle** allow to create or manipulate `Figures`, either as a whole (select, move) or focusing on a specific property (size, radius). Tools and handles are notified of user interactions by the drawing view. They too can spawn a large tree of derived classes depending on the application.

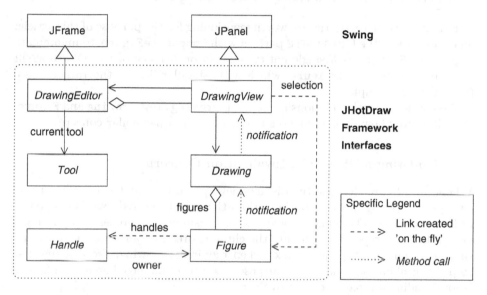

Fig. 1. A synthetic diagram of main interfaces and relationships in JHotDraw. The inheritance relationship between Swing class `JFrame` and JHotDraw interface `DrawingEditor` is a shortcut to the real relationship between `JFrame` and a `DrawApplication` class implementing `DrawingEditor`. The same is true for `JPanel` and `DrawingView`.

2.2   Design Patterns Involvement

We now quickly sketch how design patterns are involved in this general architecture (Fig. 1) and in the underlying implementation. The design patterns exposed here are documented in the code. The list below shows the importance of patterns to define relationships (MEDIATOR, OBSERVER) as well as to extend the framework (STATE, PROTOTYPE, STRATEGY, ADAPTER, FACTORY METHOD). These patterns build up the JHotDraw framework *base*.

- **Mediator:** `DrawingEditor` is a mediator between the current tool and the drawing view.
- **Strategy:** some `DrawingView` activities such as painting the drawing or grid constraining are configured with strategies.
- **Observer:** there are two occurrences of the OBSERVER pattern. One is lying between figures and the drawing, the other between a drawing and a drawing view. They basically serve to update the drawing and the view in response to figure modifications. One such concern is detailed in Sect. 2.3.
- **State & Prototype:** by switching between tools for the current tool state, the user changes the behavior he wants to apply in the drawing view context. Creation tools create figures by copying a prototype figure.
- **Adapter & Factory Method:** `Handler` adapts the `Figure` interface to respond to mouse events. The strong link between a figure and its specific handles is enforced by a factory method in `Figure`.

Finally two other patterns are worth mentioning for the purpose of this article: an occurrence of the COMPOSITE pattern with `CompositeFigure`, to manipulate a group of `Figures` as a single entity; and an occurrence of the DECORATOR pattern with `DecoratorFigure`, which adds singularities on the target figure (a border for example).

We now focus on the relationship between `DrawingView`, `Drawing` and `Figure`. We will survey how design patterns are involved in a particular concern.

2.3   Updating a View: The Invalidation Concern

Whenever a figure changes, the display view has to be updated to reflect those changes. Following a classic optimization, the area to be redrawn is clipped in order to speed up refreshing and avoid screen flashing. The process of updating a view takes two steps: first compute the clipping area and announce it to Swing, then draw on the graphics context when required by Swing. We call the first step the invalidation concern: its purpose is to collect damaged area from figures before sending a repaint request to Swing.

The obvious way to do that is to let figures announce their own clipping area whenever they change. They should notify their `Drawing`. The clipping area of a figure can be simply defined by its bounding rectangle. The clipping area for the drawing can be defined by the union of all clipping areas notified between two updates.

Obviously, this concern can be implemented with an OBSERVER occurrence between `Figure` and `Drawing`:

- when a figure is added to a drawing (after its creation for example), the drawing is registered as an observer for the figure;
- when performing some actions (such as move, change color), the figure notifies its drawing with its bounding box;
- when notified, the drawing adds the bounding box to its clipping area;
- when a figure is deleted, it deregisters the drawing as observer.

Another occurrence of OBSERVER stands between `Drawing` and `DrawingView`:

- a drawing registers its drawing view as observer;
- on request the drawing sends its clipping area to the drawing view (which forwards to Swing); after this point the clipping area can be reset.

Notice how the invalidation concern is itself decomposed in two steps: collecting the clipping area in `Drawing` and notifying Swing in `DrawingView`. This relationship is summarized in Fig. 1 by the two arrow lines for notification.

3   Study of Pattern Density in JHotDraw

The functionalities described in Sect. 2 define the JHotDraw framework base. We examine two additions to this base, both related to design patterns and the invalidation concern. Our goal is to understand how the current framework (which already contains these additions) differs from the basic one and to examine the impact in term of implementation. We do this in the spirit of incremental evolution exposed in the introduction.

3.1   Impact of Composite and Decorator on Invalidation

In the base framework all figures are direct children of the drawing and refer to it for the invalidation process. When the COMPOSITE pattern is used to manipulate a group of figures as a single entity, figures trees can be constructed (`GroupFigure`, Fig. 2). The same is true for the DECORATOR pattern with `BorderDecorator`. Then, since we can have any number of levels between the drawing and figures, does it affect the invalidation concern?

We first consider `GroupFigure`. It just merges clipping areas of figures underneath. There is no difference in merging at the group level or at the drawing level. So invalidation concern is not affected: figures can directly notify the drawing, and `GroupFigure` is not involved in this OBSERVER pattern. This solution is labelled A in Fig. 2.

On the contrary, `BorderDecorator` has the property to redefine the clipping area of the figure underneath. It enhances the bounding box by the size of its border. How do we notify the drawing that the clipping area of a figure should be enhanced? Obviously, solution A does not work since `BorderDecorator` does not have a chance to notify its change. We can think of other solutions:

- B: all `Figures` notify the `Drawing` each time a command is transmitted;
- C: base `Figures` notify their direct parent `Figure` of the change; parent can change the notification; recursively, the notification traverses the hierarchy to the `Drawing`;
- D: in some cases, a parent `Figure` can directly notify the `Drawing`.

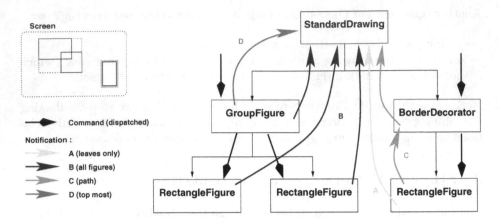

Fig. 2. Figures organized in a tree with COMPOSITE and DECORATOR patterns. In the upper left corner is a sample of figures display. The object diagram shows different strategies to deal with notification of invalidation (Sect. 3.1).

Solution B is very easy to implement, since all figures classes can inherit from an abstract class with the link to drawing. However, GroupFigure and BorderDecorator will trigger notifications every time: they can trigger false notifications since they do not know when their children really change. Notifications of children are redundant with those of GroupFigure and BorderDecorator yet it is impractical to inhibit them for temporary time.

Solution C is much more elegant with respect to false notification: GroupFigure and BorderDecorator will notify only if they receive notifications from children. This is the time for BorderDecorator to grow the clipping area. However, this has a cost in term of implementation: GroupFigure and BorderDecorator are subjects but also observers. This deeply changes the design as we now have many observers which are linked together in a chain, up to the drawing. In fact, the design for the invalidation concern is now that of a CHAIN OF RESPONSIBILITY pattern [1].

Solution D aims at reducing redundancy. A command such as "move figures" will automatically trigger changes in target figures. Then a GroupFigure can trigger the notification at the top level, computing the clipping area, and avoid notifications in levels underneath. The difficulty is to temporarily disable such notifications: however, the benefits seem too low for the cost of implementation in object-oriented languages.

The current JHotDraw framework chooses solution C. Figure 3 gives some details on the implementation of this solution. It allows to easily redefine for each Figure observer how it handles notifications (CompositeFigure, lines 17–18) and, in particular, if it changes them (BorderDecorator, lines 26–29). However, code complexity is increased. First, we notice that the change is only needed for the purpose of invalidation with BorderDecorator; but the change also affects the composite class, due to the chaining solution. Second, as said above, the

impact of the COMPOSITE and DECORATOR patterns is to transform the OB-
SERVER pattern into a CHAIN OF RESPONSIBILITY pattern, where each handler
can be seen as an observer of its children.

```
1   abstract class AbstractFigure implements Figure { // Subject role
        private FigureChangeListener observer;
3       (...)
        public void moveBy(int dx, int dy){ invalidate(); (...) }
5       public void invalidate(){
            Rectangle r = displayBox(); // clipping area
7           observer.figureInvalidated(new FigureChangeEvent(this, r));
        }
9       public abstract Rectangle displayBox();
    }
11  interface FigureChangeListener { // Observer role
        public void figureInvalidated(FigureChangeEvent e); }
13
    class CompositeFigure extends AbstractFigure // Composite role
15    implements FigureChangeListener {
        (...)
17      public void figureInvalidated(FigureChangeEvent e){
            observer.figureInvalidated(e);} // simple forward
19  }
    class GroupFigure extends CompositeFigure {...}// Composite extension
21
    class DecoratorFigure extends AbstractFigure // Decorator role
23    implements FigureChangeListener {...}
    class BorderDecorator extends DecoratorFigure {// Decorator extension
25      (...)
        public void figureInvalidated(FigureChangeEvent e){
27          Rectangle r = e.getInvalidatedRectangle();
            r.grow(factorx, factory); // grow by size of border
29          observer.figureInvalidated(new FigureChangeEvent(this, r));}
    }
```

Fig. 3. Implementation of the OBSERVER pattern impacted by COMPOSITE and
DECORATOR patterns in the current JHotDraw framework. `AbstractFigure` defines
main parts of the *Subject* role, including the reference (line 2) to the *Observer* role,
which is reified by the `FigureChangeListener` interface. `figureInvalidated` (line
12) is the notification method for the invalidation concern. Both `CompositeFigure`
and `DecoratorFigure` inherit from `AbstractFigure` to be subjects and implement `FigureChangeListener` to be observers. While the default behavior for
`figureInvalidated` is to forward the event (see `CompositeFigure`, lines 17–18),
`BorderDecorator` must redefine this method to take account of its specifity (lines
26–29).

3.2   Evolving to Multiple Drawing Views

The base JHotDraw framework allows to build single-window applications
(Fig. 6, left). There is only one drawing view, which can be managed by a
SINGLETON pattern. This considerably simplifies the implementation of the OB-
SERVER pattern between a drawing and its drawing view (Fig. 4).

```
   class StandardDrawing (...) implements Drawing {
2      (...)
       public void figureInvalidated(FigureChangeEvent e){
4          StandardDrawingView.instance().drawingInvalidated(
               new DrawingChangeEvent(this,
6                                      e.getInvalidatedRectangle()));}
   }
```

Fig. 4. Simple implementation of the *Subject* role for the `Drawing–DrawingView` OB-
SERVER pattern, with `DrawingView` as a SINGLETON pattern

An extension of JHotDraw allows to build MDI (Multiple Document Interface)
applications, allowing multiple drawing views on the same drawing (Fig. 6, right).
The implementation is primarily supported by Swing and internal frames. The
extension is almost modular since the base framework for single windows is
not modified – except for the OBSERVER pattern in Fig. 4 which does not allow
multiple observers per drawing. We need to change its implementation according
to Fig. 5. This new implementation works in both singleton and multiple cases,
but we have lost the simple choice of the single window framework.

```
1  class StandardDrawing (...) implements Drawing {
       (...)
3      private Vector<DrawingView> observers
           = new Vector<DrawingView>();
5      // when a view is linked to a drawing, it must call this method
       // to register itself as an observer
7      public void addObserver(DrawingView view) { ... }
       public void removeObserver(DrawingView view) { ... }
9      public void figureInvalidated(FigureChangeEvent e){
           for( DrawingView view: observers )
11             view.drawingInvalidated(
                   new DrawingChangeEvent(this,
13                                          e.getInvalidatedRectangle()));}
   }
```

Fig. 5. Implementation of the *Subject* role for the `Drawing–DrawingView` OBSERVER
pattern, modified to handle multiple `DrawingView`s. For brevity, the original code has
been rewritten using Java 5 generics and the new `for` loop.

3.3   Impact of Pattern Density

Pattern density is a sign that the program design becomes complex, but it does
not mean that patterns themselves are complex: the combination of the COM-
POSITE, DECORATOR and OBSERVER patterns which form a CHAIN OF RE-
SPONSIBILITY pattern is fairly easy to configure. The OBSERVER pattern is even
simpler with a SINGLETON pattern. However, our short study shows that such a
combination can have deep impact on implementation.

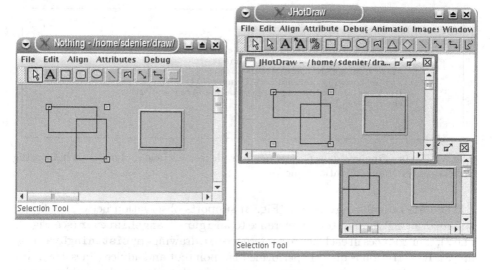

Fig. 6. Two JHotDraw applications: on the left, single view per drawing; on the right, multiple views on the same drawing

4   Pattern Density with Aspects

We now investigate the invalidation concern and the above additions with AspectJ. We want those additions to be both incremental and reversible. The process is three-fold and can be summed up as:

1. a "classic" aspectization of OBSERVER patterns for the invalidation concern;
2. configuration of OBSERVER pointcuts to deal with COMPOSITE and DECO-RATOR patterns;
3. use of modularity and pluggability of aspects to deal with the presence or absence of the SINGLETON pattern.

4.1   Aspectization of the Invalidation Concern

We extract the whole invalidation concern from the base classes (resp. inter-faces): `AbstractFigure` (resp. `Figure`), `StandardDrawing` (resp. `Drawing`), and `StandardDrawingView` (resp. `DrawingView`). This also includes many call points to the `invalidate` method (see `AbstractFigure.moveBy` in Fig. 3), scattered through the `Figure` hierarchy[2].

The `DrawingDamage` aspect (Fig. 7) structurally modifies `Drawing` classes to introduce a field called `damageArea` (line 2) and its control logic. The introduced `addDamage` method saves and merges clipping areas in this field (lines 3–5). The introduced `getAndResetDamage` method retrieves the clipping area of the drawing and resets it on purpose of the refresh process (lines 6–8).

---

[2] We count up to forty-one invalidating calls scattered across seventeen classes, with standard extension such as `GroupFigure` and `BorderDecorator` included.

```
  aspect DrawingDamage {
2      private Rectangle Drawing.damageArea;
       void Drawing.addDamage(Rectangle newDamage){
4          if (damageArea == null) damageArea = newDamage;
           else damageArea.add(newDamage); }
6      Rectangle Drawing.getAndResetDamage(){
           Rectangle r = damageArea; damageArea = null;
8          return r; }
  }
```

Fig. 7. The `DrawingDamage` aspect, which introduces new field and methods in `Drawing` subclasses for the invalidation concern

The `GetFigureDamage` aspect (Fig. 8) supports observation between a figure and its drawing. Similar to the reference to a `FigureChangeListener` (see Fig. 3, line 2), it introduces in each figure a reference to a drawing (`myListeningDrawing`, line 3). Registration is directly performed *via* pointcut and advice (lines 4–8). Notification pointcuts extract all previous method calls to `invalidate` which where scattered in `Figures` methods (lines 12–20). The description by pointcuts is not especially shorter but is localized in the aspect. Finally the invalidate action triggered by advice makes use of the damage interface introduced in `Drawing` by `DrawingDamage` (lines 24–27).

The `RepairSingleView` aspect (Fig. 9) supports the second observer and the refresh logic (refresh logic was not shown in Sect. 3.2 but follows the same principle). We consider the singleton case for the drawing view: there is no need for an observer reference. Pointcuts extract requests for screen update (usually after an user operation — line 3). The advice notifies the singleton observer (lines 8–10) which then performs the Swing request (lines 15–16).

The code above shows no more than common benefits we expect from aspects: scattered code for notifications, structure and methods relevant to the invalidation concern are localized in aspects. We should note that the invalidation concern and the OBSERVER pattern are typical examples of crosscutting concerns. We now examine issues from Sects. 3.1 & 3.2 with the help of AspectJ.

4.2   Revisiting Composite and Decorator Interactions

We consider the four strategies envisionned in Sect. 3.1 for invalidation of figures. Code from Fig. 8 implements **solution B** by default. Indeed `GroupFigure` and `BorderDecorator` are `Figure` *via* their respective superclass. The `GetFigure-Damage` aspect is oblivious to the dynamic type of `Figure` instances.

It follows that **solution A** requires more effort. We must explicitly exclude `CompositeFigure` and `DecoratorFigure` from invalidate pointcuts. For example the `changed` pointcut must be rewritten as:

```
pointcut changed(Figure f):
     this(f) && execution(void Figure+.setAttribute(..))
     && !this(CompositeFigure) && !this(DecoratorFigure);
```

```
 1   aspect GetFigureDamage {
         // Registration of drawing (observer) in figure
 3       private Drawing Figure.myListeningDrawing;
         pointcut registerFigure(Drawing d, Figure f):
 5           execution( Figure CompositeFigure.add(Figure) )
             && this(d) && args(f);
 7       after(Drawing d, Figure f): registerFigure(d, f) {
             f.myListeningDrawing = d; }
 9       (...)

11       // Notification of changes
         pointcut willChange(Figure f):
13           (execution(void Figure+.displayBox(Point, Point))
             || execution(void Figure+.moveBy(..))) && this(f);
15       before(Figure f): willChange(f){ invalidate(f); }
         after(Figure f):  willChange(f){ invalidate(f); }
17
         pointcut changed(Figure f):
19           this(f) && execution(void Figure+.setAttribute(..));
         after(Figure f):  changed(f){ invalidate(f); }
21       (...)

23       // Action on notification
         void invalidate(Figure f){
25           if( f.myListeningDrawing!=null ){
                 f.myListeningDrawing.addDamage( f.displayBox() );
27           } (...) }
     }
```

Fig. 8. Sample from `GetFigureDamage` aspect, which supports the observer relationship from figures to their drawing. Pointcuts and advice are used both for registration and notification of the observer. Pointcut `willChange` (lines 12–15) stands for actions which invalidate both the old bounding box (where the figure used to be) and the new bounding box: such actions (move, resize) are advised before and after their execution (lines 15–16). Pointcut `changed` (lines 18–19) is used solely for actions which modify the inner appearance of the figure but not its bounding box: then notification occurs only after action (line 20).

```
     aspect RepairSingleView {
 2       // Notifications (request for update)
         after(): execution(void StandardDrawingView.mousePressed(..)){
 4           repairDamage(StandardDrawingView.instance().drawing()); }
         (...)
 6
         // Action on notification
 8       private void repairDamage(Drawing d){
             Rectangle r = d.getAndResetDamage();
10           StandardDrawingView.instance().repairDamage(r); }
     }
12
     class StandardDrawingView extends JPanel implements DrawingView {
14       (...)
         public void repairDamage(Rectangle r) { // Swing request
16           if (r != null) { repaint(r.x, r.y, r.width, r.height); }}
     }
```

Fig. 9. Sample from `RepairSingleView` aspect with singleton view configuration

This strategy is initially not interesting and loses even more appeal following such constraints. The this(Type) predicate can be translated as a dynamic this instanceof Type test in some cases.

Solution C is interesting: we do not need to transform the OBSERVER pattern into the CHAIN OF RESPONSIBILITY pattern to get the same effect. The case involves solely BorderDecorator: we only target figures which have a Border-Decorator in the chain of parents. If there is to be a change down in the chain, necessarily the clipping area will be that of the top most decorator. The process of detecting the top most decorator and passing it down to the triggering figure can be managed by pointcuts:

```
pointcut targetaction():
    execution(void BorderDecorator.setAttribute(..));
pointcut topmostdecorator(BorderDecorator bd):
    this(bd) && targetaction()
    && !cflowbelow(targetaction());
pointcut changed(Figure f):
    execution(void Figure+.setAttribute(..))
    && cflowbelow(topmostdecorator(f));
after(Figure f): changed(f) { invalidate(f); }
```

The topmostdecorator pointcut captures any execution of method set-Attribute which are *not* in the control flow of another BorderDecorator: the decorator is then the top most. The changed pointcut will capture any execution of setAttribute which are under a BorderDecorator. But, instead of notifying invalidate with the current figure, it will use the parameter of topmostdecorator. The clipping area retrieved by invalidate (Fig. 8, line 26) will be that of the decorator.

The changed pointcut captures all executions below the top most decorator, including other decorators. This is not intended: only "leaves" (such as RectangleFigure) will trigger real modifications. Currently there is no mean in the AspectJ language to capture leaves in the control flow. An extension to the language is proposed in [8]. We could also use !this(DecoratorFigure) such as in solution A.

Solution D is more simple. We do not want all figures to trigger notifications, when we are sure that they will change. We simply trigger notifications for top most calls. For example move command can be notified at the top most level, by a figure, a composite or a decorator. The willChange pointcut can be rewritten:

```
pointcut action(): execution(void Figure+.moveBy(..));
pointcut willChange(Figure f):
    this(f) && action() && !cflowbelow( action() );
```

Preliminary conclusion shows that the AspectJ pointcut language is expressive enough to implement the four notification strategies. Contrary to the object solution, there is no need to change Figure subclasses, CompositeFigure and Decoratorfigure. However, there is the hidden cost of using AspectJ dynamic construct such as `cflow`. Currently we lack quantitative benchmarks on the performance of `cflow` with respect to the CHAIN OF RESPONSIBILITY solution, although this is not perceptible in the context of JHotDraw.

4.3 Pluggability of Aspects: Revisiting Multiple Views

Same as the observer in Fig. 4, `RepairSingleView` does not work with multiple views. Yet, we simply build a new `RepairMultipleViews` aspect (Fig. 10). Contrary to Fig. 5, `StandardDrawing` is not changed. The framework user can choose at weaving time which configuration (singleton or multiple views) he needs. A drawback is that there is no reuse between `RepairSingleView` and `RepairMultipleViews`, so that some change in base code could impact both aspects. However, it is possible to share some definitions (such as pointcuts for notification) using AspectJ abstract aspect and extension mechanism.

```
1   aspect RepairMultipleViews {
        // (De)registration of drawing views in drawing
3       private List<DrawingView> Drawing.listeningViews
            = new LinkedList<DrawingView>();
5       pointcut linkViewToDrawing(DrawingView view, Drawing drawing):
            execution(void DrawingView+.setDrawing(Drawing))
7           && this(view) && args(drawing);
        before(DrawingView v, Drawing d): linkViewToDrawing(v, d){
9           (...)
            v.drawing().listeningViews.remove(v);
11          d.listeningViews.add(v); }

13      // Notifications (request for update)
        after(DrawingView v): this(v)
15          && execution(void StandardDrawingView.mousePressed(..)){
            repairDamage(v.drawing()); }
17      (...)

19      // Action on notification
        private void repairDamage(Drawing d){
21          Rectangle r = d.getAndResetDamage();
            for (DrawingView view : d.listeningViews) {
23              view.repairDamage(r); }}
    }
```

Fig. 10. Sample from `RepairMultipleViews` aspect for multiple views (MDI) configuration. `Drawing` manages a list of drawing views which are its observers (lines 3–11). Since a view displays one drawing at a time, its registration on a new drawing involves its deregistration from the previous drawing (lines 10–11). Another change from Fig. 9 is the capture of the contextual view during notification (line 14).

5   Discussions

Before concluding, we present two subjects of discussion inspired by this work. They are complementary to this study but, to this day, rely much on subjective opinion.

5.1 Specificity of the AspectJ Solution

The specificity of the cflow-based AspectJ solution in Sect. 4.2 can be compared to a language where inspection of the execution stack is possible. Of course, a cflow construct can be easily emulated in such a language. However, the cflow construct combined with aspects allows to easily "compose" modules and patterns without modifying the base code. The fact that such a modification can be modularized simply with a stack inspector remains to be evaluated.

Intertype declaration (previously introduction) is another feature of AspectJ which is frequently used in pattern implementation (see Figs. 7, 8 or 10). This feature can partially emulate mixin or trait-like reuse [9].

5.2 Avoiding Implementation Overhead in a Field of Patterns

Without a reusable pattern library, programmers need to implement design patterns over and over: this leads to "implementation overhead" [10] when it comes to patterns with heavy, repetitive elements. When pattern density rises and the same pattern is being used over the same classes, there is a natural tendency in object-oriented languages to fuse concerns together in order to reuse pattern implementation and reduce the overhead. Thus reusability is enhanced at the depends of separation of concerns. We expose two such cases:

- the OBSERVER pattern in `Figure` is reused in a "figure connection" concern. Such connections are transversal to the invalidation concern. Typically observers in connection concern implement void methods for the invalidation notification and vice-versa;
- `StandardDrawing` implements the COMPOSITE pattern to manipulate `Figure`. In fact, it extends the `CompositeFigure` to reuse its structure and behavior, redefining some methods to accomodate for its nature of `Drawing`. This leads `Drawing` to copy the interface of `CompositeFigure` in a brittle relation. `StandardDrawing` also inherits from `Figure` a nonsensical subject role.

6   Related Work

The OBSERVER pattern serves as an exercise of choice for aspect languages features. The instantiation model of Caesar [11] follows more closely the object model of design patterns. Reflex [12] offers a metaphor of metaobjects as observers of hooksets. Many works, such as [13] and [14], deal with modularity and reusability of aspects in the context of design patterns: they contain valuable ideas on the way to configure generic aspects for use.

Few other patterns have been studied. One interesting case is the MEMENTO pattern, for which different attempts with AspectJ have been made [15]. To date the sole extensive study of single design patterns implementation with aspects is in [3]. It also contains some evaluation on "composition transparency" for those new implementations, that is the property to define multiple occurrences of the same pattern while keeping them separate. However, it does not explore the issues of density and composition with other patterns.

[16] revisits the case of pattern density in JUnit [2]. It follows a different guideline than ours by not aspectizing the pattern but the supported concern. It remains to be shown whether such solutions can be generalized as design patterns.

7 Conclusion

Summary of problems we review about pattern implementation includes cross-cutting of implementation, invasive modification of a pattern by application of another pattern, and tangling of concerns when reuse occurs to reduce overhead. One could argue that such problems are not specific to the implementation of design patterns. However, these are symptoms following the density of design patterns. These problems must be studied at the level of patterns and software design to promote their reusability. Software designers should be aware of such impacts:

 - composition of patterns mean you have to reconsider forces so that you select another pattern, with the same concern (see Sect. 3.1);
 - lack of reusable patterns itself could lead to tangling concerns in order to reduce implementation overhead.

Overall, there is a feeling that the difficulty in a dense field of patterns does not lie within pattern themselves (which remain what they are) but between them.

We notice AspectJ provides a sum of technologies, some of which (cflow, introduction) are not specific to aspects and exist in other languages. Nonetheless, this sum allows to cleanly modularize new concerns and compose them back and forth. It allows to avoid transformations of patterns described above, so that we were able to retain the basic JHotDraw framework and configure it by selecting aspects. We believe such an approach is valuable in software engineering to trace design choices during the development process.

The case of implementation overhead (Sect. 5.2) links to a reusable pattern library. We have implemented a composition of COMPOSITE, ITERATOR, and VISITOR patterns which remains to be evaluated in the context of JHotDraw (`StandardDrawing` and `CompositeFigure`). The approach is to build reusable compositions based on the reusable single patterns.

Aspectization of patterns opens a new perspective: traceability is enhanced and, in particular, we could benefit from interaction detection [17] and visualization tool[3]. Detection of interactions can lead to automation:

 - presence of the SINGLETON pattern links to a simple implementation of the OBSERVER pattern;
 - automatic configuration of pointcuts with cflow-like construct whenever COMPOSITE or DECORATOR patterns are detected;
 - automatic registration of the OBSERVER pattern based on registration in the COMPOSITE pattern.

---

[3] See AspectJ plugin for Eclipse – `http://www.eclipse.org/ajdt/`

Acknowledgements. We would like to thank the anonymous reviewers for their comments, which help to improve the quality of this article.

References

1. Gamma, E., Helm, R., Johnson, R., Vlissides, J.: Design Patterns: Elements of Reusable Object-Oriented Software. Addison Wesley, Massachusetts (1994)
2. Gamma, E., Beck, K.: JUnit: A Cook's Tour (2002) http://junit.sourceforge.net/doc/cookstour/cookstour.htm.
3. Hannemann, J., Kiczales, G.: Design pattern implementation in Java and AspectJ. In: Proc. of OOPSLA 2002, ACM Press (2002) 161–173
4. Soukup, J.: Implementing patterns. In: Pattern languages of program design. ACM Press/Addison-Wesley Publishing Co., USA (1995) 395–412
5. Zimmer, W.: Relationships between design patterns. In Coplien, J.O., Shmidt, D.C., eds.: Pattern Languages of Program Design. Addison-Wesley (1994)
6. Kiczales, G., Hilsdale, E., Hugunin, J., Kersten, M., Palm, J., Griswold, W.G.: An overview of AspectJ. In Knudsen, J.L., ed.: Proc. of ECOOP 2001, LNCS 2072, Springer-Verlag (2001) 327–353
7. Colyer, A., Clement, A., Harley, G., Webster, M.: eclipse AspectJ. the eclipse series. Addison-Wesley (2005)
8. Douence, R., Teboul, L.: A crosscut language for control-flow. In: Proc. of GPCE 2004, LNCS, Springer-Verlag (2004)
9. Denier, S.: Traits programming with AspectJ. RSTI - L'objet **11**(3) (2005) 69–86
10. Bosch, J.: Design patterns as language constructs. Journal of Object-Oriented Programming **11**(2) (1998) 18–32
11. Ostermann, K., Mezini, M.: Conquering aspects with Caesar. In Akşit, M., ed.: Proc. of AOSD 2003, ACM Press (2003) 90–99
12. Tanter, É., Noyé, J., Caromel, D., Cointe, P.: Partial behavioral reflection: Spatial and temporal selection of reification. In Crocker, R., Steele, Jr., G.L., eds.: Proc. of OOPSLA 2003, ACM Press (2003) 27–46
13. Clarke, S., Walker, R.J.: Composition patterns: An approach to designing reusable aspects. In: Proc. of ICSE 2001. IEEE Computer Society (2001) 5–14
14. Lieberherr, K., Lorenz, D.H., Ovlinger, J.: Aspectual collaborations: Combining modules and aspects. Computer Journal of the British Computer Society **46**(5) (2003) 542–565
15. Marin, M.: Refactoring JHotDraw's undo concern to AspectJ. In: Proceedings of the 1st Workshop on Aspect Reverse Engineering (WARE 2004). (2004)
16. Isberg, W.: Aop pointcut patterns in the JUnit Cook's Tour (2005) http://junit.sourceforge.net/doc/cookstour/cookstour.htm.
17. Douence, R., Fradet, P., Südholt, M.: A framework for the detection and resolution of aspect interactions. In Batory, D., Consel, C., Taha, W., eds.: Proc. of GPCE 2002. LNCS 2487, Springer-Verlag (2002) 173–188

A Model for Developing Component-Based and Aspect-Oriented Systems

Nicolas Pessemier[1], Lionel Seinturier[1],
Thierry Coupaye[2], and Laurence Duchien[1]

[1] INRIA Futurs, LIFL, Jacquard project/GOAL,
Bâtiment M3, 59655 Villeneuve dAscq, France
{pessemie, seinturi, duchien}@lifl.fr
[2] France Telecom R&D,
28 chemin du Vieux Chêne, BP98
38243 Meylan, France
thierry.coupaye@rd.francetelecom.com

Abstract. Aspect-Oriented Programming (AOP) and Component-Based Software Engineering (CBSE) offer solutions to improve the separation of concerns and to enhance a program structure. If the integration of AOP into CBSE has already been proposed, none of these solutions focus on the application of CBSE principles to AOP. In this paper we propose a twofold integration of AOP and CBSE. We introduce a general model for components and aspects, named Fractal Aspect Component (FAC). FAC decomposes a software system into regular components and aspect components (ACs), where an AC is a regular component that embodies a crosscutting concern. We reify the aspect domain of an AC and the relationship between an AC and a component, called an aspect binding, as first-class runtime entities. This clarifies the architecture of a system where components and aspects coexist. The system can evolve from the design to the execution by adding or removing components, aspects or bindings.

1 Introduction

Component-Based Software Engineering (CBSE) proposes to structure a program by separating concerns into clearly defined entities, called components. Reusable components with contractually specified interfaces are defined and composed together [20]. Subsequently, Architecture Description Languages [12] can be used to specify the component compositions and interactions.

Aspect-Oriented Programming (AOP) [9] identifies the code tangling and the code scattering which arise in applications. Some concerns mixed within an entity (code tangling), and some concerns scattered across several entities, are said to be crosscutting. These concerns hinders the reusability, the maintainability, and the evolvability of applications. AOP proposes artifacts (aspect, pointcut, advice) to modularize crosscutting concerns.

It has been shown that the issues of code tangling and scattering arise at the level of CBSE as well [8,11]. This is why merging AOP and CBSE makes sense.

W. Löwe and M. Südholt (Eds.): SC 2006, LNCS 4089, pp. 259–274, 2006.
© Springer-Verlag Berlin Heidelberg 2006

The integration of AOP into CBSE has already been proposed in [10,13,19], by providing a support for AOP in a component-based system. However, the application of CBSE principles to AOP is rarely proposed. In particular the implicit link between advice code and the base program where the advice applies is frequently hidden behind pointcut declarations (PcDs). Generally defined with a pattern language, PcDs select a set of joinpoints among those offered by the system. Unfortunately, once woven to the system, the implicit relationships created between a piece of advice code and the advised entities are never explicitly discernible and can surely not be individually manipulated at runtime.

In this paper, we propose a general and symmetrical model for mixing components and aspects. The approach is symmetric by considering aspects as plain components. The approach improves the component approach by giving a support for AOP, and improves the aspect approach by applying CBSE concepts to AOP. Our proposal relies on three main notions: aspect component, aspect domain, aspect binding. Aspects are contractually specified components called **aspect components** (ACs), and the relationships between ACs and regular components are reified with **aspect domains**, and **aspect bindings**. An AC embodies a crosscutting concern and can be reused in different contexts. An aspect domain is the reification of the components picked out by an AC. An aspect binding is a binding between a regular component and an AC. Thus, the model supports two levels of composition: regular components are composed together using regular bindings, and an AC is composed with regular components using aspect bindings.

We experiment this model by extending a reflective and general component model, named Fractal [4] and its ADL. In our extension, called Fractal Aspect Component (FAC for short), we introduce the notions of aspect component, aspect binding and aspect domain to the component model itself and to the Fractal ADL.

The rest of this paper is organized as follows. Section 2 introduces our general model for component and aspect. Section 3 presents the mapping of our model to the Fractal component model. Section 4 presents related work around the merging of components and aspects and some reference component models. Section 5 concludes and gives some open issues.

2   A General Model for Components and Aspects

This section describes the three main concepts we introduce to support AOP in a component model: *aspect component*, *aspect binding*, and *aspect domain*. Section 2.1 gives the motivations of our approach. The concepts are presented in the remaining three sections.

2.1   Motivations

When merging Aspect-Oriented Programming (AOP) and Component-Based Software Engineering (CBSE) two dimensions have to be considered: the integration of aspect-oriented principles into component-based systems, and the application of component-based principles to Aspect-Oriented Programming. The integration of AOP into CBSE is motivated by the code tangling issue inherent in CBSE [8,11]. On the other hand the application of CBSE concepts to AOP is less investigated. Some approaches focus on the representation of an aspect as a component to contractually specify aspects and to increase their reusability [10,18].

In our proposal we realize a twofold integration of CBSE and AOP. We introduce three main concepts: aspect component, aspect domain, and aspect binding. These three notions are closely related to the three main concepts of the component approach: component, composite, and binding.

2.2 Aspect Component

An aspect component (AC for short) embodies a crosscutting concern. It is a regular component providing as a service a piece of around advice code. This service represents the behavior which will be woven around a set of regular components. This notion is similar to the notion of Aspectual Component proposed in 1999 by Karl Lieberherr et al [11] to express each aspect separately in a modular structure.

Our approach is symmetric by making no differences between an aspect and a component. Thus, an aspect which is represented as a component, becomes a reusable contractually specified entity. Another consequence of the symmetric approach is that regular and aspect components are composed the same way using the same rules. This facilitates the adaptation to new requirements when the system evolves.

2.3 Aspect Binding

Two kinds of binding exist within our model: regular and aspect binding. A regular binding expresses that a component is using a service provided by an other component. An aspect binding expresses that a component is aspectized by an aspect component. It is the reification of the individual relationship between an aspect component (AC) and a regular component where the AC applies.

In most existing AOP languages, the relationship between an aspect and the objects containing joinpoints picked out by the aspects is explicit in the source code but is implicit at runtime. Indeed, this relationship is structurally defined by a pointcut in the source code, but is lost when the woven code is executed. By introducing the notion of an aspect binding, we reify at runtime this relationship.

Because our approach is symmetric, all possible interactions between regular components and aspect components require full consideration. In a system using components and aspects, the possible interactions are described below.

- The *component to component* interaction is the classical *client-server* interaction. The client component uses a service provided by a server component

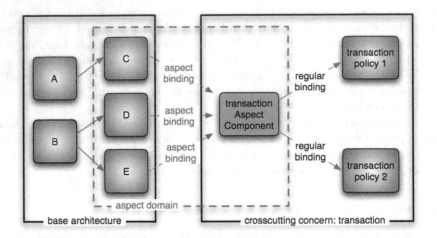

Fig. 1. Aspect binding best practice

interface. This kind of interaction exists in every component model using the notion of binding.

– The *component to AC* interaction is our notion of an aspect binding. It expresses the fact that an aspect component is woven on a component. In Figure 1 we can see this type of interaction between C, D, E and the transaction aspect component.

– The *AC to component* interaction, using a regular binding, is used as an AOP best practice. In Figure 1 we can see this kind of interaction between the transaction aspect component and various transaction policy components. In this example, changing a transaction policy is performed through a reconfiguration between the transaction AC and the components providing transaction policies.

– The *AC to AC* interaction can express a collaboration between two aspects using regular bindings, or the fact that the second aspect is woven on the first one. In asymmetric approaches this type of relationship is frequently unconsidered. Few techniques are given to make two aspects collaborate such as the use of context passing. The possibility of weaving aspects on other aspects is also uncommon.

2.4   Aspect Domain

An aspect domain is the reification of the components picked out by an AC. The goal of an aspect domain is to keep an overview on all the components affected by an aspect. It offers an abstraction on each AC woven on a set of components. A benefit that can be derived from the aspect domain notion is that the crosscutting interactions of a component-based system are clearly specified and are easily manipulable as regular interactions.

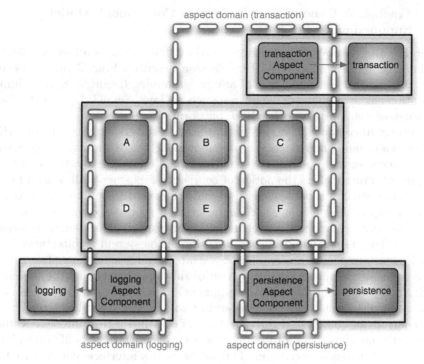

Fig. 2. FAC overview: weaving of three crosscutting concerns

Figure 2 illustrates the notion of aspect domain on a generic component-based application (components A to F). The aspect domains are represented as dotted rectangles, aspect bindings have been omitted for clarity sake. This application contains several crosscutting concerns: a logging, a persistence, and a transaction concern. These concerns are well known to be scattered and not cleanly modularized into one specific module. Their integration into an application is a hard task. In a full-fledged component, obtaining the same result requires numerous and tricky modifications. Moreover, once integrated to a system, it is difficult to remove one of these concerns in an easy and proper way. Once woven to a set of components the aspect domains of the ACs appear, offering reification on crosscutting relationships over the system.

3   Mapping onto the Fractal Component Model

This section presents the mapping of the main notions presented in the previous section onto the Fractal component model, which is a general and extensible component model supporting dynamic (regular) bindings. Our extension of Fractal is called FAC for Fractal Aspect Component. Section 3.1 presents the Fractal component model, and Section 3.2 proposes our extension FAC.

3.1   Fractal: A General and Reflective Component Model Supporting Dynamic Bindings

Fractal is an ObjectWeb consortium[1] project that proposes an extensible and modular component model [4]. This Section describes Fractal main features. Note that Fractal is independent of any programming language. Several implementations exist in different languages such as Java, SmallTalk, C, C++, and the languages supported by the .NET platform.

Contrary to component models for application servers such as EJB or .NET, Fractal is a general and reflective component model for developing complex software systems, such as operating systems and middleware. Besides the notion of a component, Fractal offers the notion of *composite-component* (allowing different views and abstractions on a system), *shared component* (a component nested by several composite components), *dynamic binding* (between components). Fractal is a reflective component model and offers introspection (system monitoring), and reconfiguration capabilities (modification of the system architecture).

A Fractal component has two parts: a *content* and a *membrane*. The *content* of a composite component is built as a set of sub-components, and the *content* of a primitive component (black box component) implements its provided services.

A component *membrane* offers a level of control and a level of interception. The control can be accessed through a set of so-called control interfaces which manage the non-functional properties of a component such as its life cycle, bindings, content, name, or attributes. This set of control interfaces can be extended with new control interfaces that can be added to a component membrane. The interception mechanism reifies messages sent by and received on component interfaces. These messages can be modified, discarded or delivered to the component.

An interface is an access point to a component comparable to the notion of a *port* in several component models such as ArchJava [2] or CCM [14]. A Fractal component offers external and internal interfaces. External interfaces are accessed from the outside of the component, while internal interfaces are only accessible from the composite's sub-components.

A binding is a communication channel between a client interface and a server interface. A client interface uses operations provided by a server interface. Fractal architectures can be described with Fractal ADL, which is an XML language to describe and to instantiate a Fractal component assembly.

Figure 4 presents the Fractal ADL syntax defining the architecture of Figure 3. Lines 2–3, 4, and 9 show the definition of server interfaces (role="server"). Lines 3–7 define the component A and Lines 8–11 the component B. Lines 12–13 are binding declarations of the binding between the server interface r of the composite and the server interface r of component A, and the binding between the client interface s of the component A and the server interface s of the component B.

Although component approaches such as Fractal offer several artifacts for the strong encapsulation of entities, the reification of dependencies, and the building of architecture from high level point of view, these approaches suffer from code

---

[1] http://objectweb.org

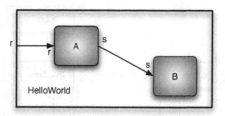

Fig. 3. Fractal-ADL: helloworld application

```
01 <definition name="HelloWorld">
02   <interface name="r" role="server" signature="java.lang.Runnable"/>
03   <component name="A">
04     <interface name="r" role="server" signature="java.lang.Runnable"/>
05     <interface name="s" role="client" signature="Service"/>
06     <content class="AImpl"/>
07   </component>
08   <component name="B">
09     <interface name="s" role="server" signature="Service"/>
10     <content class="BImpl"/>
11   </component>
12   <binding client="this.r" server="A.r"/>
13   <binding client="A.s" server="B.s"/>
14 </definition>
```

Fig. 4. Fractal-ADL: XML description of the helloworld application

tangling and code scattering. These two issues seriously limit the evolution of a system. Thus, when a crosscutting concern has to be plugged to a Fractal component assembly, the amount of reconfigurations that must be performed may become quite heavy. The next section details the mapping of our concepts of *aspect component, binding*, and *domain* onto the Fractal component model.

3.2 Fractal Aspect Component (FAC)

FAC is our mapping of the general model exposed in Section 2 onto the Fractal component model. It uses existing notions of the Fractal model and introduces new ones.

Figure 5 presents the FAC metamodel. It is based on the Fractal metamodel. The mapping of the three main notions (*aspect component, aspect domain*, and *aspect binding*) is straightforward. An aspect component is defined as a regular component; it provides as a service a piece of advice code (see the AspectComponent Interface). An aspect domain is a composite component that contains a set of ACs representing a crosscutting concern, and the components impacted by the ACs. Within the context of an aspect domain, aspect bindings can be

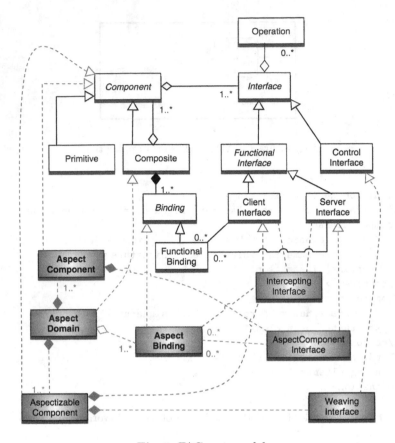

Fig. 5. FAC metamodel

defined between components and the AC. The following sub-sections describe the concepts of *aspect component interface*, and *weaving interface*. We then detail the FAC pointcut language. Finally, we discuss the two implementations of FAC.

3.3   FAC Join Point Model

Two different types of join points are supported by FAC: incoming calls on server interface operations, and outgoing calls on client interface operations. This choice is motivated by the fact that we consider AOSD in a component world.

As components are black boxes, it is rather natural to consider only join points on externally visible elements, i.e., exported and imported interfaces. Taking into account other kinds of join points, such as the ones on implementations, would break component encapsulation. Yet, for cases where this would be necessary, we believe that a best practice is to use a combination of component-based and implementation (e.g. object) based aspect-oriented tools.

The level of interception defined by FAC is very similar, at the component level, to the composition filters approach ([1]), which defines IN and OUT filters on objects to intercept messages.

3.4   FAC Pointcut Language

The FAC pointcut language is used to select join points. A pointcut expression is divided in two parts:

- A keyword that specifies if the incoming calls (keyword SERVER) or outgoing calls (keyword CLIENT) or both of them (no keyword) must be selected,
- Three regular expressions separated by semicolons that specify which components, interfaces, and operations must be selected.

Figure 6 gives some examples of PcDs. The regular expressions relies on the *java.util.regexp* package.

Pointcut Expressions	Captured Elements
;;deposit*:void	Every incoming and outgoing method returning void that start with deposit in any component and interface
CLIENT B;*;deposit*	Every outgoing method named deposit in any interface of a component named B
SERVER B;ITransfert;*	Every incoming method in ITransfert interface of a component B

Fig. 6. FAC pointcut language: Examples

3.5   The Aspect Component Interface (ACI)

The Aspect Component Interface (ACI) follows the AOP Alliance API[2], which is an open source initiative to define a common API for AOP frameworks. Figure 7 presents the *AspectComponent* Java interface and an example of an *AC*.

ACs apply on component methods exposed by client and server interfaces. The parameter of the *invoke* method is a reification of a Fractal interface invocation. It provides a set of methods to introspect a join point. The argument of the invocation can be modified, the intercepted method can be called (*proceed*), and the reference of the intercepted component can be retrieved.

Writing an *AC* requires implementing the *AspectComponent* interface. The *invoke* method describes the behaviour of the aspect. The code written in this method will be executed around the join point, i.e., a method call or execution on a component interface.

---

[2] http://aopalliance.sourceforge.net/

```
/**
 * Interface provided by an Aspect Component
 * to define an advice.
 */
public interface AspectComponent extends
              org.aopalliance.intercept.Interceptor {
  /**
   * Define an advice executed around incoming
   * and/or outgoing method invocations reified by m
   * @param m the reification of the method invocation
   * @return the result of the advice
   */
  Object invoke(FcMethodInvocation m) throws Throwable;
}


/**
 * An example of an AC with before and after code.
 */
public class GenericAC implements AspectComponent {
    Object invoke(FcMethodInvocation m) throws Throwable {
       System.out.println("before "+m.getMethod());
       Object ret = m.proceed();
       System.out.println("after "+m.getMethod()+" invoked");
       return ret;
    }
}
```

Fig. 7. The *AspectComponent interface*

The *proceed* call denotes the original method call. The code written before and after *proceed()* represents the before and after advices of AOSD. If more than one aspect applies on a given join point, the *proceed* call will trigger the next aspect, till the original method code is reached. If *proceed* is omitted the original method call will not apply. This can be useful to prevent, for example, the execution of the intercepted method.

3.6   Weaving Interfaces

The *Weaving Interface (WI)* of a component plays a key role in FAC. It manages the weaving of ACs around the interfaces of the component it controls. In the context of Fractal, we chose to represent the *WI* as a Fractal control interface in the component membrane. The *WI* uses the interception mechanism, which is provided by the membrane of components to intercept incoming and outgoing calls on its functional interfaces, and then, delegates the calls to the aspect components bound to (with an aspect binding) these operations. The *weaving interface* in FAC has three main objectives:

– Set/unset *aspect bindings* to *aspect components*,

```
void setAspectBinding(Component comp, ItfPointcutExp regExp,
                                      AspectComponent ac);
void unsetAspectBinding(AspectComponent ac);
```

– Automatically weave an *AC* around a set of components following a pointcut declaration (this weaving task will automatically create an *aspect domain*, add the components which match the pointcut declaration into this *aspect domain*, and bind with aspect bindings the *AC* and the impacted components),

```
void weave(Component rootComp, AspectComponent ac,
                              ItfPointcutExp pExp,
                              String aspectDomain);
void unweave(Component rootComp, Component ac);
```

– Provide a set of operations to order/re-order *ACs* which apply on an interface operation.

```
String[] changeACorder(String acName, int newPosition);
```

In FAC, a component supporting the *weaving interface* is called an aspectizable component. Otherwise, no aspects can be woven to this component. Since the weaving of an *AC* using the *weaving interface* is recursive and traverse the component hierarchy, if the component controlled by the *WI* is a composite component the weaving is also performed by its sub-components. A weaving operation can be initiated on the system as a whole (top-level composite) or on any sub system (intermediate composite).

All the operations provided by the interface can be invoked either with the Fractal ADL (extended with FAC notions) or directly at runtime.

The following piece of XML code presents the architecture of a Fractal assembly where a directive (tag <weave>) weaves a *traceAC* component (defined lines 2–4) to each component of the composite C (rootComp="this" line 12), which has an interface operation starting with "s" and returning "void". The aspect domain of this weaving will be automatically created and the composite representing this domain will be named "D" (adomain="D" line 12).

```
01 <definition name="C">
02 <component name="traceAC"/>
03    <interface name="ACI" role="server"  signature="AspectComponent"/>
04 </component>
05 <component name="A"/>
06    <interface name="itf1" role="client"  signature="Itf1"/>
07 </component>
08 <component name="B"/>
09    <interface name="itf1" role="server"  signature="Itf1"/>
10 </component>
11 <binding client="A.itf1" server="B.itf1"/>
12 <weaving ac="traceAC" pcd="*;*;s*:void"  rootComp="this" adomain="D"/>
13 </definition>
```

Every reconfiguration operation including the ones of our extension (setting/unsetting of aspect binding, weaving of an AC are dynamic operations).

3.7 Implementation Issues

The mapping of our general model for component and aspect on the Fractal component model has been validated with two different implementations in Java. Our first implementation extends the reference implementation of the Fractal component model in Java called Julia [4]. Julia uses a mixin [3] mechanism to program the level of control of components. The second implementation extends another implementation of the Fractal component model in Java, called AOKell [17], which uses AspectJ [9] aspects to implement control membranes.

4   Related Work

In this section, we compare FAC with different kinds of approaches. Firstly, we focus on approaches using the notions of component and aspect at a programming language level. Secondly, we investigate approaches using a symmetric representation of components and aspects. Thirdly, we study others component models.

4.1   Component and Aspect at the Programming Language Level

CaesarJ [13] is a Java based programming language, defined as an extension of the AspectJ language. The components are implemented as collaborations of classes. A collaboration defines a provided part and an expected part. The provided part is implemented with reusable CaesarJ components that are a set of virtual classes. A virtual class in CaesarJ is a kind of inner class, which can be overridden in the subclasses of the enclosing class. When overriding an inner class the new functionalities are directly usable by the parent class. With this mechanism the provided operation of a collaboration interface can be delayed to virtual sub-classes. On the other hand, the expected part is achieved by CaesarJ bindings, which are aspects woven afterward during a deployment phase. The main advantage of CaesarJ is its ability to stay close to the programming language and to be a superset of the AspectJ language.

JAsCo [19] is an AOP language originally designed for component-based systems. It introduces two main notions: aspect bean and connector. Aspect beans are reusable Java beans describing the extra behavior to apply to components. Aspect beans uses hooks that are similar to inner classes describing the advice code and the pointcut declaration. Connectors are used to deploy hooks (some kind of access points to join points) within a specific context.

Contrary to FAC, CaesarJ and JAsCo are programmatic approaches. In the case of CaesarJ, aspects are dedicated to the expression of the relationships between components. The problem is that these aspects manage the bindings of all the components of the system. In the case of JAsCo, only crosscutting relationships are expressed thanks to connectors, and the management of dependencies between base entities is missing.

4.2 Symmetric and Unified Approaches: Aspects Conceived as Components

FuseJ [18], which is the follow-up project by the JAsCo team, mainly focuses on the nature of an aspect that is represented as a regular bean. The approach is symmetric: all the concerns are implemented as plain components. Components in FuseJ are equiped with gates. A gate is a kind of interface to specify component services: aspect-oriented and regular. The connectors (extension of JAsCo connectors) specify the types of interaction between gates. FuseJ defines regular and aspect-oriented connectors. Regular connectors are in charge of functional connections between gates, and aspect-oriented connectors are in charge of weaving a component behavior to another component. All the connections defined by a component can be locally consulted. FuseJ does not yet propose a global description of a component architecture with its connections. The model does not support the managing of aspect domain and aspect binding as FAC does.

DyMAC [10] is a component and aspect-based middleware framework. It uses aspect-oriented composition to connect the application logic to the middleware services. Similarly to FAC, an aspect component in DyMAC encapsulates an advice. However around advices are not supported. Special kinds of connectors are statically described in XML files to write technical services of the middleware layer. Connectors in DyMAC looks like aspect bindings in our approach. Nevertheless, aspect ordering is static in DyMAC whereas FAC provides an API for aspect component ordering.

4.3 Other Component Models

OpenCOM [6] is a lightweight reflective component model and as such close to the Fractal component model. The key concepts of the model are interfaces, receptacles and connections. A component has a set of receptacles and interfaces. Interfaces are used to express provided services and receptacles to express required services (comparable to Fractal client and server interfaces). Unlike Fractal, OpenCOM defines a fixed meta-object protocol for components. The meta objects in OpenCOM can be compared to aspect components (ACs) in FAC. However, this meta level is fixed and thus does not support the dynamic adding and removing of meta objects.

K-Component [7] is a component model for building context-adaptive applications. Instead of using an Architecture Description Language to statically describe a component architecture, the model reifies the structure of the application and describes adaptation contracts written with an Adaptation Contract Description Language (ACDL) to dynamically reconfigure the application. The representation of the architecture is defined with a typed graph. Thus, the reconfiguration of the architecture is performed through a graph transformation. The K-Components are defined using the OMG-IDL3 language and C++ idioms. The main drawback of this approach is that adaptation is always realized through reconfiguration of the component architecture. An interception mechanism is missing to add an AOP support to the approach.

JBoss AOP [5] is a Java framework for AOP. It can be used in the context of the JBoss application server or standalone. As JAC [15], JBoss-AOP offers a set of pre-programmed aspects that can be used directly. JBoss AOP aspects can be woven with annotations, classic pointcut declarations or in a dynamic way at system runtime. When applied to the JBoss application server, aspects are woven to components. Similarly to FAC, dedicated XML fragments are used to deploy aspects. However, in FAC, XML files are used to describe a component assembly, with bindings. The notion of binding in EJB component model is missing. Components are coarse-grained components, encapsulated by containers, which do not express relationships between each other.

5   Conclusion

In this paper we have presented a general model for components and aspects called FAC and its mapping onto the Fractal component model. This model introduces three main notions: aspect component, aspect domain, and aspect binding. A crosscutting concern is embodied by a regular Fractal component called an aspect component. We have shown that an aspect component is an encapsulation of advice code. An aspect domain is the reification of the notion of a pointcut: the components picked out by an aspect component. The implicit relationship between a woven aspect component and the component in which the aspect component applies is a first-class entity called an aspect binding.

The main contribution of our approach is to bring aspect-oriented concepts to the component world, and conversely, to improve aspect-oriented approach with component notions. Thus, our three main notions (aspect component, aspect binding, aspect domain) are mapped onto the Fractal component model using existing notions of component, binding, and composite component.

We also provide a runtime support for crosscutting relationship reflection, which is an open issue in the aspect-oriented community. Moreover, we offer various abstraction views on aspect components woven on components in order to help the evolution of the modular and crosscutting concerns of a component and aspect system.

The long term objective of FAC is to work with aspects at three different levels [16]. The first level is the use of AOP at the program level, namely the level of objects that are encapsulated by components. Current AOP approaches fulfill this need. The second level is FAC itself with the notions of aspect component, aspect binding, and aspect domain. Joinpoints at this level are invocations on component interfaces. And finally, we plan to consider a third level, an architectural level, where joinpoints are architectural operations and transformations.

Acknowledgments

This work was partially funded by France Telecom under the external research contract number 46 131 097.

References

1. M. Aksit, L. Bergmans, and S. Vural. An object-oriented language-database inte-gration model: The composition-filters approach. In O. Lehrmann Madsen, editor, *ECOOP'92: Proc. of the European Conference on Object-Oriented Programming*, pages 372–395. Springer, Berlin, Heidelberg, 1992.
2. J. Aldrich, C. Chambers, and D. Notkin. ArchJava: Connecting software archi-tecture to implementation. In *ICSE'02: Proc. of the International Conference on Software Engineering*, Orlando, FL, USA, May 2002.
3. G. Bracha and W. Cook. Mixin-based inheritance. In N. Meyrowitz, editor, *Pro-ceedings of the Conference on Object-Oriented Programming: Systems, Languages, and Applications / Proceedings of the European Conference on Object-Oriented Programming*, pages 303–311, Ottawa, Canada, 1990. ACM Press.
4. E. Bruneton, T. Coupaye, M. Leclercq, V. Quema, and J.-B. Stefani. An open component model and its support in Java. In *Proceedings of the International Symposium on Component-based Software Engineering*, Edinburgh, Scotland, May 2004.
5. B. Burke and al. JBoss-AOP. *www.jboss.org/developers/projects/jboss/aop*.
6. M. Clarke, G. Blair, G. Coulson, and N. Parlavantzas. An efficient component model for the construction of adaptive middleware. In *Proceedings of Middle-ware'01*, 2001.
7. J. Dowling and V. Cahill. The k-component architecture meta-model for self-adaptive software. In A. Yonezawa and S. Matsuoka, editors, *Metalevel Architec-tures and Separation of Crosscutting Concerns 3rd Int'l Conf. , LNCS 2192*, pages 81–88. Springer-Verlag, Sept. 2001.
8. F. Duclos, J. Estublier, and P. Morat. Describing and using non functional aspects in component based applications. In *AOSD '02: Proceedings of the 1st international conference on Aspect-oriented software development*, pages 65–75, New York, NY, USA, 2002. ACM Press.
9. G. Kiczales, E. Hilsdale, J. Hugunin, M. Kersten, J. Palm, and W. Griswold. Get-ting started with AspectJ. *Communications of the ACM*, 44(10):59–65, 2001.
10. B. Lagaisse and W. Joosen. Component-based open middleware supporting aspect-oriented software composition. In *CBSE*, pages 139–154, 2005.
11. K. Lieberherr, D. Lorenz, and M. Mezini. Programming with Aspectual Compo-nents. Technical Report NU-CCS-99-01, College of Computer Science, Northeast-ern University, Boston, MA, March 1999.
12. N. Medvidovic and R. N. Taylor. A classification and comparison framework for software architecture description languages. *IEEE Transaction on Software Engi-neering*, 26(1):70–93, January 2000.
13. M. Mezini and K.Ostermann. Conquering Aspects with Caesar. In *Proceedings of the 2nd International Conference on Aspect-Oriented Software Development (AOSD'03)*, pages 90–100. ACM Press, March 2003.
14. OMG. CORBA Components, v3.0 (full specification), Document formal/02-06-65, june 2002.
15. R. Pawlak, L. Seinturier, L. Duchien, G. Florin, F. Legond-Aubry, and L. Martelli. JAC : An aspect-based distributed dynamic framework. *Software Practise and Experience (SPE)*, 34(12):1119–1148, Oct. 2004.
16. N. Pessemier, O. Barais, L. Seinturier, T. Coupaye, and L. Duchien. A three level framework for adapting component-based systems. In *Second International Work-shop on Coordination and Adaptation Techniques for Software Entities (WCAT05)*, Glasgow, Scotland, July 2005.

17. L. Seinturier, N. Pessemier, L. Duchien, and T. Coupaye. A component model engineered with components and aspects. In *Proceedings of the 9th International SIGSOFT Symposium on Component-Based Software Engineering (CBSE06)*, Lecture Notes in Computer Science, Stockholm, Sweden, jun 2006. Springer. To appear.
18. D. Suve. FuseJ web site. `http://ssel.vub.ac.be/fusej/`.
19. D. Suve, W. Vanderperren, and V. Jonckers. JAsCo: an aspect-oriented approach tailored for component based software development. In *Proceedings of the 2nd International Conference on Aspect-Oriented Software Development (AOSD'03)*, pages 21–29. ACM Press, 2003.
20. C. Szyperski.   *Component Software: Beyond Object-Oriented Programming.* Addison-Wesley Longman Publishing Co., Inc., 2002.

FROGi: Fractal Components Deployment over OSGi

Mikael Desertot[1,3], Humberto Cervantes[2], and Didier Donsez[1]

[1] Laboratoire LSR-IMAG, 220 rue de la Chimie,
Domaine Universitaire, BP 53, 38041, Grenoble, Cedex 9, France
{mikael.desertot, didier.donsez}@imag.fr
[2] Universidad Autonoma Metropolitana-Iztapalapa (UAM-I),
San Rafael Atlixco N 186, Col. Vicentina, C.P. 09340, Iztapalapa. D.F., Mexico
hcm@xanum.uam.mx
[3] Bull SAS,
1 Rue de Provence, 38130, Echirolles, France

Abstract. This paper presents FROGi, a proposal to support continuous deployment activities inside Fractal, a hierarchical component model. FROGi is implemented on top of the OSGi platform. Motivation for this work is twofold. On one hand FROGi provides an extensible component model to OSGi developers and eases bundle providing. FROGi-based bundles are still compatible with legacy OSGi bundles that offer third party services. On the other hand, FROGi benefits from the deployment infrastructure provided by OSGi which simplifies conditioning and packaging of Fractal components. With FROGi, it is possible to automate the assembly of a Fractal component application. Partial or complete deployment is also supported as well as performing continuous deployment and update activities.

1 Introduction

Component-based software engineering (CBSE) is a development methodology that promotes the idea that software can be built through the assembly of reusable software units called components [14]. Components are characterized by the fact that they explicitly define a set of provided functionalities along with dependencies that allow the components to be assembled (i.e. composed). CBSE assumes that component development and component assembly are clearly differentiated activities. Moreover these activities can be performed by different actors. This differentiation implies that delivery and deployment aspects must be taken into account early in the development life-cycle. To support these activities, components are typically packaged in a unit which includes everything that is needed by the component to function, except whatever the component declares as an explicit dependency. Dependencies can be fulfilled either through composition or at deployment time. A component model is also associated to an execution environment which is responsible for controlling several aspects associated to the components at run-time. These aspects include life-cycle

W. Löwe and M. Südholt (Eds.): SC 2006, LNCS 4089, pp. 275–290, 2006.

management and the support of non-functional requirements such as persistence or security.

Currently, many component models exist; the majority of them are targeted toward specific application domains such as the construction of user interfaces or the construction of server-side applications (for example, the Corba Component Model (CCM) and Enterprise Java Beans (EJB)). The Fractal component model, however, aims to be a general-purpose model and to address a wide spectrum of domains [3]. The Fractal specification defines the component model characteristics, and different implementations for this specification exist. One of them is Julia, which is the reference Java-based implementation (http://fractal.objectweb.org). An important particularity of the Fractal component model is that it supports hierarchical composition, where a composition itself can be seen as a component that can be used in other compositions. Another particularity of this model is that it is extensible; this characteristic allows this model to be independent from a particular application domain. Although the Fractal specification defines clearly the characteristics of Fractal components, it does not cover deployment aspects which, as previously mentioned, need to be taken into account early in the development lifecycle. This paper presents FROGi [6] which is an extension of the Fractal component model that supports deployment features and dynamic service-orientation. FROGi introduces the concept of a deployment unit which is not covered in the original Fractal specification. Furthermore, FROGi deployment units address the problem of deployment at both the component and the composition level, necessary to support Fractal's hierarchical model. FROGi also addresses the issue of supporting continuous deployment activities, which represent the fact that deployment activities, which include installation, activation, update and un-installation of components occur continually. Supporting continuous deployment is facilitated by introducing concepts from Service Orientation [2,7] into the component model.

FROGi implements these concepts by combining the Julia reference implementation of the Fractal component Model and the OSGi services platform (http://www.osgi.org). FROGi simplifies Fractal-based application deployment and also allows these applications to support continuous deployment activities. This paper describes the concepts and the implementation of FROGi and discusses some issues related to its realization. It is structured in the following way. Section 2 presents the Fractal component model and its reference implementation Julia. Section 3 presents FROGi concepts. It describes how a Fractal application is delivered as a set of deployment units. Section 4 discusses implementation details, including OSGi. Section 5 presents related work and finally section 6 provides a conclusion and gives some perspectives to this work.

2   The Fractal Component Model

This section discusses the principles behind the Fractal component model and its reference implementation Julia.

2.1 Fractal

The Fractal component model is intended as a general-purpose component model. Fractal components are defined as entities that provide and require functional interfaces and that can be composed hierarchically. Fractal components can also provide or require various named instances of an interface of a same type (similar to CCM's facets). To support multiple application domains, Fractal components allow an undefined number of control interfaces to be implemented by the components. Control interfaces are used at run-time for various purposes. The Fractal specification defines several control interfaces which cover aspects such as life-cycle control (LifeCycleController LC), the management of connections between components (BindingController BC), the configuration of the component attributes (AttributeController AC) and the management of composite contents (ContentController CC). Furthermore, different instances of a Fractal component can be created from a factory associated with a particular component type. Figure 1 illustrates an example of a composite component containing two component instances. These instances, which represent a client and a server, are bound together and an interface provided by the client instance is exported outside the composition. Additionally, the two instances and the composite provide several control interfaces.

The Fractal specification defines a standard API that allows component types to be defined programmatically. The API also allows component instances to be created, configured and connected.

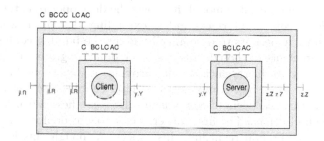

Fig. 1. Graphical representation of a Fractal composite

2.2 Julia

Julia (http://fractal.objectweb.org) is the Java-based reference implementation of the Fractal framework which implements the Fractal API. Julia aims to simplify the construction of Fractal applications through the generation of support classes, which allow standard Java classes to adhere to the Fractal component model. A developer using Julia who wishes to create a Fractal component must only provide code associated to application logic (the code that implements the functional interfaces or *component implementation*). Julia generates a set of classes which include implementations of control interfaces as well as interceptors between functional interfaces and the component implementation. Support classes are generated either in a static or in a dynamic way through mixin and byte code injection techniques. It must be noted that Julia is not the only Fractal implementation; other implementations of Fractal are also available for other languages and frameworks such as C, C#, Smalltalk, JavaScript, etc.

2.3   Construction of Fractal Applications Using Julia

A Fractal application is typically built from a set of classes implementing the application logic contained in the components, one or more coordination classes, as well as a primary class (bootstrap) responsible for performing the application startup. Coordination classes interact with the Fractal framework to create the different component types, component instances and instance connections required by the application. Coordination logic can be written either programmatically or declaratively using the Fractal Architecture Description Language (ADL). It must be noted that the ADL only allows static compositions between component instances to be described; as a consequence, dynamic changes must be programmed explicitly in the application code.

3   FROGi

As previously described, the Fractal component model intends to be general and allow many types of applications to be constructed, either distributed or not. Construction of applications using this model is beneficial for several reasons. First, Fractal is an extensible model; it allows the developer to extend it by providing additional control interfaces and by extending its ADL as well. Fractal is also flexible since it permits to dynamically adapt the binding configuration between the components (although this has to be done programmatically through the API). Finally its hierarchical model provides a way to build coarse components by composing finer components. Fractal enables also the management of the non-functional aspects of components. Despite these advantages, Fractal still has some limitations. The first concerns component deployment since nothing is specified in Fractal regarding this aspect. Although this issue has been addressed by some recent work, proposed solutions are limited because they do not support component unloading when components are not used anymore (see related work section). The second limitation concerns component packaging. As deployment is not currently addressed, no deployment unit has been specified. As a result, a Fractal application is delivered a set of classes. Although these classes can be packaged together in a JAR file (Java ARchive), the components themselves cannot be delivered independently. The last limitation concerns the versioning of the components constituting the application. It is not currently possible to support multiple versions of components running simultaneously as classes or package versioning is not supported, although this is more a limitation of standard Java.

On the other hand, Service-Oriented Architectures (SOA) [2,7] are built following a different model. Services are similar to components in the sense that they are composed to build applications. Services, however, are specifically designed to be shared at runtime. Services are usually discovered using a service registry before being used in a composition. Web services are the most common incarnation of SOA, however, other frameworks which are based on the SOA principles also exist. OSGi is one of them and is presented later in this article. OSGi was initially designed to build applications running inside home gateways; this kind of environment is typically shared by several providers and must run continuously.

The construction of a component-based application or a service-based application requires different concerns to be addressed. The main difference is that in component models, bindings are static and explicitly described (naming) whereas in service architectures bindings are dynamic as services are referenced in a registry (trading) and can appear or disappear at runtime. Moreover, components tend to be fine-grained assembly units. It is possible to create a considerable amount of component instances inside an application. For instance, a large number of components can be deployed in an application server. On the other side, services are usually designed to be coarse-grained entities. A reason for this is that in service orientation the program must deal with the inherent dynamism. Therefore the lookup and adaptation required to support dynamic service availability tend to be resource consuming activities which are too costly for fine grained components.

FROGi introduces an approach where concepts from component orientation and service orientation are mixed. FROGi components (either single components or compositions) are used to provide services. This approach allows applications to be constructed as hierarchical compositions where bindings are dynamic. Dynamic binding is supported through the introduction of service orientation concepts. Furthermore, the introduction of support for dynamic binding also allows dynamic deployment activities to be performed.

FROGi is built by introducing the OSGi service platform into Fractal. FROGi intends to illustrate that OSGi can be used to deploy applications build using different component models and furthermore to be able to make these applications interact. This interoperability can occur, for example, between a Fractal component and another like an EJB. The authors have already demonstrated in [8] the dynamic deployment of J2EE applications and technical services on Java EE application servers running on the top of OSGi platform. In this case, FROGi offers a deployment container that takes in charge bindings between components using inversion of control [9], in a similar way to PicoContainer [11]. Finally, FROGi also allows Fractal-based applications to benefit from all the legacy services already offered by the OSGi platform. For instance, Comanche HTTP, a web server implemented with Fractal, can use the Log service specified in OSGi.

4   FROGi Implementation

This section discusses the implementation of FROGi by describing the OSGi framework upon which FROGi is built. It also discusses how components are packaged, an ADL that is used for deployment and finally a generation chain.

4.1   The OSGi Framework

The Open Services Gateway Initiative (OSGi) Alliance [16] is an independent, non-profit corporation working to define and promote open specifications originally intended for the delivery of managed services to networked environments, such as homes and automobiles. These specifications include the definition of the OSGi Services Platform, which consists of two pieces: the OSGi framework and a set of standard service definitions. The OSGi framework is a Java-based deployment and execution environment for components. The OSGi framework was originally conceived to be used inside restricted environments, such as set-top boxes. The OSGi framework can however be used in other domains, as for example, an infrastructure to support underlying release 3.0 of the Eclipse IDE and of the Eclipse RCP.

The OSGi framework supports uninterrupted deployment of components that are delivered inside of *bundles*. The framework also provides a service registry that allows the components to interact following a service-oriented approach. In OSGi, each bundle is used to deploy a single component that results in a unique instance at run time (singleton). The continuous deployment activities supported by the framework include bundle installation, activation, deactivation, update and de-installation of the bundles. The framework ensures that deployment dependencies at the bundle level are satisfied before allowing the bundle to be activated. Bundle activation results in the creation of the component instance deployed inside the bundle.

Physically, a bundle is packaged a jar file that contains binary code as well as resources needed by the component. The jar file manifest file provides meta-information that describes the bundle's dependencies and the name of an activation class. This class is instantiated by the framework upon bundle activation. The bundle's dependencies are divided between deployment-time and run-time dependencies. Deployment-time dependencies are code dependencies described as packages that are exported and imported by the bundles. Run-time dependencies describe the services that are provided or required by the component that is deployed inside the bundle.

Component instances can publish or discover services provided by other component instances at run-time. In OSGi, a service is published from a service interface, a reference toward the component implementing the service and a set of properties. Those properties, defined as keys and values, allow clients to differentiate two equivalent service offers (i.e. two services with the same interfaces). Moreover, the registry allows constraint searches to be made using filters based on the properties following LDAP syntax. Because service publication or departure can occur at anytime, the service registry supports a notification mechanism that allows service clients to be aware of a particular service arrival or departure events. In OSGi application assembly occurs at execution time as a result of the interaction between components and the service registry.

4.2   Component Packaging

In FROGi, a Fractal application is packaged as one or more bundles. It is important to notice that inside a single bundle, FROGi components are bound together following the standard Fractal approach. However, when components are delivered in separate bundles, components become service providers and binding is performed using the service-oriented interaction pattern which is facilitated by the OSGi platform.

Because a Fractal application is built as a hierarchical composition, FROGi supports independent packaging of primitive components as well as composites. As a consequence, it is possible to perform independent delivery as well as independent update of the components. The example of figure 2 presents the application from figure 1 packaged as a set of bundles. In this example, each component is delivered in a different bundle: B0 for the composite, B1 for the client and B2 for server.

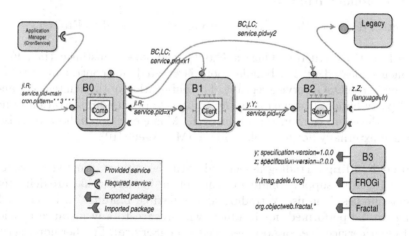

Fig. 2. Fractal application packaged as a set of OSGi bundles

It is important to notice that once published, service interfaces become stable contracts which evolve slowly while their implementations can evolve more frequently. As a consequence, service interfaces used for the binding between components should be delivered in separate bundles (for example bundle B3 in the figure 2 contains the interfaces implemented by the components in the other bundles). The bundles that implement interfaces have a deployment-time dependency towards the bundle that contains them. The independent delivery of service interfaces allows implementation bundles to be updated without impact on the other bundles. If services interfaces were delivered with their implementation, a bundle update would lead to stopping and restarting (i.e. refresh) of the bundles that depend on those services interfaces. This situation can be problematic when applications run in non-stop environments. In FROGi, the Fractal API as well as the Julia runtime are themselves delivered inside a bundle (fractal.jar); this bundle exports packages that must be imported by bundles containing Fractal components.

FROGi uses standard OSGi mechanisms for managing deployment activities of a bundle-based Fractal application. During bundle installation, the OSGi framework resolves in an automatic way deployment dependencies corresponding to packages containing service interfaces as well as the Fractal API. When those dependencies are resolved, the bundle can be activated. Activation of a FROGi bundle results in the instantiation and activation of an object from a generic class, FrogiBundleActivator, contained in each FROGi bundle. This class is responsible for configuring Julia execution environment (notably by specifying that the classloader to use is the bundle one). It then instantiates a primary class (i.e. BootStrap) that is responsible for creating the component(s) instance(s) delivered by the bundle.

4.3   Component Runtime

This section describes the runtime environment associated to FROGi.

Controller Publication. Once a FROGi component instance (i.e., Fractal components located at the bundle root) is created, its control interfaces are published in the OSGi service registry. The publication of those interfaces allows a third party bundle (its encapsulating composite or an administration bundle) to control the component instance's lifecycle. Management can, however, also be performed externally, for example using a JMX Agent [10].

Instance Binding. Trading associated with the service oriented approach is used in FROGi to support binding of component instances that are delivered in different bundles. The use of trading allows flexible bindings to be created. A binding can be performed, for instance, with regard to any instance providing a particular service (i.e. org.osgi.service.log.LogService). Furthermore, services are characterized by a set of registration properties (such as "'language=en'" or "'cron.pattern=***3***'" in figure 2). Trading also allows 'static' bindings to be created. In that case a service request must contain the unique instance identifier (i.e. the property service.pid) towards which the binding must be created.

Life-cycle and Binding Management. FROGi proposes two policies to manage the life-cycle and binding of the components: a composite-driven policy and an autonomic policy. The instance life-cycle of a root component can be managed either by its composite (delivered in another bundle), either by itself in an autonomous way. Life-cycle management by the composite requires the instance control interfaces to be published as services in OSGi service registry. Each service is identified by the service.pid properties. This properties identifies the instance that provides the service in a unique and persistent way. The composite creates bindings between instances through the BindingController services they expose. Once those binding are created, the composite activates the instances with the help of their LifeCycleController services.

The alternative to this policy is to consider the bundle as an autonomous life cycle management unit of the instance with regard to its composite. This policy is inspired from the Service Binder (see section 6.2). The instance is started as soon as mandatory services dependencies are available in the registry. This last policy is used for connecting components to legacy bundles that are devoid of life cycle and binding controllers.

Dynamic reconfiguration. Whatever policy is used, it is necessary to support dynamic reconfiguration when the framework notifies that new components are introduced or removed from the environment. If an arriving component is required by another one, the binding must be performed. If a component leaves, the components that depend on it must check in the registry that the mandatory services they depend on are still available. In the case of the autonomous policy, provided services are systematically unregistered of OSGi registry at component stopping time. They are registered again (still with the same service.pid attribute) during the component instance restart.

Application Activation. A Fractal application is a component/composite that can be activated from one of its functional interfaces by Fractal support classes such as org.objectweb.fractal.adl.Launcher. In OSGi, the application concept doesn't really exist: the application is built as a set of bundles that create connections as they are installed or removed from the framework. Bundles can, however, be classified into two categories: support bundles (i.e., which provide services), and coordination bundles (which may not provide services but use services provided by other bundles). Coordination bundles are closer to the concept of an application, however, these bundles may themselves provide services to other bundles and become part of a bigger application. In FROGi, an application manager is responsible for activating the Fractal application deployed on OSGi. This can be for instance a Cron Service calling the run() method of a component or an administrator command executed on the terminal console.

4.4   Extensions to the Fractal ADL

Fractal provides an Architecture Description Language (ADL) that allows component assemblies to be described. As previously mentioned, this ADL is extensible. FROGi extends this ADL to take into account the deployment aspects of the components, i.e. Packaging them within bundles.

The extended ADL is specified as shown in figure 3. This example presents the Fractal ADL description used to obtain the FROGi packaging of figure 2 for the application depicted in figure 1. The <bundle> sub-element of the <component> and <definition> elements define how components are packaged inside the

```
<definition name="HelloWorld">
  <bundle name="B0"/>
  <interface name="main" role="server" signature="java.lang.Runnable">
    <property name="cron.pattern" value="** * 3 * * *"
        type="java.lang.String"/>
  </interface>
  <component name="client">
    <bundle name="B1"/>
    <interface name="x1" role="server" signature="java.lang.Runnable"/>
    <interface name="cy2" role="client" signature="y.Y"
        version="1.0.0" bundle="B3"/>
    <content class="ClientImpl"/>
  </component>
  <component name="server">
    <bundle name="B2"/>
    <interface name="y2" role="server" signature="y.Y"
        version="1.0.0" bundle="B3"/>
    <interface name="cz3" role="client" signature="z.Z"
        cardinality="collection" contingency="optional"
        version="2.0.0" bundle="B3"/>
    <content class="ServerImpl"/>
  </component>
  <binding client="this.x1" server="client.x1"/>
  <binding client="client.cy2" server="server.y2"/>
  <binding client="server.z3" server="this.cz3"/>
  <binding client="this.z3" serverfilter="(language=fr)"/>
</definition>
```

Fig. 3. The Extended Fractal ADL

bundle identified by the `name` attribute. The `version` attribute specifies the overall implementation version. It corresponds to the bundle's `Bundle-Version` manifest attribute in OSGi. All the elements that are declared after a `bundle` element are packaged together in the same bundle and this occurs until another `<bundle>` element is encountered.

The `bundle` attribute under the `<interface>` element indicates that the interface must be packaged inside another bundle whose name is specified by the name value. If the bundle attribute value is an empty string, the interface is not packaged by FROGi: it is already available in another bundle, generally a legacy bundle. By default, if nothing is specified, service interfaces are packaged in the same bundle as their component implementation. The `version` attribute of the `<interface>` element declares the package specification version (i.e. contract) of the interface. The default version value is 0.0.0.

The sub-element `<property>` of the `<interface>` element defines some properties that are associated to the service interface and which are used when the interface is published in the service registry. Those properties are used for service trading and and to provide information to application managers.

The sub-element `<binding>` of the `<component>` and `<description>` elements is used simultaneously to create standard Fractal bindings between instances created in the same bundle, bindings between instances created into separate bundles and bindings between instances and legacy OSGi services. The `server` attribute can be substituted by a `filterserver` attribute whose value is a LDAP expression that the requiring service must match to perform the binding. This attribute is not available for standard Fractal bindings (i.e. intrabundle). We can notice that the `serverfilter="(service.pid=server.y2)"` attribute is equivalent to `server="server.y2"`.

4.5   Generation and Deployment Chain

The extended ADL presented in the previous section allows packaging tasks to be automated using a generation and deployment chain. Once Fractal components are packaged inside bundles, the facilities provided by the OSGi platform are used to perform their deployment.

The first step in the chain is concerned with bundle generation. This activity is performed by the FROGi packager (left of figure 4). The packager parses the ADL and packages interfaces and implementations following the ADL descriptor. The packager tries to separate interfaces from implementations since this is essential to support dynamic component updates.

The deployment is managed by another tool dedicated to OSGi deployment (right of figure 4). This tool manages OSGi gateways distributed over several nodes. It reads deployment files that are produced by the FROGi packager (xml files). These files contain both the localizations of the generated bundles and the gateway on which they must be deployed. The description also contains the dependencies between the bundles. The tool deploys the FROGi bundles and, if necessary, depending of the state of the targeted OSGi platform, it also deploys required OSGi legacy bundles. Those bundles, and possibly their dependencies, are made available from bundle repositories (such as the Oscar Bundle Repository, Oscar (http://oscar.objectweb.org) being the open source OSGi implementation we are using for demonstration purposes).

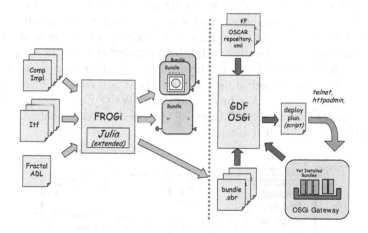

Fig. 4. Generation and deployment chain

4.6   Security

Service oriented architectures and service deployment require security aspects to be taken into account. In the context of FROGi, it is necessary to ensure that an architecture that is deployed using the ADL functions properly after installation. The components that interact with legacy OSGi services must be able to trust them. This concern is exacerbated by the fact that the OSGi environment is designed to be operated by different actors, and a FROGi-based application may coexist with unsafe bundles from a different provider.

FROGi currently relies on the mechanisms provided by the OSGi framework to handle security. These mechanisms allow bundles to be signed so that other bundles can verify their origin. This offers an initial level of security. The second level occurs at the service level. OSGi provides a mechanism that allows services to be traded according to security policies. Furthermore, those policies can be updated dynamically. Security mechanisms at the service level are adequate for FROGi because they bring additional capabilities to the component model. Finally, It must be noted that Fractal does not support these concepts (which is understandable as it targets mono-operated applications).

5   Experimentation

This section presents an experimentation which compares the creation of an HTTP server using a "'standard"' approach versus a FROGi-based approach. The experimentation is inspired from the comanche HTTP server discussed in the Fractal tutorial.

5.1   Using Standard Fractal

Figure 5 depicts a minimal HTTP server. This server is assembled as a composite component that is responsible of receiving, analyzing and dispatching requests (to simplify, only the external composite is shown, not the contained components). This component requires a Log component and one or more handlers towards which the requests will be directed. Before a call arrives to a handler, the request may go through different filters that are capable of adapting the requests or that can be used as probes for example to collect information. To realize this example in standard Fractal, all the needed components are described in the ADL along with their bindings.

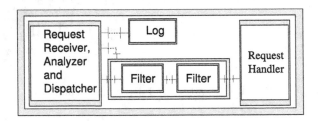

Fig. 5. A minimal HTTP server with Fractal

Once deployed and during execution, it is still possible to adapt the bindings between the components. For example it is possible to disconnect the Log component if we do not want to trace the requests anymore. It is also possible to adapt the filter chain between the requests manager and the request handler by connecting or disconnecting filters. This adaptation is taken in charge by the requests analyzer and dispatcher. What is not possible, however, is to add dynamically a new filter that was not previously described in the ADL. This is simply because the implementation classes of this filter are not deployed with the original application. The same problem occurs if a filter needs to be updated, for example for performance reasons. It is possible to disconnect the filter properly but no mechanism is available to perform an update of the filter's implementation and maintain the coherency.

5.2   Using FROGi

The construction of the same example using FROGi illustrates three key points: the capability of using legacy OSGi services, of dynamically deploying new components and of updating components without restarting the application.

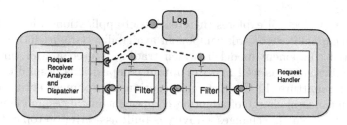

Fig. 6. A minimal HTTP server with FROGi

Figure 6 depicts how the HTTP server application is assembled and deployed using FROGi components. The capability of using legacy OSGi services is illustrated by replacing the previous Fractal log component with the Log service defined in the OSGi specification. Deployment concerns are now addressed since the components are packaged into different bundles which are later managed by OSGi framework. In this example, the filter components are packaged and delivered in different bundles. As a result new filters can be deployed easily. Using the trading mechanisms, the Dispacher is able to select, among the set of filters, the ones that it requires to create the filter chain. Updating a component is also possible and is supported by the OSGi update mechanism. First of all, bindings with the corresponding component are relieved. Then the update mechanism manages the download, replacement and reactivation of the component embedded in the bundle. During this period, Fractal's interception capabilities are used to hold the calls towards the components until it they are reactivated. It is interesting to notice that as soon as a component is not used anymore, it is possible to uninstall it and completely free the resources it was using. F This simple example shows that the FROGi's features introduce important benefits into the standard Fractal model.

6   Related Works

This section presents different related works concerning the OSGi use as an infrastructure for deploying components as well as Fractal components packaging.

6.1   Beanome

Using OSGi as a component deployment infrastructure is explored in the Beanome component model [4]. In Beanome, OSGi bundles are used to deploy COM-like components. Moreover, the OSGi service registry is used to publish components factories when the bundle is activated. A benefit of registering component factories as services is that factories can be located based on the functionalities of the components they create and not only from a unique identifier as in COM. Beanome, however, does not provide support for dynamic changes.

6.2   Gravity

The Gravity project [5] explores the creation of applications with autonomous adaptation capabilities towards component availability. Gravity introduces a service oriented component model in which trading is used at run time to bind component instances as well as to maintain compositions despite components arrival and departure. In Gravity, an execution environment entity, called the Service Binder, is in charge of adapting component instances and compositions with respect to dynamic changes. Gravity is built as a layer on top of OSGi, and the Service Binder is deployed as a bundle inside the service platform. A drawback of Gravity is that is uses a particular component model that is nevertheless not far from Fractal. Many of the ideas introduced in the Service Binder have been recently added to the OSGi specification's 4th release under the name of Service Component Runtime (Declarative Services). This component is also the subject of the JSR 291 (Dynamic Component Support for Java SE) submitted to the JCP by several members of the OSGi Alliance.

6.3   Fractal Packages and Deployment Activities

Some discussions on the Fractal mailing list mention the definition of a packaging mechanism for Fractal components and some work has been realized concerning this mechanism. The proposals that have been made also rely on OSGi but only for packaging purposes (packaging units are .FAR)[1]. An XML manifest that contains the metadata is added to the archive. Deployment is supported but it is impossible to update components at runtime. This proposal does, however, not consider the existence of an infrastructure to perform continuous deployment activities. This issue is addressed in another work [12]. This proposal uses a layer that supports the creation of Java classloaders to bring additional components to an application at runtime. This work does, however, not support component uninstall.

6.4   JSR277

Packaging an application is one of the most recurrent problems to facilitate deployment. JSR277 (Java Module System http://www.jcp.org/en/jsr/detail?id=277) aims to specify an unified packaging model for all Java software for J2SE 1.7 (2007). JSR277 intends to overtake JNLP, J2EE EAR, OSGi R4 packaging formats. It will be based on the JAR file format and the Manifest will be augmented by explicit versioned package dependencies. In fact, the chapter "Module Layer" of the recent OSGi R4 specifications already covers all of JSR 277 requirements. Moreover, JSR277 does not address the OSGi service layer which enables to build dynamic service-oriented architectures of Java applications as SCR, JSR 291 or FROGi. If this JSR is integrated in Java, FROGi would already be compliant at the packaging level with future Java versions.

7   Conclusions and Perspectives

This paper has presented FROGi, a proposition that is based on the introduction of some characteristics of the OSGi service platform in the Fractal component model. With FROGi, a Fractal application is packaged inside one or more OSGi bundles; this allows the components to be delivered and deployed individually and continuously. Moreover, binding between components instances can be realized either through the 'standard' Fractal connexion technique, either by the publication of functional interfaces in the services registry and the use of OSGi proper trading technique. In addition, FROGi proposes Fractal ADL extensions to automate packaging and deployment. It must be pointed out that FROGi, as well as the different works described in the fifth section, show that OSGi is an ideal platform to perform component deployment, application update and code versioning. Nevertheless, some points have not been considered in the work realized until now:

Multiple instances creation mechanism: Fractal supports the creation of a variable number of component instances. The work presented here focuses on a singleton based approach. A way to resolve this, still being compatible with the OSGi environment, is to publish components factories through services (similar to the approach followed by Beanome and described in 6.1).

Architecture introspection: as we assume that different kinds of components can be deployed and bound on OSGi, it is desirable to expose the architecture of the application independently of the technologies we are using. An example of such architecture viewer is Fractal Explorer but it only manages pure Fratal applications.

Finally, as it was mentioned in the second part, there is currently not a clear vision of the difference between component models and service oriented architectures. Most of the time, these approaches are considered either as orthogonal aspects, either as similar approaches. We have already cited some tracks on the subject and this is the focus of our current research. For instance we are currently working on the interoperability we can have between Fractal and EJB components model inside an application server and on component deployment on heterogeneous platforms [13].

References

1. Abdellatif, T., Kornas, J. And Stephani, J-B.: J2EE Packaging, Deployment and Reconfiguration Using a General Component Model. Proceedings of Component Deployment, CD, Grenoble 2005
2. Bieber, G., Carpenter, J.: Introduction to Service-Oriented Programming. OpenWings whitepaper, Septembre 2001, http://www.openwings.org/download/specs/ServiceOrientedIntroduction.pdf
3. Bruneton, E., Coupaye, T. and Stefani, J.B.: The Fractal Composition Framework Version 2.0-3. Object Web Consortium, July 2004.
4. Cervantes, H. and Hall, R.S.: Beanome, A Component Model for the OSGi Framework. Proceedings of the workshop Software Infrastructures for Component Based Applications on Consumer Devices, Lausanne, 2002
5. Cervantes, H. and Hall, R.S.: Automating Service Dependency Management in a Service-Oriented Component Model. Proceedings of CBSE 6, Portland, USA, 2003
6. Cervantes, H., Desertot, M. And Donsez, B.: FROGi: Dploiement de composents Fractal sur OSGi. Proceedings of Decor'04, CoRR, Grenoble 2004
7. Cervantes, H. and Hall R. S.: Chapter I: Service Oriented Concepts and Technologies. In the book "Service-Oriented Software System Engineering: Challenges and Practices" (ISBN 1-59140-426-6) edited by Zoran Stojanovic and Ajantha Dahanayake, Idea Group Publishing, 2005.
8. Desertot, M., Escoffier, C. And Donsez, D.: Autonomic administration of J2EE Edge Servers. Proceedings of the International Worshop of Middleware for Grid Computing (MGC), Grenoble, 2005
9. Fowler, M.: Inversion of Control and the Dependency Injection Pattern. Online Document, 2004. http://martinfowler.com/articles/injection.html
10. Frnot, S. And Stefan D.: Instrumentation de plate formes de services ouvertes Getion JMX sur OSGi. Ubimob, Nice, 2004
11. Hammant, P., Hellesoy, A., and Tirsen, J.: PicoContainer: a lightweight embeddable container. http://www.picocontainer.org
12. Kornas, J., Leclercq, M., Quema, V. And Stephani, J-B.: Support pour la reconfiguration d'implantation dans les applications a composants Java. Proceedings of Decor'04, CoRR, Grenoble 2004
13. Marin, C. And Desertot, M.: SensorBean: A Component Platform for Sensor-Based Services. Proceedings of the International Worshop of Middleware for Pervasive and Ad-Hoc Compouting (MPAC), Grenoble, 2005
14. Szyperski, C.: Component software: beyond object-oriented programming. ACM Press/Addison-Wesley Publishing Co., 1998.

Modular Design of Man-Machine Interfaces with Larissa

Karine Altisen, Florence Maraninchi, and David Stauch

Verimag, Centre équation - 2, avenue de Vignate, 38610 GIÈRES — France

Abstract. The man-machine interface of a small electronic device like a wristwatch is a crucial component, as more and more functions have to be controlled using a small set of buttons. We propose to use Argos, an automaton-based language for reactive systems, and Larissa, its aspect-oriented extension, to show that several interfaces can be obtained from the same set of basic components, assembled in various ways. This is the basis of a quite general component-based development method for man-machine interfaces.

1 Introduction

Man-Machine Interfaces of small electronic devices. In small devices such as wristwatches, portable multimedia devices, or GPS devices, more and more functions have to be controlled using a very small set of buttons. The design of such systems usually follows an approach in which the interface is clearly separated: this is a component that accepts the button events as inputs, and translates them into complex functions, depending on its internal state, or mode. For instance, the same button of a wristwatch means "toggle alarm" or "increment minutes", depending on the running mode. We will distinguish the *interface* from the *internal* components of the system, which take a much larger set of inputs ("toggle alarm", "increment minutes", etc.). In this paper, we concentrate on the design of the *interface* component of such small electronic devices. We propose to use aspects in order to help modular design and reuse.

Programming Man-Machine Interfaces. Man-machine interfaces are typical interactive, or reactive systems. Using reactive languages for programming or modeling them is quite natural. Moreover, among the formalisms and languages that are used to describe reactive systems, those that are based on explicit automata, like Statecharts [8], are particularly well adapted. The user documentation of a small electronic device is often given with partial graphical automata, because it is the more natural way of thinking of it.

The family of *synchronous languages* [5] has been very successful in offering semantically founded languages, adapted to the needs of the programmers. It is comprised of several dataflow languages (Lustre, Signal), a textual imperative language (Esterel), and several variants of graphical automaton-based languages (Argos, Safe State Machines, some variants of Statecharts). Their main structure is the parallel composition; components synchronize and exchange data via

W. Löwe and M. Südholt (Eds.): SC 2006, LNCS 4089, pp. 291–306, 2006.

the so-called synchronous broadcast. All these languages may be compiled into sequential cyclic code for a direct implementation on embedded processors, or into synchronous circuits, for ASIC or FPGA implementations. Moreover, the internal structure used in the compilation or synthesis process can be used as input by various formal verification tools (model-checkers, abstract-interpretation tools, theorem-proving tools).

In this paper, we use a simple version of Argos [14]. Argos was first designed as a variant of Statecharts having a pure synchronous semantics. The hierarchy of states inherited from Statecharts is very convenient for the description of a watch interface that has several running modes.

Aspect Oriented Programming. Programming languages usually have mechanisms to *structure* the code of programs. For any program P, whatever be its modular structure, it is always possible to think of some functionality F that P should provide, in such a way that F cannot be implemented only by some modular modifications of P by e.g. simply adding some new components to it. This is the case when F is a *crosscutting* feature, that indeeds requires modifications in several components of the original program. Aspect oriented programming (AOP) has emerged recently as a response to this problem. It provides facilities to design F as a new kind of component – F is then called an *aspect* – and to compile F and P together – this process is called the *weaving* of the aspect F into the program P. Some aspect languages like AspectJ [9] are becoming increasingly popular. A number of case studies (see for instance [2,3]) have shown that they can considerably improve the code structure of large systems.

Aspects may be used to describe functionalities like tracing, debugging, profiling. In this case, they do not aim at modifying the behavior of the original program; they only add code that *observes* it. They should be given a complete view of the entities of the program. On the other hand, aspects may sometimes be used in order to modify the behavior of the original program. For this kind of aspects, the way they modify the program has to be clearly defined. Aspect weaving can also be required to have some good properties, like the preservation of a behavior equivalence (if two programs P and Q behave the same, then the result of weaving an aspect A into P should behave the same as the result of weaving the same A into Q). In this paper, we use the formally defined language Argos, and its aspect extension Larissa [1]. The aspects allowed have a clear semantics and the weaving process preserves the usual behavior equivalence.

Contributions and structure of the Paper. We show the interest of using aspect oriented programming in the particular context of developing man-machine interfaces of small electronic devices: we illustrate it by studying several variants of watches. We propose an approach in which these interface components may be described by assembling smaller components, thus improving reuse.

We consider aspects as components in this assembling process. This is made possible by two important points: first, our mechanism for aspect weaving behaves exactly as the operators of the base language, and has the same properties regarding the respect of a behavior equivalence; this allows to combine pieces of programs and aspects freely, in any order. Second, our specification of aspects is independent of the internal structure and names of the base program, and only refers to the elements of its interface; this means that a component on which an aspect is applied may be safely replaced by another one, provided its interface is the same and its behavior is equivalent to the old one.

The structure of the paper is as follows: Section 2 describes the base language Argos; Section 3 describes our aspect extension of Argos, from the user point of view; Section 4 is the case study; Section 5 comments the case study; Section 6 is a non-exhaustive list of related work and Section 7 concludes and lists the main perspectives.

2   The Argos Language

An Argos program describes the *reactive kernel* of a system. A reactive system is a computer system that communicates with the environment it is embedded in: it has input signals coming from the environment and output signal it emits towards the environment. In Argos, input and output signals have Boolean values. Whereas the environment evolves in a continuous manner, the fact that the reactive system is a program implies that, from the program(mer)'s point of view, the time is sampled into instant. At each instant, an Argos program reacts to inputs by sending outputs and updating its internal memory. Such a reaction is *atomic*: the system does not read inputs while computing outputs and updating its memory. This property mainly characterizes synchronous languages of which Argos is a member.

Argos is an automata based language. Its base components are automata with transitions labelled by inputs and outputs; more complex components can be obtained by connecting components with operators, i.e. the parallel product between automata, the encapsulation (hiding variables), the inhibition (freezing a program for a while) and the hierarchy (a state of an automaton may contain a program). The communication between components is achieved by parallel product and encapsulation. Two programs communicate by exchanging local signals which are inputs of one program and outputs of the other. The communication is the *synchronous broadcast*: it is non blocking (unlike the *rendez-vous* mechanism, for instance).

Argos programs are (as programs should always be) deterministic and complete, i.e. for any given sequence of inputs there exists a unique execution of the program. The semantics of Argos is formally defined by using traces of the execution. Those traces are only defined by the values of the inputs and outputs at each instant (the states reached – value of the memory – are not part of the information of a trace). A semantic equivalence between programs is also defined as being the equality of traces.

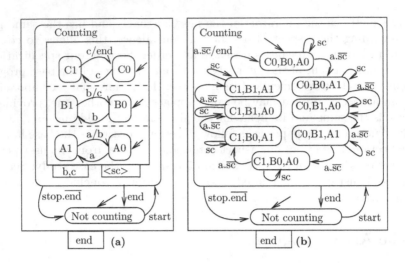

Fig. 1. Two Argos programs for the modulo-8 a-counter

2.1   Syntax of the Main Constructs

The complete language is described in [14]. In this paper, we partially describe it using an example. Figure 1(a) is an Argos program using four automata to describe a modulo-8 a-counter.

Single automata. Rounded-corner boxes are automaton states; arrows are transitions. A set of states and transitions which are connected together constitutes an automaton. The four basic components of the program have the following sets of states: {Counting, Not counting}, {A0, A1}, {B0, B1}, {C0, C1}. Transitions are labeled by a Boolean condition on input signals, and a set of emitted signals. We use the concrete syntax: condition / emitted signals. In the condition, negation is denoted by overlining and conjunction is denoted by a dot (examples: c/end, stop.end). When the output set is empty, it can be omitted. The initial state is designated by an arrow without source. States are named, but names should be considered as comments: they cannot be referred to in other components nor are used to define the semantics of the program. An arrow can have several labels — and stand for several transitions, in which case the labels are separated by a comma. By convention, every automaton is complete: if a state has no transition for some input valuations, we suppose that there is a self-loop transition with these valuations as triggering condition and no outputs.

State refinement. The automaton whose states are Counting and Not counting is said to be *refined*. The Counting state contains a sub-program built from the three other automata.

Parallel product. Three automata whose states are respectively {A0, A1}, {B0, B1}, {C0, C1} are put *in parallel*: they are drawn separated by dashed lines.

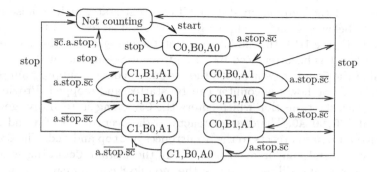

Fig. 2. The behavior of the modulo-8 a-counter

Encapsulation. Rectangular boxes are used for unary operators. The external box, whose cartridge contains **end**, is the graphical syntax for the declaration of a local signal **end**. The box defines the scope in which **end** is known. This signal is used as input by the refined automaton; it is used as output by one of the three other ones: a communication will take place between the two. The same operator is used in order to limit the scope of signals **b**, **c** to the program constituted by the three unrefined automata.

Inhibition. The inhibition is another unary operator: the notation is another cartridge containing a *fresh* variable between "<" and ">". The parallel product of the three non refined automata are inhibited by the inhibition variable **sc**.

Interface of a program. All signals which appear in a left-hand (resp. right-hand) side of a label plus inhibition variables, and are not declared to be local to some part of the program are *global inputs* (resp. *global outputs*).

2.2 Intuitive Semantics

We give here the intuitive semantics of the operators, by explaining the behavior of the counter. This behavior is a single automaton, as shown by Figure 2.

First, observe the three automata embedded in a parallel structure, and the operator which defines the scope of **b** and **c**. This constitutes a subprogram whose only input is **a**, and whose only output is **end**. The global behavior of this subprogram is defined by: the global initial state is C0,B0,A0; when it has reacted to input **a** n times, the program is in state C_k,B_j,A_i, where $i+2j+4k = n$ mod 8; **end** is emitted every 8 **a**'s.

This behavior is achieved by connecting three one-bit counters. The first one (A) reacts to external input **a**, and triggers the second one (B) with signal **b**, every two **a**'s. The second one, reacting to **b**, triggers the third one (C) with **c**, every two **b**'s. The third one emits **end** every two **c**'s. The communication being *synchronous*, a reaction to which the three bits participate, is indeed *one* transition in the global behavior (e.g., reaction to **a** from C0,B1,A1 to C1,B0,A0). Finally, inhibition by **sc** (for "stop counting") is applied: in each state, either sc is true and the automaton stays in its current state, or it is false and the automaton behaves as before applying inhibition. The result of those operators is shown in Figure 1(b): the modulo-8 counter subprogram modularly described in Figure 1(a) has been replaced by an equivalent 8-state automaton.

Refining the Counting state with the modulo-8 counter subprogram provides a way to describe how the counter can be started and stopped. Provided that start is true, the transition which enters the Counting state always goes to its initial state C0,B0,A0. The counter reacts to the occurrences of a and sc; and the refined automaton reacts to the occurrences of stop and end. The Counting state is left if end and/or stop occurs. At the instant Counting is left, the refining subprogram still reacts. Thus, the modulo-8 counter can terminate itself by emitting end. The program goes to state Not counting when stop occurs at any time in state Counting, and also when it is in state C1,B1,A1 and a and $\overline{sc}$ occur, because end is emitted. end is also emitted when stop, a and $\overline{sc}$ occur together in state C1,B1,A1.

As we did for the example, the semantics of each Argos operator is given by a flattening operation that transforms any complex program (made of automata composed together) into an equivalent single flat automaton. The semantics of a flat automaton is then given by defining the set of all its execution traces, (inputs and outputs at each instant).

3   Larissa: An Aspect Extension to Argos

Argos operators are already powerful. However, there are cases in which they are not sufficient to modularize all concerns of a program: some small modifications of the global program's behavior may require that we modify all parallel components, in a way that is not expressible with the existing operators.

The goal of aspects being precisely to specify some cross-cutting modifications of a program, we proposed an aspect-oriented extension for Argos [1], which allows the modularization of a number of recurrent problems in reactive programs, like the reinitialization. This leads to the definition of a new kind of operators (corresponding to the weaving of aspects) for which we took care of ensuring some nice properties: they preserve determinism and completeness of programs and also the semantic equivalence between programs.

All the aspect extensions of existing languages (like AspectJ [9]) seem to share two notions: pointcuts and advice. The *pointcut* describes a general property of program points where a modification is needed (all the methods of the class X, all the methods whose name contains visit, etc.); the pointcut, applied to a particular program, selects a set of concrete *join points*, where the aspect has to be applied. The *advice* specifies what has to be done at each of these join points (execute some piece of code before the normal code of the method, for instance). For Larissa, we adopted this approach: an aspect is given by the specification of its pointcut and its advice.

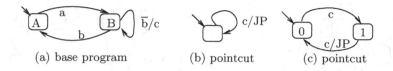

(a) base program   (b) pointcut   (c) pointcut

Fig. 3. Example pointcuts

3.1 Join Point Selection

In Larissa, we decided not to express pointcuts in terms of the internal structure
of the base program. For instance, we do not allow pointcuts to refer explicitly
to some state name (as AspectJ can refer to the name of a private method).
As a consequence, pointcuts may refer to the observable behavior of a program
only, i.e., its inputs and outputs. In the family of synchronous languages, where
the communication between parallel components is the synchronous broadcast,
observers [7] are a powerful and well-understood mechanism which may be used
to describe pointcuts. Indeed, an observer is a program that may observe the
inputs and the outputs of the base program, without modifying its behavior,
and compute some safety property (in the sense of safety/liveness properties as
defined in [10]).

In Larissa, pointcuts are expressed as observers, which select a set of *join point
transitions* by emitting a single output JP, the *join point signal*. A transition T
in a program P is selected as a join point transition when in the concurrent
execution of P and the pointcut, JP is emitted when T is taken. Technically,
we perform a parallel product between the program and the pointcut and select
those transitions in the product which emit JP. Figure 3 illustrates the pointcut
mechanism. The pointcut (b) specifies any transition which emits c: in base
program (a), the loop transition in state B of the base program is selected as
a join point transition. The pointcut (c) specifies every second time c is true:
no transition of the base program (a) corresponds directly to this condition.
However, as the join points are selected on the parallel product of the base
program and the pointcut, the pointcut introduces new memory: the automaton
memorizes if c has been emitted an even or an odd number of times.

Pointcuts can be built by composing other pointcuts with Argos operators.
E.g., some pointcuts can be put in parallel with an automaton which takes their
join point signals as inputs and emits the join point signal of the composed
pointcut. Thus, expressions like "pointcut A and not pointcut B" or "pointcut
A until a and then pointcut B" can be written modularly.

3.2 Specifying the Advice

The advice usually expresses the modification applied to the base program. In our
setting, we consider that the base program has been flattened first, as explained
in Section 2.2. In Larissa, we defined two types of advice: in the first type, an
advice replaces the join point transitions with *advice transitions* pointing to some

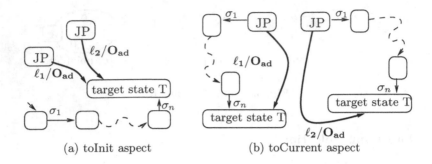

(a) toInit aspect   (b) toCurrent aspect

Fig. 4. Schematic toInit and toCurrent aspects (Advice transitions are in bold)

existing target states; in the second type, an advice introduces a full program between the source state of the join point transition and some existing target state. In both cases, target states have to be specified without referring explicitly to state names.

We consider three ways of specifying the target state T, among the existing states of the base program P: 1) T is the state of P that would be reached by executing some finite input trace from the initial state of P, called a *toInit* advice; 2) T is the state of P that would be reached by executing some finite input trace from the join point itself, called a *toCurrent* advice; 3) we first define some recovery states, among the states of P; then T is the recovery state that was passed last. The third type will not be used in the paper (see [1] for further details). For the first two types, specifying the advice includes giving a finite input trace to define the target state. Since the base program is both deterministic and complete, executing an input trace from any of its states is an effective way of defining exactly *one* state.

Advice Transition. The first type of advice consists in replacing each join point transition with an advice transition. Once the target state is specified by a finite input trace $\sigma = \sigma_1 \ldots \sigma_n$, the only missing information is the label of these new transitions. We do not change the input part of the label, so as to keep the woven automaton deterministic and complete, but we replace the output part by some *advice outputs* O_{ad}. These are the same for every advice transition, and are thus specified in the aspect. Advice transitions are illustrated in Figure 4.

Advice Program. It is sometimes not sufficient to modify single transitions, i.e. to jump to another location in the automaton in only one step. It may be necessary to execute arbitrary code when an aspect is activated. In these cases, we can insert an automaton between the join point and the target state.

Therefore, we use an *inserted automaton* A_{ins} that *terminates*. Since Argos has no built-in notion of termination, the programmer of the aspect has to identify a final state **F** (denoted by filled black circles in the figures).

Inserting an automaton is quite similar to inserting a transition. We first specify a target state T by a finite input trace, starting either from the initial

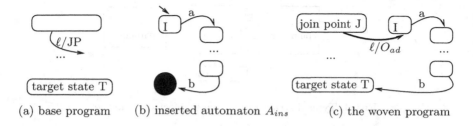

(a) base program   (b) inserted automaton A_{ins} (c) the woven program

Fig. 5. Inserting an advice automaton

state or from the source state of the join point transition. Then, for every T, a copy of the automaton A_{ins} is inserted, which means: 1) replace every join point transition J with target state T by a transition to the initial state I of this instance of A_{ins}. As for advice transitions, the input part of the label is unchanged and the output part is replaced by the *advice outputs* O_{ad}; 2) connect the transitions that went to the final state F in A_{ins} to T. See Figure 5.

3.3 Fully Specifying an Aspect

As stated above, an aspect is given by the specification of its pointcut and its advice: $Asp = ($PC-program, *Advice*$)$. PC-program is an Argos program with a single output JP used as the pointcut program. *Advice* is a tuple which contains 1) the advice outputs O_{ad}; 2) the *type* of the target state specification (*toInit* or *toCurrent*); 3) the finite trace σ over the inputs of the program; and optionally 4) when adding an advice program, ADV-program, the advice program itself (when adding advice transitions, this slot is left empty).

As a summary, when adding an advice transition, $Advice = \langle O_{ad}, type, \sigma \rangle$, when adding an advice program, $Advice = \langle O_{ad}, type, \sigma,$ ADV-program$\rangle$, with $type \in \{toCurrent, toInit\}$.

3.4 Formal Setting and Implementation

In [1], we define the aspect language formally, and prove the main properties: aspect weaving preserves the usual behavior equivalence, and also preserves the determinism and completeness of the base program. Let us note $P \lhd Asp$ the result of weaving an aspect Asp into a program P.

The preservation of the equivalence, noted $\sim$, means that, if $P \sim Q$ then, for any Asp, $(P \lhd Asp) \sim (Q \lhd Asp)$. With these properties, aspect weaving can indeed be considered as a new operator. This new operator can be used freely in expressions of the form: $((P||(Q \lhd A_1))||R) \lhd A_2$, for instance ($||$ denotes the parallel composition). Then, any of the components appearing in this expression may be replaced by an equivalent one without changing the behavior of the global program.

A compiler [11] for Larissa was developed, as an extension of an existing Argos compiler: it performs the weaving of an aspect Asp into an Argos program P

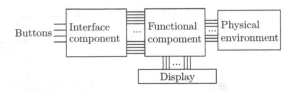

Fig. 6. Typical structure of a small electronic device

as shown above. This tool is connected to simulation, test, debug and formal verification tools like the model-checker Lesar [6].

The formal definition of aspects also allows to study interference problems in a clean setting. This question is treated in [16].

4   Case Study: A Suunto[1] Watch

4.1   Global Scheme

In this section, we model the interfaces of small electronic devices with Argos and Larissa. These devices – e.g. wristwatches, alarm clocks or car radios – usually have a small number of buttons which control a large number of functionalities. These buttons have different meanings depending on the state in which the device is currently.

Therefore, controllers of such devices usually have a structure like the one shown in Figure 6: it contains an *interface component*, which interprets the meaning of the buttons the user presses, and then calls the corresponding function in the underlying *functional component*. The functional component obtains the necessary information of the environment of the device (e.g. a quartz crystal to measure time), reads and writes persistent memory, and updates the display.

Hierarchic automata languages like Argos are very well suited to model interface components. However, some additional functions are difficult to express in a modular way.

Our case study shows two of these functions: shortcuts, and additional modes. A shortcut is the possibility, in some given modes, to use a single button to activate a function that would otherwise need a long sequence of buttons. Adding shortcuts modifies the interface, but not the internal components.

Furthermore, interfaces for similar devices often use the same components for large parts of their functionalities. We show that aspects can be used to compose and configure components so that the same components can be used for different devices.

4.2   Suunto[1] Watches

As a case study, we implement the interface components of two complex wristwatches, the Altimax[1] and the Vector[1] models by Suunto[1]. Both share the

---

[1] Suunto, Altimax and Vector are Trademarks of Suunto Oy.

same casing, display, and a large set of their functionalities: time, altimeter and barometer functions are nearly equal in both models, but the Vector also has an integrated compass. Carefully following the documentation, we propose Argos components and aspects to describe the interfaces of the two watches.

The Base Program. In both watches, each main functionality is represented by a main mode, which in turn has several submodes, that offer numerous functionalities. The interfaces of both watches contain four buttons, the `Mode`, the `Select`, the `Plus`, and the `Minus` button. The `Mode` button circles between the main modes, or, in a submode, returns to the main mode. The `Select` button selects a submode, and the `Plus` and `Minus` buttons modify current values. All main modes and many submodes have an associated configuration mode, where settings for the mode can be modified. A configuration mode can be reached by holding the select button pressed for two seconds in the corresponding mode.

Figure 7 shows the implementation of the interface component for the modes both wristwatches have in common. The input `s2s` occurs when the `Select` button is pressed for two seconds. This part of the interface is called the *base program*. Figure 7 is not complete: most of the states arc further refined, and only some of the outputs (i.e. the commands to the functional component) are shown, namely `Time-Mode`, `Bari-Mode`, `Alti-Mode` and `mainMode`. The signal `toMainMode` is encapsulated: the submodes can emit it to force a return to their main mode. To save space, the encapsulation is not included in Figure 7.

The Fast Cumulative Shortcut. The altimeter in the watches can record vertical movements in so called *logbooks*, so that the user can evaluate his performance after a hike. A logbook records the distances the user vertically ascends and descends from the moment it is started until it is stopped, and the number of runs accomplished in this period, i.e. the vertical movements of at least 50 meters. However, a logbook can only be read after recording stopped, and it is quite complicated to display the logbook (one has to go to the third submode of the altimeter main mode). Therefore, the Altimax model has the *fast cumulative shortcut*: in any main mode, when the `Minus` button is pressed, some information from the current logbook is displayed. First the total vertical ascend rate is shown until the `Minus` button is pressed, then the total vertical descend rate and then the number of runs, before the watch returns to the main mode in which it was.

The fast cumulative mode is a typical shortcut and is implemented with an aspect. The pointcut `main-modes-PC` in Figure 8 (a) chooses transitions which have a main mode of the base program as source state and `minus` as input part of the label. Visiting the current logbook is done in several steps: it first displays the ascend rate (output `showAsc`), then the descend rate (`showDesc`), and then the number of runs (`showNbRuns`). Therefore, the aspect outputs first `showAsc` and then inserts the automaton `visit-logbook`, shown in Figure 8(b). As target state, we choose an empty trace from the current state, so that the program continues in the main mode in which it was when the aspect was activated. The aspect for the fast cumulative shortcut is fully specified by `Fast-Cumulative` = (`main-modes-PC`, {`showAsc`}, *toCurrent*, ϵ, `visit-logbook`).

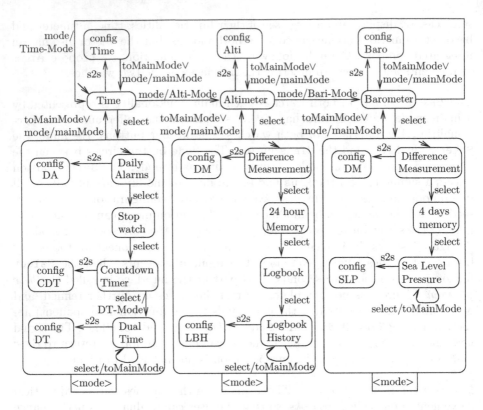

Fig. 7. The base-program component. Its interface is: inputs = {Mode, Select, plus, minus, s2s}, outputs = {Time-Mode, Bari-Mode, Alti-Mode, mainMode}, toMain-Mode is encapsulated.

The Altimax Model. The controller of the Altimax watch is the base program (Figure 7) with the fast cumulative aspect woven to it: Altimax = base-program◁ Fast-Cumulative.

The Compass Mode. We program a controller for the Vector wristwatch by applying three aspects to the base program, which are explained in the sequel. The Vector has a fourth main mode, the compass mode. We add it to the base program with an aspect. The transition going from the Barometer main mode to the Time main mode is the sole join point transition (chosen by the pointcut baro-mode-PC in Figure 9 (a)). The only advice output is Comp-Mode which displays the compass. The aspect inserts the automaton Compass (see Figure 9 (b)), which contains the interface for the compass. After leaving the compass mode, the interface goes back to the Time main mode, thus the target state is set to the initial state: this is a *toInit* advice with σ being the empty trace ϵ. The resulting aspect is thus Compass-Mode = (baro-mode-PC, {Comp-Mode}, *toCurrent*, ϵ, Compass).

The Compass Shortcut. When the Minus button is pressed in a main mode, the Vector does not show information from the current logbook, but goes directly to

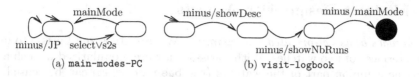

(a) `main-modes-PC`   (b) `visit-logbook`

Fig. 8. Pointcut (a) and inserted automaton (b) for the Fast-Cumulative aspect

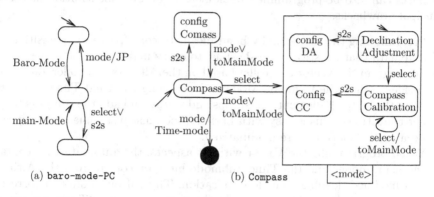

(a) `baro-mode-PC`   (b) `Compass`

Fig. 9. Pointcut (a) and inserted automaton (b) for the Compass-mode aspect

the compass mode. This is useful when the user is hiking cross-country and wants to check regularly the bearing of the compass. Thus, the Vector does not contain the fast-cumulative aspect, but an aspect that adds advice transitions from the main modes to the compass main mode: Fast-Compass = (main-modes-PC, {Comp-Mode}, *toInit*, mode.mode.mode.mode). Note that this aspect must be applied after the Compass-Mode aspect, because it uses the compass mode. Indeed, after the compass mode has been added, it can be reached by pressing four times the Mode button from the initial state. The trace mode.mode.mode.mode ends in state Compass; it is the target state of the advice transitions.

No Dual Time Submode. As a last difference with the Altimax, the Vector lacks the Dual Time submode (the fourth submode of the Time main mode of the base program in Figure 7), which allows the user to simultaneously view the time in two different time zones. We cut it out of the base program with an aspect. We choose as join points all transitions which emit DT-Mode, the signal that tells the underlying component to display the information related to the Dual Time mode. The corresponding pointcut, Countdown-PC, consists of a single state with a loop transition with label DT-Mode/JP. Instead of going to the Dual Time mode, the Vector goes to the Time main mode, thus the target state is defined by the empty trace. The aspect is thus defined by No-Dual-Time = (Countdown-PC, {Time-Mode}, *toInit*, ϵ).

The Vector Model. The controller for the Vector can thus be built by weaving the three aspects into the base program: Vector = base-program ◁ Compass-Mode ◁ Fast-Compass ◁ No-Dual-Time.

5 Modular Design with Aspects

Advantages of aspect-oriented programming. We use Argos and Larissa to model the interfaces of two watches. With Larissa, they are modularized in such a way that the common part of the watches (the `base-program`) can be reused, and the behavior that is specific to a single watch can be added with aspects. The interfaces can also be programmed without aspects, but this solution has three principal drawbacks:

1) Programming the shortcuts by hand means to copy/paste the transitions or automata that constitute the shortcut to every main mode.
2) To program the Vector controller based on the Altimax controller, one must, besides adding the Compass Mode and removing the Dual Time Mode, remove the logbook shortcut transitions and states, and add the compass shortcut transitions. This is easy with Larissa (one must just replace the aspect), because the shortcuts are modularized.
3) When programming the Vector without aspects, the automata that contain the main modes and the Time Submode must be copied from the Altimax and modified, leading to code duplication. Thus, if one wants to correct a bug or change something in one of these, the same modification must be applied twice.

Note that the design of aspects itself is modular: the `Fast-Cumulative` aspect has the pointcut program `main-modes-PC` (see Figure 8(a)) which has been reused for the pointcut of the `Fast-Compass` aspect.

Aspects as components. In our setting, we want to consider aspects as normal components. We claim that to be able to do so, the two following properties should hold: *1) aspect weaving should behave as an ordinary composition operator, so as to be freely mixable with ordinary components; 2) the aspect definition should allow component substitutability.* Larissa obeys these properties:

1) The aspect weaving operator ◁ is an ordinary operator of the language. Indeed, weaving an Argos program and an aspect results in another Argos program. This allows the construction of arbitrary expressions made of Argos operators, aspects and programs. For instance, the `Vector` model is obtained by weaving several aspects. This means that the `Compass-Mode` aspect is woven into the `base-program`, producing an Argos program into which the `Fast-Compass` aspect is woven, etc.
2) The aspect definition only refers to the interface of the program it has to be woven into. Thus, we can replace a component by another one with the same interface, and the aspect can still be applied. Moreover, the semantics of the weaving does not depend on the way the program is implemented (e.g. local variables or internal names like state names), but only on its semantics. Thus, when we replace a component with an semantically equal one, we obtain a semantically equivalent program. For instance, if the `base-program` is replaced by a semantically equivalent, but more efficient one, the `Altimax`

and the `Vector` are obtained by replacing the base program by the new one, with the guarantee that they execute as before.

6   Related Work

Concerning automata-based language, the closest work is an extension of Statecharts [12]. Aspects are modeled as normal Statecharts, and a transition in an aspect is taken before or after a certain transition in the base program. This approach does not have the semantical properties we are looking for, but has the advantage of being closer to AspectJ.

As for the integration of aspects and components, interesting approaches have been proposed, e.g. in the ACP4IS workshop. Most approaches, e.g. [4,18], use aspects as a tool in component-based frameworks, for instance for adapting components to a given context of use. Others, e.g. [15], consider aspects as components which are woven into the components they are assembled with. This is close to our setting, in which aspects are ordinary pieces of programs.

The third direction to which our work relates is the use of AOP to build man-machine interfaces, but we found very few papers there. [17] uses aspect-oriented programming to reduce the constraints imposed by the model-view-controller paradigm, which is central in many man-machine interfaces.

7   Conclusion

With a case-study on the design of small electronic device interfaces, we illustrated the use of the aspect-oriented extension of an automaton-based language for reactive systems. This case-study mainly serves for exploring the idea that aspects should be freely mixed with other kinds of components, and that weaving is a particular assembling mechanism. The first step in this direction is to have a clean and formal semantics of aspects. Aspects that do not refer explicitly to the internals of programs are more likely to be the basis for the definition of *aspect components*.

We think that our automaton-based language can easily be used as the core of a component-based approach for reactive systems, since its programs have well-defined interfaces, and it contains clean notions of encapsulation (information hiding), composition between programs, and substitutability of component behaviors. Furthermore, a number of approaches have been proposed to specify components with *contracts*. A contract is a kind of assume-guarantee predicate that characterizes the behavior of a component. The main point we will study in the near future relates to the specification of contracts, in the idea of [13], for aspect components. This rises many questions, such as: how do we define the behavior of an aspect, independently of the program it is woven with? Can we define a semantic equivalence between aspects, in such a way that aspects are substitutable, as usual components are? We need to clarify those notions before being able to introduce contracts for aspects and to fully consider aspects as components in our framework.

References

1. K. Altisen, F. Maraninchi, and D. Stauch. Aspect-oriented programming for reactive systems: Larissa, a proposal in the synchronous framework. *Sci. Comput. Programming, Special Issue on Foundations of Aspect-Oriented Programming*, 2006. To appear.
2. Y. Coady and G. Kiczales. Back to the future: A retroactive study of aspect evolution in operating system code. In *AOSD'03*, pages 50–59, 2003.
3. A. Colyer and A. Clement. Large-scale AOSD for middleware. In *AOSD'04*, pages 56–65, 2004.
4. P.-C. David and T. Ledoux. An approach for developing self-adapting fractal components. In *5th International Symposium on Software Composition*, Vienna, Austria, Mar. 2006.
5. N. Halbwachs. *Synchronous programming of reactive systems*. Kluwer Academic Pub., 1993.
6. N. Halbwachs, F. Lagnier, and C. Ratel. Programming and verifying critical systems by means of the synchronous data-flow programming language LUSTRE. *IEEE Trans. Softw. Eng., Special Issue on the Specification and Analysis of Real-Time Systems*, Sept. 1992.
7. N. Halbwachs, F. Lagnier, and P. Raymond. Synchronous observers and the verification of reactive systems. In M. Nivat, C. Rattray, T. Rus, and G. Scollo, editors, *3rd Int. Conf. on Algebraic Methodology and Software Technology, AMAST'93*, June 1993.
8. D. Harel. Statecharts: A visual formalism for complex systems. *Sci. Comput. Programming*, 8(3):231–274, June 1987.
9. G. Kiczales, E. Hilsdale, J. Hugunin, M. Kersten, J. Palm, and W. G. Griswold. An overview of AspectJ. *LNCS*, 2072:327–353, 2001.
10. L. Lamport. Proving the correctness of multiprocess programs. *IEEE Trans. Softw. Eng.*, SE-3(2):125–143, 1977.
11. Compiler for Larissa. http://www-verimag.imag.fr/~stauch/ArgosCompiler/.
12. M. Mahoney, A. Bader, T. Elrad, and O. Aldawud. Using aspects to abstract and modularize statecharts. In *5th Aspect-Oriented Modeling Workshop*, 2004.
13. F. Maraninchi and L. Morel. Logical-time contracts for the development of reactive embedded software. In *30th Euromicro Conference, Component-Based Software Engineering Track (ECBSE)*, Rennes, France, Sept. 2004.
14. F. Maraninchi and Y. Rémond. Argos: an automaton-based synchronous language. *Computer Languages*, 27(1/3):61–92, 2001.
15. N. Pessemier, L. Seinturier, T. Coupaye, and L. Duchien. A model for developing component-based and aspect-oriented systems. In *5th International Symposium on Software Composition*, Vienna, Austria, Mar. 2006.
16. D. Stauch, K. Altisen, and F. Maraninchi. Interference of Larissa aspects. In *Workshop on the Foundations of Aspect-Oriented Languages (FOAL)*, 2006.
17. M. Veit and S. Herrmann. Model-view-controller and object teams: A perfect match of paradigms. In M. Akşit, editor, *AOSD'03*, pages 140–149, 2003.
18. E. Wohlstadter, S. Tai, and P. Devanbu. Two party aspect agreement using a COTS solver. In *Proceedings of the Fourth AOSD Workshop on Aspects, Components, and Patterns for Infrastructure Software*, Mar. 2005.

On the Integration of Classboxes into C#

Markus Lumpe[1] and Jean-Guy Schneider[2]

[1] Department of Computer Science
Iowa State University
Ames, IA 50011, USA
lumpe@cs.iastate.edu
[2] Faculty of Information & Communication Technologies
Swinburne University of Technology
P.O. Box 218
Hawthorn, VIC 3122, Australia
jschneider@swin.edu.au

Abstract. Classboxes are a new module system for object-oriented languages defining a packaging and scoping mechanism for controlling the visibility of isolated extensions to portions of class-based systems. Unlike object-oriented specialization, the class extension mechanisms supported by classboxes preserve the identity of extended classes and, therefore, all clients of extended classes can benefit from the applied extensions. In this paper, we present a language design and a corresponding implementation strategy for classboxes in C#. A particular challenge in incorporating classboxes into C# is to preserve the identity of extended classes as the .NET framework represents classes as metadata type declarations and access to classes by static links into metadata of the host assembly. However, the local refinement of an imported class results in a new metadata type declaration. In order to guarantee the identity of extended classes, new metadata type declarations have to be incorporated into the original metadata of imported classes. But this "re-wiring" has to occur in a manner that is consistent with the Common Language Infrastructure (CLI).

1 Introduction

Today, many real-world software systems are built using mainstream object-oriented techniques and languages. However, when using object-oriented technology, one often faces an *extensibility problem* that arises from the fact that mainstream object-oriented languages provide only limited support for modular addition of both *horizontal* and *vertical* extensions to classes. While in general it is always possible to add (vertically) new classes to a system, existing classes can only be extended with new, orthogonal behaviour (horizontally) in an often non-object-oriented style, that is, by breaking the object-oriented encapsulation property (e.g., the Visitor pattern [11]). Such extensions are awkward at best, and error-prone at worst. Furthermore, the inheritance relationships in mainstream object-oriented languages are not powerful enough to capture many useful forms of incremental modifications [6, 17, 5, 3].

To address this problem, several approaches have emerged that focus on tangible techniques for evolving object-oriented software systems that do not rely on standard

W. Löwe and M. Südholt (Eds.): SC 2006, LNCS 4089, pp. 307–322, 2006.

inheritance mechanisms [7, 12, 17, 5, 15, 1]. Of special interest is the concept of *classboxes* proposed by Bergel et al. [5], a new *module system* for object-oriented languages that defines a packaging and scoping mechanism for controlling the visibility of isolated extensions to portions of class-based systems. Classboxes define *explicitly named scopes* within which (i) classes, methods, and variables are defined, (ii) classes can be extended using the "traditional" operation of subclassing, and (iii) classes can be *imported* from other classboxes. More importantly, however, classboxes also support *local refinement* of imported classes by adding and/or modifying their features, without affecting the originating classbox. As such, classboxes offer a promising approach, as they provide support for extending existing classes both vertically and horizontally.

Classboxes have been implemented for both the Smalltalk [5] and the Java environments [4]. The Smalltalk implementations of classboxes mainly rely on a modified, "classbox-aware" virtual machine for dynamic class and method lookup and a reification of the method call stack, respectively. Central to the modified virtual machine is a graph search algorithm that implements the local rebinding of methods at runtime, an approach that cannot be easily mapped to languages who's runtime environment does not offer the same amount of flexibility. Classbox/J [4], on the other hand, is a prototype classbox implementation for Java that is based on preprocessor directives and reification of the method call stack. It uses an implementation scheme that may reveal extensions of classes to clients, which should not be able to see them (i.e., new class members are inserted into the original class without any additional visibility control [4, §6.1]).

But is it possible, to incorporate classboxes into an industrial-strength programming language without relying on a "classbox-aware" virtual machine or a preprocessor, respectively? To answer this questions, we present a backward-compatible implementation strategy for classboxes in C# in this work. Our implementation shows that the metadata concept of the Common Language Infrastructure (CLI) [14] plays a crucial role in integrating class extensions seamlessly into the C# language without the need to modify the underlying runtime infrastructure. Furthermore, to facilitate code reuse and to assist in building families of classes that are subject to the same change, we introduce the notion of *reusable class extensions* to the classbox concept. Our results not only demonstrate the expressive power of classboxes in an industrial-strength programming language such as C#, but also illustrate how reusable class extensions substantially improve the specification of incremental modifications in classboxes.

The rest of this paper is organized as follows: in Section 2, we present an example to illustrate the concept of classboxes, followed by our model and implementation of classboxes in C# in Section 3. We conclude this paper in Section 4 with a summary of the presented work and outline future work in this area.

2   Applying Classboxes

In order to illustrate the concept of classboxes and the associated expressive power, consider the example given below that motivates the need to restrict the impact of a modified class.

A class Point implements the behaviour of two-dimensional points. It contains two private instance variables x and y, two public properties X and Y to get/set the corresponding point coordinates, a public method MoveBy to move a point by a given offset (dx,dy), and a public method MoveByXY that doubles the values of the x and y coordinates by invoking MoveBy (using dynamic method lookup). The class BoundedPoint is a direct specialization of Point that ensures that the y coordinate of an instance never exceeds a given upper bound yBound. This bound is a constant in BoundedPoint, but this behaviour can be altered by overriding the property Bound, as show below.

In order to define a non-constant bound, we can specialize the class BoundedPoint by overriding the property Bound to return X. That is, the resulting class LinearBoundedPoint implements a behaviour guaranteeing that the value of the y coordinate is always smaller than the value of the x coordinate. As this specialization does not affect either the class Point nor the class BoundedPoint, any clients of these two classes will not be affected.

If we want to add color to our point-class hierarchy (i.e., adding a private instance variable color and a corresponding property Color to all classes), we can simply add the corresponding features to the class Point. As the additional behaviour is *orthogonal* to the existing behaviour, none of the clients of any of the point classes will be affected by this modification.

However, if we suddenly need to alter the behaviour of bounded points (i.e., restricting the x coordinate instead of the y coordinate), we cannot simply modify the class BoundedPoint, as such a modification would affect all clients of BoundedPoint and the (implicit) contract between BoundedPoint and LinearBoundedPoint would be broken. Hence, "traditional" subclassing fails to provide us with the required expressive power. What we need is an approach where we can *restrict* the modified behaviour of bounded points to well-encapsulated parts of our application, leaving all existing clients unaffected by this modification.

Classboxes provide us with a solution to this problem, as they provide a framework in which we can control both the scope and the impact of change [5,4,13]. In particular, classboxes exhibit the following main characteristics [5]:

- A classbox is an explicitly named unit of scoping in which classes (and their associated members) are defined. A class belongs to the classbox it is first *defined*, but it can be made visible to other classboxes by either *importing* or *extending* it.
- Any extensions to a class are only visible to the classbox in which they occur first and any classboxes that either explicitly or implicitly import the extended class. Hence, overriding a particular method of a class in a given classbox will have no effect in the originating classbox.
- Although class extensions are only locally visible, their embodied refinements extend to all collaborating classes within a given classbox, in particular to any subclasses that are either explicitly imported, extended, or implicitly imported.

In order to illustrate how classboxes address the problems associated with implementing the point class hierarchy illustrated above, consider the four classboxes depicted in Figure 1, namely *OriginalCB*, *LinearCB*, *ColorCB*, and *TraceCB*, respectively.

The classbox *OriginalCB* contains the class Point as well as the class BoundedPoint as a direct specialization of Point. The classbox *LinearCB* introduces the class

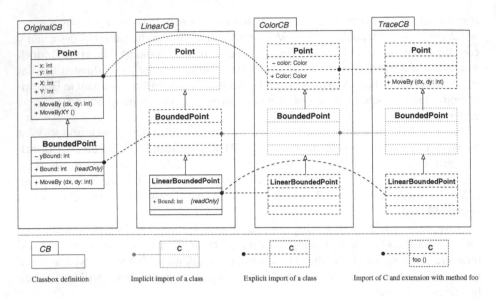

Fig. 1. Sample classboxes

LinearBoundedPoint, which, in order to define a non-constant bound, specializes BoundedPoint by overriding the property Bound to return X. LinearBoundedPoint is defined as a subclass of BoundedPoint *imported* into *LinearCB* from *OriginalCB*. As a consequence, the class Point is *implicitly* imported also, making it visible as the direct superclass of BoundedPoint, but not accessible to clients of the classbox *LinearCB*.

The classbox *ColorCB extends* the class Point from *OriginalCB* by adding a private instance variable color and a corresponding property Color. As a consequence, all instances of Point in *ColorCB* as well as the instances of any of its subclasses posses this additional behaviour. Therefore, the class LinearBoundedPoint *imported* from *LinearCB* also possesses the color feature, but all classes in *OriginalCB* and *LinearCB* remain unaffected by this alteration. The reader should note that the explicit import of LinearBoundedPoint from *LinearCB* also triggers the implicit import of BoundedPoint from *LinearCB*.

Finally, the classbox *TraceCB* defines an extended version of the class Point from *ColorCB* by overriding the method MoveBy to add a tracing facility (i.e., each invocation of MoveBy is monitored by a console message).

3   Classboxes in C#

In previous work on formalizing classboxes [13], we have identified four unique classbox operations, namely (i) *import* of classes, (ii) introduction of *subclasses*, (iii) *refinement* of classes, and (iv) *inclusion* of new behaviour. The latter two operations are deduced from the original extend operator [5] by revising the notion of extending classes. That is, the refinement operator should exhibit a behaviour similar to C#'s new modifier [8, §17.2.2], which can be used to hide any super-class method by declaring a new method with the same signature in a subclass, whereas the inclusion operator roughly corresponds to *mixin application* [6] in which the extended class takes the role of an *abstract subclass*.

In addition, both *refinement* and *inclusion* are modeled in a way that enforces a separation of the incremental modification defined by these operations from the underlying extension mechanism [13]. As a result, incremental modifications become reusable software artifacts. Within a classbox, this allows for an approach in which we can compose these software artifacts with multiple imported classes simultaneously.

In the following, we outline the design and implementation of classboxes in C#. As a proof-of-concept, we have implemented our classbox model in standard C# by means of source code transformations, refactoring [16], and locally updating metadata type declarations. While our ultimate goal is to define an approach in which class extensions can be compiled into existing classes without source code access, using refactoring has produced valuable insights into the compilation process.

3.1 Classboxes as C# Namespaces

In our model, classboxes are represented by C# *namespaces*. A namespace in C# is a compile-time construct that defines a scope to organize source code and *globally-unique* types [8]. All namespaces have implicitly public access. Moreover, namespaces are open-ended and can be divided into separate compilation units, which then all contribute to the same declaration space [8, §16.2]. However, once a type has been defined, it can only be extended by means of "traditional" subclassing, a technique that does not suffice to express the incremental modifications used, for example, in the classboxes *ColorCB* and *TraceCB*, respectively. Therefore, we refine the notion of namespace to be an *open* scoping mechanism that enables the local redefinition of type declarations. However, to retain complete backward compatibility with the extant C# language, a corresponding compilation scheme for our extended C# language has to target the standard CLI.

At the technical level, C# is compliant with the *Common Language Infrastructure* (CLI), a specification that provides a basis for a *virtual execution system* insulating programs from the underlying operating system [14]. In CLI, new types are introduced via **read-only** metadata type declarations.[1] Moreover, metadata contains information to locate and load classes, lay out instances in memory, resolve method invocations, and enforce security constraints. Consider, for example, the classbox *OriginalCB*: it defines two types Point and BoundedPoint, respectively, both defined within the namespace OriginalCB. The two types are represented by TypeDef metadata tokens as shown in Figure 2. TypeDef tokens encode the name of a type, its declaration namespace, the super type (index into a TypeDef or TypeRef table), and a list of the type's members. In addition, OriginalCB's metadata contains a TypeRef token that encodes an index into the TypeDef table of the assembly defining System.Object. This token is required, since Point's super type is System.Object, the root of every reference type in C#.

A particularly difficult problem in representing classboxes in the .NET framework is induced by *fully qualified class names*, as they are encoded as pointers into *metadata*

---

[1] The reader should note that without loss of generality, we will only consider TypeDef and TypeRef tokens in this work. These tokens normally utilize other metadata tokens to correctly establish references to the defining assemblies.

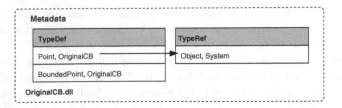

Fig. 2. *OriginalCB*'s metadata

associated with every assembly and, therefore, hard-wire classes with their corresponding direct parent-classes. However, the key provision for providing support for classboxes in C# is that we need to be able to locally *update* metadata type declarations. This requirement arises from the fact that the local refinement of an imported class results in a new metadata type declaration. To restore the identity of extended classes, this new metadata type declaration needs to be incorporated into the original metadata of imported classes.

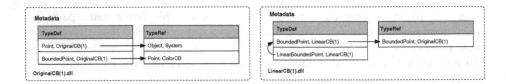

Fig. 3. Updated metadata of *OriginalCB(1).dll* and *LinearCB(1).dll*

Consider again the classbox *ColorCB* that defines an extended version of the class **Point** imported from *OriginalCB*. Compiling this code yields a new assembly, called `ColorCB.dll`, that contains the classes **Person** and **LinearBoundedPoint** (explicitly imported from *LinearCB*) and their corresponding metadata (c.f., Figure 4). However, the inheritance chain between both classes and the implicitly imported class **BoundedPoint** is not preserved.

In order to link the extended class **Point** with the implicitly imported class **BoundedPoint** in *ColorCB*, we need to *update* **BoundedPoint**'s metadata type declaration in the assemblies of both *OriginalCB* and *LinearCB*, respectively. More precisely, we need to create new versions (marked (1)) of their corresponding assemblies, in which the super-class type declaration of **BoundedPoint** refers to **ColorCB.Point** (see Figure 3). To add **ColorCB.Point** in *OriginalCB* we need to extend the **TypeRef** table with a new token for **ColorCB.Point** and rewire **BoundedPoint**'s super type index to the newly added token. In *LinearCB*, we need to "patch" the original **Point** TypeRef token in order to connect it to **ColorCB.Point**. Adding a new token does not work, since this would break the link between **Point**'s **TypeRef** token and its applications in the member lists of **BoundedPoint**. This process results in a *physical* structure consisting of three assemblies for the *logical* structure defined by the classbox *ColorCB*.

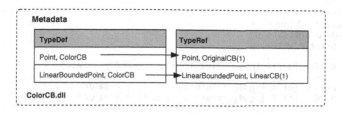

Fig. 4. Metadata of *ColorCB.dll*

Classes in .NET assemblies are represented as metadata type tokens and references to classes are encoded as pointers to these metadata type tokens. To change the link structure in metadata, we need to create new assemblies, since .NET assemblies do not allow these links to be changed dynamically. Altering the metadata structure, as shown in Figure 3, guarantees that the local refinement of the imported class Point in classbox *ColorCB* (the resulting metadata is shown in Figure 4) does not impact the originating classbox *OriginalCB* and its clients.

This approach works for all *managed* assemblies [14]. Unfortunately, some namespaces in the .NET framework are only available in *native* code (e.g., the System namespace) and classes defined in those namespaces cannot be extended due to the lack of metadata.

3.2 Import and Subclassing

Both, import and subclassing do no require any language changes. The available language abstractions suffice to specify these operations. However, the import operation may require a local update of the metadata type declaration associated with an imported class, as outlined in Section 3.1.

Consider the classbox *OriginalCB* defining the classes Point and BoundedPoint, which are in an inheritance relationship. The corresponding implementation of *OriginalCB* is shown in Listing 1. Compiling *OriginalCB* yields a dynamic link library (DLL) or *assembly* called OriginalCB.dll. This library defines two public types OriginalCB.Point and OriginalCB.BoundedPoint, both recorded as type declarations in *OriginalCB*'s metadata.

The classbox *LinearCB* can be defined similarly in standard C#, as shown in Listing 2. *LinearCB* explicitly imports BoundedPoint from *OriginalCB*. We use the *alias* form of the using directive to specify class imports [8, §16.4.1]. An alias for a type is a user-defined name that is only available within the namespace body introducing it. However, to enable a local rebinding of features of explicitly imported classes, we create an "empty" subclass with the same name for each imported class in the importing classbox. This empty subclass does not define any new functionality, but it enables clients of the importing classbox to use the explicitly imported class as it had been defined in the importing classbox. This technique corresponds to the approach proposed by Bergel et al. [5], in which importing a class into a classbox is the same as extending this class with an empty set of methods. The newly created subclass for an imported

```
namespace OriginalCB {
  public class Point {
    private int x, y;

    public Point( int ix, int iy ) { x = ix; y = iy; }

    public int X { get{ return x; } set{ x = value; } }
    public int Y { get{ return y; } set{ y = value; } }

    public virtual void MoveBy( int dx, int dy ) { X += dx; Y +=dy; }
    public virtual void MoveByXY() { this.MoveBy( X, Y ); }
  }

  public class BoundedPoint : Point {
    private int yBound;

    public BoundedPoint( int ix, int iy, int ibound ) :
      base( ix, iy ) { yBound = ibound; }

    public virtual int Bound { get{ return yBound; }}

    public override void MoveBy( int dx, int dy )
      { if ( Y + dy < Bound ) base.MoveBy( dx, dy ); }
  }
}
```

Listing 1. The namespace OriginalCB

class is linked to its original image by a type reference (i.e., a TypeRef metadata token) in the importing classbox (c.f. Figure 4). Therefore, clients of the classbox *LinearCB* can access the imported class BoundedPoint as it had been originally defined in classbox *LinearCB*, even though BoundedPoint's behaviour is actually being defined by the class OriginalCB.BoundedPoint hosted by OriginalCB.dll.

```
namespace LinearCB {
  using BoundedPoint = OriginalCB.BoundedPoint;

  public class LinearBoundedPoint : BoundedPoint {
    public LinearBoundedPoint( int ix, int iy, int ibound ) :
      base ( ix, iy, ibound ) { }

    public override int Bound { get{ return X; } }
  }
}
```

Listing 2. The namespace LinearCB

In order to compile *LinearCB*, we need to add OriginalCB.dll as a *reference* to look up the metadata associated with the class OriginalCB.BoundedPoint. The result is the assembly LinearCB.dll that defines one public type LinearCB.LinearBoundedPoint. The reader should note, however, that due to the implicit import of OriginalCB.Point and the explicit import of OriginalCB.BoundedPoint, clients must have access to both OriginalCB.dll and LinearCB.dll in order to use the classbox *LinearCB*.

3.3   Reusable Class Extensions

The original classbox concept defines the extension of classes as an operation that works like import, except that the imported class is instantaneously altered in order to add and/or change its features [5]. More precisely, a particular local refinement is exclusively associated with the imported class. Thus, if we want to apply the same refinement to another class, then we need to *duplicate* its corresponding specification. However, it is more desirable to separate the local refinement from the import of classes to facilitate code reuse and to assist in structuring the specification of incremental modifications to classes within a classbox [17, 18].

Therefore, we propose the introduction of a new linguistic facility, called *explicit class extension*, that is based on the concept of *mixins* [6]. However, while mixins are *class-to-class functions* [10], we define explicit class extensions as *open mixins*, which are parameterized over a "composition" mechanism. The purpose of the composition mechanism is to determine how a given extension is to be merged in an imported class. In this work, we shall consider two composition mechanisms: *refinement* and *inclusion* [13]. The syntax for *extension-declarations* is given below:

```
extension-declaration:
      extension identifier class-body ;opt
```

An *extension-declaration* consists of the keyword **extension**, an *identifier* that names the extension, a *class-body* [8, §17.1.3], followed by an optional semicolon.

At present, extensions are a pure mechanism to create incremental modifications. Thus, extensions can only be type-checked after they have been applied to a class and this class is *linearized* (or "flattened") [6, 18]. We plan, however, to add *required* interfaces [18, 15] to extensions in future work to address this shortcoming. In this work, we shall assume that extensions are always well-typed.

The linearization process involves two steps: (i) *closing* the extensions using a corresponding extension composition mechanism, and (ii) *applying* the closed extensions to the imported class. Assume, for example, the extensions Δ_1 and Δ_2, the extension composition mechanisms W_1 and W_2, and the imported class C. Then the extended imported class C' is defined as

$$C' = \Delta_2(W_2) \oplus (\Delta_1(W_1) \oplus C)$$

where $\oplus$ is a non-commutative *class-to-class* mixin composition operator [6], and both $\Delta_1(W_1)$ and $\Delta_2(W_2)$ denote extensions closed by their corresponding extension composition mechanism W_1 and W_2, respectively. However, if conflicts arise due to composing an imported class with extensions that provide identical named members, these conflicts have to be resolved manually.

The classboxes *ColorCB* and *TraceCB* each import the class Point and define an extension to it. *ColorCB* defines the extension Color, as shown in Listing 3. This extension defines a Color property and an associated private instance variable color. In order to define the Color extension, we also need to import the namespace System.Drawing that provides the definition for the type Color. In addition, the reader should note that every public member in an extension is virtual by default. However, it is the extension composition mechanism that determines the actual required modifier (e.g., new in case of refinement, and override in case of inclusion).

```
using System.Drawing;

extension Color
{
    private Color color;

    public Color Color { get{ return color; } set{ color = value; } }
}
```

Listing 3. The extension Color

Similarly, *TraceCB* defines the extension TraceMoveBy, which is shown in Listing 4. This extension captures a specialization of the method MoveBy that (i) prints a message to the console and (ii) transfers the control to the *original* base method MoveBy. Hence, the extension TraceMoveBy requires that the class it is eventually applied to defines at least a public virtual method MoveBy. This property is verified when TraceMoveBy is composed with a given imported class.

```
extension TraceMoveBy
{
    public void MoveBy( int dx, int dy )
        { Console.WriteLine( "MoveBy: {0}, {1}", new object[] { dx, dy } );
          base.MoveBy( dx, dy ); }
}
```

Listing 4. The extension TraceMoveBy

3.4   Refinement and Inclusion

Refinement and *inclusion* both consist of three elements: (i) an imported class, (ii) a corresponding extension composition mechanism, and (iii) some explicit class extensions. To facilitate the specification of the corresponding classbox operations, we propose a linguistic facility that combines these elements in a single language construct – the *using-extension-directive*. The syntax for the *using-extension-directive* is given below:

```
using-extension-directive:
    using identifier = type-name extension-application

extension-application:
    includes_opt refinements_opt

includes:
    include type-list ;

refinements:
    append type-list ;
```

The *using-extension-directive* introduces an identifier that serves as an alias for a type within the immediately enclosing namespace body. The *using-extension-directive* works like the *using-alias-directive* [8, §16.4.1], except that a non-empty *extension-application* specification is required. The *extension-application* may contain *includes*, *refinements*, or both.[2] *Includes* and *refinements* are processed in the order they are specified. However, the linearization process requires that all members occurring in the extensions have pairwise distinct names.

```
namespace ColorCB {
  using System.Drawing;
  using Point = Original.Point append Color;
  using LinearBoundedPoint = LinearCB.LinearBoundedPoint;

  extension Color
  {
    private Color color;

    public Color Color { get{ return color; } set{ color = value; } }
  }
}
```

Listing 5. The classbox ColorCB

To illustrate the use of the *using-extension-directive*, consider the implementation of the classbox *ColorCB*, as shown in Listing 5. *ColorCB* explicitly imports the classes Point and LinearBoundedPoint. Furthermore, it defines the extension Color, which is applied to the imported class Point with the specification

using Point = Original.Point **append** Color;

where **append** Color defines a *refinement* of the class Point.

The *refinement* operation defines an information hiding protocol that, when applied to a concrete class, renders the features of the extensions invisible to the class' behaviour. Hence, *refinement* yields a membrane for a class that permits calls originating from extensions, but prevents the class' behaviour to see the extensions.

To implement this behaviour, we mark all public members defined by a *refinement* extension with the new modifier [8, §17.2.2] to shield them from the imported class. Secondly, the resulting specifications are then used to construct a subclass of the imported class. When using subclassing to incorporate extensions into a class, former clients generally have to be modified as well in order to benefit from the refinements [9]. However, by "re-wiring" the metadata type declarations, as illustrated below, this problem disappears, because the identity of imported classes is restored. To illustrate this process, consider Listing 6, which shows the corresponding source code of the class Point in *ColorCB*.

---

[2] *Type-list* is like the base class specification [8, §17.1.2], except that the elements are extension type names. We follow the scheme applied in the Mono compiler in which *type-list* is used to denote a list of both class and interface type names.

```
// Color(append) ⊕ Original.Point
public class Point : OriginalCB.Point {
  private Color color;

  public new virtual Color Color { get{ return color; } set{ color=value; } }

  // required constructor(s)
  public Point( int ix, int iy ) : base( ix, iy ) { }
}
```

Listing 6. Transformation of class ColorCB.Point

The class Point in *ColorCB* behaves like Original.Point, except that all clients of class ColorCB.Point now have access to the property Color. Moreover, since Color is declared new in *ColorCB*, existing clients of Original.Point remain unaffected by this change. However, to compile *ColorCB*, we need to *rewire* the metadata inheritance chain of all implicitly or explicitly imported classes in *ColorCB*. In particular, we need to link LinearCB.BoundedPoint with ColorCB.Point and ColorCB.LinearBounded-Point with the updated LinearCB.BoundedPoint (see Figure 3). Therefore, we have to create new versions of OriginalCB.dll and LinearCB.dll, say OriginalCB(1).dll and LinearCB(1).dll, respectively, in which the metadata type definition for class Point refers to ColorCB.Point. Using OriginalCB(1).dll and LinearCB(1).dll as references, we build ColorCB.dll that implements the desired functionality of the classbox *ColorCB*.

```
namespace ColorCBX {
  using System.Drawing;

  public class Point : OriginalCB.Point {
    private Color color;

    public new virtual Color Color
                     { get { return color; } set { color = value; } }

    public Point( int ix, int iy ) : base( ix, iy ) { }
  }

  public class BoundedPoint : Point
  { /* Point members */ }

  public class LinearBoundedPoint : BoundedPoint
  { /* BoundedPoint members */ }
}
```

Listing 7. Implementation of classbox ColorCB by refactoring

The effect of compiling the classbox *ColorCB* in this way results in an assembly, whose functionality is equivalent to the code extract illustrated in Listing 7. Here, source code refactoring [16] is used to construct the namespace ColorCBX, which defines a functionality that corresponds to the one provided by the classbox *ColorCB*.

The classbox *TraceCB* (see Listing 8) defines an *inclusion* extension to the class Point and an explicit import of the class LinearBoundedPoint from the classbox *LinearCB*. Inclusion enables *down calls* to class extensions. Thus, unlike refinement, inclusion extensions may be visible throughout the extended class, as they can override existing members. However, the visibility of this effect is confined to the defining classbox and its clients; the originating classbox remains unaffected.

```
namespace TraceCB {
  using Point = ColorCB.Point include TraceMoveBy;
  using LinearBoundedPoint = LinearCB.LinearBoundedPoint;

  extension TraceMoveBy
  {
    public void MoveBy( int dx, int dy )
      { Console.WriteLine( "MoveBy: {0}, {1}", new object[] { dx, dy } );
        base.MoveBy( dx, dy ); }
  }
}
```

Listing 8. The classbox TraceCB

We implement *inclusion* by marking all public members with override (or virtual if no member with the same signature exists in the imported class). The transformed extensions are then again used to construct a subclass of the imported class (e.g., class Point, as shown in Listing 9).

```
//  TraceMoveBy(include) ⊕ ColorCB.Point
public class Point : ColorCB.Point {
  public override void MoveBy( int dx, int dy )
  {
    Console.WriteLine( "MoveBy: {0}, {1}", new object[] { dx, dy } );
    base.MoveBy( dx, dy );
  }

  // required constructor(s)
  public Point( int ix, int iy ) : base( ix, iy ) { }
}
```

Listing 9. Transformation of class TraceCB.Point

Once more, in order to compile *TraceCB*, we need to rewire the inheritance chain originating from TraceCB.Point. Therefore, we need to create new versions (marked (2)) of the assemblies for the classboxes *OriginalCB*, *LinearCB*, and *ColorCB*, respectively. Please note that the new assemblies *OriginalCB(2).dll*, *LinearCB(2).dll*, and *ColorCB(2).dll* are all derived from the versions that were created to compile the classbox *ColorCB*. Hence, we only need to patch the corresponding metadata type tokens to link BoundedPoint's superclass type to TraceCB.Point.

4 Conclusions and Future Work

Classboxes provide a feasible solution to the problem of controlling the visibility of change in object-oriented systems without breaking existing applications, as they strictly limit both its scope and impact to clients of the extending classbox. Consequently, classboxes can significantly reduce the risk for introducing design and implementation anomalies due to the need to adapt a software system to changing requirements [5].

In this paper, we have presented an approach to augment C#, an industrial-strength programming language, with the classbox concept. In our model, classboxes are represented by C# *namespaces* and the corresponding operations are defined using a small extension to the C# language. The integration of this extension is achieved by means of source code transformations, refactoring, and locally updating the metadata type declarations in assemblies. This approach allows us to preserve the identity of extended classes in classboxes, resulting in a seamless integration of classboxes into the .NET framework.

Although omitted due to the lack of space, our implementation of classboxes guarantees that different versions of a class can *co-exist* in the same classbox. This is achieved by representing the different versions of a class by unique metadata type tokens and appropriately linking the corresponding superclass types. Furthermore, due to the fact that class extensions are linked into the classes at *compile-time*, our approach does not add any runtime overhead in order to perform method calls. This contrasts with the existing Smalltalk implementations where, compared to "normal" method lookup, a 25% to 60% runtime overhead is added in the classbox-aware virtual machine [5].

In order to facilitate code reuse and to assist in building families of classes that are subject to the same change, we have also added the notion of *explicit class extensions* to the classbox concept. In contrast to the approach taken by Bergel and Ducasse [3] that combines classboxes with *traits*, in our model explicit class extensions are mixin-like code abstractions that combine both behaviour and state. Furthermore, explicit class extensions can be composed with imported classes using a refined C# *using-alias-directive*, giving us the flexibility to specify how and in which order specific extensions should be integrated into a given class. Explicit class extensions allow us to explicitly separate the local refinement from the import of a class and, as a consequence, substantially improve the specification of incremental modifications to classes within a given classbox.

In our extended classbox model, both refinement and inclusion extension provide a linguistic means for *separation of concerns*. However, in contrast to aspects that can be defined in a separate specification unit [12], these class extensions are *explicitly* applied to the imported classes and are *confined* to the declaration space within which they occur. The aspect-oriented programming model, on the other hand, employs a much looser coupling between extensions (i.e., aspects) and the locations of their application, denoted by advises. This can result in *surprises*, since (possibly unseen) code is executed in response to a method invocation simply because the method's signature matches a corresponding advise, usually specified elsewhere [7].

To address this problem, Clifton [7] recently proposed the "MAO discipline" that encompasses both a design discipline and language features for modular reasoning in aspect-oriented programs. In MAO, we distinguish between two categories of aspects: *assistants* and their associated *concern maps* that can change the behaviour of modules to which they apply, and *spectators* that do not affect other modules, as they only *view* methods. Both categories, even though not completely, correspond to our model of explicit class extensions. Inclusion can be characterized as an instance of an assistant, whereas refinement corresponds to a spectator.

In this work, we have focused on a seamless integration of classboxes into the C# language and have explored the concept of *explicit class extensions* to further enhance separation of concerns. Besides the definition of an extended C# compiler in which class extensions can be compiled into existing classes without source code access, there are a number of open questions that need to be addressed in future work.

In our model, both classes and explicit class extensions specify their "own" state whereas the trait model by Bergel and Ducasse [3] only allows the explicit extension of behaviour, but not state. Hence, in future work, we plan to investigate how to decouple behaviour and state by introducing *state-only* abstractions as first-class entities into the model. This would allow us to express classes and explicit extensions as compositions of explicit state, behaviour, and compositions thereof. As a consequence, both traits and Scala-style class composition [15] could be seamlessly integrated into the classbox model. A natural extension of such a model would then be to allow classboxes to import (and possibly extend) any of the abovementioned first-class entities. The implications of such an extension to the classbox model in the .NET framework is however not yet fully understood.

Our current model lacks the notion of *required* interfaces [18, 15] for explicit class extensions. As a consequence, explicit class extension can solely be type-checked in the context of an application to a class, but not as standalone entities. Hence, future work will need to address this issue. Similarly, we plan to investigate the implications and applicability of having classboxes as first-class values as well as parameterized (i.e., generic) classboxes.

Finally, an area where further investigations are needed is *method overloading*. Whereas we do not need to worry about this in languages such as Smalltalk, both, Java and C# allow developers to overload methods. In such a context, a correct implementation of a classbox model needs to be able to determine which of the overloaded methods is refined by an (explicit) extension. This will very probably require some form of additional type annotation to method names. A similar problem arises when instance variables with restricted visibility are *shadowed* by extensions, both issues that need to be addressed in future work.

Acknowledgement. The authors thank Alexandre Bergel and the anonymous reviewers for their valuable comments and discussions.

References

1. Davide Ancona, Giovanni Lagorio, and Elena Zucca. Jam – Designing a Java Extension with Mixins. *ACM Transactions on Programming Languages and Systems*, 25(5):641–712, September 2003.

2. Alexandre Bergel. *Classboxes — Controlling Visibility of Class Extensions*. PhD thesis, University of Bern, Institute of Computer Science and Applied Mathematics, November 2005.
3. Alexandre Bergel and Stéphane Ducasse. Supporting Unanticipated Changes with Traits and Classboxes. In *Proceedings of Net.ObjectDays (NODE'05)*, pages 61–75, Erfurt, Germany, September 2005.
4. Alexandre Bergel, Stéphane Ducasse, and Oscar Nierstrasz. Classbox/J: Controlling the Scope of Change in Java. In *Proceedings OOPSLA '05*, pages 177–189, San Diego, USA, October 2005. ACM Press.
5. Alexandre Bergel, Stéphane Ducasse, Oscar Nierstrasz, and Roel Wuyts. Classboxes: Controlling Visibility of Class Extensions. *Journal of Computer Languages, Systems & Structures*, 31(3–4):107–126, May 2005.
6. Gilad Bracha and William Cook. Mixin-based Inheritance. In Norman Meyrowitz, editor, *Proceedings OOPSLA/ECOOP '90*, volume 25 of *ACM SIGPLAN Notices*, pages 303–311, October 1990.
7. Curtis Clifton. *A Design Discipline and Language Features for Modular Reasoning in Aspect-oriented Programs*. PhD thesis, Iowa State University, Department of Computer Science, July 2005.
8. European Computer Machinery Association. *Standard ECMA-334: C# Language Specification*, third edition, June 2005.
9. Robert Bruce Findler and Matthew Flatt. Modular Object-Oriented Programming with Units and Mixins. In *Proceedings of the ACM SIGPLAN International Conference on Functional Programming (ICFP '98)*, volume 34 of *ACM SIGPLAN Notices*, pages 94–104. ACM Press, 1998.
10. Matthew Flatt, Shriram Krishnamurthi, and Matthias Felleisen. Classes and Mixins. In *Proceedings POPL '98*, pages 171–183, San Diego, January 1998. ACM Press.
11. Erich Gamma, Richard Helm, Ralph Johnson, and John Vlissides. *Design Patterns*. Addison-Wesley, 1995.
12. Grégor Kiczales, Erik Hilsdale, Jim Hugunin, Mik Kersten, Jeffrey Palm, and William G. Griswold. An Overview of AspectJ. In Jørgen Lindskov Knudsen, editor, *Proceedings ECOOP 2001*, LNCS 2072, pages 327–355, Budapest, Hungary, June 2001. Springer.
13. Markus Lumpe and Jean-Guy Schneider. Classboxes – An Experiment in Modeling Compositional Abstractions using Explicit Contexts. In Mike Barnett, Steve Edwards, Dimitra Giannakopoulou, Gary T. Leavens, and Natasha Sharygina, editors, *Proceedings of ESEC '05 Workshop on Specification and Verification of Component-Based Systems (SAVCBS '05)*, pages 47–54, Lisbon, Portugal, September 2005.
14. James S. Miller and Susann Ragsdale. *The Common Language Infrastructure Annotated Standard*. Microsoft .NET Development Series. Addison-Wesley, 2003.
15. Martin Odersky, Philippe Altherr, Vincent Cremet, Burak Emir, Sebastian Maneth, Stéphane Micheloud, Nikolay Mihaylov, Michel Scinz, Erik Stenman, and Matthias Zenger. An Overview of the Scala Programming Language. Technical Report IC/2004/64, École Polytechnique Fédérale de Lausanne, School of Computer and Communication Sciences, 2004.
16. William F. Opdyke. *Refactoring Object-Oriented Frameworks*. PhD thesis, University of Illinois at Urbana-Champaign, Department of Computer Science, 1992.
17. Nathanael Schärli, Stéphane Ducasse, Oscar Nierstrasz, and Andrew Black. Traits: Composable Units of Behavior. In Luca Cardelli, editor, *Proceedings ECOOP 2003*, LNCS 2743, pages 248–274, Darmstadt, Germany, July 2003. Springer.
18. Charles Smith and Sophia Sophia Drossopoulou. Chai: Traits for Java-Like Languages. In Andrew P. Black, editor, *Proceedings ECOOP 2005*, LNCS 3586, pages 453–478, Glasgow, Scotland, July 2005. Springer.

Automatic Control Flow Generation from Software Architectures

Kung-Kiu Lau and Vladyslav Ukis

School of Computer Science, The University of Manchester
Manchester M13 9PL, United Kingdom
{kung-kiu, vukis}@cs.man.ac.uk

Abstract. In a traditional software architecture, control originates in components and flows to other components via connectors. The system's control flow is fixed at design time, when components and their inter-connections are specified. Code generated from the design inherits this control flow, and consists of component code and glue code that tightly couples connected components. This means that code generated from a given software architecture is system-specific, and is therefore neither generic nor reusable. In this paper we describe an approach which allows separate reuse of component code and connector code, and thus making it possible to build architectures from pre-existing components and generic connectors. Furthermore, we show we can implement such architectures by generating control flow at run-time automatically.

1 Introduction

In a traditional software architecture [15], control originates in components (boxes) and flows to other components via connectors (lines). The system's control flow is fixed at design time, when components and their inter-connections are specified, in an Architecture Description Language (ADL), e.g. Acme [7].

Mostly ADLs do not provide any support for creating code for the system from its architecture. When they do, as in ArchJava [3,1] (based on Acme), code generated from the architecture inherits the control flow fixed at design time, and consists of component code and glue code that tightly couples connected components. This means that code generated from a given software architecture is system-specific, and is therefore neither generic nor reusable.

In this paper we describe an approach which allows separate reuse of component code and connector code, and thus making it possible to build architectures from pre-existing components and generic connectors. Furthermore, we show that we can implement such architectures by generating control flow at run-time automatically.

To achieve this we take a different approach to system construction. We take control out of components and put it into connectors. That is, in our approach, control in the system does not originate in components but in their connectors. This makes components completely encapsulated, and therefore independent and easier to reuse. Furthermore, our connectors are generic, like the Bus connector in C2 [17], and we can reuse them among different systems. To construct a system, we choose a set of pre-existing, independent components required for the system, connect them with a set of (pre-existing)

W. Löwe and M. Südholt (Eds.): SC 2006, LNCS 4089, pp. 323–338, 2006.

generic connectors, and generate control flow of the system automatically at run-time. Thus our approach obviates the need for generating glue code to put together components and connectors, in contrast to ArchJava. In addition, our components as well as connectors can be used in different systems with different control flows. Our automatic runtime control flow generation not only instantiates components and connectors, like the C2 Bootstrapper, but, unlike the C2 Bootstrapper, also generates the whole control flow of the system automatically at run-time.

In this paper we describe how we can generate control flow at run-time. We begin by briefly surveying current approaches for code generation from software architectures (Section 2). Next, we introduce our connectors as origins of control flow in a system (Section 3.1), and explain architectures containing our connectors (Section 3.4). Subsequently, we explain how to automatically generate control flow at runtime (Section 3.5) and provide an example (Section 4). Finally, we briefly evaluate our approach (Section 5).

2   Code Generation from Traditional Software Architectures

Among existing ADLs, Acme/ArchJava [3,1] and C2 [17] are representative examples of ADLs that support code generation from architectures.

Acme/ArchJava (Fig. 1 (a) shows an example architecture) allows automatic generation of code from an architecture. Components and connectors are generated afresh for each system. That is, neither components nor connectors pre-exist or are reused from system to system.

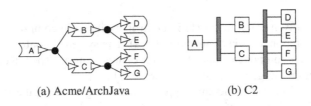

(a) Acme/ArchJava   (b) C2

Fig. 1. Software architecture examples

In C2 (Fig. 1 (b) shows an example architecture) components have to be coded first. Components communicate by sending events to each other. Their code must explicitly identify events they can deal with and provide corresponding actions. Events are transported by buses between components. The bus is a generic connector, and is not generated afresh for every system but is reused in all systems. To implement an architecture, C2 provides a Bootstrapper, which allows instantiation of components and connectors at run-time. These instances together with event-handling constitute the runtime system. Thus in C2 the bus is reused but not the components, because the latter are 'hard-wired' to events for a specific system.

No ADL inherently intends both component and connector reuse from an architecture description. This is exactly what our approach endeavours to achieve. We want to have pre-existing components as well as pre-existing connectors, and reuse them to build many architectures.

In the ArchJava example in Fig. 1 (a) for instance, component A knows connector AB. The connector AB in turn knows component B. Thus, A cannot be reused independently without AB and AB without B. Furthermore, component B knows connector BD. The connector BD in turn knows component D. Thus, B cannot be reused without BD and BD without D. In other words, neither components nor connectors in ArchJava are independently reusable entities.

In the C2 example in Fig. 1 (b), connectors AB and BD etc. are constructed from one generic bus connector template and, unlike in ArchJava, are not coded afresh for each component connection. Thus connectors AB, BD etc. are generic and independently reusable. However, component A sends a specific event with a specific format, say AB_Event, to the connector AB. The connector AB dispatches the AB_Event to component B. Component B is waiting for the arrival of this specific event, knows its format and how to handle it. Moreover, once component B has processed the AB_Event, it originates another event, say BD_Event, to the bus connector BD. The bus connector BD dispatches the BD_Event to component D. Component D is waiting for the arrival of the BD_Event, knows its format and how to handle it. In other words, components in C2 wait for specific incoming events from and send (or originate) specific outgoing events to other components. Therefore, components in C2 are not independently reusable encapsulated entities.

By contrast, we want to be able to reuse components A, B, D etc. independently as well as connectors AB, BD etc.

3 Our Approach

In this section we explain our approach. The key characteristics of our approach are that (i) components pre-exist and are reusable; (ii) connectors (pre-exist and) are generic and reusable; (iii) run-time systems can be generated from architectures by automatically generating control flow.

To make our components reusable, we make them encapsulated and thus independent, by taking control out of them. Thus in our approach, components are units of computation (linked by connectors). A component is a unit of software with (i) an *interface* that specifies the services it provides (i.e. its methods) and the services it requires, and the dependencies between the two sets of services; and (ii) *code* that implements the provided services. In essence it is similar to Szyperski's definition [16]. However, our components do not invoke methods or services in other components. Rather, they only perform their provided services (methods) when they are invoked from outside, by connectors. Thus our components encapsulate computation.

We put control in connectors. Connectors are composition operators that compose components into systems. They are *exogenous*, i.e. they initiate and coordinate method calls in components, and handle their results. Thus they determine control flow and data flow, i.e. they encapsulate communication in general, and control in particular. Exogenous connectors play a fundamental role on our approach.

3.1 Exogenous Connectors

Exogenous connectors were introduced in [12]. Here, we briefly explain them.

The distinguishing characteristic of exogenous connectors is that they encapsulate control. In traditional ADLs, components are supposed to represent *computation*, and

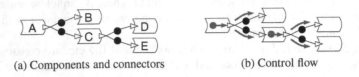

(a) Components and connectors   (b) Control flow

Fig. 2. Traditional ADLs

connectors *interaction* between components [13] (Fig. 2 (a)). Actually, however, components represent computation as well as *control*, since control originates in components, and is passed on by connectors to other components. This is illustrated by Fig. 2 (b), where the origin of control is denoted by a dot in a component, and the flow of control is denoted by arrows emanating from the dot and arrows following connectors.

In this situation, components are not truly independent, i.e. they are tightly coupled, albeit only indirectly via their ports, and the control flow between components is fixed at their design time.

By contrast, in exogenous connection, control originates in and flows from connectors, leaving components to encapsulate only computation. This is illustrated by Fig. 3.

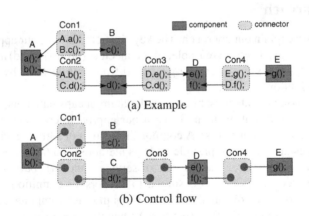

(a) Example

(b) Control flow

Fig. 3. Connection by exogenous connectors

In Fig. 3 (a), components do not call methods in other components. Instead, all method calls are initiated and coordinated by exogenous connectors. The latter's distinguishing feature of control encapsulation is clearly illustrated by Fig. 3 (b), in clear contrast to Fig. 2 (b).

Exogenous connectors thus encapsulate control (and data), i.e. they *initiate* and *co-ordinate* control (and data). With exogenous connection, components are truly independent and decoupled.

Exogenous connection is not provided by any existing ADLs. However, exogenous connection has been defined as exogenous coordination in coordination languages for concurrent computation [2]. Also, in object-oriented programming, the courier pattern [6] uses the idea of exogenous connection whereby a courier object links a producer-consumer pair of objects by calling the *produce* method in the producer object and then calling the *consume* method in the consumer object with the result of the *produce* method.

3.2 Connector Type Hierarchy

The concept of exogenous connection entails a type hierarchy of exogenous connectors. Because they encapsulate all the control in a system, such connectors have to connect to one another (as well as components) in order to build up a complete control structure for the system. For this to be possible, there must be a type hierarchy for these connectors.

In the connector type hierarchy for our approach, components are obviously a basic type. Because components are not allowed to call methods in other components, we need an exogenous *method invocation connector*. This is a *unary* operator that takes a component, invokes one of its methods, and receives the result of the invocation. To structure the control and data flow in a set of components or a system, we need other connectors for sequencing exogenous method calls to different components. So we need *n-ary* connectors for connecting invocation connectors, and *n-ary* connectors for connecting these connectors, and so on. In other words, we need a hierarchy of connectors of different arities and types.

Example 1. (Exogenous Connector Hierarchy). Consider a system whose architecture can be described in Acme [7] and C2 [17] as in Fig. 1 (a) and (b) respectively. Using exogenous connectors in our approach, the corresponding architecture is that shown in Fig. 4.

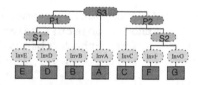

Fig. 4. Exogenous connection example

At the lowest level, level 1, we use *invocation* connectors that connect to individual components and make calls into them. There are no other kinds of connectors at this level. In Fig. 4, the invocation connectors are InvE, InvD, InvB etc.

At the next level, level 2, we need a *selector* connector to implement branching in the system. Such a connector connects connectors and makes a call into a selected one of the connectors. In Fig. 4, at level 2, selector S1 connects InvE and InvD, and decides whether to call E or D depending on the selection condition it receives from its parent connector P1. Similarly, S2 connects and selects from F and G.

At level 3, we need a *pipe* connector to implement sequential control. Such a connector connects connectors and makes consecutive calls into these connectors in the order in which they are connected to it. In Fig. 4, P1 is a pipe connector. It connects to InvB (which calls a method in B) and passes the result to the selector S1. S1 uses the result as a selection condition to select component E or D. Similarly, the pipe P2 effects sequential control between C and selector S2.

Finally, at level 4, the top level, there is only one connector. This is a selector S3, which selects P1 or P2 depending on the top-level (user) input.

In general, connectors at any level other than the first can be of variable arities; connectors at any level higher than 2 can be of variable arities *and* types; and we can define any number of levels of connectors. Connectors at level n for any $n > 1$ can be defined in terms of connectors at levels 1 to $(n - 1)$. At the top level, there is always just one connector. A detailed definition of the hierarchy can be found in [12,11].

3.3   Implementing Generic Connectors

Exogenous connectors can be implemented as generic connectors, such that: (i) generic connector templates can be defined and stored; (ii) these connector templates can be deployed to a system; and (iii) connector instances can be created and used to build the control structure of any specified system (with exogenous connectors). In particular, we want to do so for *any* connector at *any* level. In [12] we show an implementation in Java that is generic only in the sense of (i), and that only defines connectors for *specific* levels. Here we describe how we can define connectors at *any* level that are generic in the sense of (i), (ii) and (iii). We use C# in .NET for the implementation.

We implement three kinds of connectors (*invocation, pipe* and *selector*) as a hierarchy of classes, with a base class *Connector*.

The *Connector* class has several *Execute* methods for executing either a single given method (with its parameters) or a given set of methods (with their parameters). These are the following `public virtual void` methods:

```
... Execute (string method, object[] params);//(1)
... Execute (string[] methods, object[] params);//(2)
... Execute (int cond, string method, object[] params);//(3)
... Execute (int cond, string[] methods, object[] params);//(4)
```

Using the *Connector* class, we can define a generic connector at any level of the hierarchy. Such a connector inherits from *Connector*, and implements the appropriate *Execute* method(s).

Only the invocation connector makes calls into components from within its *Execute* method (1).

The selector connector's *Execute* method can be passed a list of methods (4). Consider the case of just one method (3). In this case, the *Execute* method of a selector connector is used for calling one method on the connector inside the selector which gets selected according to the condition *cond* which is passed into the method. In our current implementation, the selection condition is an integer but it can easily be extended to other types in future.

The selector assumes that all the connectors in it can in principle deal with the method passed into it. Therefore it is also sufficient to provide only one list of parameters. Whichever connector gets selected, the method *method* and parameters *params* will be passed to it.

The *Execute* method of a pipe connector (2) is represented by a loop, which sequentially processes all the connectors in it. Basically, the pipe connector takes the first connector, makes a call into it, obtains the result and makes a call into the second connector passing the result obtained from the first connector as a parameter into the second one and so on until the end of the loop is reached.

In the loop the first thing is to check whether we are at the beginning of the loop. If we are, then the parameters passed into the *Execute* method can be used as they are, to be passed into the first connector. On the other hand, if we are in the middle of the loop, the parameters to be passed on to the next connector are the results from the previous one.

Next if the connector to be called in the current loop iteration of the pipe is a selector connector, we have to extract the first parameter from the *Execute* method's parameter list if we are at the beginning of the loop, or the first element of the result array from the previous invocation if we are in the middle of the loop, and pass it to the selector connector as a condition.

Then if we are at the first loop iteration we can call into the selector straight away, but otherwise we have to adjust the method array and remove the first element from it because the first method has already been processed in the previous loop iteration.

If the connector in the current loop iteration is not a selector, we do not have to bother with the first element in the parameter list to be processed as a selection condition, and can call the *Execute* method straight away considering the necessary method array adjustment for each loop iteration.

Eventually the Result is retrieved from the connector processed in the current iteration, and will be used in the next iteration as parameter list for the next connector in the pipe. Once the end of the loop is reached, the Result is returned by the pipe.

The connectors we present here are generic because they are independent, self-contained and can be used by any application. As shown in the above description, no application-specific logic has been put into the connectors. In fact, in a general sense they could even be thought of as light-weight components in the system.

Exogenous connectors form a hierarchy and thus can contain one another. Thus, pipe and selector connector can contain invocation, pipe or selector connectors. It is possible to add a connector to the "host" connector after the "host" connector has been created when building a connector hierarchy. This allows for "late-binding" of connectors, which is used for system control flow generation.

3.4 Architectures with Exogenous Connectors

Having implemented generic exogenous connectors, in this section we show how architectures can be defined using them. Just as exogenous connection entails a connector type hierarchy, so the latter in turn entails a strictly hierarchical way of constructing systems by composing components. As illustrated by Figure 4, in such a system, components form a flat layer, and the entire control structure (of connectors) sits on top of this. Beyond level 1, the precise choice of connectors, the number of levels of connectors, and the connection structure, depend on the relationship between the behaviour of the individual components and the behaviour that the whole system is supposed to achieve. Whatever the control structure, however, it is strictly hierarchical, which means that there is always only one connector at the top level. This is the connector that initiates control flow in the whole system.

Example 2. (The Bank Example). Consider a bank system, whose architecture is described in Acme in Figure 5 (a). The system has just one *ATM* that serves two bank

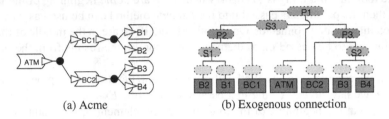

(a) Acme   (b) Exogenous connection

Fig. 5. Architecture of the bank example

consortia ($BC1$ and $BC2$), each with two bank branches ($B1$ and $B2$, $B3$ and $B4$ respectively). The *ATM* passes customer requests together with customer details to the customer's bank consortium, which in turn passes them on to the customer's bank branch. The bank branches provide the usual services of withdrawal, deposit, balance check, etc.

At level 1, each component has an invocation connector. At level 2, there is a selector connector $S1$ that is used to select the customer's bank branch from banks $B1$ and $B2$, prior to invoking that branch's methods requested by the customer. Similarly, there is a level-2 selector connector $S2$ for choosing between $B3$ and $B4$, prior to invoking their methods requested by the customer. To pass values from one bank consortium to one of its banks we need a pipe connector; at level 3, we have two pipe connectors $P2$ and $P3$, for $BC1$ and $BC2$ respectively. At level 4, $S3$ is a selector connector that selects the customer's bank consortium from consortia $BC1$ and $BC2$. Finally, at level 5, the top level, the pipe connector $P1$ initiates the bank system's operational cycle by passing customer requests and card information to the *ATM*, invoking the *ATM*'s methods, and then passing the resulting value to connector $S3$.

3.5 Automatic Control Flow Generation

Separation of control flow and computation using exogenous connectors means that control flow is not kept inside components like in current ADLs but can be managed outside. Having implemented generic exogenous connectors, in this section we show how a system's control flow can be generated automatically, given its architecture, i.e. the connection structure for the components.

As depicted in Figure 6 (which should be read from bottom to top, as indicated by the arrow on the left), to generate a system's control flow we need 3 kinds of entities: (a) independent components; (b) generic exogenous connectors; and (c) an XML description of the system's architecture, i.e. the connection structure of the system. These

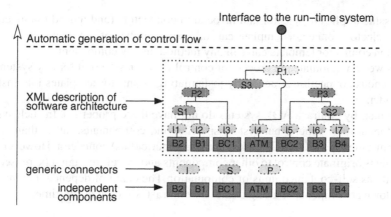

Fig. 6. Automated control flow generation

3 entities are independent from one other, i.e. components can be connected by any connectors depending on a specific system's needs, and connectors can take part in any connection structure.

The output of the control flow generation is a run-time system constructed in accordance with the given connection structure description, along with an interface, which is the top-level connector in the architecture. The system constructed provides all control flow paths possible in the system specified by (c). A particular run-time request to the system may not use every control flow path available. Nevertheless, the system construction ensures that all possible control flow paths are available to serve all requests placed on the system through the top-level connector in the architecture.

Application-*independent* templates for connectors can be created as shown in Section 3.3 and reused for different applications by creating application-specific instances. Note that connector template instances are not ordinary class instances in the sense of object-oriented programming. When a connector template is instantiated it gets adapted to the current place in the connection structure. The generic exogenous connectors can be deposited in a repository and retrieved on demand for each application. Furthermore, for any specific application with an exogenous control or connection structure, the generic connectors can be instantiated, on the fly, into the instances in the latter's connection structure. This means that it is possible to generate the control flow of a system dynamically and automatically from its architecture.

To illustrate this, consider the connection structure of the Bank example in Figure 6. The system contains three pipe connectors and three selector connectors (as well as seven invocation connectors). Each of these connectors hosts different connector types (and in different numbers). For example, the pipe $P1$ hosts a selector $S3$ and an invocation connector $I4$ for the component ATM, whereas the pipe $P2$ hosts a selector $S1$ and an invocation connector $I3$ for the component $BC1$. Although the two pipes are doing completely different things, they have been constructed from the same template. The template is generic enough to embody different instances. So, $P1$ is an instance of the pipe template that hosts the selector $S3$ and the invocation connector $I4$, and $P2$ is an instance that hosts the selector $S1$ and the invocation connector $I3$.

The same applies to selector and invocation connectors (and indeed to any connector). A selector connector template can take any number of any connectors, and an invocation connector template can call any method on any component.

Thus we can automate the process of control flow construction for any system with an exogenous connection structure by instantiating connector templates into instances in the latter.

Note that, by contrast, ADL systems do not have these properties. In such systems, connectors are not generic but system-specific, and components, rather than connectors, form a hierarchy. Only C2 makes use of a generic (bus) connector. However, in C2 components originate control to other components and therefore cannot be reused independently as self-contained units of computation. The chain of dependent components is laid down at components' design time. By contrast, we do it at run-time.

3.6 Connection Structure Description

In order to build up a control structure on the fly, it needs to process a system's connection description. We choose to write the description in XML because: (a) XML itself is hierarchical, and so is particularly suited to expressing our connector hierarchies; (b) the system description can be automatically checked against a pre-defined XML schema, thus eliminating (some) errors right at the beginning; (c) there is good tool support for XML, e.g. we use XMLSpy from Altova; (d) the system integrator can be guided by a tool while developing a system control structure description according to the XML schema; (e) XML schemas are extensible in a consistent manner [5]; this is important because when the schema is extended to include new connector types, for instance, old system descriptions, which have been checked against the old schema, will be able to pass the schema check using the new schema. Using XML for system description is also favoured by XML ADLs [14,8,4].

The XML schema we use for system control structure description is depicted in Figure 7. The top-level XML element is called "ExADL" and has two child elements: (i) connector_types and (ii) system, in that order. (i) contains an extensible specification of exogenous connector types which are generic and not system-specific; whilst (ii) contains a (system-specific) specification of the system using these connector types. Connector types presented here include invocation, pipe and selector connectors.

A system can contain any number of connector types which can contain one another. The connector type hierarchy defined in the schema is of course the same one that we used for implementing these connectors.

Note that connector types presented here are not the only ones possible. We show only these connector types here because they are used in the Bank Example. In general, any exogenous connector types are conceivable. For example, a repeater connector, which repeats some invocations into a component, or a sequencer connector, which has the semantics of the pipe connector but does not pipe values from one component to another one. What is important is that all these connectors can be described using system control structure description and instantiated at runtime. That is, the infrastructure for building systems using exogenous connectors is defined by the extensible XML schema for system control structure description.

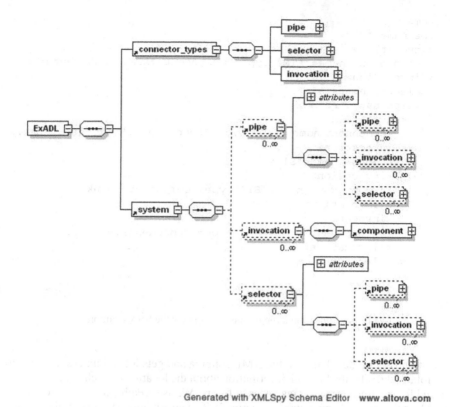

Generated with XMLSpy Schema Editor www.altova.com

Fig. 7. XML schema for system connection structure description

As an example of system connection structure description, the bank system can be described by the outline in Figure 8.This can be read as: 'A pipe $P1$ contains an invocation connector and a selector $S3$. The invocation connector contains a component ATM. The selector $S3$ contains a pipe $P2$, which contains a component $BC1$, and so on'.

3.7 Implementation of Control Flow Generation

To generate a system's control flow, its XML description is processed. First of all the XML description is checked against the schema shown in Figure 7. If the XML system description does not pass the schema check, the system will not be created. This enforces the connector hierarchy to be always well-defined by the schema. During the processing of the system element, the connector types are retrieved first and stored for future use. A connector type is instantiated each time a specific connector occurs in the system connection structure description. For example, each time a pipe element occurs in the XML description of the system, an instance of a pipe is created from the information stored before.

To describe the implementation, we follow the sequence of operations that are carried out to process a system control structure description. First, the system control flow

```
<system>
  <pipe name="P1">
    <invocation>
      <component name="ATM" type="Components.ATM, Components"/>
    </invocation>
    <selector name="S3">
      <pipe name="P2">
        <invocation>
          <component name="BC1" type="Components.BankConsortium ...
        </invocation>
        <selector name="S1">
          <invocation>
            <component name="B1" type="Components.Bank ...
          </invocation>
          <invocation>
            <component name="B2" type="Components.Bank ...
          </invocation>
        </selector>
      </pipe>
      ...
```

Fig. 8. Connection structure description for the bank example

description gets validated against the XML schema and gets loaded unless the description violates the schema. Second, information about the location of each connector class is stored for creating connector instances in future. We use XPath expressions to retrieve the XML nodes (e.g. "//connector_types/pipe"). The information stored is a piece of text containing the class name and a .NET assembly name containing the class. Using this information .NET runtime (CLR) can load the assembly into a process and create an instance of the class inside. Third, the top-level connector is identified and created, Then system control flow construction begins. The complete system is created beneath the top-level connector, using a recursive method:

```
private void LoadSystem(XmlNode theXmlNode,
                        Connector theCurrentConnector) {...}
```

This recursive method has 2 parameters: (i) the current XML node in the system control structure description to be processed; and (ii) the current connector, which will take the connectors created from the child nodes of the XML node passed into the method as child connectors. Thus when entering the method we always have a connector created in the previous iteration and its XML representation. The method iterates through the child nodes of that node, creates connectors out of them and puts each of these connectors as a child connector into the connector passed into the method.

The recursion itself can only occur when processing either a pipe or a selector connector. An invocation connector cannot cause the recursion since the only XML node that can be beneath invocation is component, according to the XML schema. On the other hand, we do not know which XML node will occur after pipe or selector. The schema only enforces that it will be either pipe, selector or invocation. In order to investigate what is below a pipe or a selector we engage in a recursion passing the necessary parameters, namely the current connector and its XML representation, and in the next iteration explore the child nodes. The recursion ends when an invocation connector is found.

During the construction of the system control flow all possible control flow paths in the system are laid down, while a particular request to the system does not necessarily makes use of all of them but follows some paths necessary to answer the request.

4   Example

Now we illustrate the use of exogenous connectors for automatic runtime control flow generation, using the bank example (Example 2), with the architecture described in Figure 5 (b).

The first step is to implement the components. In our implementation, components are C# classes with public methods (that can be invoked by the invocation connectors) for the usual ATM operations like insert card, enter password, withdraw, deposit, check balance, etc. The objects (of these classes) do not call methods in other components.

The second step is to specify the system in XML following the XML schema. We have already done this in Figure 8.

The third step is to actually construct the system according to the process outlined above. The result is the running system with control flow as shown in Figure 6.

Now we briefly explain how the automatically generated bank system works, and therefore how it can be used to provide services, by means of an example. Consider the service request of getting the balance of an account. The get balance operation (illustrated for card 4711) is implemented by using *TopLevelConnector* of the bank system, as follows:

```
TopLevelConnector.Execute(new string[] {"GetBankConsortiumID_",
  "GetBranch_", "GetBalance"}, new object[] {4711});
```

The top-level connector $P1$ gets a list of methods, namely *GetBankConsortiumID_*, *GetBranch_* and *GetBalance*, and parameters to be propagated through the system. Only invocation connectors in ATM, $BC1$ and $B1$ respectively call these methods. The connectors themselves draw on various *Execute* methods offered by their base class *Connector* to propagate the necessary information down towards invocation connectors. Where the control flow can pass (at which connector and component) was specified before in the system description. The concrete control flow for a request depends on request parameters. For example, a particular bank is selected for executing an operation on an account according to the account number of the customer.

For the get balance operation, the control flow involved is shown in Figure 9.

Note that the control flow for get balance operation does not use all possible control flow paths laid down on system construction but rather uses a part of them. Figure 6 shows that the system contains all the possible control flow paths. Figure 9 depicts control flow paths necessary for serving the request to get an account balance. Another request may need completely different paths than those used when serving account balance request.

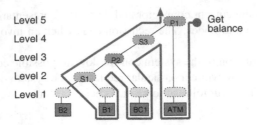

Fig. 9. Control flow for get balance

Other operations to be performed by the Bank System like deposit and withdraw can be implemented as follows:

Deposit $100 onto account the card 4711 belongs to:

```
TopLevelConnector.Execute(new string[]
  {"GetBankConsortiumID", "GetBranch", "Deposit"},
  new object[] {"100", "4711"});
```

Withdraw $100 from account the card 4711 belongs to:

```
TopLevelConnector.Execute(new string[]
  {"GetBankConsortiumID", "GetBranch", "Withdraw"},
  new object[] {"100", "4711"});
```

Besides the Bank Example we have implemented a complex Automated Train Protection System (ATP) using exogenous connectors. In that system we implemented some other connectors in addition to those presented in this paper and we could reuse connectors from this paper in the ATP system. For lack of space we do not discuss the ATP System here.

5   Discussion and Concluding Remarks

In this paper we have presented an approach to automatic runtime system control flow generation from software architectures using exogenous connectors. In particular, we showed our procedure for control flow construction. As far as we know, our approach is unique because it generates control flow of systems consisting of independent, reusable components automatically.

Code generators like the one in ArchJava generate code with components originating control flow to other components. Tools like Bootstrapper in C2 do not create control flow of the system at runtime but only instantiate components and connectors, with control flow already implemented in components and via connectors. In other words, traditional ADLs do not allow automatic runtime control flow generation for a system.

Furthermore, ADLs do not have generic and hierarchical connectors. XML-based ADLs like xADL 1.1 [8] and xADL 2.0 [4], which have XML descriptions of their architectures, do not generate control flow automatically at runtime.

Table 1 summarises related approaches and shows the differences to our proposed approach.

Table 1. Comparison with related architectures

Approach	Access to component	Control origin	Component reuse	Connector reuse	Automated control flow generation
ArchJava/ACME	by method call	component	no	no	no
xADL	by method call	component	no	no	no
C2	by event	component	no	yes	no
Exogenous	by method call	connector	yes	yes	yes

Our future work is concerned with predictability of system properties resulting from composing components using connectors into a system. We have shown that automatic composition is possible by constructing system's control flow on the fly. However, it is highly desirable as well to be able to predict the result of this automated control flow construction before it actually takes place. Therefore we are working on Deployment Contracts [10] for components, which is metadata [9] attached to the components, with a view to being able to analyse that metadata before the actual composition takes place. The analysis should flag incompatible components for composition. By having this, we will be able to predict conflicts by doing some compositional reasoning.

References

1. J. Aldrich, C. Chambers, and D. Notkin. ArchJava: Connecting software architecture to implimentation. In *Proc. ICSE 2002*, pages 187–197. IEEE, 2002.
2. F. Arbab. The IWIM model for coordination of concurrent activities. In P. Ciancarini and C. Hankin, editors, *Lecture Notes in Computer Science 1061*, pages 34–56. Springer-Verlag, 1996.
3. ArchJava web page. http://archjava.fluid.cs.cmu.edu/index.html.
4. E.M. Dashofy, A. van der Hoek, and R.N. Taylor. A highly-extensible, XML-based architecture description language. In *Proc. Working IEEE/IFIP Conference on Software Architecture*, pages 103–112. IEEE Computer Society, 2001.
5. L. Dykes, E. Tittel, and C. Valentine. *XML Schemas*. Sybex Inc, 2002.
6. E. Gamma, R. Helm, R. Johnson, and J. Vlissides. The courier pattern. *Dr. Dobb's Journal*, Feburary 1996.
7. D. Garlan, R.T. Monroe, and D. Wile. Acme: Architectural description of component-based systems. In G.T. Leavens and M. Sitaraman, editors, *Foundations of Component-Based Systems*, pages 47–68. Cambridge University Press, 2000.
8. R. Khare, M. Guntersdorfer, P. Oreizy, N. Medvidovic, and R. N. Taylor. xADL: Enabling architecure-centric tool integration with XML. In *Proc. 34th Hawaii Int. Conf. on System Sciences*, 2001.
9. K.-K. Lau and V. Ukis. Component metadata in component-based software development: A survey. Preprint 34, School of Computer Science, The University of Manchester, Manchester, M13 9PL, UK, October 2005.
10. K.-K. Lau and V. Ukis. Deployment contracts for software components. Preprint 36, School of Computer Science, The University of Manchester, Manchester, M13 9PL, UK, February 2006.

11. K.-K. Lau, V. Ukis, P. Velasco, and Z. Wang. A component model for separation of control flow from computation in component–based systems. In *Proceedings of the 1st International Workshop on Aspect-Based and Model-Based Separation of Concerns in Software Systems, ENTCS, www.elsevier.nl/locate/entcs*, Nuremberg, Germany, November 2005.

12. K.-K. Lau, P. Velasco Elizondo, and Z. Wang. Exogenous connectors for software components. In *Proc. 8th Int. SIGSOFT Symp. on Component-based Software Engineering, LNCS 3489*, pages 90–106, 2005.

13. N.R. Mehta, N. Medvidovic, and S. Phadke. Towards a taxonomy of software connectors. In *Proc. 22nd International Conference on Software Engineering*, pages 178–187. ACM Press, 2000.

14. S. Pruitt, D. Stuart, W. Sull, and T.W. Cook. The merit of XML as an architecture description language meta-language. Microelectronics and Computer Technology Corporation, 1998.

15. M. Shaw and D. Garlan. *Software Architecture: Perspectives on an Emerging Discipline*. Prentice Hall, 1996.

16. C. Szyperski, D. Gruntz, and S. Murer. *Component Software: Beyond Object-Oriented Programming*. Addison-Wesley, second edition, 2002.

17. R. N. Taylor, N. Medvidovic, K. M. Anderson, E. J. Whitehead Jr., J. E. Robbins, K. A. Nies, P. Oreizy, and D. L. Dubrow. A component- and message-based architectural style for GUI software. *Software Engineering*, 22(6):390–406, 1996.

Author Index

Lecture Notes in Computer Science

For information about Vols. 1–4028

please contact your bookseller or Springer